Researching Online For Dummies®

W9-AVT-187

Research Jargon to Remember

Search words or **search terms:** The words or phrases you select to describe the topic you're researching

Boolean operators: AND, OR, and NOT, used to define a logical relationship between your search terms

Proximity connectors (operators): ADJ, pre/, (w) and others, used to specify how close to each other in a document your search terms must appear

Field searching (restricting): Limiting your search terms to a certain portion of a document

Search statement or **search query:** The words or phrases you select *plus* any Boolean or proximity operators, field restrictions, and so on you decide to use

Phrase searching: Using two or more words commonly found together, such as *usual suspects,* as a search term

Hits: Items retrieved by your search

Result set or **hit list:** *All* the items retrieved by your search

Set searching: Combining the results of one search with the results of another, or running a second search within the results of an earlier search

Refining: Making your search results more relevant

Wild card: A character (such as *) used to stand for one or more letters in a search word

Truncation: Searching on a portion of a word to pick up alternate forms: *bank** may pick up *banks, banker, banking, bankruptcy*, and so on

Word stem or **word root:** The portion of a word — such as *bank** — used in a search

Case-sensitivity: Whether a search engine pays attention to upper- and lowercase: *Apple* or *apple*

Relevance ranking: Displaying search results in order of their apparent usefulness

...For Dummies: #1 Computer Book Series for Beginners

Researching Online For Dummies®

Cheat Sheet

Key Search Connectors

AND — Narrow your search by looking for documents that include both (or all) terms: *total AND solar AND eclipse*

OR — Broaden your search by looking for documents that include any (one or more) terms: *solar OR sun*

NOT — Narrow your search by excluding documents in which certain terms appear: *solar NOT lunar*

adj, pre/, (w) — Term A must appear within so many words of Term B, in the order specified: *total pre/2 eclipse*

same, w/, (n) — Term A must appear within so many words of Term B, in any order: *solar w/5 eclipse*

( ) — Parentheses let you group search terms together so you can enter more complex search statements: *(solar or sun) and eclipse*

Note: Not all search engines support all of these connectors, and some express them in different ways. See the Bonus Appendix on the CD for more about these important connectors and how to use them.

Stellar Starting Points for Researching Online

Subject catalogs

Yahoo!: www.yahoo.com

Argus Clearinghouse: www.clearinghouse.net

WWW Virtual Library: vlib.stanford.edu/Overview.html

Internet Public Library: www.ipl.org/

Search engines

AltaVista: www.altavista.digital.com

Infoseek: www.infoseek.com

Hotbot: www.hotbot.com

Excite: www.excite.com

Lycos: www.lycos.com

DejaNews: www.dejanews.com

Liszt: www.liszt.com

Research services and mega-sites

Dialog: www.dialogweb.com

Dow Jones Interactive: www.djnr.com

Fedworld: www.fedworld.gov

Thomas (Legislative Information on the Internet): thomas.loc.gov

U.S. Library of Congress: lcweb.loc.gov/loc/libserv/

AJR NewsLink: www.newslink.org/

Virtual Reference Desk: thorplus.lib.purdue.edu/reference/index.html

Usenet Hypertext FAQ Archive: www.faqs.org/faqs/

...For Dummies: #1 Computer Book Series for Beginners

™

References for the Rest of Us!®

BESTSELLING BOOK SERIES FROM IDG

Are you intimidated and confused by computers? Do you find that traditional manuals are overloaded with technical details you'll never use? Do your friends and family always call you to fix simple problems on their PCs? Then the *...For Dummies*® computer book series from IDG Books Worldwide is for you.

...For Dummies books are written for those frustrated computer users who know they aren't really dumb but find that PC hardware, software, and indeed the unique vocabulary of computing make them feel helpless. *...For Dummies* books use a lighthearted approach, a down-to-earth style, and even cartoons and humorous icons to diffuse computer novices' fears and build their confidence. Lighthearted but not lightweight, these books are a perfect survival guide for anyone forced to use a computer.

> *"I like my copy so much I told friends; now they bought copies."*
> — Irene C., Orwell, Ohio

> *"Quick, concise, nontechnical, and humorous."*
> — Jay A., Elburn, Illinois

> *"Thanks, I needed this book. Now I can sleep at night."*
> — Robin F., British Columbia, Canada

Already, millions of satisfied readers agree. They have made *...For Dummies* books the #1 introductory level computer book series and have written asking for more. So, if you're looking for the most fun and easy way to learn about computers, look to *...For Dummies* books to give you a helping hand.

™

IDG BOOKS
WORLDWIDE

RESEARCHING ONLINE FOR DUMMIES®

by Reva Basch

IDG Books Worldwide, Inc.
An International Data Group Company

Foster City, CA ♦ Chicago, IL ♦ Indianapolis, IN ♦ New York, NY

Researching Online For Dummies®

Published by
IDG Books Worldwide, Inc.
An International Data Group Company
919 E. Hillsdale Blvd.
Suite 400
Foster City, CA 94404
www.idgbooks.com (IDG Books Worldwide Web site)
www.dummies.com (Dummies Press Web site)

Library of Congress Catalog Card No.: 98-85684

ISBN: 0-7645-0382-0

Printed in the United States of America

10 9 8 7 6 5 4 3 2 1

1B/RZ/QW/ZY/IN

Distributed in the United States by IDG Books Worldwide, Inc.

Distributed by Macmillan Canada for Canada; by Transworld Publishers Limited in the United Kingdom; by IDG Norge Books for Norway; by IDG Sweden Books for Sweden; by Woodslane Pty. Ltd. for Australia; by Woodslane (NZ) Ltd. for New Zealand; by Addison Wesley Longman Singapore Pte Ltd. for Singapore, Malaysia, Thailand, Indonesia and Korea; by Norma Comunicaciones S.A. for Colombia; by Intersoft for South Africa; by International Thomson Publishing for Germany, Austria and Switzerland; by Toppan Company Ltd. for Japan; by Distribuidora Cuspide for Argentina; by Livraria Cultura for Brazil; by Ediciencia S.A. for Ecuador; by Ediciones ZETA S.C.R. Ltda. for Peru; by WS Computer Publishing Corporation, Inc., for the Philippines; by Unalis Corporation for Taiwan; by Contemporanea de Ediciones for Venezuela; by Computer Book & Magazine Store for Puerto Rico; by Express Computer Distributors for the Caribbean and West Indies. Authorized Sales Agent: Anthony Rudkin Associates for the Middle East and North Africa.

For general information on IDG Books Worldwide's books in the U.S., please call our Consumer Customer Service department at 800-762-2974. For reseller information, including discounts and premium sales, please call our Reseller Customer Service department at 800-434-3422.

For information on where to purchase IDG Books Worldwide's books outside the U.S., please contact our International Sales department at 650-655-3200 or fax 650-655-3297.

For information on foreign language translations, please contact our Foreign & Subsidiary Rights department at 650-655-3021 or fax 650-655-3281.

For sales inquiries and special prices for bulk quantities, please contact our Sales department at 650-655-3200 or write to the address above.

For information on using IDG Books Worldwide's books in the classroom or for ordering examination copies, please contact our Educational Sales department at 800-434-2086 or fax 817-251-8174.

For press review copies, author interviews, or other publicity information, please contact our Public Relations department at 650-655-3000 or fax 650-655-3299.

For authorization to photocopy items for corporate, personal, or educational use, please contact Copyright Clearance Center, 222 Rosewood Drive, Danvers, MA 01923, or fax 978-750-4470.

is a trademark under exclusive license to IDG Books Worldwide, Inc., from International Data Group, Inc.

About the Author

Reva Basch is a writer, editor, and consultant to the online industry. She operated her own online research business for more than 10 years. Prior to that, she was vice president and director of research at Information on Demand, a pioneering independent research company in Berkeley, California. She is a frequent speaker on topics related to information retrieval, virtual communities, the Internet and the World Wide Web, and has keynoted at international conferences in Australia, Scandinavia, and the United Kingdom, as well as Canada and the U.S.

Reva is a columnist for *Online* magazine and *The CyberSkeptic's Guide to Internet Research*. She has been a contributing editor to several publications, and wrote the Cybernaut column for *Computer Life* magazine and the Compleat Searcher column for *Online User*. Her feature articles have appeared in those publications and many others. She has written three other books, *Secrets of the Super Net Searchers* (Pemberton Press, 1996), *Secrets of the Super Searchers* (Pemberton Press, 1993), and *Electronic Information Delivery: Evaluating Quality and Value* (Gower, 1995). She has edited and contributed chapters, introductions, and interviews to several other books about the Internet and information retrieval, including Carla Sinclair's *Net Chick,* Pamela Kane's *Hitchhiker's Guide to the Electronic Highway,* Sue Rugge and Alfred Glossbrenner's *Information Broker's Handbook,* Mary Ellen Bates's *Online Deskbook,* Betty-Carol Sellen's *What Else You Can Do With a Library Degree,* and Michael Banks's *The Internet Unplugged.*

Reva won the 1990 UMI/Data Courier Award for her two-part article on the user "wish list" in *Online* magazine. She was the 1993 recipient of the Dun & Bradstreet Online Champion Award. She was the subject of a profile in the May 1995 issue of *WIRED* magazine, which called her "the ultimate intelligent agent." She is a past president (1991-1992) of the Association of Independent Information Professionals, a member of the Northern California Chapter of the Southern California Online Users Group (SCOUG), and a founding member of Information Bay Area. She taught a course called "Information Brokering: Is this career for you?" at the University of California, Berkeley, Extension.

Reva has a degree in English Literature, *summa cum laude,* from the University of Pennsylvania, and a Masters degree in Library Science from the University of California at Berkeley. She began her career as a corporate librarian, and has been online since the mid-1970s. She logs off occasionally to eat, sleep, and perform other essential functions.

She is an active participant in The WELL, one of the first virtual communities online, and has hosted several conferences there. She lives on the rugged northern California coast with her husband, Jerry Shifman, their three differently-specied children, Abbie, Flash, and Tigray; and a 6,300-watt generator for when the power goes out but the work must go on.

ABOUT IDG BOOKS WORLDWIDE

Welcome to the world of IDG Books Worldwide.

IDG Books Worldwide, Inc., is a subsidiary of International Data Group, the world's largest publisher of computer-related information and the leading global provider of information services on information technology. IDG was founded more than 25 years ago and now employs more than 8,500 people worldwide. IDG publishes more than 275 computer publications in over 75 countries (see listing below). More than 90 million people read one or more IDG publications each month.

Launched in 1990, IDG Books Worldwide is today the #1 publisher of best-selling computer books in the United States. We are proud to have received eight awards from the Computer Press Association in recognition of editorial excellence and three from *Computer Currents'* First Annual Readers' Choice Awards. Our best-selling *...For Dummies*® series has more than 50 million copies in print with translations in 38 languages. IDG Books Worldwide, through a joint venture with IDG's Hi-Tech Beijing, became the first U.S. publisher to publish a computer book in the People's Republic of China. In record time, IDG Books Worldwide has become the first choice for millions of readers around the world who want to learn how to better manage their businesses.

Our mission is simple: Every one of our books is designed to bring extra value and skill-building instructions to the reader. Our books are written by experts who understand and care about our readers. The knowledge base of our editorial staff comes from years of experience in publishing, education, and journalism — experience we use to produce books for the '90s. In short, we care about books, so we attract the best people. We devote special attention to details such as audience, interior design, use of icons, and illustrations. And because we use an efficient process of authoring, editing, and desktop publishing our books electronically, we can spend more time ensuring superior content and spend less time on the technicalities of making books.

You can count on our commitment to deliver high-quality books at competitive prices on topics you want to read about. At IDG Books Worldwide, we continue in the IDG tradition of delivering quality for more than 25 years. You'll find no better book on a subject than one from IDG Books Worldwide.

IDG BOOKS WORLDWIDE

John J. Kilcullen
John Kilcullen
CEO
IDG Books Worldwide, Inc.

Steven Berkowitz
Steven Berkowitz
President and Publisher
IDG Books Worldwide, Inc.

Eighth Annual Computer Press Awards ≥1992

Ninth Annual Computer Press Awards ≥1993

Tenth Annual Computer Press Awards ≥1994

Eleventh Annual Computer Press Awards ≥1995

Acknowledgments and Dedication

This is where I get to play out my Academy Awards fantasy, thanking everyone who's helped me in any way with this book. The list is a long one, and I can't possibly single out every person who inspired me or provided practical or emotional support. But I must start with Sue Rugge and Barbara Bernstein, who first hired me as a freelance researcher, taught me how to do it right, and got me started on my own career as an independent information professional. I'm also very grateful to my friend and colleague Mary Ellen Bates for her impeccable and hugely helpful technical review of this book, and for her unflagging support, encouragement, and good humor. I don't know what we'd have done without e-mail, <mebs>. Thanks, too, to Bill Helling, project editor, and Rowena Rappaport, copy editor; we managed to communicate amazingly well through those "query" fonts and colors in Word. Thanks to Matt Wagner as well, for bringing me the opportunity to do this book in the first place.

My friends and neighbors, Janet Hubbard, Rich Kuehn, and Dean Schuler, went far beyond my expectations in sharing their favorite online starting points for genealogy and birding, respectively, that appear in the Recreational Researching chapter on the CD. Thanks to them, and to my WELL pals who reacted with alacrity, wit, and their usual stunning expertise to my repeated requests for reality-checking that usually began with the phrase, "Would it make sense to say . . . ?"

I especially want to thank Libbi Lepow, Linda Cooper, Carol Gould, Thaisa Frank, Kay Hardy, Rita Hurault (can we go shopping now?), Tina Loney, Drew Trott, Eric Rawlins, David Gans, Bryan Higgins, Jen Avian, Mary Carter, Linda Castellani, Colleen Evans, and the dozens of other dear friends (you know who you are) who patiently endured my online whining and always knew exactly what to say. Also, thanks to Hertha Basch, for reminding me not to work too hard. I don't always listen, Mom, but I appreciate the advice and the spirit in which you gave (and undoubtedly will continue to give) it.

Most of all, I thank Jerry Shifman for the grace with which he shouldered the household and relationship responsibilities during the four months in which what we laughingly refer to as "normal life" turned even more bizarre than usual. I owe you big time, Jer — and I dedicate this book to you, with my love and gratitude.

Publisher's Acknowledgments

We're proud of this book; please register your comments through our IDG Books Worldwide Online Registration Form located at http://my2cents.dummies.com.

Some of the people who helped bring this book to market include the following:

Acquisitions, Editorial, and Media Development

Project Editor: Bill Helling

Senior Acquisitions Editor: Jill Pisoni

Copy Editor: Rowena Rappaport

Technical Editor: Mary Ellen Bates

Media Development Technical Editor: Marita Ellixson

Associate Technical Editor: Joell Smith

Permissions Editor: Heather Heath Dismore

Associate Permissions Editor: Carmen Krikorian

Editorial Manager: Elaine Brush

Media Development Manager: Megan Roney

Editorial Assistant: Paul E. Kuzmic

Production

Project Coordinators: Regina Snyder, Valery Bourke

Layout and Graphics: Lou Boudreau, Angela F. Hunckler, Brent Savage, Linda M. Boyer, J. Tyler Connor, Jane E. Martin, Anna Rohrer, Janet Seib, M. Anne Sipahimalani, Kate Snell

Proofreaders: Christine Berman, Kelli Botta, Michelle Croninger, Rachel Garvey, Nancy Price, Rebecca Senninger, Janet M. Withers

Indexer: Sherry Massey

Special Help

Publication Services, Oran Sands

General and Administrative

IDG Books Worldwide, Inc.: John Kilcullen, CEO; Steven Berkowitz, President and Publisher

IDG Books Technology Publishing: Brenda McLaughlin, Senior Vice President and Group Publisher

Dummies Technology Press and Dummies Editorial: Diane Graves Steele, Vice President and Associate Publisher; Mary Bednarek, Director of Acquisitions and Product Development; Kristin A. Cocks, Editorial Director

Dummies Trade Press: Kathleen A. Welton, Vice President and Publisher; Kevin Thornton, Acquisitions Manager

IDG Books Production for Dummies Press: Michael R. Britton, Vice President of Production; Beth Jenkins Roberts, Production Director; Cindy L. Phipps, Manager of Project Coordination, Production Proofreading, and Indexing; Kathie S. Schutte, Supervisor of Page Layout; Shelley Lea, Supervisor of Graphics and Design; Debbie J. Gates, Production Systems Specialist; Robert Springer, Supervisor of Proofreading; Debbie Stailey, Special Projects Coordinator; Tony Augsburger, Supervisor of Reprints and Bluelines

Dummies Packaging and Book Design: Robin Seaman, Creative Director; Jocelyn Kelaita, Product Packaging Coordinator; Kavish + Kavish, Cover Design

◆

The publisher would like to give special thanks to Patrick J. McGovern, without whom this book would not have been possible.

◆

Contents at a Glance

Cartoons at a Glance

By Rich Tennant

page 7

page 179

page 261

page 35

page 285

Fax: 978-546-7747 • E-mail: the5wave@tiac.net

Table of Contents

. . . .

Introduction

The Wide World of Researching Online

*W*ay back in the dark ages of the online realm — around 1992 or so — "research" was something associated with scientists in white lab coats, scholars in book-filled libraries, and eager librarians helping the public from behind their reference desks. Thanks to the rise of the Internet, and particularly the Web, "research" has taken on a different meaning. It's a do-it-yourself project now. Research has acquired an aura of hipness, the same way that computer geeks, with their taped-together eyeglasses and plastic pocket protectors, are now considered cool. Every one of us can be our own researcher. Oh joy. Or can we? On one level, the answer is a definite *yes*. The Net has empowered us, given us the tools we need to find information and make decisions, large and small, about our lives. It's eliminated the middleman. It's done away with the need to wait in line, whether at the public library or in voice-mail limbo, until it's *our* turn to have our questions answered. The Net has given us instant research gratification — assuming, that is, that we can actually *find* what we're looking for online. That's where this book comes in.

What Librarians Know

In eliminating the middleman, whether librarian or other research professional, we've cut ourselves off from a lot of valuable expertise. Librarians know how the world of human knowledge is organized, from broad disciplines like humanities and social sciences down to the most minute individual fact. That means that they know where to start looking for information instead of floundering around in a sea of possibilities. It's like the difference between starting out with your friends' address — or, at the very least, a map of their neighborhood and a description of their house — and meandering through the streets of their town with no idea of where you're going or how to recognize your goal when (and if) you get there.

Librarians also know how to choose keywords and index terms that help focus in on the precise information they're seeking, instead of being overwhelmed by hundreds or even thousands of mostly-irrelevant references. If their first strategy doesn't work as expected, they've got more tricks up their sleeve. Lots more. You'll find most of them in this book.

Searching versus Surfing

Searching online isn't the same thing as *surfing*. Surfing merely skims the surface. Searching is a lot more like scuba diving; it goes deep. It can still be fun and exhilarating, but getting the results you want takes thought, care, and planning. Success depends on more than just how the waves happen to be breaking that day.

I don't promise to turn you into a professional researcher. You probably wouldn't want that, anyway. You have your own life; at least I hope you do. But here's where I'm coming from: As a trained librarian and professional researcher, I watched the Internet grow up around me. At first I was skeptical. I had my own resources — including some of the industrial-strength online databases that I talk about in this book — that I was accustomed to using. But gradually, the Net lured me in. As I got to know my way around, I realized that there were pockets of incredibly valuable information that I couldn't get anywhere else, or that would take much longer or cost much more to get through my usual means. I also realized that there was a lot of junk on the Internet, and that finding the good stuff wasn't always easy. I was seduced by the Net, but not so completely that I didn't recognize its shortcomings. I've identified what I call The Four Myths of Online Research:

- ✔ Everything is online.
- ✔ It's all free.
- ✔ You just "plug it into your computer and pull it out."
- ✔ It's all there for the taking.

Would that it were so. It's just not true that everything worth knowing has made its way to the electronic realm. Not everything online is free, especially if you value the time it takes you to find it. Finding what you need takes a bit more effort — despite the occasional miracle — than keying in a word or two and automagically retrieving the answer. And *using* what you find isn't just a matter of plug and play; you have to think about issues like copyright, giving credit where it's due, and verifying that the information is accurate, current, and complete.

What Makes a Good Researcher?

It doesn't take a library science degree, years in academia, or advanced training in some specialized field, to be a good researcher. Formal education doesn't hurt, and if you've gotten some research experience in school or on the job, you're ahead of the game. But if I had to choose the single most important characteristic for a successful online searcher, I'd pick *curiosity*. Good researchers love to pursue information for its own sake. The thrill of the chase is almost as important as the goal. Many of my colleagues in the research biz are avid crossword puzzlers, word-game enthusiasts, or mystery novel readers. A couple of them even *write* mysteries in their spare time. Give them a challenge, or a clue, and they're off and running.

Practice doesn't make perfect, but it helps. You're not going to become a top-notch online searcher simply by reading this book. You've got to get out there and try it for yourself. It's like on-the-job training — *theory* is worthless until you start using what you've learned. Check out the tools, techniques, and resources I recommend throughout the book. Plug in your own search terms; look for what interests *you*. When you catch yourself thinking "I wonder if *this* will work . . . ?" or "Wouldn't it be *better* if I . . . ?" you'll know that you're on your way to thinking like a researcher. The best researchers use both halves of their brain — the left side, which is supposed to be the logical, linear part, and the right side, which is said to embody intuition and creativity. My goal throughout the following chapters is to show you how to do the same.

And You Are . . . ?

What you're *not* is a Dummy. Not really. You're a regular person, and undoubtedly an intelligent person, too, because you clearly know that one way to come up to speed and acquire new skills is to listen to someone who knows more about the subject than you do. (That's me, she said, curtseying modestly.) You're obviously a person of great discernment, too, because you turned to *this* particular book for help.

I'm assuming that you've already spent at least a little bit of time online, know how to connect to the Internet, and are familiar with basic concepts such as *Web browser, linking,* and *search engines* — even if you're not entirely comfortable with using them. Ideally, you've spent enough time trying to find information online to have become just a wee bit frustrated with the process, and to be wondering, right about the time you picked up this book, whether there isn't a better way.

There is a better way. There are many better ways. And I'm delighted to make your acquaintance.

How This Book Is Organized

If you're interested enough in how *my* mind works to start with Chapter 1 and read your way straight through, I'm flattered. This book unfolds in a way that makes sense to me — obviously, or I wouldn't have organized it that way. But it works just as well as a reference book. You can dip into it when, where, and for as long as you like. Although you'll find that some discussions refer to or build on material covered in earlier sections, each chapter also stands on its own. If you feel that you need to fill in the gaps somewhere along the way, you can always go back and do so. Nobody's keeping track of how you use this book. I know *I'm* not, anyway.

We're big on chunky-style around here. You'll find chapter-size chunks, and chunklets of easily-digestible information, checklists, and fun factoids within each chapter. The book itself is divided into five mega-chunks: Getting Started, The Tools of the Trade, Putting It All Together, The Broader Picture, and the mysteriously-named Part of Tens. You'll also find a directory, printed on yellow paper in the middle of the book, full of bite-size descriptions of selected research sites, services, and other useful resources. The URLs (Web addresses) for just about all these sites, and more than 100 others that may interest you, are on the CD that's packaged with this book. Sound good? Good.

Part I: Getting Started

In this part, I talk about both the mental skills and the online resources that successful online researchers should master. There's more to "online" than the Web; even the Internet doesn't encompass it all.

Part II: The Tools of the Trade

This part covers search engines, indexes, quick reference aids, proprietary databases, and many other types of research tools, including human expertise. The CD in the back of the book includes an important bonus appendix that covers Boolean searching and other power search tips and techniques.

Part III: Putting It All Together

In this part, you get to see how the online tools and techniques you've learned about actually work in real-life research situations. You also get an in-depth look at some of the best — and sometimes best-*hidden* — resources in popular subject areas like news, business, technology, and government information. Check the CD for two bonus chapters on researching real-life decisions and interests.

Part IV: The Broader Picture

Approximately 47 minutes into your career as an online researcher, you'll start bumping up against some major issues: How do I keep up with all this stuff? Can I just go ahead and use what I find any way I want? Is there a way to judge the quality of the information I'm getting? In this part, I tackle the big questions that come *after* "How do I find . . . ?" The answers aren't always clear-cut, but the more time you spend researching online, the more you'll encounter them.

Part V: The Part of Tens

Is it just me, or does "The Part of Tens" sound like something from the Letterman show or a mystical incantation from some CD-ROM medieval adventure game? Whether or not you get the same weird associations I do, this is where I get to reduce everything I've learned about research — well, maybe not quite *everything* — into bite-size morsels, and you get to graze, nibble, and otherwise eat between meals. Here's the section to turn to if you have a really short attention span, or are the kind of person who licks the filling out of their Oreos first. I look at the Part of Tens as a supplement to, not a substitute for, other parts of the book — a snack, rather than the main course. But I think you'll find these goodies tasty no matter how or when you consume them. Speaking of CD-ROMs, you'll find a bonus "Ten" there: Ten Simple Tune-ups for Streamlined Searching.

Signs and Symbols

> My eyes glaze over when I see
> an icon bearing down on me.

Not really; we English majors *love* symbolism. This book uses just a few simple conventions throughout to call your attention to certain kinds of material. Bear with me; this may be tedious but it'll be over soon. Read fast:

- ✔ URLs and other online addresses are indicated in a boring typeface like this: `www.mypage.com`
- ✔ <u>Hypertext links</u> are <u>underlined</u>, just as they appear in your Web browser. Just don't try clicking on them.
- ✔ Keywords and search terms appear in **bold,** the better to distinguish them from the non-keywords and non-search terms that surround them.
- ✔ New terms are *italicized* the first time they appear. This is a clue that you haven't missed anything but maybe you'd better pay attention *now*.

This icon is for gems of hard-earned understanding and insight that are even more valuable than the usual pearls of wisdom that I so liberally disperse.

This icon signals the nitty-gritty steps involved in using a particular re-search tool.

This icon lets you know when I'm heavily into talking like a researcher. You can pick up phrases and sprinkle them into your conversations to impress, amuse, or scare your friends.

This icon indicates advanced research techniques or technical stuff — which I define as something you don't need to know unless you're curious about how it really works.

I expect you to commit the entire book to memory. This icon is for material that will be on the final.

This book comes with a CD at no extra charge. Such a deal. It has some great stuff on it, including free software, plus three bonus chapters of this book, and an appendix on Boolean searching and other power research techniques that I refer to throughout the book. When I mention something that's on the CD, you see this icon.

If disregarding something I say might produce unfortunate or unexpected results, I'll try to tag it with this icon. If I forget, please don't sue me. One person's problem is another person's challenge, you know? Here's a real-life example coming up right now:

Note: Research sites and services change their appearance all the time, especially on the Web. Sometimes all it takes is a new sponsor or partner-ship deal. Functionality and content — the way sites work, and the sort of information you can expect to find at them — change more slowly. But everything does change. Some sites may look different when you visit them than I depict them in this book. You may not find all the features I describe exactly where I left them. It's the way of the Web. Consider it a challenge. I do.

One More Thing

Under "What Makes a Good Researcher" earlier in this intro, I said some-thing about the thrill of the chase. Every searcher I've ever asked has told me that, above all else, research has to be *fun*. You can learn the basics anywhere. But if I can convey what it's like to approach the online world from inside the mind of a virtuoso researcher who truly enjoys her work, I'll consider this book a huge success — for both of us.

Part I
Getting Started

The 5th Wave   By Rich Tennant

"This afternoon I want everyone to go online and find all you can about Native American culture, history of the old west, and discount air fares to Hawaii for the two weeks I'll be on vacation."

In this part . . .

*I*n this part, you find out what it takes to become an effective online researcher. Anyone is capable of learning how to think like a researcher, using your own unique combination of logic and creativity to track down information in a systematic way.

This part introduces the tools and techniques that are available to you online. You discover how and when to use them, when to think about alternatives, and how to tell when it's time to try a different tactic altogether.

In this part, you find that "online" means more than just the Web, and that the Web itself includes many hidden and elusive treasures. I show you how to tap into them, and how to uncover new ones on your own.

Chapter 1
The Many Faces of Online

In This Chapter

▶ Unearthing the hidden online
▶ Investigating fee-based services
▶ Contacting the Net's human resources

*A*mazing as it may seem, the online world was alive and thriving long before the arrival of the World Wide Web. Yes, the Web has grabbed the spotlight as a glamorous, fun-loving, party animal — every would-be information junkie's dream date. But for all its multimedia glitter and flash, the Web is a newcomer to the online world, and a derivative and ditzy one at that.

Harsh words? Not really. I adore the Web. The Web is fast becoming the preferred route for information publishing of all kinds. But the Web is not synonymous, quite yet, with *online*. The Web is an overlay on a much older, quieter and less chaotic environment — the Internet itself. Early Net denizens developed an extensive array of electronic archives, or collections of specialized information, and the research tools needed to plumb them. You can now access many of these resources through the Web, but you may want to bypass the Web at times and go direct. See the section, "The Net beneath the Web," later in this chapter for the when, why, and how of accessing these electronic archives directly.

The Online World: Library, Bookstore, or Shopping Mall after an Earthquake?

Coming up with creative ways to describe the online world could be a full-time job for a wordsmith. For all I know, a roomful of English majors are sitting around somewhere, busily minting metaphors on the subject. Make them stop, please, and tell the one who came up with the term "web-surfing" to stand in the corner, right next to the guy who invented "Information Superhighway." Thanks. I feel better now.

Actually, metaphors can be useful. They help you create a mental map of the territory you're getting into. Someone — one of those English majors, probably — once called the Web "the world's biggest library." If only it were all as orderly and logical as a real-world library. Some sections, like the Library of Congress site (`lcweb.loc.gov/loc/libserv/`), really are library-like. Other parts are far more chaotic.

Some people prefer a bookstore metaphor to describe the online world. A bookstore can be as orderly as a library, or can be a chaotic jumble of idiosyncratic offerings that reflect the proprietor's taste and opinions. Parts of the online world really are like bookstores. You find neatly organized rows of information at `www.yahoo.com`, and highly selective offerings in *web rings* and at *guru pages* and *mega-sites* (see more about these resources in Chapters 5 and 6).

You might even find the online equivalent of helpful bookstore clerks and fellow browsers. We take a quick glance in this chapter at the human side of online research — the kinds of information you can get from real, live experts who hang out in various places on the Net. Chapter 10 goes into a lot more detail about how to use these people-resources effectively.

Just to complicate the question of what the online world is really like, dozens of well-organized online services have developed independently of the Internet and still haven't fully merged with it. You can find professional database services, such as Dialog, LEXIS-NEXIS, and Dow Jones Interactive. You can also find popular (or once-popular) online venues, such as America Online and CompuServe. Each of these services has something unique to offer information-wise, and its own way of organizing it and making it available. We do a brisk survey of them in this section, and go into more detail in Chapter 9.

My favorite metaphor for the online world is "a shopping mall after an earthquake." This implies a worst-case scenario. Go in expecting total chaos, and you're pleasantly surprised when you stumble across a section that hasn't been thoroughly trashed, and that still bears some semblance of order and rationality.

Much of the Web *is* a shopping center, earthquake-jumbled or not. You've got piped-in music and video entertainment along with retail opportunities galore. From a research standpoint, parts of the Web are totally content-free. No wonder you can't find the information you're looking for. When you get frustrated with your lack of results online, look around you: Are you even in the right neighborhood? You wouldn't expect to buy a Big Gulp in a bookstore, let alone a library; what makes you think you can find useful data in a cyber-mall? Get ye to another corner of the online world, posthaste. And don't forget your map.

The Net beneath the Web

Duck below the glossy surface of the Web and take a look at the raw, unvarnished Net, where it all began — plain text on a blank background, no graphics, just information, in its pure, unadulterated form. The sight is kind of spooky, and beautiful, in its own austere way. If nothing else, it gives you an appreciation for how much the online research environment has evolved in just a few short years.

Gopher it!

One of the earliest ways of organizing information on the Net was through something called *Gopher*. A gopher is just a menu-based way of filing and finding information online. Gopher is a lot like the Web, but without the fancy multimedia effects. The grandmother of all gophers was developed at the University of Minnesota — the name came from the state mammal and the University's mascot. Gopher is also a pun on "go-for," as in errand-runner. You figured that out, right? To see what a gopher of the non-furry variety looks like, type `gopher://peg.cwis.uci.edu/` into your Web browser.

Since most Web browsers no longer require you to type http:// at the beginning of a Web address or URL, we generally don't include them here. However, for some other protocols, like Gopher or telnet, a prefix is required. When one's needed, we show it.

Figure 1-1 introduces you to PEG, a Peripatetic, Eclectic Gopher, serving your Internet research needs since 1992. Lovely, isn't it? Don't those folders look organized? And, if you're a Windows 95 user, don't they look awfully *familiar?*

Figure 1-1:
A typical
gopher.

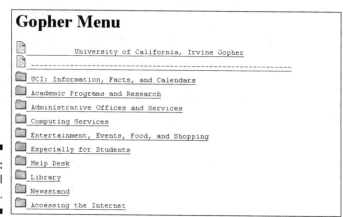

Gopher Menu

University of California, Irvine Gopher

UCI: Information, Facts, and Calendars
Academic Programs and Research
Administrative Offices and Services
Computing Services
Entertainment, Events, Food, and Shopping
Especially for Students
Help Desk
Library
Newsstand
Accessing the Internet

Now, click the folder labeled <u>Accessing the Internet</u>. Figure 1-2 looks like a list of destinations on the Net, and that's exactly what it is.

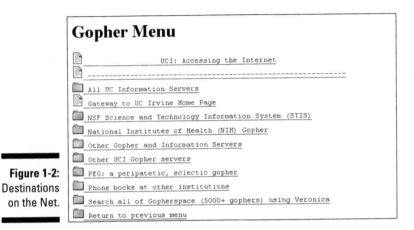

Figure 1-2:
Destinations
on the Net.

Notice the icons mixed in that look like pages rather than folders. Those icons represent files or documents — destinations in themselves. Folders, like directories on your hard drive, contain other files and pointers to other destinations.

Just for fun, click <u>Other Gopher and Information Servers</u> and, on the next screen, <u>All the Gopher Servers in the World</u>. The next page may take a while to load, and for a good reason, too: The page is a list of 80 bazillion or so individual collections of information, ranging from the American Association for the Advancement of Science to ZAMNET, the Zambian National Gopher.

Searching in Gopherspace

Veronica is the gopher equivalent of a web search engine, such as Infoseek or AltaVista. If you glance back at Figure 1-2, you see a folder labeled <u>Search all of Gopherspace (5000+ gophers) using Veronica</u>. From here, you can do a keyword search and find gophers, anywhere in the world, that contain information on your topic.

Another type of search engine, called *Jughead*, is roughly equivalent to a Web page "search-this-site" feature. Jughead lets you search for information on the gopher site where you're currently parked, or sometimes in a collection of related sites. In case you're wondering, Veronica is allegedly an acronym for Very Easy Rodent-Oriented Net-wide Index to Computerized Archives. Jughead supposedly stands for Jonzy's Universal Gopher Hierarchy Excavation and Display.

You can also browse Gopherspace using specialized software programs, such as QVT/Gopher or WSGopher for Windows, or TurboGopher for the Mac. www.shareware.com will lead you to other free and low-cost gopher clients you can try out for yourself.

The bad news about gophers is that they're yesterday's technology, largely supplanted by the Web. The people who used to maintain them are now putting the same information up on public Web servers and corporate intranets. As a result, many gophers are stagnant relics containing reams of outdated and no-longer-useful information. In fact, of those 80 bazillion gopher entries on the worldwide list we just pulled up, an astounding number are no longer in service.

The other bad news is that Veronica and Jughead are real wimps compared to today's search engines. They're slow and awkward to use, and they only search the titles of documents, not the complete text. A title search is only as good as the title is descriptive, and often that's not good enough. For that reason, I'm not going to spend time here explaining how to use Veronica and Jughead. You can find help a click away online, often in a file called **How to compose Veronica [or Jughead] queries,** or something similar.

Why spend any time on gophers, then? The *good* news is that they're still a fast and convenient way to store and retrieve data, particularly lengthy texts and information that doesn't change very often. Many countries that don't yet have the communications bandwidth to support graphics and multimedia still maintain much of their information on gopher sites. If you know what you're looking for, and have at least a general idea of where to find it, then you can rejoice that gophers aren't extinct.

Where's Archie?

If you're old enough to remember the comic book characters Jughead and Veronica, you've probably been wondering: Is there an Archie, too? There certainly is. Archie is a tool for searching ARCHIvEs of software and other files that you can access through something called *FTP,* or File Transfer Protocol. You can find Archie on some gopher menus, such as the one at the University of Minnesota (gopher://gopher.tc.umn.edu). When you download software or a large document from a Web site, you're sometimes FTPing without knowing it. Since the research we do in this book doesn't involve finding files with Archie or manipulating them with FTP, I won't spend time on them here.

Check the CD-ROM for software packages like Anarchie for the Mac or WS_FTP for Windows, to help you with Archie and FTP.

We have WAIS to make you talk

Another kind of retrieval mechanism called WAIS, for Wide Area Information Server, addresses some of the shortcomings of gopher searching. WAIS is the equivalent of a "deep" search engine, like AltaVista, HotBot, or InfoSeek, that purports to search not just titles, but every word in a document, and that displays the results based on how many times in each document your keyword appears. WAIS showed great promise in the early days, when searchers were desperate for something more powerful than Veronica and Jughead. It never caught on the way it should have. Nowadays, you're most likely to encounter WAIS without even knowing it, as a customized search engine embedded in a particular Web site or other online database. See Chapter 3 for more about these engines.

Hytelnet

No, Hy Telnet wasn't the slick-haired cohort of Archie, Veronica, and Jughead. That was Reggie, and I hate myself for remembering that. The word *Hytelnet* is actually a smooshed-together construction of *hypertext* and *telnet*. Hytelnet is a program that lets you look up library catalogs and other useful resources by geographic area or type of library, and then connect to them using the telnet protocol by means of a hypertext link.

The creator of Hytelnet, Peter Scott, has announced that he plans to stop development on the program and replace it with something new and even more useful. I hope so, because Hytelnet is a great shortcut to some incredibly useful information. For the moment, you can still use it through the Web at `galaxy.einet.net/hytelnet/START.TXT.html`. Figure 1-3 shows the Hytelnet Welcome page. See Chapter 8 to find out more about telnet and library catalogs.

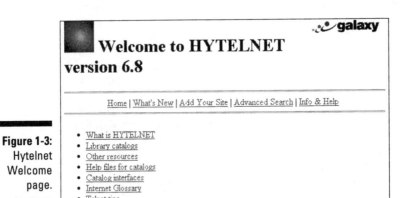

Figure 1-3: Hytelnet Welcome page.

Hot links, cool Lynx

When the Web first got started, it wasn't the multimedia circus it is now. Originally, it was designed to make it easier to move between related text documents through hyperlinks. You don't need Netscape Navigator or Internet Explorer to read simple text; all you need is a browser that displays the documents and allows you to link from a document you're reading to another document that may be pertinent to it in some way. If you happen to find yourself on, or with access to, a UNIX-based computer system (if you are, you probably know it) you can experiment with a text-based browser called *Lynx* that comes already installed on many UNIX systems. Just type **lynx** followed by a space and the full URL (*Uniform Resource Locator,* or Web address) of the site you want to visit, like this:

```
lynx http://www.yahoo.com
```

Figure 1-4 shows the text-only version of the Yahoo! Welcome screen. See Chapter 5 for more on Yahoo!.

```
                                                      Yahoo! (p1 of 2)
Yahoo!

   [ Reuters News Headlines | What's New | Cool Sites ]

   [ Write Us | Add URL | Random Link | Info ]

   _____ Search Options
         * Arts -- Humanities, Photography, Architecture, ...
         * Business and Economy [Xtra!] -- Directory, Investments,
           Classifieds, ...
         * Computers and Internet [Xtra!] -- Internet, WWW, Software,
           Multimedia, ...
         * Education -- Universities, K-12, Courses, ...
         * Entertainment [Xtra!] -- TV, Movies, Music, Magazines, Books,
           ...
         * Government -- Politics [Xtra!], Agencies, Law, Military, ...
         * Health [Xtra!] -- Medicine, Drugs, Diseases, Fitness, ...
         * News [Xtra!] -- World [Xtra!], Daily, Current Events, ...
-- press space for more, use arrow keys to move, '?' for help, 'q' to quit
  Arrow keys: Up and Down to move. Right to follow a link; Left to go back.
H)elp O)ptions P)rint G)o M)ain screen Q)uit /=search [delete]=history list
```

Figure 1-4: Text-only version of the Yahoo! Welcome screen.

The term *text-only* means that text is all you get — no images, movies, audio clips, or other special effects. Lynx uses the **Up** and **Down** arrow keys on your keyboard to move around the screen, and the **Left** and **Right** arrow keys to navigate back and forth (or forth and back) between links. You can find built-in help, the ability to print or save documents, and even a way to create and maintain a bookmark file — just as you can with Netscape or Internet Explorer.

Lynx isn't very exciting to look at, but boy is it *fast*. Without all those huge graphics and multimedia files to clog up your download, pages viewed in Lynx appear almost instantly. What a relief from the World Wide Wait. I sometimes use Lynx when I'm after truth, not beauty — when I know that the pictures at the site I'm visiting aren't necessarily going to be worth a thousand words.

The elephants' burial ground?

Are you starting to think that I've led you into a morgue, or some Internet backwater of dead and dying technologies? You may never use Gopher, Veronica, Hytelnet, or Lynx. But you may run into references to them as you move around the Net, and a knowing nod is much more impressive than a blank stare. Also, knowing this information is a "remember your ancestors" kind of deal; these are the foundations on which the Web was built.

Knowing about the forerunners of the World Wide Web is also a matter of perspective: Don't you feel more confident already, knowing that you'll be working with much more powerful tools than the Net-gurus of just a few short years ago had available to them; and that most of the useful information encapsulated in these now-underground sources is available to you, one way or another, through much easier means? I thought so.

Gated, Not Open; Fee, Not Free

Three of the most enduring misconceptions about online research are:

- ✔ The information is all out there on the Net.
- ✔ Everything on the Net is free.
- ✔ All you have to do is type a couple of words into your favorite search engine, *et voilà* — instant, on-target edification.

You mean there's more to it than that? I'm afraid so, and here's why:

- ✔ Some online resources are *proprietary* — they're self-contained, and not part of the Net at large.
- ✔ Some make you register first; access is by password only.
- ✔ Some require you to pay a monthly or annual subscription fee, or charge you every time you use the service, and/or for each item you retrieve.

I call any online resource that matches one or more of these conditions a *gated* site or service, because the site is set off from the Web at large. Gated sites are *closed,* and the rest of the Web is *open.* Most Web spiders (spiders are special software programs used by search engines to crawl around and index the Web) can't climb the walls of a gated site, so whatever information is stored inside the gates is invisible from the outside. To get access to what's behind the walls, you have to be on the inside yourself.

Gated resources come in two flavors — proprietary and Web-based.

Probing proprietary services

The Internet has been around for a long time. But so have dozens of other good-sized computer systems with names like *Dialog, LEXIS-NEXIS,* and *Dow Jones.* These are called *proprietary* online services. None of these services had anything to do with the Net until quite recently, and you can still reach them by dialing up and connecting directly to their computers, without going through the Internet at all. Before you can search them, you have to set up an account, agree to pay a pre-determined amount for the information you're going to receive, and supply a user ID and password every time you log in to look for information. Proprietary services use their own methods of organizing material into giant collections of information called *databases.* They require special protocols that are different from the query languages used by Web search engines to run searches and retrieve information.

Proprietary services sound like a pain to deal with, don't they? But they have a couple of distinct advantages:

- ✔ They often contain information you won't find anywhere else online, such as legal cases, conference papers, dissertations, and obscure scholarly journals.

- ✔ They're masters of *aggregation.* Proprietary services collect and make available, under one roof, sources that you would otherwise have to wander the great, wide Web to cover on your own. You can search hundreds, even thousands, of unique and valuable research resources at the same time.

Aggregation means that instead of visiting two dozen different newspaper sites to gather articles on the Rolling Stones' last tour, you can cover them all, plus hundreds more, with a single search query, if — big IF — you're willing to pay for it. These proprietary services don't come cheap. We talk about the costs, and about when and whether it makes sense to use them, in Chapter 9.

Gated sites on the Web

You find two different kinds of gated Web sites:

- ✔ Some sites just require you to register. You may have to supply some information about yourself when you first sign up, but after that, you typically just type your name and a password, and you're in. Hundreds of Web sites require registration now, often because advertisers are interested in the data on age, gender, income, occupation, and spending habits that you're sometimes asked to provide.

> ✔ Other sites make you register *and* pay a fee. This may be a subscription fee ranging from a couple of dollars to $50 or more a month, or a charge (often nominal) for every item you view, download, or print. Some subscriptions offer a certain amount of free usage; then you must pay for each additional item. Dozens of Web sites charge for access, from the *Wall Street Journal Interactive Edition* (www.wsj.com/) to *Engineering Information Village* (www.ei.org/eihomepage/village/intro.html) to the full-text special collection at the *Northern Light* search site (www.nlsearch.com/).

Whether free or not, gated sites all have one thing in common: A standard search engine won't touch them, and many Web indexes miss them, too. You may miss a lot if you ignore this sad fact, because gated sites are far too valuable to overlook. Chapter 9 has a lot more on gated sites, how to find them, and what they can do for you.

The Human Side of the Net

You probably think that the goal of your research project — the answer to your question — will come from something fixed and formal in nature, such as a product brochure, a company financial statement, a government report, a list of references or article summaries, a scholarly journal, or a story from a magazine or newspaper. It may even be a video clip, a sound file, or a piece of software. Every one of these things is a *publication* — something that someone has produced and published for the world to see and react to. Web sites are publications consisting of documents and pages.

But information comes in the form of *conversation,* too. Conversation is fast, and often fleeting. The online world is full of conversation pits, informal gathering places where people chat, tell stories, and express their opinions. Some of these people actually know what they're talking about, and some of them may be willing to share their knowledge with you.

Tapping into human expertise online calls for a different set of research skills, involving psychology, and some anthropology and sociology, too. Every online hangout has its own culture and set of behavioral norms. You can find knowledgeable folks hanging out in newsgroups, in mailing lists or listservs, in chat rooms, electronic conferences, and other virtual communities. You can converse with them publicly, or go one-on-one in e-mail.

People made the Net what it is today. Sometimes, it makes sense to go directly to the source. Chapter 10 explains how to find, interact with, and get the information you need from other people online.

Chapter 2

Thinking and Working Like a Researcher

*W*hat's your preferred tactic for getting what you want? Do you walk into your boss's office and blurt out that you want a raise? Or do you do some calculations, add a cost-of-living factor, and present him with the facts? If you've got a role in a play, do you study your lines and try to get inside the character's head, or do you walk onstage opening night and trust that the universe will channel divine inspiration directly into your brain?

Any good performance takes preparation. For a researcher, half the effort takes place before you even sit down at the computer. It was once a matter of survival: If I'm paying $200 an hour just to stay connected to a big marketing database, you know I won't waste any of that time staring at my monitor and just thinking. I do my thinking *offline,* so that when I do go online, I know exactly where I'm going and can make maximum use of my time. We used to call it the *Ticking Meter Syndrome*. Visualizing those dollars mounting up was a powerfully effective way to sharpen the mind.

You're unlikely to encounter a $200-an-hour database in your research travels, but you will do a better job and may even have more fun if you're prepared and focused going in. You'll be more resourceful and less likely to get distracted if you've got a clear picture in your mind of the goal you're trying to reach and your options for getting there. This chapter presents some techniques for defining your research goal and coming up with a plan for reaching it.

Reference-Interviewing Yourself

Research is more than coming up with a list of keywords, plugging them into a search engine, and standing back to see what it spews out. Librarians and professional researchers routinely do something called a *reference interview.* What they ask themselves, and their clients or patrons, is exactly what you should ask yourself at the beginning of any research quest:

✔ **What are you really looking for? (What, exactly, is your topic?)**

Keywords or phrases, such as *internal combustion engine,* are just a starting point. Do you want a basic description of how an internal combustion engine works, or technical information on the kind and quantity of emissions it puts out? Do you want an objective history of internal combustion engines? Examples of how they're used? A reasoned analysis of why they're one of the greatest advances of the 20th century, or, contrariwise, the devil's own invention?

Every research topic has at least two parts: The subject itself, and the *angle* — the aspect of the subject that you really want to know about. If you search on the subject alone — unless the topic is something new, rare, unusual, or seldom talked about — you may be overwhelmed with information, and much of it will be useless to you.

✔ **How else can you describe the topic?**

The English language is rich with synonyms, jargon, and figures of speech. You can usually find more than one way of expressing the same concept: A dip in *employment* is the same as a rise in *unemployment.* If you're looking for statistics on one or the other, consider the mirror image as well.

It works the other way, too: The same word sometimes stands for two totally different concepts. Are you interested in *apple* the fruit or *Apple* the computer company? If the meaning is ambiguous or can possibly be misconstrued, you've got to qualify your search query somehow.

✔ **What is the project, or goal, for which you are gathering the information?**

Are you researching for a high school term paper or a doctoral dissertation? Do you want to build a working model of that internal combustion engine, or file for a patent on a new, improved version? Are you just looking to satisfy your curiosity, or gathering information to help you make a major life decision? Your reason for asking the question determines not only where you need to look for the answer — an engineering manual, an encyclopedia, or *Joe's Picture Gallery of Internal Combustion Engines I Have Known and Loved* — but how much time and effort, and sometimes money, you want to spend.

✔ **Where have you already looked?**

Librarians and professional researchers ask this question to avoid duplicating what their clients have already done. Consider it a reality check: Are there some other logical starting points, such as a phone book, almanac, or neighborhood expert, that you should consult first? Don't overlook the obvious. You may be tempted to jump online immediately, but maybe you can find an easier way.

✔ **If you could sum up your answer in one ideal article, what would that article be called?**

Have some fun: Try to visualize the single, perfect answer to your question — one document that tells you everything you need to know. Then assign a title to that document: "The Internal Combustion Engine: A Detailed History." Or "The Internal Combustion Engine: Environment-Polluting Spawn of Satan." Whatever. Don't forget to factor in those synonyms — Satan = Devil = Lucifer. Okay, silly example. But remember what I said about alternate ways of expressing the same idea. Come up with two or three variations on the ideal title that mean essentially the same thing.

The idea behind the "ideal article" exercise is to capture the most important concepts and to clarify your goal. Do you notice how the title for the internal combustion engine project immediately suggests some key words to hang your research on? Not that you're going to hold out for an exact match, but it gives you a yardstick for measuring your results and for evaluating the good and the not-so-good answers.

What if you can't come up with a title at all? That's important information, too. I've heard a saying: "Writing is nature's way of letting you know how sloppy your thinking is." Being unable to put something in writing, or at least in words, is an indication that you don't quite know what you're looking for. A vague idea produces vague results. "I'll know it when I see it" doesn't cut it in the online research game.

The professional researcher also asks mundane questions during a reference interview, such as "How quickly do you need it?" and, if the client is paying for her services, "How much do you want to spend?" She also asks whether the client wants recent information only, or references that go back many years. The researcher doesn't even assume — unless the client tells her — that the answer has to be in English. Sometimes the best work in a field is in Japanese, Russian, or Swahili.

And the professional researcher listens *closely* to the answers. She listens before she looks. Even when you're just talking to yourself, asking yourself the same questions, be sure listen to the answers carefully before you go online.

Asking the right questions

This happens to me a lot. I was working in the garden and a neighbor meandered up, shaking his head. "I don't know how you do it, this Internet stuff. I spent *six hours* online last night, and I couldn't find what I was looking for." He explained that his son and daughter-in-law were in the process of adopting a Bosnian orphan baby. They were concerned that the child might be seriously underdeveloped; the height and weight measurements they'd been given were far lower than those for an American child of the same age. My neighbor, the concerned granddad-to-be, had promised to surf around the Net to see whether he could find any comparable figures for European children, or kids in war-torn or otherwise stressed environments. He'd fired up a search engine and entered terms such as **height**, **weight**, and **children**. He'd gotten thousands of hits, including a handful of references having to do with kids who'd reached a certain height, or weighed so many pounds or kilograms. But he found nothing even remotely useful for his purpose.

As a researcher, my first thought wasn't about keywords. It was about what my neighbor was really hoping to find: He wanted his information in a form that would list and compare height and weight in relation to age. That insight suggested a much larger concept to me — what he was really looking for was a *table* or *chart*.

Later that day, I threw the terms **height**, **weight**, **children**, and **chart** into the same Web search engine that my neighbor had used. I made sure to specify, which he probably hadn't, that *all* — not just *any* — of those words had to appear in the documents I retrieved. Number 2 on the list I pulled up was a reference to *growth charts for Chinese children*. Browsing further down, it was clear that **growth charts** was the key term I wanted. So I added that phrase to my search, along with **height**, **weight**, and **children**, and got dozens of useful hits.

My neighbor was beside himself with gratitude. "I live to serve," I said modestly, blowing the smoke from my pearl-handled revolver and twirling it around my trigger finger, and then slipping it back in its holster.

Where Do You Start?

One of the biggest time-wasters in the research game is starting off on the wrong track. You can spend hours pursuing dead ends and wondering why you keep coming up empty-handed. All too often, the problem goes right back to the beginning: You may have made a wrong assumption about how, where, and whether to proceed.

Assumptions may be hazardous to your mental health. For quick relief of nausea, pain, and stress, take one or more of these simple correctives as needed:

- ✔ There's no such thing as a comprehensive online search.

- ✔ Information takes different and sometimes unexpected forms.

- ✔ No single search tool works throughout the online universe.

- ✔ No one approach is best. Sometimes it takes a combination.

- ✔ Just because it worked the last time doesn't mean it works now.

- ✔ You can always try something different.

Mental-mapping your online resources

Every one of the search aids and techniques covered in this book has its own strengths and weaknesses. This section includes a quick summary of these aids and techniques, their pros and cons, and which chapters contain more information about them.

Search engines

General-purpose search engines, such as Infoseek, Excite, AltaVista and HotBot, work best when you know — or strongly suspect — that what you're looking for is available on the open Web. The open Web refers to sites that don't require registration or charge a fee, such as company or personal Web sites, or most sites put up by government agencies, trade associations, clubs, or interest groups. Search engines work well in a variety of situations:

- ✔ Search engines make sense when you're looking for the proverbial needle in a haystack, or when you really need to get a great deal of information on a topic.

- ✔ If you're looking for information in a particular form, such as articles in newspapers or computer magazines, hold off — unless you find a search engine that specifically lets you search that kind of material. (See Chapter 13 for some examples of this type.)

- ✔ If you're looking for yellow- or white-page-type listings, maps, or software; or you're looking for what people are saying in online discussion groups, you can probably find a specialized search engine to do the job. (See Chapter 4.)

- If you're looking for news that happened yesterday, or information that's more than a few years old, don't waste your time. Most search engines take a while to update, and the Web as a whole is a bad bet for historical data.

- Search engines like to chomp on unique, specific, and unambiguous terms. If you're researching a person or company with an unusual name, or can include a phrase that's distinctive and meaningful, such as "unidentified flying objects," that query is a good bet for a search engine search.

- If you're having trouble with terminology or you can't pin it down, if you're finding too much out there to sort through, or if you want just a few good references or some general background on a subject, then a search engine is probably not your best bet.

Check out Chapters 3 and 4 for more about the types of search engines described in this section.

Subject catalogs

Subject catalogs, such as Yahoo!, have two things to recommend them: They're organized (usually by subject, no surprise) and they're *selective*. They don't try to include the entire known universe of Web sites, but rather a subset that somebody, often a team of actual human beings, has decided are worthy of inclusion. It's helpful to know when to use — and when *not* to use — subject catalogs:

- It doesn't make sense to mess around with subject catalogs unless you're pretty sure that what you're looking for is out there on the Web at large, and that it's fairly current but not brand new.

- The selectivity factor I mentioned makes subject catalogs *un*suitable for needle-in-haystack and no-stone-unturned searches; for all you know, what you're looking for has already been weeded out.

- Subject catalogs are great when your search terms are vague, your interest is general and unfocused, or you just want a sense of what's out there.

- Turn to a subject catalog first when you know that a great deal of information on your topic exists (a topic such as Internet commerce, for example) and you want to find the sites that are authoritative and devoted exclusively, or extensively, to the subject.

Check out Chapter 5 to read more about subject catalogs.

Guru pages, mega-sites, and web rings

Guru pages and *mega-sites* are more focused, and sometimes more personalized, variations on the subject catalog idea. Guru pages are usually assembled by individuals with an interest in a topic. Mega-sites tend to be more official, often the work of a government agency or other institution. Instead of covering the Web from A to Z like a typical subject catalog does, guru pages and mega-sites focus on a single topic or group of related topics. They include collections of links that the creator of the page or site (I'm using those two words interchangeably here) has visited and found worthwhile. Sometimes you find additional content and editorial commentary there, but a guru page or mega-site is often a gateway to more information on the topic, rather than a goal in itself.

Guru pages and mega-sites may turn up when you do a search engine or subject catalog search. You may hear about them through word-of-keyboard. An actively-maintained guru page or mega-site will often point you to new sites and current information that the search engines and catalogs haven't gotten to yet, and to weirder, more specialized, and more esoteric links. If you find a good one, maintained and updated by someone who seems to know what they're talking about, bookmark it — it may be an incredibly useful shortcut when you're doing research on that subject.

A *web ring* is an interlinked circle of individual pages, all on the same or somewhat related subjects. Instead of just presenting a collection of links, like a regular subject catalog, guru page, or mega-site, a web ring lets you move around the circle directly, from one linked site to another. Web rings have a social component that you won't find in subject catalogs or the other research tools described in this section. Web rings give you human interaction along with your information.

Check out Chapter 6 for more on guru pages, mega-sites, and web rings.

Library catalogs and archives

An online library catalog contains references to resources that are not on the Web, but are physically housed in a particular library. If you're looking for a book or journal article that's already been published in another, non-electronic form, library catalogs are a good place to start. You can search by title and author, and usually by subject, to get the information you need to compile a bibliography, borrow or order the book, or request photocopies from the institution that carries the original.

Library catalogs can't be beat if you're looking for historical information — not just printed documents, but original manuscripts, maps, music scores and recordings, and other special material. They point you to valuable scholarly resources that you won't readily find elsewhere.

Digital archives are usually maintained by libraries and universities, too. They provide a direct link with the past, letting you look at letters, photographs, drawings, plans, and other primary source material used by scholars or people with a deep interest in a field. A digital archive is seldom your first stopping point when you're researching online, but if your subject is historically important and you find an archive devoted to it, you're golden.

Don't look to libraries when what you're seeking is current, fast-changing, or is just for fun. They require concentration and a different sort of approach. You're often dealing with books, original manuscripts, and rare documents that are priceless when researching in certain subject areas. And you may have to master a particular library's peculiarities in order to get access to its treasures.

Check out Chapter 8 to read more about library catalogs and archives.

Ready reference

Librarians use the term *ready reference* to describe questions that can be answered with a simple fact — a statistic, date, or quotation. If you'd normally turn to a commonly-used reference book, such as an encyclopedia, directory, atlas, or almanac, for the answer to your question, consider the Net equivalent — a virtual reference collection or online bookshelf containing the counterparts of those useful and familiar volumes.

Most general-purpose search engines don't dig down in documents where the cold, hard facts are often buried. If you've got a quick, fact-based question in mind, seek out a ready reference collection, go to the exact volume you want, and then look up your answer.

Don't take the ready reference approach if your research goal is broad, vague, complex, or multifaceted, or if you're interested in opinion and analysis from several different perspectives. Also, if you're trying to locate a company or person, hold off — specialized sources exist for that kind of research. I talk about some of these in Chapter 4. See Chapter 7 for more on ready reference.

Proprietary and gated sites

When does it make sense to pay for information, or to seek it out behind a password-protected barrier, as opposed to searching the Net at large?

> ✔ **When you want scope.** Commercial database services, such as Dialog, contain in-depth information, going back many years, on topics ranging from astronomy to zoology, with hundreds of stops in-between. Most of the material in these databases originally appeared in print form, in academic journals, trade publications, magazines, or newspapers. You can sometimes find summaries from expensive and hard-to-get sources, such as brokerage house analyst reports and market research studies.

> ✔ **When you want efficiency.** Proprietary database services allow you to search anywhere from a dozen to several thousand sources at once, with a single search query. If you don't know, or care, what publication is likely to cover your topic, a database search can save you hours, even days, of effort.

Propietary database search engines are precise and powerful. They allow you to search by author or standardized keywords, custom-tailor your output, and do other research tricks that you can't do on the open Web. But you'll have to master some terse and sometimes puzzling commands, like the ones I describe in Chapter 9, and you'll end up paying anywhere from a few bucks to several hundred dollars per search. You may not want to go this route unless you're willing to spend some money and commit to the training it takes to become proficient at searching.

You can also find some database-type information on consumer online services, such as CompuServe and AOL. If you're already a member of one of these services, you may want to poke around to see what you can discover there. CompuServe in particular has some useful research databases. In general, though, you can find better, more complete information in the professional database services and at selected sites on the Web.

Some Web sites, such as *The Wall Street Journal Interactive Edition,* for example, require you to sign up before they grant full access to their contents. These sites are called *gated* sites. Sometimes gated sites charge a fee, sometimes not. Signing up is worth doing if you know that you need this kind of information on a regular, or even intermittent, basis. The content of gated sites seldom, if ever, turns up in a general Web search engine. If a key publication or collection of publications in your area of interest exists on a controlled-access site, it makes sense to register and even pay (ouch) to subscribe. Bonus: Some members-only sites provide access to experts as well. See Chapter 9 for more on proprietary and gated sites.

Human resources

Finding the right expert online can help you figure out how to tackle a research project, brainstorm alternative approaches, or jumpstart a project that's stalled. But, unless you've already established a good working relationship with some invisible buddies in cyberspace, you may not want this to be your first resort. Net denizens are knowledgeable and generous with their time, but don't think you can use them as a substitute for doing the work yourself. Before you ask for help, make an effort on your own. If you come to a series of dead-ends and can honestly say you've run out of ideas, then it's time to call for help.

People are also a good way to track down *soft* news — rumors, *new* news, opinions — news that isn't even news yet, and may never be. For more on locating and tapping into human expertise online, see Chapter 10.

Reality-Checking

Step back and look at the big picture. Chances are you're not going to subscribe to a database service or take the time to master the intricacies of the Library of Congress catalog if you just want to satisfy your curiosity, prove a point, refresh your memory, or bring yourself up to speed on an issue that's been in the news. Real-life, practical concerns, such as planning a trip to Hawaii, getting background on Whitewater, looking up the known side-effects of aspirin, or figuring out what movies Kevin Spacey was in before *L.A. Confidential,* call for a Web search or a quick trip to a supersite you already know, such as the Internet Movie Database (us.imdb.com).

See the Bonus Chapters 1 and 2 on the CD-ROM for loads of tips on how to research hobbies, personal interests, and life decisions like planning a major trip, choosing a college, or finding a job.

The bucks start here

But suppose you're researching something that involves investments, key business decisions, legal matters, or even human lives. You can do a Web search to familiarize yourself with the territory, or to make sure you're doing a comprehensive search. But you're asking for trouble if you stop with the open Web. Serious research, such as the kind required for a doctoral dissertation, patent application, lawsuit, business acquisition, or medical investigation, calls for heavy-duty resources that you find only in proprietary databases, library catalogs and archives, and some specialized, members-only sites on the Web. Sometimes you can't avoid using database services, despite the fact that a sizable investment in time (and fees of anywhere from $9.95 a month to a couple of hundred dollars per search) may stand between you and the answer.

Research is a combo plate

In reality, you may often use a combination of approaches while researching online. You may start with a subject index and move on to a web ring, and from there go to an Internet newsgroup where experts on the topic hang out. Or you run a keyword through a search engine, click on a page that turns out to be full of links on the topic, follow a pointer to a library catalog, and immerse yourself in the virtual stacks.

You may use the Web for current information, and do a database search to fill in the historical blanks. Or you may gather some experts' names from newsgroups and Web sites, and run a database search to get a list of everything those experts have written.

After a while, it becomes a mostly seamless process. You don't even think about it as you glide from one kind of site to another, trying out different tools, tactics, and approaches to your question. You *do* feel a little bump when you move between the open Web and sites where you have to stop and key in a password. You feel an even bigger bump (ooof!) when you decide you have to go from free sites to a site that charges by the search or for every item you look at. But the more practice you have thinking like a researcher, the easier it becomes to make that transition.

When Bad Things Happen to Good Searchers

The moment of truth has arrived: You've thought about your research goal and what you really want to accomplish. You've visualized what the perfect answer looks like. You've chosen your search terms and keyed them in. Now you just sit back and wait for the answers to pour out, right? El wrong-o. The "pour out" part may be accurate; it's the "answers" part that's problematic.

Most of the research tools you've been introduced to in this chapter have their own built-in ways of ensuring that you don't get overwhelmed with information, and that the information you do get is relevant.

Search engines don't work that way — at least not automatically. Whether you use them on the Web or as part of a proprietary online service like Dialog and the others in Chapter 9, search engines are notorious for giving you exactly what you asked for. Sometimes that's way too much to handle. Sometimes it's way too little, or way off target. All kinds of things can go wrong, or at least not totally right, during the course of an online search. Here's what can go wrong, and what you can do about it.

A *hit* is researcher jargon for an item retrieved by an online search that matches — or seems to match — the keywords and other conditions you've specified. Your *results list* is made up of *hits*. A hit may be an answer, or part of an answer, or totally useless. Hits retrieved for unforeseen reasons, such as typos, search terms that mean something else in a different context, or mistakes in search logic, are called *false hits,* or, for reasons buried in the dim past of mainframe computing, *false drops*. Experts call this kind of hit "garbage." If you want to be elegant, put the accent on the second syllable.

If at first you don't succeed . . .

Back before the days of PCs, I worked at a research company where the "search room" was a separate office containing an old-fashioned printing terminal as big as a desktop. You'd hear the printer-head clacking across the paper, and the *ziiiiip* as it moved back to the left side of the page — over and over and over again. Every now and then, there'd be a loud WHOOP! or YEEHAW!! or All RIGHT!!! and one of the searchers would emerge, flushed with triumph and trailing a wide paper streamer as long as the train on a wedding gown. More often, though, the zipping and clacking noises would go on for an hour, and the person who emerged from the room was quiet and subdued, carrying a stack of folded printout. She'd gotten "pretty much" what she was looking for, or knew that she'd be able to piece together an answer from the various sources she'd had to check — or she was resigned to having to go back to her desk and rethink the entire problem from a different angle. Even the pros seldom get it perfect the first time.

Yikes, 42,178 hits! What do I do now?

What you *don't* do is look at all 42,178 of them. Unless you specify otherwise, most web search engines use what's called *relevance ranking* when they present you with your results. Relevance ranking means that the best answers, or the ones that the engine *thinks* are best, will appear toward the top of your list. If you don't find what you want among the top 50 to 100 items, chances are that it won't appear farther down. Time to try a different search engine or some new search terms.

Some search engines offer *Boolean* searching as an alternative to relevance ranking. For proprietary database systems, such as Dialog and LEXIS-NEXIS, Boolean searching is the default mode.

- ✔ When you tell a search engine explicitly that you want documents in which ALL your terms appear, or you string terms together using AND — **apples AND oranges** — you're doing a Boolean search.

- ✔ When you tell a search engine that you want documents in which ANY of your terms appear, or you string terms together using OR — **apples OR oranges** — you're also doing a Boolean search.

In the AND case, you're telling the search engine that you want documents in which both **apples** and **oranges** appear. In the OR case, you're telling it that it's okay to show you documents that contain either **apples** or **oranges**, or both.

The more terms you string together with ORs, the more hits you get. The more you string together with ANDs, the fewer hits you retrieve. OR is *inclusive.* AND is *exclusive.* So, adding more relevant concepts to your search request, and stringing them together with ANDs, is one way to cut down on the volume of results. The Bonus Appendix on the CD tells you more about Boolean searching.

When you do a Boolean search on a web search engine, the results may not be relevance-ranked. Don't assume, before checking, that the items at the top of the list are going to be the best ones.

Set searching is another way to cut down on the number of hits you retrieve. In Dialog and some other proprietary online services, you can do a search in stages, and combine the results of an earlier search (Set 1) with those of one or more follow-up searches (Sets 2, 3, and so on). On the Web, you can sometimes run a second-stage search on a set of existing results. Infoseek, for example (www.infoseek.com) gives you the option of refining your results by doing a second search *only within* the pages you've already retrieved.

You can also focus your results by using features that automatically restrict your search to certain kinds of information. Dialog, Dow Jones Interactive, and LEXIS-NEXIS all let you limit your results in advance to documents published on a certain date or in a particular time period. They generally allow you to limit by language and sometimes geographic region, too. Most web search engines allow various kinds of restrictions, also. But be careful with date-limiting on the Web, since the date often has nothing to do with when the information itself was first published.

Waah! How come I didn't get anything?

A zero hits scenario isn't always a disaster. If you've invented something and want to patent it, or need to find a unique topic for your dissertation, you may be delighted to discover that nobody's thought of it before. Sometimes, there really *is* nothing on a particular subject. But "no results" may be bad news, too, and you can do something about it:

- ✔ Double-check your search terms. A typo or misspelling will throw off your results.

- ✔ Think of synonyms for your search term, or other ways of expressing the concept you're looking for.

- ✔ Don't overqualify at the outset; try adding one term at a time.

- ✔ Make sure you're in the right database, or haven't inadvertently told the search engine to check newsgroups or company directories only, for example, when you intended to do a Web-wide search.

Why on earth did I get this?

Search engines work in mysterious ways, especially on the Web. Some relevance-ranking engines place more emphasis on words that they consider unique, unusual, or distinctive — even if *you* don't think they're the most important concepts in your search. Some place more emphasis on the words at the beginning of your search query, and less on those at the end. A search engine that assigns more relevance to the terms you enter first gives you different results if you type **height weight children** than if you type **children height weight**. You can deal with these tendencies by:

- ✔ Entering your most important terms first
- ✔ Specifying that the terms *you* consider most important are *mandatory,* meaning that they *must* appear in the results

Other reasons why you might get odd and unexpected results:

- ✔ Your keyword may appear just once, in passing, in a very long document. Chances are that the keyword is irrelevant, but the search engine doesn't know that. You may find it easy to overlook these fleeting mentions, but the search engine is just doing what it's told.
- ✔ Your keyword may have an entirely different meaning in another context; for example, banking CDs and audio CDs. If you're researching investments and you're turning up music sites, well, there *could* be a band called **High Yield**. . . .
- ✔ Some Web site promoters engage in a tacky kind of spamming. They load their sites with invisible keywords, such as **sex, Hawaii, sports, money,** and other popular search terms. When you search, you pull up their site, which may have nothing to do with your topic. Many search engines are now smart enough to detect this invisible spamming, but some sites still slip through.

Don't waste time trying to figure out why you turned up a handful of weird items in a search that otherwise looks okay. Loads of possible explanations exist, and it's not worth the effort to try to debug the Web. But if the weird hits outnumber the reasonable ones, heed the signal to rethink your search.

Evaluating what you get

The most tedious and time-consuming part of a search may be paging through your results list. You can speed things up considerably by remembering these three tips:

✔ **Set the display options.** If the search engine you're using offers this option, set it to show the maximum number of hits at once. Paging through 50 or 100 items is much more efficient than clicking the **Next 10** button time after time after time. . . .

✔ **Don't automatically click on every single link that your search engine delivers — not even the ones at the top of the list.** Look at the titles, headlines, or brief descriptions, and follow only the ones that sound most promising.

✔ **Use your intuition.** You can knock out many foreign language sites at the get-go (unless, of course, you're fluent in Swedish, Portuguese, or whatever). If you're looking for authoritative sources, you can quickly discount sites that seem to have been put together by kids, jokers, or cranks. You can skip repeated mentions of the same site, and breeze right past other types of sites, such as commercial, promotional, or technical, that just aren't a match for the kind of research you're doing.

One of the joys of the Web is that anyone can publish on it. One of the dangers of the Web . . . is that anyone can publish on it. Don't assume that what you've found, no matter how good it looks, is valid — not until you've read what Chapter 15 has to say about information quality and how to assess it.

Knowing When You're Done

If you're doing research in your local public library, your resources may be defined by what lies within those four walls. If you're searching a propri-etary database, your resources are limited to the number of records it contains. That number may be huge, but it's manageable. The Net, though, is deep, open to everyone, and potentially unlimited. You could conceivably spend your entire life there, trying to track down every last bit of informa-tion on a topic. And by the time you get through it once, it's time to start over and look at all the *new* stuff. What a gruesome possibility.

How you can tell when an online research project is done?

✔ You run out of time.

✔ You run out of money (if you're searching on a fee-based system).

✔ You run out of patience.

✔ You find the perfect answer.

✔ You reach the point of diminishing returns.

The first three points are self-explanatory. It's all too easy, though, to stay online a lot longer than you have to, wasting time, money, *and* patience, in pursuit of the perfect answer — whatever that may be. A point comes where you have to hang it up, call it quits, declare it done, and get on with your life. A good rule of thumb is that when you start seeing the same information over and over again, recycled through various Web sites, repeated in different magazines, you've probably reached the end of the research line.

Remember that reference interview earlier in this chapter? Don't lose sight of what you set out to accomplish, whether the goal is a definition of beta blockers, a map of Boston, or five good articles on the U.S. economy. Found it? Fine; now *stop*.

Using What You Find

Just because you found it online doesn't mean that the information is totally free for the taking. Using information for your own private edification is one thing. Incorporating it into something that you plan to sell, publish, promote, or distribute to others is quite another.

Before you snarf that well-written article for your own report, cop that cool quote for your Web site, or grab that great graphic for your PowerPoint presentation, check Chapter 15 for the legal lowdown, professional "best practices," and just-plain good manners guidelines for using information you find online.

Part II
The Tools of the Trade

The 5th Wave   By Rich Tennant

"Now when I need a simple answer, I use a search engine that takes me to a subject index from where I link to an online guide that sends me to a web ring and from there I finally arrive at a gateway site. Or I just flip a coin."

In this part . . .

*I*n this part, you take a detailed look at search engines, subject catalogs, research database services, newsgroups, and the other resources available to you online.

In each chapter, you find my pick of the best and most interesting research tools around, together with tips on how to use them effectively and examples of the kinds of research to which each one is best suited.

Be sure to check the CD for an important Appendix covering Boolean logic, field searching, and other professional research tips and techniques that I mention in this part.

Chapter 3

The Search Engine Sweepstakes

In This Chapter

▶ Building an effective search query

▶ Exploring advanced search engine features

▶ Touring the top general search engines

▶ Shortcutting your search with meta-engines

*S*earch engines are the media darlings when it comes to researching on the Web. Before you picked up this book, perhaps you thought that's what online research was all about. A good general search engine can be an invaluable research aid, especially when you have unique keywords to feed it, or you're hoping to find everything on a subject, or you haven't been able to find *anything* on your topic through any other means.

I'll be honest with you, though — there's no such thing as brand loyalty when it comes to search engines. Even professional researchers tend to go with the one that produced good results the last time around, and to chuck it away like last month's leftovers — or at least put it aside for a while — if it doesn't continue to deliver.

Web-based search engines operate in ways that even the pros don't understand. Each one uses a different complex mathematical scheme — called an *algorithm* — to retrieve the results it thinks you're interested in. Each one indexes Web sites and Web pages in a different way. No one search engine covers the entire Web.

You can influence the results up to a point, by taking advantage of the powerful features that are sometimes concealed on pull-down menus or behind a button or link innocuously labeled Help or Search Tips. But you can't predict or totally control the outcome of your search. If one engine doesn't do the job for you, move on.

By all means experiment with the major search engines I talk about in this chapter. Take a look at the sample help file on the CD-ROM. Go online and experiment with them. You'll develop your own favorites. Or maybe not.

Most important of all, though — remember that the search engines I talk about in this chapter are just one small part of the online research picture. You have many, many other tools at your disposal.

Meet the three main types of search engines:

- ✔ **General:** cover — or claim to cover — the entire Web.
- ✔ **Meta-:** can run the same search through several engines at once.
- ✔ **Specialized:** focus on a particular site or kind of research query.

We talk about general and meta-engines in this chapter, and about specialized engines in Chapter 4. *Note:* The search engines I talk about here are ones that I tend to come back to because they produce good results. These are just a few of the dozens of search engines in existence. Your mileage may vary, and that's fine with me.

Timeless Tips for Effective Searching

Regardless of which search engine you use, you can use a few pointers to get you started:

- ✔ Keep It Simple to Start (KISS, sort of): The first time you use a search engine, go for the default search link, whether it's called <u>Quick Search</u> or <u>Simple Search</u> or something equally elementary. Let the search engine do its own thing before you complicate matters with ANDs and ORs, required terms, parentheses, and other advanced options. Before you try something fancy, get a basic grip on how the whole thing works.
- ✔ Enter your most rare and important search terms first: **Tarantino movies** instead of **movies Tarantino.**
- ✔ Use phrases or proper names whenever possible. Enclose them in quotes if necessary: **"chocolate chip cookies"** and **"Chelsea Clinton."**
- ✔ Click the <u>Help</u>, <u>Search Tips</u>, <u>Power Searching</u>, or <u>Advanced Search</u> link (every search engine has one) to find out more about what it can do.

What to Consider When Choosing a Search Engine

The mechanics of how search engines actually process your search are boring to write about, and even more boring to read about — until you actually need them.

At this point, you might want to refer to the Bonus Appendix on the CD, which explains the nitty-gritty of such basic research concepts like Boolean logic, proximity operators, mandatory terms, set searching, case-sensitivity, truncation, and wild cards. Wheee! Understanding at least a little about these features, and knowing how and when to use them, can make the difference between research success and failure.

The following questions should help you evaluate which search engine is right for the job — or whether any one is a clearcut candidate for first place. Remember that the answers to these questions are usually just a click away, under that button labeled Advanced Turbo Mega Power Searching Help Tips.

- ✔ Does the search engine cover just the top level or two of each site, or probe all the way down to every document on every page?

- ✔ Does the search engine include newsgroups, FAQs (Frequently Asked Questions lists), or specialized sources, such as newswires and business directories, in addition to the Web itself?

- ✔ Does the search engine do *field* searching, which lets you restrict your search terms to the title, summary, first paragraph, or URL? All these variables can help focus your results.

- ✔ Can you specify, by using plus (+) and minus (–) signs, a pull-down menu, or some other means, when certain words *must* appear, *could* appear, or should *not* appear in your results?

- ✔ Can you do Boolean searching, which lets you look for sites that mention **Smashing Pumpkins** AND **Nine-Inch Nails; Smashing Pumpkins** OR **Nine-Inch Nails;** or **Smashing Pumpkins** BUT NOT **Nine-Inch Nails?**

- ✔ Can you search for literal phrases, such as "Your mileage may vary"?

- ✔ Can you restrict your results by language, geographic region, or other useful limitations?

- ✔ Is the search engine case-sensitive? No, case-sensitivity isn't an allergy that lawyers develop. It has to do with whether a search engine recognizes upper- and lowercase letters. Some even interpret two capitalized words in a row as a proper name, such as **Tiger Woods** or **Apple Computer**, so that you don't get everything that's available on tigers and woods, or apples and — heaven help you — computers.

- ✔ Does the search engine automatically look for plurals, such as **dog** and **dogs,** or let you use a *wildcard* to stand in for one or more letters if you want to search for alternate forms of a word (**aviat*** = **aviator, aviators, aviation**)?

- ✔ Does the search engine give you the option of refining your search by looking for new terms within the results you've already retrieved?

- ✔ Can you increase the number of results that display per page, or specify whether you want to see more, or less, information about each item?

Exploring General Search Engines

Every time I fire up a search engine I haven't used in a while, I find that I've got to re-familiarize myself with the controls. The software mechanics who build these machines are constantly tinkering with them, trying to improve their performance and make them easier to use. Some of the search engine features I describe here, and the screen shots that accompany these descriptions, may have changed somewhat by the time you read this. Scuzi. As they say on the information superhighway signs, "Temporary inconvenience, permanent improvement."

AltaVista

AltaVista (`altavista.digital.com`) was the first really deep search engine, meaning that it penetrated below the top level of a Web site to pull up references buried one or more levels down. Although it's not the only in-depth player out there anymore, AltaVista is still a good starting point for a comprehensive search.

- ✔ AltaVista enables you to search Usenet newsgroups as well as the Web.
- ✔ It enables you to search in a couple of dozen languages other than English.
- ✔ It allows you to look for people and businesses via the Switchboard directory service.
- ✔ It enables you to browse by subject category, as shown in Figure 3-1, as well as run a regular keyword search. If you think this looks like a subject guide (see Chapter 5 to read about subject guides) rather than a search engine, you're right; many search engines now incorporate both.

Figure 3-1: AltaVista subject categories.

You can target your AltaVista search more precisely by limiting it to:

- ✔ The title of a Web page; for example **title:Dummies**
- ✔ The URL; for example **url:msn**

Limiting your search term to the title is a quick-and-dirty tactic for locating pages devoted exclusively to your subject. Downside: The best resources on a topic won't necessarily be labeled this clearly. But this tactic is worth a try — especially if you're overwhelmed with hits and need some way to cut down on the number.

Limiting your search term to the URL is an even quicker-and-dirtier way to find pages exclusively on your topic. But using the URL alone has an even deeper downside: Although a URL, such as `www.puppies.com`, may be about those cuddly little canines, it may just as well be a lame site for which someone was lucky enough to score and register the obvious name. Only one `www.puppies.com` URL is permitted on the entire Web, and it may not have been assigned to the best possible resource on the subject. (*Note:* When I checked, the `puppies.com` domain was not in use; go for it, and bow wow wow.)

Refining your search in AltaVista

Click AltaVista's Refine button to cut down on the number of hits you've gotten, and to sharpen the relevance of your results.

The Refine screen shown in Figure 3-2 displays other topics associated with your search term (in this case, Kevin Spacey) and their relevance (maybe) to your search. You can click any topic that you specifically want to include or exclude in the next go-round. Click Graph to include or exclude individual terms within each of those categories.

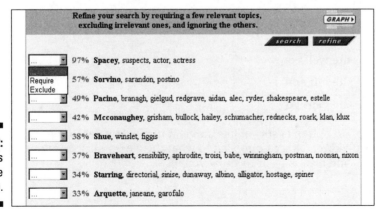

Figure 3-2:
AltaVista's
Refine
option.

Refine your search by requiring a few relevant topics, excluding irrelevant ones, and ignoring the others. [GRAPH▸]

search *refine*

97% **Spacey**, suspects, actor, actress

Require
Exclude

57% **Sorvino**, sarandon, postino

49% **Pacino**, branagh, gielgud, redgrave, aidan, alec, ryder, shakespeare, estelle

42% **Mcconaughey**, grisham, bullock, hailey, schumacher, rednecks, roark, klan, klux

38% **Shue**, winslet, figgis

37% **Braveheart**, sensibility, aphrodite, troisi, babe, winningham, postman, noonan, nixon

34% **Starring**, directorial, sinise, dunaway, albino, alligator, hostage, spiner

33% **Arquette**, janeane, garofalo

Infoseek

Infoseek (`www.infoseek.com`) has always been a solid performer in the search engine sweeps. It's another good bet for a deep, fairly comprehensive search.

- ✔ Infoseek lets you search in French (*et voilà!*) as well as in English.
- ✔ Infoseek covers newsgroups, as well as the Web.
- ✔ If news stories or company descriptions are what you're looking for, confine your search in Infoseek to wire services, industry journals, national newspapers, and other Web-based news sources.
- ✔ Infoseek offers a subject-catalog alternative, called channels (see Chapter 5 for more about subject catalogs).
- ✔ You can refine your Infoseek search, after getting your first round of results, by clicking the **search only within these pages** button and entering some additional terms.

Infoseek is smart enough to assume that two or more capitalized words in succession may be a proper name, a company, or another entity, such as United States Postal Service. The good news is that you don't have to put phrases in quotes like you do with some other search engines. The not-so-good news is that if you're looking for two or more capitalized words that you don't want to be searched as a phrase, you have to separate them with commas: **Netscape Navigator, Internet Explorer.**

Site searching with Infoseek

Infoseek's Site option enables you to pull up all the available pages at a particular Web site. You can then browse to see what the site has to offer or what kind of folks hang out there. After doing a site search, you can enter keywords to search for specific information within the site.

Try:

> **site:well.com**
>
> **site:mit.edu**
>
> **site:usps.gov**

The Site option is sort of like surgery, to me. You get to see what's really inside a Web site, as opposed to what the glossy surface and pre-planned links and menus want to show you.

HotBot

HotBot (www.hotbot.com) gets my vote for the most colorful search form on the Web. This site uses the type of slick, colorful graphics that its sponsor, *Wired* magazine, is notorious for. Figure 3-3 doesn't do justice to its, er, vibrance. Fortunately, the screen is legible, though you probably don't want to peruse it on a moving bus. Even more fortunate, under its rather whimsical surface, HotBot is a lean, mean research machine.

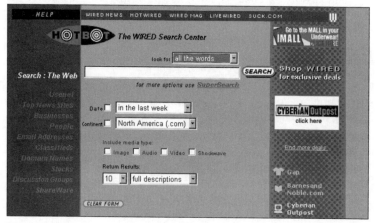

Figure 3-3: HotBot.

✔ HotBot lets you do several different kinds of specialized research right off the bat by restricting your search terms to certain Net resources, such as newsgroups and other discussion forums, current news sites, business and residential directories, e-mail listings (via a link to BigYellow), classified ads, stock quotes, and even Internet domain registrations.

✔ HotBot's pull-down menus and check boxes make it easy to limit your search by date, geography, and media type (including images and multimedia).

✔ HotBot lets you restrict your search term to the title of a Web page.

✔ HotBot lets you tailor your search results by specifying how many items you want to browse at once, and whether you want to see full or brief descriptions, or just URLs.

Refining your search with HotBot

HotBot's <u>SuperSearch</u> link leads to an array of options for narrowing down a search you've already done, or for starting a new search. For instance,

- ✔ You can add or exclude additional words and phrases.
- ✔ You can qualify the search by domain, geographic region, or media type.
- ✔ Not only can you search for general file types, such as **images**, but you can specify extensions, such as **.gif** or **.jpg**, to get exactly the formats you need.

Excite

Excite (www.excite.com) comes across as a subject guide rather than as a search engine. Your first view, as shown in Figure 3-4, is of a catalog of topics ranging from A almost to Z.

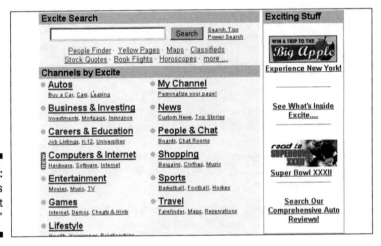

Figure 3-4: Excite's subject "channels."

In addition, Excite offers specialized searching for people, businesses, stock quotes, classified ads and other spending opportunities, news, sports, weather, horoscopes, maps, and more. Click on that more . . . to discover dozens of helpful links to reference books, government information, and other handy resources. Excite also lets you search newsgroup postings via a link to DejaNews. (Check out Chapters 4 and 10 for more on DejaNews.)

Concept searching with Excite

What about the Excite search engine itself? Excite's main claim to fame is what it calls *concept searching*. Like other search engines, it looks for documents containing the search terms you've supplied. But it takes a giant step beyond that, linking your keywords to its own internal database of synonyms and related concepts, and then searching automatically for those terms and concepts as well. This extra step means that if you enter a keyword such as **teenager,** Excite looks for references to adolescents, youths, and young people, as well. Amazing, isn't it?

After you've run your search, Excite suggests additional words you might want to include, and lets you check any that you want to add. Figure 3-5 shows how Excite does that.

Excite not only saves you from having to think up synonyms, but it also gives your brain cells a boost when you're having trouble narrowing down your search. If, while browsing your results, you find one or more items that are very close to what you're looking for, click the <u>More Like This</u> link. Excite uses the terms and concepts in that document as a model for your ideal answer, and refines your search accordingly.

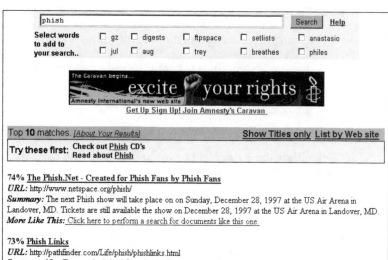

Figure 3-5:
Excite
suggests
additional
words.

Excite extras

Click Excite's <u>Power Search</u> link to uncover a range of other features.

- Search the Web, news sources, international versions of Excite, or a subset of sites that Excite has deemed worthwhile.
- Specify words or phrases that your results can, must, or must not contain.
- Tweak your search output to show you more or less description for each item or to sort results according to the Web site where they appear.

Northern Light

The Northern Light search engine (www.nlsearch.com) is unusual in more ways than name alone. For one thing, it allows you to search not just the Web, but its special collection of articles from nearly 2,000 publications, databases, and other sources, most of which are not readily available elsewhere on the Web. This search engine is also unusual in that it charges a nominal monthly subscription fee covering up to 50 items, or a pay-as-you-go fee, usually in the $1.00 to $4.00 range, for individual items from the Special Collection that you may want to read, print, or download in their entirety. These fees are actually pretty reasonable as subscription fees go, and they're made more so by Northern Light's money-back guarantee.

To get an alphabetical or subject list of the publications that make up Northern Light's Special Collection:

1. **Click Support.**

2. **Then click the Special Collection tab at the top of the following page.**

3. **Click either the <u>by subject</u> or <u>alphabetically</u> link near the bottom of the page that comes up next.**

4. **Finally, click a subject category or a letter of the alphabet to see specific titles.**

Some sample publications in the trade journal area alone include *Bakery Production and Marketing, Communication World, Graphic Arts Monthly, Journal of Coatings Technology, Machine Design, Oil & Gas Journal, Online, Professional Builder,* and *Robotics World.*

Northern Light attempts to refine and make sense out of your search results by organizing them into Custom Search Folders. It creates these folders on the fly, based on the Web sites and the types of information it turns up. You have the choice of browsing a standard, relevance-ranked results list, or clicking any of the folders on the left side of the screen, as shown in Figure 3-6, to read documents grouped by site or type of site (such as nonprofits or personal home pages), by publication title, by language, or by a particular slant on, or treatment of, your topic.

Figure 3-6:
Northern
Light
Custom
Search
Folders.

Making Your Mark with Meta-Engines

A meta-search engine, or *meta-engine,* is an umbrella site: You enter your query just once, and the meta-engine runs it in anywhere from a handful to a couple of dozen search engines, more or less simultaneously. You can cover a lot of ground quickly with a meta-engine, and save yourself huge amounts of time and effort. Sounds terrific, doesn't it?

The downside of using a meta-engine is that it has a lowest-common-denominator effect on your search. It uses only those features that all of the search engines it covers have in common. Not all search engines support features such as phrase searching, Boolean AND/ORs, or wildcard searching for word stems and variations. Individual search engines handle details such as capitalization and punctuation differently, too. Meta-engines therefore ignore many of the variations and refinements that you can take advantage of when you go directly to an individual search engine site. Meta-engines do only the most basic kind of search at each one.

Meta-engines also return a limited number of results from each site they search, at least in the first go-round. If you get to see only 10 or 20 hits, you might miss the perfect item that's ranked at #11 or #21.

What lowest common denominator means for you is a return to the KISS principle: Keep it simple, searcher. This ensures that you don't confuse, or get unexpected results from, any of the search engines involved. Doing a simple search means that your results may be broader than you want, but they should more accurately reflect your intentions.

Inference Find

Using Inference Find (`www.inference.com/ifind/`) couldn't be easier: Enter your search term and hit the search button. That's it. If you really want to put the pressure on, you can use the pull-down tab to vary the maximum number of seconds you want Inference Find to spend on your search. (I can't imagine anyone being in that big a rush; my sympathies if your life really is that harried.)

Inference Find goes out to half a dozen of the top search engines, submits your search to each of them, and brings back the hit list from each one. Before presenting the results to you, Inference Find merges them, removes the duplicates (it gets big points from me for that!), and neatly clusters the remaining items according to their main emphasis or the type of site that they came from. Sometimes that's useful, sometimes not.

SavvySearch

SavvySearch (`http://guaraldi.cs.colostate.edu:2000/form`) is an experimental meta-engine. The form shown in Figure 3-7 includes check boxes for limiting your search to certain types and categories of information (you can select as many as you want). A pull-down menu enables you to specify whether you want any or all of your terms to appear in any context, or whether you want to search them just as you entered them, as a phrase. A couple of dozen language options for the SavvySearch interface appear at the bottom of the screen.

You can tune SavvySearch so that it shows you more or fewer references at once, and more or less information about each one. The Integrate results box, when checked, tells SavvySearch to merge results and present them in a single continuous listing. Leaving it unchecked gives you a separate hit list from each individual engine searched. Whichever way you go, SavvySearch presents you with a Search Plan, which predicts which of the search engines it uses is likely to be most productive for your current topic.

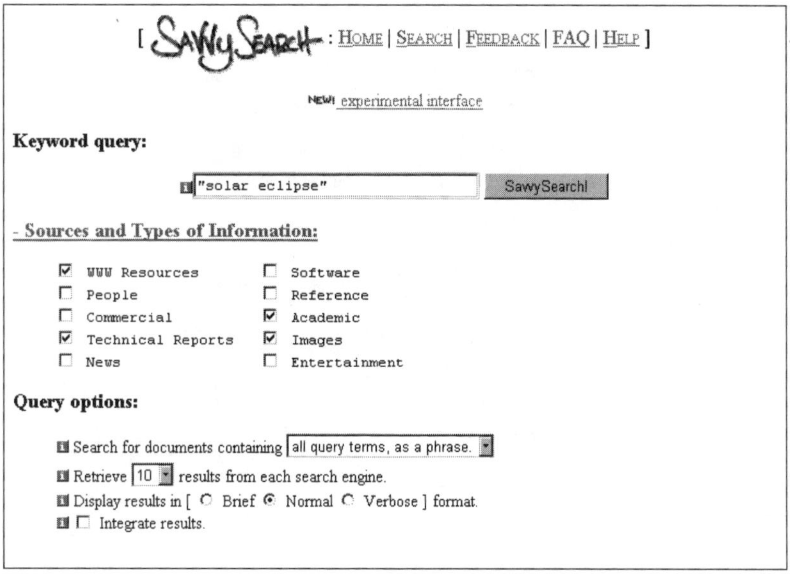

[SavvySearch : HOME | SEARCH | FEEDBACK | FAQ | HELP]

NEW! experimental interface

Keyword query:

"solar eclipse"   SavvySearch!

- Sources and Types of Information:

☑ WWW Resources   ☐ Software
☐ People   ☐ Reference
☐ Commercial   ☑ Academic
☑ Technical Reports ☑ Images
☐ News   ☐ Entertainment

Query options:

▪ Search for documents containing [all query terms, as a phrase. ▾]
▪ Retrieve [10 ▾] results from each search engine.
▪ Display results in [○ Brief ⦿ Normal ○ Verbose] format.
▪ ☐ Integrate results.

Figure 3-7:
SavvySearch
search
form.

Leaving the Integrate results box unchecked allows you to judge more easily the kind of information each search engine is turning up.

Internet Sleuth

The Internet Sleuth engine (www.isleuth.com) takes a different approach — actually, several different approaches in a single meta-engine:

✔ It enables you to select up to six of the major search engines and directories, as shown in the top box in Figure 3-8.

✔ It enables you to run your search instead in up to six of the "top," "reviewed," "new," and "best-of-the-web" sites shown in the second box in Figure 3-8.

✔ It enables you to run your search through specialized news, business and finance, software, or newsgroup sources, by means of additional boxes you can scroll down to on the same screen. These boxes don't show in Figure 3-8.

✔ It maintains its own index, on the left side of the page, to hundreds of specialized databases, guides, and references in particular subject areas. Click **List all Categories** at the top of the index (it's not visible in Figure 3-8) for a more detailed subject breakdown, or on any single category for an expansion of that one.

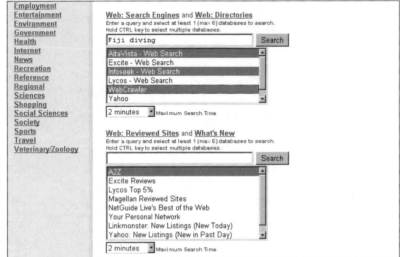

The Internet Sleuth includes a handy chart (www.isleuth.com/ hts-chart.html) showing which of the major search engines support advanced features such as Boolean AND/ORs, wildcards, mandatory terms, and title searching.

Ask Jeeves

Ask Jeeves (www.askjeeves.com) is a meta-engine with a twist. First, it attempts to find the answer to your plain-English question in its own vast collection of Internet resources. Figure 3-9 shows what happens when I ask Jeeves "Where can I find out about travel to New Zealand?" It displays a list of closely-matching questions that it understands. The first question happens to be an exact match, and when I click it, Jeeves takes me to a fine collection of New Zealand travel sites.

But, as they say on the late-night TV infomercials, "that's not all!" Following the list of questions, Jeeves shows me a list of search engines that, er, it has gone ahead and checked on its own (give that machine a bonus for initiative!), along with the number of hits for each one. I can browse all the hits by clicking the arrow to the right of each box, and go directly to the full results list at each site by clicking the search engine name.

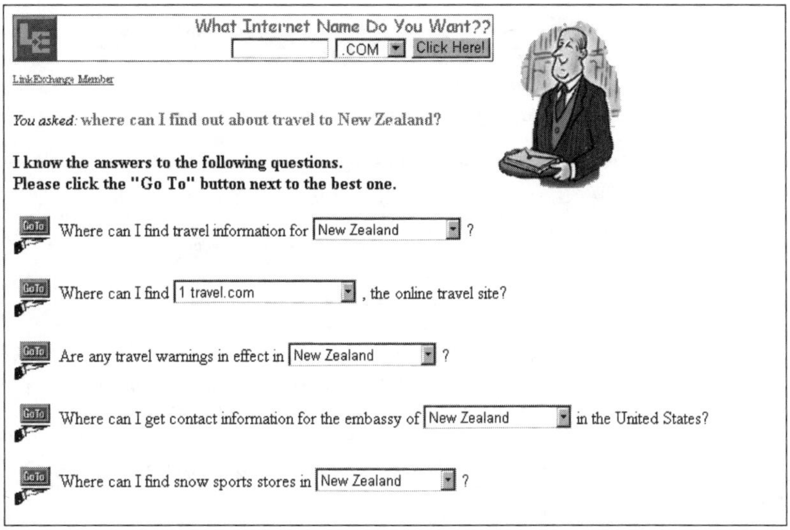

What Internet Name Do You Want??
[   ] .COM ▼ [Click Here!]

LinkExchange Member

You asked: where can I find out about travel to New Zealand?

I know the answers to the following questions.
Please click the "Go To" button next to the best one.

[Go To] Where can I find travel information for [New Zealand ▼] ?

[Go To] Where can I find [1 travel.com ▼] , the online travel site?

[Go To] Are any travel warnings in effect in [New Zealand ▼] ?

[Go To] Where can I get contact information for the embassy of [New Zealand ▼] in the United States?

[Go To] Where can I find snow sports stores in [New Zealand ▼] ?

Figure 3-9:
Ask Jeeves
rephrases
my
question.

ProFusion

Brought to you by those fun-loving folks at the University of Kansas, the ProFusion meta-engine (www.designlab.ukans.edu/profusion/) shown in Figure 3-10 runs your search through any or all of its selection of top search engines. You can let ProFusion choose the best search engine, based on the type of search you're doing, or you can make your own selection. ProFusion also offers an automatic updating service: Tell it what you're interested in, and ProFusion promises to notify you of any new information it finds on a weekly, biweekly, or monthly basis.

Dogpile

I saved the best one, or at least the best name, for last — Dogpile (www.dogpile.com). This puppy runs your search through as many as 25 search engines at once. Its Custom Search feature enables you to choose and prioritize your favorites. You can use the same query in general search engines such as Infoseek and AltaVista, newsgroup search engines such as DejaNews, and even specialized FTP file-finding tools.

Because Dogpile searches so many engines, and each one has its own features, quirks, and limitations, it's best to keep your search query as simple as possible. Be sure to read Dogpile's *Help with Syntax* section before you get yourself in deep doggy, uh, trouble.

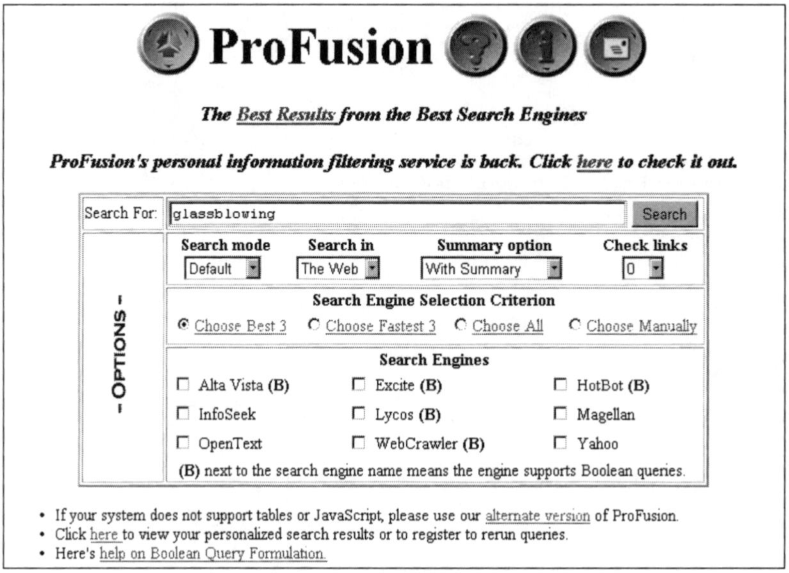

Figure 3-10:
ProFusion
search
form.

Watching the Web with Search Engine Watch

Search Engine Watch (searchenginewatch.com) is like Consumer Reports for truly dedicated Web searchers. It monitors and compares the performance of all the major players you've met in this chapter, and keeps you up-to-date on new developments in the field. I devour every edition of the Search Engine Report, a free monthly newsletter sent out via e-mail. But then, I get my jollies in some pretty strange ways.

Chapter 4
Using Specialty Search Engines

● ●

In This Chapter

▶ Exploring specialty search engines

▶ Searching online discussion groups

▶ Finding people, companies, maps, and software

● ●

*T*he half dozen or so search engines whose names you see every time you read an article about the Net are only a small part of the picture. General and meta-engines, such as the ones outlined in Chapter 3, are fine when you want to cover the entire Web. But the Swiss Army Knife approach isn't always the best one. You may be researching in an area where information is organized in a particular way, such as a phone directory, a shareware catalog, or a collection of maps. You may need to penetrate into sites and special collections that standard Web search tools can't reach. Sometimes you need a tool that's designed to do just one job, and to do it well.

How do you find a specialty search engine that'll do that job for you? Luckily, a number of Web sites have taken it upon themselves to catalog and keep track of the expanding population of search engines. Some sites even include a collection of search forms, one for each specialty engine they've identified, so that you can enter your search without leaving the site. Others provide a set of links, so that you can click and go.

These sites are different from meta-engines. They don't actually take your search and run it through multiple search engines, nor do they process any of your results. These sites simply provide a convenient, one-stop interface to a variety of different search engines — more than any of the meta-engines cover; more than you probably dreamed existed.

The All-in-One Search Page

One of the oldest sites of its type on the Web, the appropriately named All-in-One Search Page (`www.albany.net/allinone/`) presents a dozen or so broad categories of search engine types, including <u>People</u>, <u>News/Weather</u>, and <u>Technical Reports</u>.

Other Interesting Searches/Services, a miscellaneous, catch-all category, lists nearly 50 individual search engines, most of which are accompanied by a search form on the All-in-One page itself. Try the FedEx or UPS package tracking service, the Searchable Online Recipe Archive, or Money magazine's stock quote service.

Search.Com

Search.Com (`search.com/`) compiles research tools from hundreds of different sites Net-wide. You can search any of a handful of top search engines from Search.Com as well. But check out the A-Z List of live links to get an idea what's out there *beyond* the usual suspects: How about the AmeriCom Long Distance Area Decoder? America's Job Bank? The Auto Trader Online Dealer Search? And those are just a few of the **As**!

Beaucoup Search Engines

Beaucoup (`beaucoup.com`) boasts links to more than 1,000 search engines, aids, and indexes. You can browse through a couple of dozen broad categories, from the all-purpose to the highly specialized, and then link to the categories that you want to search. Beaucoup provides a terrific summary of hard-to-find resources in education, politics, science, music, art, and *beaucoup* other research areas. That's *a lot,* just in case you don't speak French.

Searching Newsgroups with DejaNews

Newsgroups — you may hear Net.graybeards refer to them as *Usenet* or *netnews* — are a sprawling, global collection of ongoing conversations about everything under, and beyond, the sun. Picture a humongous party with knots of people all talking at once about subjects ranging from medieval armor to microchip technology.

The last time I checked, I found more than 50,000 individual newsgroups, each one devoted to a particular subject. Undoubtedly, more than that exist by now. No matter how you look at it, there's a whole lot of schmoozing going on. Those umpteen-thousand groups are organized into several broad categories. Within each category, individual groups are arranged hierarchically, from general discussions down to the ultra-specific. Some categories are several layers deep. If I talk about the `rec.sport` hierarchy, I'm already one layer beneath the surface. `rec.sport.football` is a layer below that. You might think I've hit bottom, but no — the `rec.sport.football` hierarcy goes even lower — to `rec.sport.football.australian`, `rec.sport.football.canadian`, `rec.sport.football.college`, `rec.sport.football.fantasy`, and `rec.sport.football.pro`.

Newsgroups are an excellent source for fresh, timely news, opinion, and advice. Chapter 10 tells you more about how to find newsgroups in certain subject areas, and how to act when you get there. Right now, I want to concentrate on mining that vast conversation pit for specific, focused information.

The DejaNews search engine (`www.dejanews.com`) is a fine tool for digging into newsgroups. DejaNews offers both a **Quick Search** and a **Power Search** mode.

Quick searching

For a quick search on DejaNews, you just key in your topic and go. Unless you tell it otherwise, DejaNews runs your search in everything but the job-posting and "adult" newsgroups. That's DejaNews' considerate way of screening out unwanted distractions. Of course, if you're *looking* for job opportunities or "adult" material, or wouldn't mind running across them in your search, you can choose accordingly from the pull-down menu. Go ahead; I won't tell your boss. Or your mom.

Power searching

For power searching, DejaNews gives you several more options:

- ✔ Using **Keywords matched: All** or **Any**

- ✔ Limiting your search to recent newsgroup postings (roughly the latest month's worth) or to older ones

- ✔ Limiting your search to a particular newsgroup or newsgroup hierarchy

- ✔ Limiting your search to postings by a particular individual (author)

- ✔ Limiting your search to postings made on a certain date or during a specific time period

- ✔ Seeing more or fewer postings at once, and more or less information about each posting

- ✔ Sorting the results of your search by relevance, or by date, author, subject headers, or the newsgroup in which they were posted

If you've discovered a Net guru or a newsgroup that's been particularly helpful in the past, you can enter their names in DejaNews' Power Search Author(s) or Group(s) box, respectively, and look for pearls of wisdom exclusively from that source.

Figure 4-1 shows the Power Search screen, and my search for newsgroup postings about diving in Fiji.

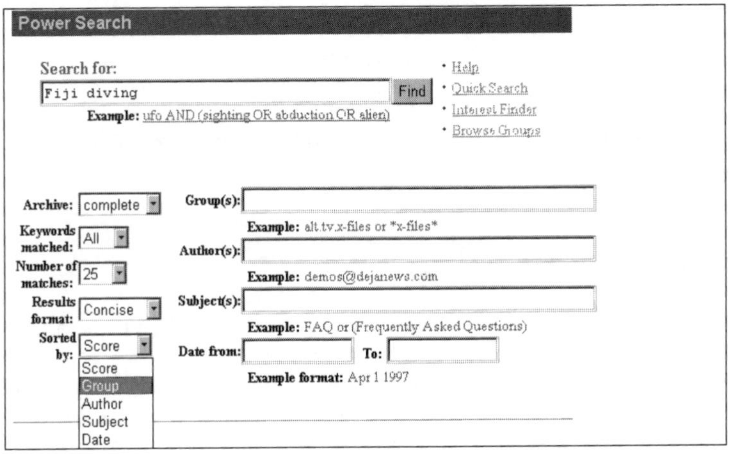

Figure 4-1:
DejaNews
Power
Search
screen.

Power Search	
Search for:	• Help
Fiji diving [Find]	• Quick Search
Example: ufo AND (sighting OR abduction OR alien)	• Interest Finder
	• Browse Groups

Archive: complete
Keywords matched: All
Number of matches: 25
Results format: Concise
Sorted by: Score
 Score
 Group
 Author
 Subject
 Date

Group(s): [   ]
Example: alt.tv.x-files or "x-files*"
Author(s): [   ]
Example: demos@dejanews.com
Subject(s): [   ]
Example: FAQ or (Frequently Asked Questions)
Date from: [   ] To: [   ]
Example format: Apr 1 1997

Figure 4-2 shows the results of that search. After your results come up, scan the list of subject headers, and then click any header to read the actual message. Once you're reading messages, it's a matter of clicking your way through the online conversation, message by message, listening to what people are talking about. From my simple two-word search on diving in Fiji, I found out more than I wanted to know about scuba outfitters, boat operators, the logistics of getting there, cyclone season, Fijian culture (including *kava,* a popular Fijian liquid refreshment) and — most intriguing of all, if I were really planning a trip and not just indulging in a pleasant mid-winter fantasy — what underwater sights I must see.

Refining your DejaNews search

You can include any of these elements in your DejaNews search query:

✓ Boolean operators, such as AND/OR (equivalent to the **Power Search** option: **Keywords matched: All** or **Any**)

Power Search Results Help **?** free homepages

25 Matches for search: `Fiji diving` [Find]

```
     Date     Scr      Subject              Newsgroup            Author

 1. 98/01/21 036 Capt Cook Cruises Fiji     rec.scuba            Herbert A. Lenze
 2. 98/01/21 036 Capt. Cook Cruises Fiji    rec.scuba.locations  Herbert A. Lenze
 3. 98/01/21 033 Re: Capt. Cook Cruises Fiji rec.scuba.locations George Kyriazis
 4. 98/01/08 031 Re: Fiji Snorkeling        rec.scuba.locations  Al Rider
 5. 98/01/07 031 Diving in Bahamas?         rec.scuba            Marcos H. Woehrman
 6. 98/01/17 030 Re: New Year's Eve 1999 Plan rec.travel.air     MrLFH
 7. 98/01/15 030 Re: Local News article on 3 rec.scuba          Phil Carta
 8. 98/01/13 030 Re: Help, please          rec.scuba            Kenneth A. Smith
 9. 98/01/07 030 Re: Diving in Bahamas?     rec.scuba           Bruce Christoffers
10. 97/12/31 030 Re: Fiji                   rec.scuba.locations  daniel kessler
11. 97/12/29 030 Re: Fiji                   rec.scuba.locations  jdrisko
12. 98/01/08 029 Re: Diving in Bahamas?     rec.scuba            Canadian Diver
13. 98/01/05 029 Re: Thailand scuba locations rec.scuba.locations Torben Vering Søre
14. 97/12/24 029 Re: Playa del Carmen - Cozum rec.scuba          Phil Carta
15. 98/01/14 028 Re: Vegetarian-friendly loca rec.scuba.locations Dan Volker
16. 98/01/12 028 Re: little cayman          rec.scuba.locations  Cecil Max Bloch
17. 97/12/24 028 Re: Playa del Carmen - Cozum rec.scuba.locations Jose' Kirchner
18. 97/12/20 028 Re: fiji conditions        rec.scuba.locations  charles en marij
19. 98/01/13 027 Re: Day trips from London ? rec.travel.air      Phil Carta
20. 98/01/12 027 Travel / Exploration (Af#9/1 rec.arts.books.market Thaddeus Books
21. 98/01/12 027 Travel / Exploration (Af#11/ rec.arts.books.market Thaddeus Books
22. 97/12/28 026 Travel / Exploration (Af#9/1 rec.arts.books.market Thaddeus Books
```

Figure 4-2:
DejaNews
Power
Search
Results.

✔ A **NEAR** operator, which enables you to look for two terms that occur close to each other, but not in any particular order: **women near military**

(**NEAR** is more precise than **AND,** but less restrictive than looking for the two terms as part of the same phrase)

✔ Phrase searching ("enclose your phrase in quotes")

✔ Wildcard searching (**bank*** also picks up **banks, banking, bankruptcy,** and so on)

See the Bonus Appendix on the CD for more information on Boolean operators and other ways of refining your research techniques.

Getting Discussion Group Updates with Reference.Com

Reference.Com (`www.reference.com`) is similar to DejaNews, up to a point. It enables you to

✔ Do a simple search by entering a keyword or phrase.

✔ Select advanced mode to search older postings.

✔ Limit your results to specific newsgroups, subject headers, or authors.

With Reference.Com, you can also search for postings by organization. That's one way to find newsgroup participants who are affiliated with a certain company, school, or research institution.

Reference.Com includes a couple of other valuable extras: It searches electronic mailing lists as well as newsgroups. And it enables you to set up search queries and then store them so that you can run them whenever you want.

What's a mailing list?

Mailing lists are different from newsgroups. Chapter 10 goes into mailing lists in more detail, but the main distinctions are:

- You can't just cruise by and read or post to a mailing list. You have to subscribe to have access.
- Mailing list messages come to you as e-mail.
- Mailing lists are often more business-like than newsgroups; they tend to stick to the subject.

Stored Queries with Reference.Com

You can set up a permanent search question — or as permanent as you want it to be — using Reference.Com's *Stored Query* feature. Say you have an ongoing interest in diving in Fiji (sigh . . .) and you want to know when new postings on the subject appear:

- Register by clicking Login at the top of the main Reference.Com page, and then click New users at the bottom of the next page. Fill out the form and click Register. You'll get a confirmation in e-mail; put an X in the box as instructed, and e-mail it back to Reference.Com.
- Log in again and create your search. (Test it first as a regular, real-time search to make sure that it produces the results you expect.) When you're happy with the results, click Add to Query List.
- Fill in the Add Query form. (The Query Name isn't the search itself; it's just a title that you've chosen to identify the search — like Diving in Fiji, or just Fiji, as shown in Figure 4-3.) If you have more than one stored query, choose a distinctive name for each one.

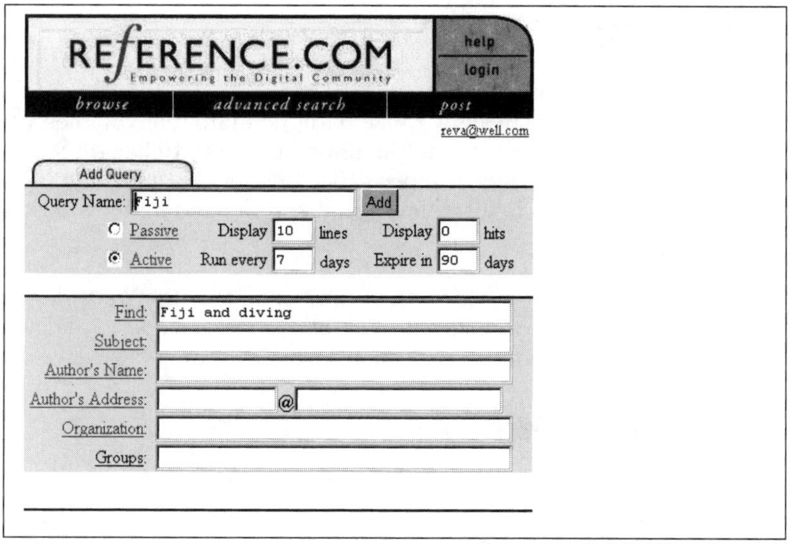

Figure 4-3:
Reference.Com
Add Query
feature.

✔ The Subject box and the boxes that follow it are additional filters you can add at this point. Unless you find that you're getting too many results, you probably want to leave these boxes blank.

✔ Choose either Passive or Active Query. What's the diff? Good question: Reference.Com saves *passive queries* so that you can run them whenever you visit the site. *Active queries* are more like an automatic clipping service: You specify on the Add Query form how often you want Reference.Com to run your search. Each time it does, it sends you a summary of your results (assuming any results do come up) in e-mail. You can read the complete messages at the Reference.Com site.

✔ When you're done filling in the form, click Add. You'll get a confirmation message from Reference.Com.

✔ To add, delete or modify a stored query, log in to Reference.Com, click the User profile tab, and then on Add query *or* the query name you want to change.

Using Reference.Com via e-mail

You can search Reference.Com using e-mail, and even set up and manage stored queries through e-mail as well. Some people prefer the e-mail approach; it's faster, and it can help in a pinch when you're stuck with a slow modem, or your Web connection is acting sluggish. For complete instructions, click <u>Help</u>, and then select <u>E-mail Access</u>. The instructions are lengthy, so if you're interested, print them out for future Reference.Com.

Pinpointing People

Finding folks in online "white pages" has some advantages over picking up the phone book (especially those pathetic mutilated volumes you find hanging forlornly in some public phone booths). Unlike directory assistance, it doesn't cost 50 cents or more a call. Best of all, though, you can do a nationwide search in just a few seconds — and sometimes pick up e-mail addresses as well.

You may run into "people finders" at sites all over the Web. Many of these link back to one of the two biggest directory providers, *Four11* and *Switchboard*.

Calling Four11

To find an e-mail address in the Four11 directory (www.four11.com):

1. **Enter the name of the person in the search form, shown in Figure 4-4. If you know the** domain **portion of their email address — such as** aol **or** netcom **or** ibm **— you can enter that, too. (Four11's SmartName feature automatically accounts for common variants, such as** Bob **and** Robert**.)**

2. **Click the Search button.**

3. **On the results list (if any), click the name of a person to get her e-mail address.**

4. **Write the person and ask for money. Just kidding.**

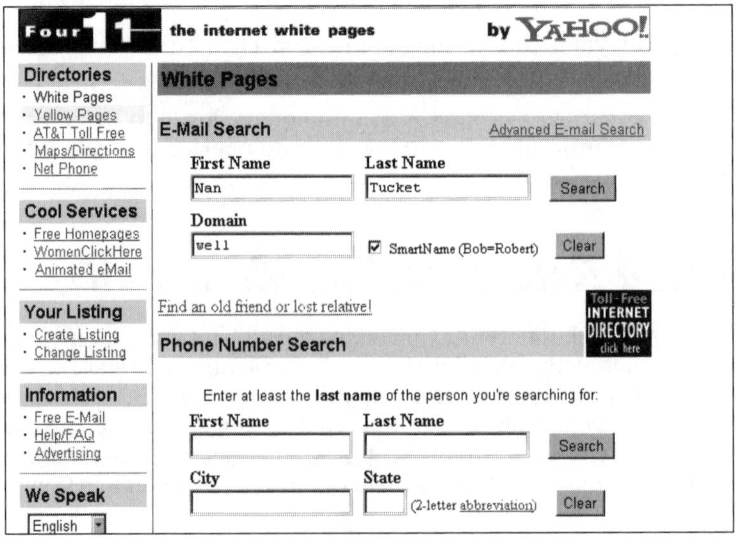

Figure 4-4:
Four11
people-
finder form.

To find a phone number (in the U.S. only):

1. **Enter the person's last name and first name or initial in the search form shown in Figure 4-4. (Remember that many people prefer to list themselves by first initial.)**

2. **Enter the city and/or state, if you're sure of it. (This helps if the person has a common name.)**

3. **Click the Search button.**

4. **On the results list, click a person's name to get his phone number.**

From Four11's main search page, click <u>Advanced Search</u> to find the names of old high school friends, people from other parts of your past, or folks who share your current interests.

Plugging into Switchboard

To find an e-mail address in Switchboard (`www.switchboard.com`):

1. **Click the Find E-mail icon.**

2. **Enter the person's last name (if the last name is very common, try entering his first name, too, or the first two or three letters of the name).**

3. **Click Search.**

4. **Click his e-mail address — are you ready for this? — to send him mail.**

To find a phone number through Switchboard:

1. **Click the Find people icon.**

2. **Enter the last name — and more, if you want.**

3. **Click Search.**

4. **Choose your victim — er, friend — from the resulting list.**

Some Tips for People-Finding

Online directories tend to be much better at finding phone numbers than at finding e-mail addresses. That's because directories get their telephone information the old-fashioned way — from published directories and the same databases used by phone companies nationwide.

The problem with e-mail listings

Online directories' e-mail listings depend largely on folks who volunteer their own listings, and that's still a very small percentage of e-mail users worldwide. Very few of my online friends are listed in either Switchboard or Four11, and some of the listings I do find are outdated. When you order new phone service, your listing is automatically updated and shows up in the next edition of the phone book — unless you've requested an unlisted number, of course. But no built-in way exists to keep your e-mail listing current — nor, for most people, is there any incentive to do so.

They're not listed — now what?

Here are some tips to keep in mind if you're not having much luck:

- ✔ If one directory doesn't work for you, try another.

- ✔ Start out with a general search, using the last name and initial, or just last name. The directory may show an initial, a nickname, or a formal name other than the one you associate with the person.

- ✔ Don't include a city at the outset. The person may have moved, but kept the same e-mail address, or even the same phone number.

- ✔ Don't expect online directories to be any more timely than the local phone book.

- ✔ Explore other avenues for finding people online:

  - Do a general Web search to see if the person has a home page.

  - Check student, faculty, and staff directories at colleges and other institutional Web sites. Many college and university sites are listed at www.mit.edu:8001/people/cdemello/univ.html or (take a deep breath) www.clas.ufl.edu/CLAS/american-universities.html.

  - Check high school and college alumni associations through weber.u.washington.edu/~dev/others.html or www.yahoo.com/Education/Organizations/Alumnae_i_Assocations.

  - Use DejaNews to search for newsgroup posts the person may have written, assuming she's a newsgroup kinda person.

  - Is she famous, or well-known in her field? Has she written books or published articles? A search in local or national newspapers, scholarly journals, and trade publications, or even online bookstores, such as Amazon.com, may turn up contact information. (More about these sources in Chapters 9, 11, 12 and 13.)

• Celebrity listings: Did you go to high school with Courtney Love? Just wanna catch up on old times? Uh-huh. Don't overlook Four11's Celebrity listing (under **Directories**). Or check out `www.yahoo.com/Reference/White_Pages/Individuals/Celebrity_Addresses/`.

Locating Businesses

Looking up companies can be tricky business. Is it listed under *IBM* or *I.B.M.* or *International Business Machines?* Is it *The Gap,* or *Gap, The,* or just plain *Gap?* Good old *Macy's,* or the more formal *R.H. Macy and Company?* Does the subsidiary or division have the same name as the parent company? Are you sure? People-searching has its complexities, too, but at least you don't have to think about who *owns* them.

Business directory searching drives librarians nuts, especially when they're paying a couple of dollars a pop in a commercial database to pull out *wrong* companies along with the right one. Web directories sometimes charge companies for the privilege of being listed, but they usually don't charge *you* to use them. That's good news, because it means you can afford to experiment if your first attempt doesn't work out.

Finding firms with BigBook

BigBook (`www.bigbook.com`) enables you to search by company name, or Yellow Pages-style, by category. It does insist on a city or state, so you can't search for every Ace Hardware in the country. But you can get a list of the 50 or so Ace Hardwares in Chicago. You can opt for a category search instead, to get *all* the hardware stores in the city, regardless of name.

Category searching

Category searching is tricky at times. Of course you can guess the name under which your business is classified, and maybe you'll hit it right. But if you browse through BigBook's category listing, you won't find hardware stores under <u>Shopping</u>; they're part of the <u>House and Garden</u> category. Moral: Think creatively, not categorically.

BigBook's **Detailed Search** mode, shown in Figure 4-5, expands your options in several different ways. You can search by category and name at the same time, though you still have to enter a city or state.

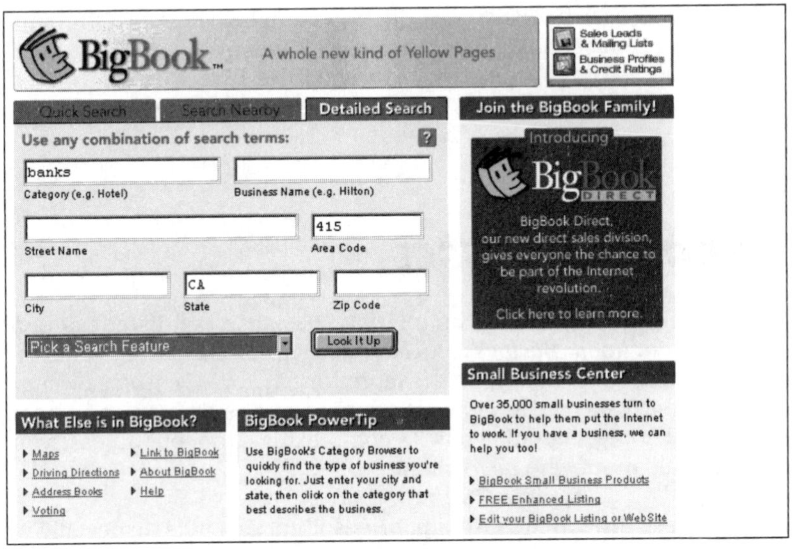

Figure 4-5:
BigBook's
Detailed
Search
form.

Suppose you want to get an address of all the banks in area code 415, or all the drug stores in zip code 19102? Key in the category and the code you want (no need for city or state with these), and your list of possibilities appears (see Figure 4-6).

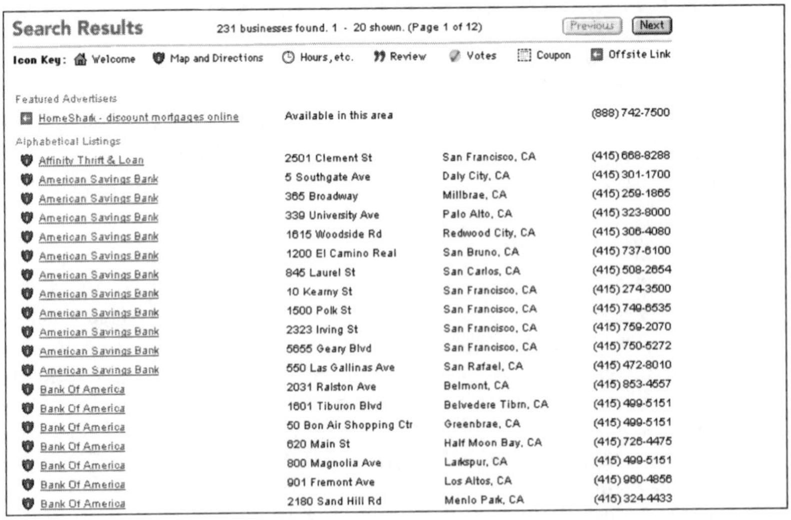

Figure 4-6:
BigBook
business
listing.

Remember that great Italian restaurant on Walnut Street in Philly? Yeah! Now, what was the name of that place? No problemo: Key **Italian restaurants** into BigBook's category box, and enter the street and city. BigBook comes back with a list of pasta-bilities. None of 'em sound right? Um, maybe it was on *Locust* Street . . . or possibly *Spruce*. Or . . .

Where's the nearest . . . ?

BigBook also enables you look for businesses by type or specific name, within a 1- to 25-mile radius of a certain address or intersection. Click Search Nearby, and then enter the business name or category and make sure the appropriate button is selected. Use the pull-down menu to specify how far to extend your search, and then supply either a full street address with the number, or just the name of the street with a cross street in the Cross Street box. Finally, enter the city and state, and click Look It Up.

Go ahead and try it. I already know I have to drive 10 miles for a pizza.

Use BigBook's Search Nearby to help you determine whether an area is already saturated with the kind of business you want to open, or whether a market opportunity exists for you. If you want to open a bookstore but discover 40 bookstores already operating within 10 miles of your intended location, perhaps you'd better think about opening a different kind of business. Or moving.

Any BigBook business listing that's accompanied by an Interstate Highway logo includes a map, and sometimes driving directions.

Going global with WorldPages

What if your interests go beyond finding a list of hometown banks, nearby bookstores, or good restaurants in a U.S. city you're planning to visit? WorldPages (www.worldpages.com/) adds Canada to the mix, to start with. This business directory site also includes specialized mini-directories of legal, government, automotive, entertainment, restaurant, and travel resources.

The key to global business research, though, is WorldPages' International Search & World Resources section, which links to company directories in more than 50 countries. So far, the resources in some areas are pretty sketchy, but I figure that's because not all countries are industrialized to the point of using company directories routinely — let alone putting them on the Web. Factor in the language barriers and problems with displaying different alphabets, and it's amazing that anyone's figured out a coherent way of getting so much of this stuff online.

WorldPages has made a good start. Just click on that <u>International Search & World Resources</u> bar at the top of the page, and then select the country you want to search from the pull-down menu, and then click Find It. Next up: a list of directories for that country (see Figure 4-7).

Figure 4-7:
International
directory
choices
from
WorldPages.

From there, you're one short step away from your quest for hotels in Stockholm or car rentals in Lund. Better make it *two* clicks — you see a button on the left labeled **English.** Ah, there you go. Much better. (Figure 4-8 shows the Svenska button, for switching back into Swedish.) Unless, of course, your Swedish is a lot better than mine.

Figure 4-8:
Swedish
company
directory
search
form.

Questing for Maps with MapQuest

I love maps. You may have heard the saying, "the map is not the territory." My reaction is "Okay, but I still love maps." As far as I'm concerned, one of the best uses of all that bandwidth brought to us by the Web is the ability to display maps online, and even draw them to order.

You can find maps and links to map sites all over the Web, including BigBook and WorldPages. At MapQuest (www.mapquest.com/), you can

- ✔ Browse through an interactive world atlas, zooming in and out from a country-wide view down to street level.

- ✔ Pinpoint an exact address.

- ✔ Get driving instructions (city to city and, for urban areas in North America, door to door).

- ✔ Locate places of interest, such as restaurants, hotels, museums, theaters, and even ATMs.

- ✔ Create maps that include markers for your friends' addresses and other likely destinations.

- ✔ Print, download, and save your personalized maps.

- ✔ Link from your own Web site to a customized map you've created and saved at MapQuest. (You have to join MapQuest for this, but membership is free.).

- ✔ Plan a trip itinerary with help from the Mobil Travel Guide.

You've gotten an invitation to your high school reunion. (If you haven't graduated from high school, use your imagination to visualize that grand event.) Years have passed since you visited your home town, and a lot has changed — new highways and buildings have gone up, and old landmarks are gone. You think you can still find your way, but wouldn't it help to have a current map?

Point your browser to www.mapquest.com, click <u>Interactive Atlas</u>, and key in the coordinates — an exact address, or the cross streets. Click Search and, almost instantly, something like Figure 4-9 appears.

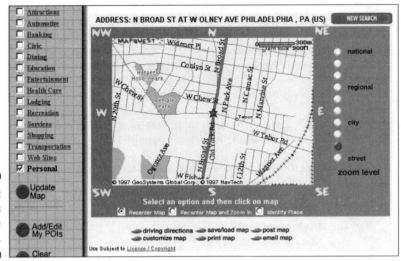

Figure 4-9:
MapQuest's
Interactive
Atlas.

The **zoom level** panel at the right enables you to click in for a closer view of the immediate area, or back up for a picture of the neighborhood. The **city** view shows you your destination in context; that is, what part of town you're headed for.

You're not planning to drive across country for this reunion, but you need some help getting there from the far-flung corner of the city where you're staying the night before. Advance-planner that you are, you click <u>driving directions</u>. Then you enter your starting point and your destination in the form that pops up next. Other options at the bottom of the screen enable you to choose what kind of map you want, or select written directions only (Text Only). One more click, and you're on your way, with custom-tailored instructions to print out and take with you — assuming you remember to grab them before you leave.

MapQuest hasn't mapped the entire country, let alone the world, down to street level. Door-to-door directions only work when your journey starts and ends in certain major urban areas. If you can't get door-to-door directions, your fallback is city-to-city.

Want to avoid the interstate, or take the fastest route, even if it involves a few more miles? Click Door-to-Door Options and select Fastest versus Shortest. Click any of the listed obstacles — such as local streets, major highways or frontage roads — that you prefer to avoid. Now if only MapQuest could tell us about construction zones and commute-hour traffic backups.

Shopping for Software with Shareware.Com

I'm a wuss and a wimp when it comes to sniffing out neat software utilities on the Net and then figuring out how to get them from *out there* onto my computer. Don't let my matter-of-fact demeanor in Chapter 1 fool you: I've anguished through Archie searches. I've fought my way through FTP. Commands such as **prog** and **mget** make my blood run cold. Searching is easier with a friendly assist from a helper program such as WS_Archie or Anarchie (check the CD for some software you can use), but you're still faced with *finding* worthwhile stuff in the first place.

My life improved — to say nothing of my self-esteem — the moment I found Shareware.Com (`www.shareware.com`). Shareware.Com is a catalog of publicly available software found in shareware archives and other distribution sites around the world. You can search it by program name, type of application, hardware platform, or operating system, and by other useful criteria.

If you know exactly what you're looking for, enter the name of the program or file in the Search For: box, and select your computer type or operating system. Click Search, and Shareware.Com displays a list of matches, with descriptions and keywords for each. Another couple of clicks and a copy of the program is en route to your hard drive.

Don't put that in your mouth; you don't know where it's been! Okay, substitute "on your disk" for "in your mouth." The point's the same: Strange software can sometimes make you sick. Unless you're very, very sure of the source, run every executable file you get from the Net — that means shareware and freeware, Java applets, anything that has the power to modify information on your hard drive — through a virus-checking program before you install it. Shareware.Com does no virus-screening, and the "reliability guide" it displays when you've opted to download a file is just a measure of how many successful connections have been made to that software archive or FTP site.

What if you don't have a particular software package in mind, but you know what you want it to do? Or you've heard of a program that you'd like to check out but you're not quite sure of the spelling? Click Power Search to bring up the form shown in Figure 4-10. Then specify your computer type or operating system, and enter descriptive words to help pin down what you're looking for.

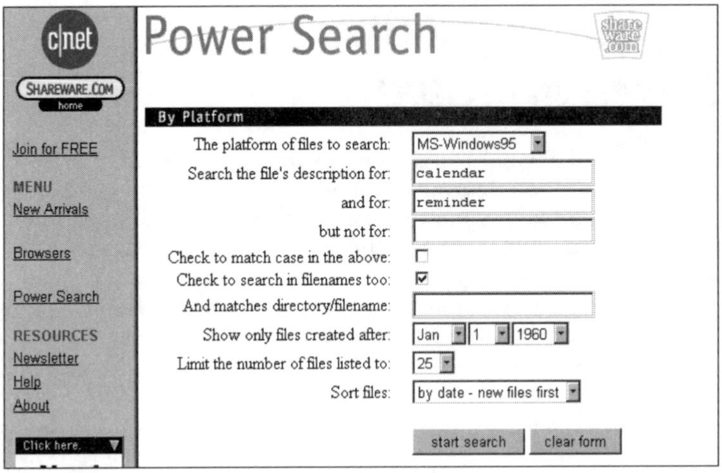

Power Search

By Platform	
The platform of files to search:	MS-Windows95 ▼
Search the file's description for:	calendar
and for:	reminder
but not for:	
Check to match case in the above:	☐
Check to search in filenames too:	☑
And matches directory/filename:	
Show only files created after:	Jan ▼ 1 ▼ 1960 ▼
Limit the number of files listed to:	25 ▼
Sort files:	by date - new files first ▼

start search   clear form

Figure 4-10: Share-ware.Com Power Search options.

Power Search extends your options a gazillion-fold. You can tell Shareware.Com to

- *Exclude* a certain word — useful when you want to eliminate whole categories, such as games or spreadsheets, from your search.

- Pay attention to capitalization — Shareware.Com is normally case-insensitive.

- Limit to files created after a certain date.

- Sort by date.

- Search particular software archives — assuming you know where you want to look.

Don't overlook the Simple Search option at the bottom of the Shareware.Com Power Search page. Despite the name, Simple Search is pretty powerful too. It lets you look for synonyms like calendar OR scheduler, which Power Search does not. The Quick Search option on the same page is similar to the basic one-word search form you see when you first navigate to Shareware.Com.

Feel like browsing rather than searching? You don't have to go beyond Shareware.Com's main page to check out its featured software packages, listed by name, category, and operating system.

Chapter 5
Subject Catalogs: The Narrow-Down Approach

• •

In This Chapter
▶ Browsing versus searching
▶ Drilling down for precision
▶ Sampling subject catalogs

• •

Remember the card catalog? I'm sure a few still exist out there. Before libraries went electronic, those wooden cabinets stuffed with 3 × 5 cards occupied a position of honor. And justifiably — they held the key to finding what you wanted, even if you didn't know exactly what you were looking for.

Without a card catalog, you'd have to wander aimlessly up and down the aisles, glancing at the titles on hundreds of book spines until some of them start to look relevant, until you finally find the right shelf and the volume or two that you need. In a large library, that could take hours. With a catalog, your fingers — and your mind — do the walking. Good thing libraries still have catalogs, though the cards today are often electronic.

Narrowing Your Search: The Drill-Down Drill

I like the term *drilling down* to describe how you can start out with a very general heading and gradually, by selecting the right subheading and perhaps an even more specific subheading after that, narrow in on precisely the subject you're looking for.

For example, the library subject catalog enables you to start with a broad topic, such as **History,** and then narrow it down by place — **European** — and time — **19th Century** — until you have a manageable number of books on the topic to deal with. You can narrow it down even farther:

History
History — European
History — European — 19th Century
History — European — 19th Century — War of 1812
History — European — 19th Century — War of 1812 — Personal Narratives

I'm making these headings up, in case any librarians out there are keeping score. But you get the idea: Start broad, then drill down through progressively more specific levels, defining your target as you go. Now, are you going to gasp with surprise when I tell you that online subject catalogs work exactly the same way that offline subject catalogs do? I didn't think so.

You may encounter the terms **subject guide, subject index,** and **subject catalog** used interchangeably on the Net. They all refer to pretty much the same thing. I use **subject catalog** in this book.

Subject Catalogs versus Search Engines

Search engines get most of the attention when it comes to researching online. But subject catalogs are just as important, and sometimes even better:

- ✔ **Subject catalogs are *selective*.** They don't claim to include everything — just the best, most important, or most focused information on a topic. Often, that information is chosen by people who are experts in the field.

- ✔ **Subject catalogs are *more controlled*.** They don't depend on you to choose the right keyword or come up with the optimal search query. Instead, they present a set of logical choices, gateways for you and your questions to flow through.

- ✔ **Subject catalogs are *built by human beings*** who think the way you do — or understand how most human beings think — while search engines are built on a foundation of math, linguistic analysis, and a lot of other abstract constructs.

When should you use a subject catalog instead of a search engine? No law says that you can't use both, of course, but it makes sense to start with the subject catalog approach when:

- ✔ You don't know quite what you're looking for, but you'll recognize it when you see it.

- ✔ You're looking for general background on a very broad topic, such as American politics.

- ✔ You can express your subject in many different ways; or you can't think of a standard vocabulary term, key phrase, or bit of jargon for a search engine to chew on.

Hybrid Subject Catalogs

Several major search engine sites have recognized the value of the subject catalog approach, and added a subject catalog to their site. You can use the search engine as you normally would, to search the entire Web, or use only the subject catalog portion of the site. I use the term *hybrid* — as opposed to *pure* — to describe subject catalogs that are part of a search engine site and integrated closely with it. Three of the biggest ones are described in the following three sub-sections.

Getting a hole-in-one with Yahoo!

Many people think of Yahoo! as a search engine, but it's actually a subject catalog, and the first Web-based catalog to attain fame and fortune. That exclamation point isn't my editorial expression of enthusiasm; it's a trade-marked part of the Yahoo! name (although it's not in the URL: `www.yahoo.com/`). Still, despite the fact that its two young developers are millionaires and I'm not, I don't begrudge 'em that gratuitous punctuation mark; Yahoo! has earned its !.

Figure 5-1 shows the main Yahoo! search form. But before you go ahead and type a search term in that box up top, take a closer look at those subject categories below it.

I used Yahoo!'s subject catalog to do some quick background research on a subject I knew nothing about. You see, some friends of mine have been leaning on me to play golf. I've been resisting. Swinging at a little white ball has always seemed to me like a sure way to ruin a perfectly good walk. Besides, my upper body strength is nil and I'm sure I couldn't hit far enough, and do they *make* people wear those ugly clothes?

Still, I admit I'm getting curious. Rather than ask my friends and betray my budding interest, I take my questions to the privacy of Yahoo!. I can just type in **golf** and see where it takes me. But I want to explore the whole terrain; get the lay — or the lie (golf joke) — of the land.

Scanning Yahoo!'s top level categories, I figure that <u>Recreation</u> is probably a good starting point. The subcategories shown underneath indicate that the category covers sports, among other things — and golf, as far as I know, is a sport. <u>Sports</u> is also a link, so I click that, and come up with an alphabetical list that includes an amazing array of activities: Baton Twirling, Camel Racing, Dogsledding, Rodeo — oh, and Golf. Reluctantly leaving behind my visions of baton twirling while camel racing, I click <u>Golf</u> and the results appear, as shown in Figure 5-2.

Figure 5-1:
Yahoo!
search form
and subject
catalog.

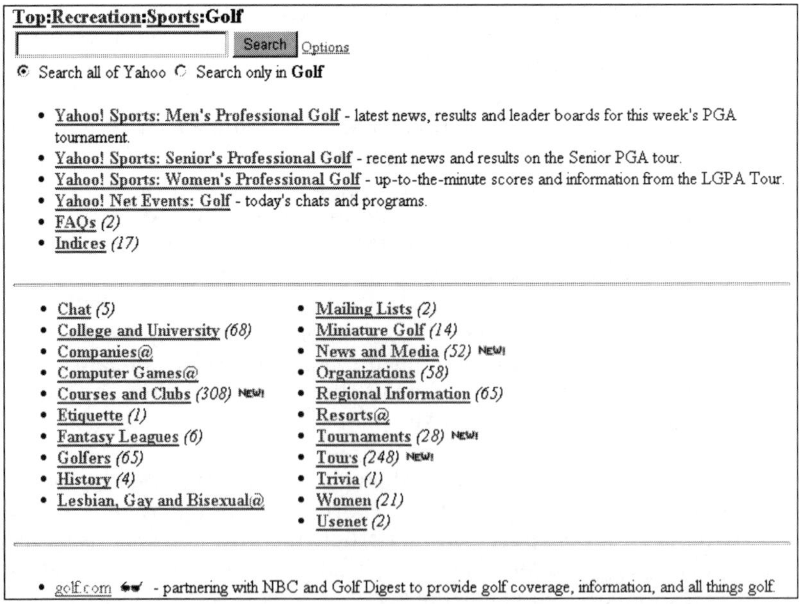

Figure 5-2:
Golf sub-
categories
in Yahoo!.

Yahoo! presents me with a neat three-part summary of golf-related resources:

- ✔ **The first part consists of sites that the Yahoo! golf pro considers especially timely and important** — PGA tour updates, scheduled golf events on the Net (yes, there are such things — real-time golf chat, celebrity golfer interviews, and so on), and pointers to two valuable research leads, **FAQs** (Frequently Asked Questions) and **Indices** (the proper plural, strictly speaking, of *Index*).

- ✔ **The second part includes themes and variations on the subject of golf,** similar to those subheadings in the library catalog I talked about earlier in this chapter — history of golf, golf resorts, golf trivia, and so on. It also covers specific kinds of information, such as chat groups, newsgroups, and mailing lists.

- ✔ **The third part is a long list of golf-specific sites** (the first item is just barely visible at the bottom of Figure 5-2). When I checked, this part contained nearly 60 sites, and every one looked like a hole-in-one.

Compare all this to the random assortment of links (no pun intended) that you get if you simply type **golf** into a search engine such as Infoseek or AltaVista. Go ahead; try it. I'll wait.

Getting an education with Excite

Excite (www.excite.com/) is known mainly as the search engine that knows what you're thinking. Well, not quite, but its concept-based searching and "get me more like this" feature *are* pretty impressive. (See Chapter 3 for more about these Excite features.) Excite's subject catalog, which it calls channels, isn't as deep or comprehensive as Yahoo!'s, but it does offer a quick route to some of the most commonly researched topics.

Again, resist the temptation to just type-and-go. Instead of entering a keyword in the search form in Figure 5-3 and letting Excite have its way with you, maintain control by taking the subject catalog approach.

The only advanced degree I'm likely to earn at this point is from the University of Life. I probably have enough credits there for my Ph.D. But when the parents of a high school sophomore asked me "Is there anything on the Internet that'll help with this college thing?" (how's that for a well-defined search question?), I jumped at the chance to educate them, and myself in the process.

I start with Careers & Education. The three narrower subheadings listed under it, Job Listings, K-12, and Universities, help define the scope of the category. Each of these subheadings is also a live link to more specific information. I click Universities, and get a screen that offers me more specific subtopics, such as Fields of Study, Financial Aid, and Student Life.

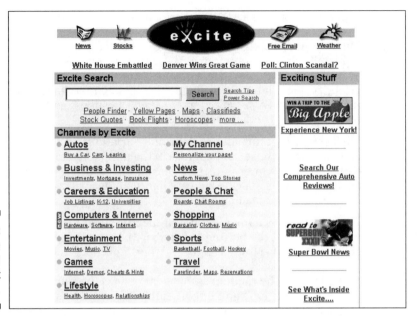

Figure 5-3:
Excite
search form
and subject
catalog.

Scrolling down a bit, I see a highly selective list of half a dozen or so **Recommended Web Sites.** At the bottom of that list is a link inviting me to <u>Click here for more sites</u>. When I do that, I find more promising-sounding resources: <u>College Bound</u>, <u>College Cost Calculator</u>, <u>CollegeNet</u>, the <u>Online Student Survival Guide</u>, and <u>Peterson's Education Center</u>. One site even offers online tours of college campuses.

And check out that California Virtual University right at the top of the page. It looks like my high school sophomore pal can get a degree without leaving home. Wait'll I break the news to his parents.

Infoseek and ye shall find

Infoseek has picked up on the subject catalog or channel idea, too. Its categories (shown in Figure 5-4) are very, very, *very* similar to Excite's, though I'm sure that's entirely coincidental. Right. But that's okay. It's sort of validating to discover that great cataloging minds *do* think alike. Besides, every subject catalog is almost certain to pick up some unique resources that you may not find, or at least not as readily, with another. As with search engines, you may need more than one subject catalog for optimal results.

Figure 5-4:
Infoseek
search form
and subject
catalog.

I chose Infoseek's <u>Business</u> channel for a quick tutorial in small business management. I know it's there because the subcategory listing under the main category heading advertises "<u>Business resources, small businesses</u> . . . " — *and more,* is what those three dots are telling me. I can shortcut the procedure at this point and click directly to the small business category, but I decide to take the indirect approach, via the broad <u>Business</u> heading, just to see what else Infoseek has in store. The **Business Web sites** listing in Figure 5-5 tells me that I may want to check subcategories such as <u>Business resources</u>, <u>Marketing</u>, and <u>Women in business</u>, too.

I can click <u>Small business</u> right from the Business Web sites listings. It takes me to the same place as if I'd selected <u>Small businesses</u> from Infoseek's broad <u>Business</u> category (see Figure 5-4). Figure 5-6 shows Infoseek's small business offerings.

✔ At the top is a list of a dozen or so small-business topics — starting, financing, and expanding a business; franchising; home offices; and more. Each one is a link leading to more specific information on the subject.

✔ These topics are followed by a list of individual Web sites. Check marks next to the top two dozen or so sites indicate Infoseek's special recommendation.

✔ The rest of the list — and it's a long one, with thousands of entries — is ungraded. The list is far more extensive than what you'd get with Yahoo! or Excite, although it may be too much of a good thing. Sometimes you may prefer a more selective approach; other times, you'll be grateful for the opportunity to browse a couple hundred — if not thousand — more hits.

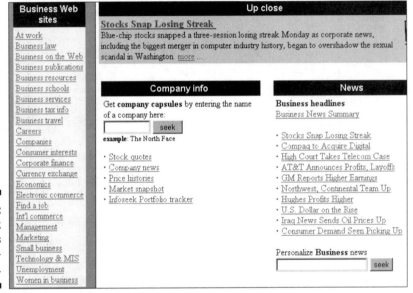

Figure 5-5: Infoseek Business sub-categories.

Figure 5-6: Infoseek's small business offerings.

Pure Subject Catalogs

Yes, pure. Don't laugh. The subject catalog approach goes back to before the dawn of the Internet, when librarians strode the earth. In that primitive era, the idea of venture capital funding for search engine startups was unheard of, and would've been laughed at — ho ho! — as absurd. Subject catalogs were woven out of bark and carved, slowly and painstakingly, in stone.

You don't believe me, do you? Okay: When I talk about a "pure" subject catalog, I mean one that's put together by experts with a focus on finding the very best and most authoritative resources online, no matter how esoteric or deeply buried they may be. These resources don't depend on search engines, or need to mesh, as the hybrid subject catalogs do, with the ever-changing Web at large. They cover academic research topics as well as popular ones, and they have "Heavy-Duty Research Tool" written all over them. The WWW Virtual Library and the Argus Clearinghouse are two of my favorite pure subject catalogs.

Scholarly sites operate at a different, usually far more leisurely, pace than the Web at large. Finding sites that haven't been updated in months, or even years, is not uncommon. Depending on the topic, this may not be a problem: Resources in a field such as medieval studies are probably fairly static compared to the rate of change in science and technology. Just be aware that some otherwise excellent subject catalogs aren't all that up-to-date because they're put together by people — who have *lives* — and not by machines. But some of the sites they *link to* may, in turn, point to more recent entries.

World Wide Web Virtual Library

Remember when they actually called it the "World Wide Web"? No matter how you tried to abbreviate it, anything that required you to say "double-u" out loud already took longer to say than saying "World Wide Web" itself. Even the hip and insider-ish "triple-dub" has as many syllables as the phrase it's supposed to replace.

The World Wide Web Virtual Library (`vlib.stanford.edu/ Overview.html`) — sometimes streamlined to the W3 Virtual Library — is the essence of cool, despite its gawky name. Why? Because it was invented by Tim Berners-Lee, the creator of the Web itself.

Figure 5-7 hints at the range of information to be found on the Virtual Library's shelves. The catalog pages for individual topics are housed on servers all over the world. Every one is different, but each is maintained by a certified expert in the field. Many pages are written in an easy-to-follow narrative style, with lots of description and personal commentary. It's almost like having a personal guide to the subject.

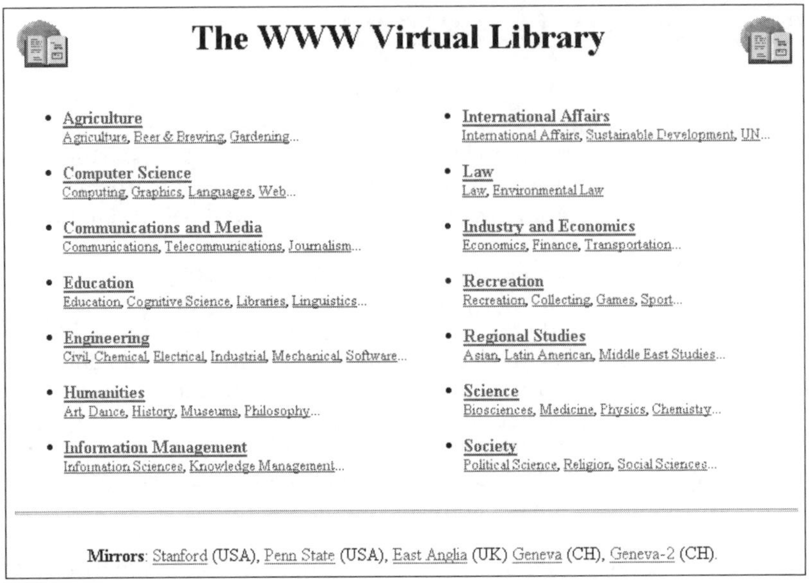

The WWW Virtual Library

- **Agriculture**
  Agriculture, Beer & Brewing, Gardening...

- **Computer Science**
  Computing, Graphics, Languages, Web...

- **Communications and Media**
  Communications, Telecommunications, Journalism...

- **Education**
  Education, Cognitive Science, Libraries, Linguistics...

- **Engineering**
  Civil, Chemical, Electrical, Industrial, Mechanical, Software...

- **Humanities**
  Art, Dance, History, Museums, Philosophy...

- **Information Management**
  Information Sciences, Knowledge Management...

- **International Affairs**
  International Affairs, Sustainable Development, UN...

- **Law**
  Law, Environmental Law

- **Industry and Economics**
  Economics, Finance, Transportation...

- **Recreation**
  Recreation, Collecting, Games, Sport...

- **Regional Studies**
  Asian, Latin American, Middle East Studies...

- **Science**
  Biosciences, Medicine, Physics, Chemistry...

- **Society**
  Political Science, Religion, Social Sciences...

Mirrors: Stanford (USA), Penn State (USA), East Anglia (UK) Geneva (CH), Geneva-2 (CH).

Figure 5-7:
The World Wide Web Virtual Library.

Yesterday I couldn't even spell engenir, and today I are one

I got that line from an engineer. *He* seemed to think it was funny. But hey, why don't we look at the Engineering category as an example of how the W3 Virtual Library works. (Am I smooth or what? Don't answer that.)

The Virtual Library lists more than two dozen subcategories under the general heading of Engineering. They range from specialties, such as Acoustics and Vibrations or Aerospace, Aeronautics and Aeronautical Engineering (yes, this *is* rocket science) at the top, to Wastewater Engineering and Welding at the bottom.

Under Telecommunications, I notice a subheading — probably because it's the only subheading on this particular list — for Amateur Radio. Back when I was a girl geek, I was

intrigued by ham radio, but lost my nerve when I discovered I'd have to learn Morse code (I was going to be a doctor, too, before calculus had the same chilling effect). Go ahead, I tell myself; click it.

The W3 Virtual Library comes through: The Amateur Radio page offers three dozen or so neatly-organized resources, many with descriptions, for hams and wannabe-hams: clubs and organizations, government regulations, frequency guides, information on packet radio, amateur satellites and other technologies, and links to sites such as the Amateur Radio Beginners Information Page (www.acs.ncsu.edu/HamRadio/FAQ/). Oh, and tests. *Dit-dit-dit dah-dah-dah dit-dit-dit....*

Subject catalogs are a good way to find *mega-sites* and *guru pages* (such as the ones described in Chapter 6) that search engines won't turn up.

Argus Clearinghouse

The Argus Clearinghouse (`clearinghouse.net/`) is — are you ready for this? — a subject catalog of subject catalogs. It began as a research project for library school students who were instructed to ferret out indexes, bibliographies, catalogs, and guides-to-the-literature in dozens of academic disciplines, wherever on the Net they existed.

Compared with the hybrid catalogs (see the "Hybrid Subject Catalogs" section earlier in this chapter), Argus's top-level categories have a definite scholarly bent. No Automobiles, Games, or Shopping here. Instead, you find groupings such as Arts & Humanities, Business & Employment, Communications, Computers & Information Technology, Education, Engineering, Environment, Government & Law, Health & Medicine, Places & Peoples, Recreation, Science & Mathematics, and Social Sciences & Social Issues.

Argus categories go deep. I'm curious to see what the Net may hold for a lit major — like I was — today. I scan the list and then click <u>Arts & Humanities</u>. That produces a list of narrower topics ranging from <u>Architecture</u> (cross-indexed, a note tells me, to the top-level <u>Engineering</u> category), <u>Cinema</u>, <u>Dance</u>, and <u>Design</u>, to <u>Music</u>, <u>Performance Art</u>, <u>Philosophy and Religion</u>, and <u>Visual Arts</u>. Ah, there, right in the middle — <u>Literature</u>.

When I click the Literature subcategory, Argus presents me with a list of about 20 literary topics. I've got <u>poets</u>, <u>postmodernism</u>, <u>science fiction</u>, <u>Shakespeare</u>, <u>world literature</u>, and <u>young adult literature</u> to choose from.

I'm now two levels down in the Argus subject catalog. I've gone from <u>Arts & Humanities</u> to <u>Literature</u> and am now about to descend one more level, into my old specialty, <u>American Literature</u>. See why I call it *drilling down?* When I click <u>American Literature</u>, Argus presents me with a general and comprehensive-sounding guide called **Researching American Literature on the Internet**. Argus applies a detailed rating system to all the resources it includes.

One more click, on `www.sccd.ctc.edu/~sbeasley/mais/maishome.html`, and I leave the confines of the Argus Clearinghouse and land at the college where Sarah Beasley has mounted her extensive list of Web sites, electronic journals, archives, mailing lists, online discussion groups, and other useful resources for students of American literature.

The Mining Company

The Mining Company (www.theminingcompany.com) takes the idea of the expert subject guide and carries it one step further. The company hires real people not only to put together collections of worthwhile resources in their area of expertise, but to interact with you and keep you up-to-date through newsletters, e-mail, bulletin-board discussions, and scheduled online chats. These experts are actually called *guides,* though they could be called *miners,* because their job is to mine the Net for premium resources and haul these resources out, into the light of day.

I'm curious about some of the herbal remedies, such as St. John's Wort, that are supposed to be natural alternatives to prescription drugs. Are they really useful? Can they be harmful instead of helpful to your health? I tried a search engine search, and it pulled up a ton of stuff about herbs and alternative medicine — some of it pretty weird. This strikes me as one research area where an experienced guide could save me a lot of grief.

From The Mining Company's home page I select the Health category, and from the Alternative Medicine submenu (the other choices at this level are Disabilities, Diseases, Fitness, Medicine, Mental Health, and Women's Health) I pick Herbs for Health. I find articles right there on a couple of the hottest herbal remedies, plus links to related subjects such as Chinese medicine, gardening, herb books and manuals, a newsletter, and sources for herb plants and seeds.

Access to chat, a discussion forum, and an e-mail link to the Herb goddess . . . , er, guide, are all part of the herbal brew. It's a comforting concoction, like having a friend say, "Here, read *this,* and let me know if you have any questions." Other parts of The Mining Company site may not be quite as mellow, but they have that same friendly, yet well-informed, feeling.

Chapter 6

Playing the Links: Guru Pages, Mega-Sites, and Web Rings

*T*he Internet has always been a barter economy. Long before anyone dreamed up the phrase *electronic commerce,* people were building useful tools, archives, and collections of information, and offering them up to their fellow Netizens, for free. If you derived value from the Net and were in a position to create something useful in return, you were expected to "give something back" — not necessarily to the person whose tools you'd used, but to the Net at large. That way, the public storehouse of software utilities, directories, and documents of all kinds continues to grow and become even more valuable. A FAQ, or Frequently Asked Questions list (see Chapter 10) is an example of someone — or several someones — giving something back.

What does "giving something back to the Net" have to do with doing research online? That's simple: Much of what people created — and continue to create — is useful information on a topic about which they happen to be the resident guru. You know the guy who's a walking encyclopedia of baseball statistics? The woman with her own personal database of every Beatles recording in existence — including the rare, early English imports? The kid who loves stamps, or dinosaurs, or vintage airplanes?

They're all on the Web. And they've put up Web pages full of information, and pointers to *more* information that they've ferreted out of the far corners of cyberspace — obsessively, in some cases — just because they love the subject. And they want to share their enthusiasm with you. Aren't you lucky?

I'm not being sarcastic. You really *are* lucky. You may not want to be cornered by a heavy-breathing philatelist at a party where you can't escape. But if stamp collecting is what you're looking for (and who am I to judge?), finding a good guru page puts you one step ahead in the information-gathering game.

Institutions like universities, libraries, government agencies, and businesses sometimes perform a similiar guru-like function, compiling pointers to useful sites for particular kinds of information, or coordinating the Web resources of their entire organization — and sometimes other, related entities, too — and presenting it in a way that helps ease your way through the bureaucratic maze. I call these concentrations of institutional wisdom *mega-sites* (*mega* meaning large) because they act as gateways to anywhere from a handful to hundreds of other individual sites.

Mega-sites are a form of guru pages, but since a guru is usually a person, I've reserved that term for Web-spun labors of love, and the more formal-sounding *mega-site* for pages put together by some official agency or institution.

Web rings are yet another way of giving something back to the Net. Like guru pages and mega-sites, web rings connect you to additional resources on a topic. But rather than just presenting you with a list of links, web rings form their own closed circle, allowing you to move from one site to others within the ring.

What guru pages, mega-sites, and web rings have in common is *links*. Each one includes — and some consist of nothing but — a compilation of links to *other* sites that someone has checked out and deemed worthy of inclusion. Often, the links are right up front; you see them as soon as you navigate to the site. If they're not obvious, you may have to click around a bit; look for pointer-type phrases such as *Useful Links, Related Sites,* or *Other Blah-Blah Resources* (for *Blah-Blah,* fill in the topic that the site is dedicated to, assuming you're not actually looking at the Ultimate Blah-Blah Page). The real value of such sites lies in their expertly-chosen links to new and potentially useful information. Finding a good guru page, mega-site, or web ring is like having a librarian hand you a ready-made list of books on your topic when you thought you'd have to compile your own from scratch.

Guru Pages: Experts, Enthusiasts, and Obsessives

Here's my guru joke: A guy goes to India on a spiritual quest, and climbs a high mountain peak to talk to the guru, reputedly the wisest man in the world. "Guru," he asks, bowing down before the ancient, bearded figure in tattered robes, "please tell me the meaning of life."

The wise old man is silent for a minute and then replies, "The meaning of life is . . . fish."

"FISH???" the seeker responds, incredulously. "You're telling me that the meaning of life is FISH?!"

The guru looks at him mildly and says "You mean it *isn't?*"

The world is full of gurus, very few of whom live on mountaintops and dress in rags. The word originally referred to a spiritual teacher, but now the term *guru* is used more broadly to refer to a genuine expert of any kind — from a competent car mechanic to an awesome Nintendo player to a corporate mentor who knows how to play *that* particular game. Gurus not only *know;* they're willing to share. Fortunately for you, the Net is full of them, too.

One way to think of a *guru page* is as a highly-specialized subject catalog that covers just a small portion of the Web. A guru page doesn't aspire to the encyclopedic reach of the subject catalogs described in Chapter 5. Instead, it focuses on a single topic or theme. See the sidebar "A grab-bag of guru pages" for examples of four different — but each very useful in its own way — guru pages.

Subject catalogs are a good way to find guru pages — a better bet than search engines, which aren't as good at distinguishing the *echt* (German for genuine) from the *ecch* (American for not-that-great). You can also read about guru pages in business and hobby magazines, and hear about them from your friends and fellow stamp — or whatever — collectors.

Bookmark it! When you find a great guru page, add it to your browser's bookmarks or Favorites list as soon as you realize you've struck gold. Don't leave the site without bookmarking it, or you may never find your way back. And, in the spirit of Giving Something Back, share the wealth — tell other people about it, too.

Mega-Sites: Stepping through the Gateway

A mega-site can be a convenient gateway into an unfamiliar subject area or a means to ensure that you don't overlook key resources in a field where you're expected to be well-versed. Many of the starting-points that I recommend in later chapters for particular kinds of research — including FedWorld for government information, Statistical Resources on the Web, Galaxy: Medicine (see Chapter 11), and AJR NewsLink (see Chapter 13), among others — are actually mega-sites as well. Here, I provide just three quick examples of mega-sites you might not otherwise encounter.

TIP

A grab-bag of guru pages

Finding a guru page is often a matter of good luck, hearsay, or poking around the Web on your own. One of my earliest discoveries was John Makulowich's Awesome List. John put the Awesome List together to answer a question he was hearing repeatedly: "But what's the Internet good for?"

The Awesome List (www.cais.com/makulow/awesome.html) is a collection of random-appearing, but carefully chosen links to several dozen URLs that demonstrate the variety of cool sites on the Web. John began his project several years ago. The Web has grown so much that, to keep up, he's had to divide his collection into two lists — the Awesome, and the Truly Awesome. Between them, you find many indispensable Net research tools listed (something to keep in mind in the unlikely event that you don't have this book within reach whenever you go online) as well as an assortment of other sites that are, well, simply awesome. Explore the Great Outdoor Recreation Pages at www.gorp.com. Check out the World Art Treasures (sgwww.epfl. ch/BERGER/index.html). Or reawaken those formaldehyde-laden memories of biology lab with the Virtual Frog Dissection Kit (george.lbl.gov/ITG.hm.pg.docs/dissect/info.html).

I almost hate to tell you this, but the Awesome List has an evil twin, The Worthless Page List, at www.bright.net/~nuke/worthless.html, if you must.

I mentioned an imaginary baseball nut earlier in this chapter. Although I didn't have anyone in particular in mind, John Skilton's obsessively thorough Baseball Links site (www.baseball-links.com/main.shtml) fits my hypothetical example like a glove. Or a mitt. This guru page lists nearly three dozen subcategories ranging from Major League Teams to Baseball History, Cards and Collectibles, and the ever-popular Stats & Analysis. Click one, and you're presented with dozens of links — out of more than 3,500, site-wide — to individual baseball-related resources on the subject.

"I get by with a little help from my friends" could be the Official Guru Page Theme Song. The Beatles, living and dead, are commemorated copiously on the Web. One of my favorite sites is Dave Haber's Internet Beatles List (www.primenet.com/~dhaber/blinks.html), which includes links to other people's Beatles pages, more specialized sites, such as a Sgt. Pepper Archive, newsletters, and song lyrics pages, sites devoted to individual members of the Fab Four (okay, Paul has a couple more than John, but John was *smarter*), official fan club pages, Beatles cover — er, tribute — band sites, collector pages, sites devoted to people and themes that are somehow intertwined with the Beatles, plus newsgroups and ftp archives.

Gurus operate in the professional realm as well. Susan Detwiler, a specialist in healthcare and medical industry research, has put together a collection of her favorite, clinically-tested sites. With pharmaceuticals and healthcare devices a bazillion-dollar business worldwide, this is a special interest that thousands of folks are following. To uncover Detwiler's hand-picked collection of useful healthcare industry resources, go to www.detwiler.com and click Healthcare Business Links. You find an annotated list of links to groups such as the American Medical Association, specialized sources such as Healthfinder (for reputable consumer-type health information), HospitalWeb, and the National Library of Medicine's PubMed database.

How do you find a useful mega-site in your particular field or occupation? Be on the lookout for articles in professional magazines, conference presentations, and continuing-education seminars that spotlight Web-based research aids. If I don't happen to touch on your specialty here, it's a sure bet that your colleagues in the field will call your attention to the resources *they've* uncovered.

Subject-oriented Web catalogs like the ones in Chapter 5 can be a good way to locate mega-sites. In Yahoo!, for instance, select your specific subject category, then look for a subcategory called **Indices.** If you don't find such a subcategory, scan the descriptions of individual sites with an eye out for ones that sound comprehensive.

It's all in your mind

Mental Health Net (www.cmhc.com/) is an awesomely deep and comprehensive guide to resources in all areas of the mental health field, from alcohol and substance abuse, to eating disorders, hypnosis, and psychotherapy. The site was designed primarily for mental health professionals, but includes quite a lot of consumer-level information, too.

Click either <u>Disorders & Treatments</u> or <u>Professional Resources</u> — or any of the direct links shown under each one — for a detailed breakdown (no pun intended) of topics. In the <u>Professional Resources</u> category, I followed the <u>Family and Marriage Therapy</u> link and found Web-based resources such as <u>The Family Relationships Page</u> and the <u>Men and Domestic Violence Index</u>, plus links to dozens of publications, organizations, and discussion groups. And that's in just one small portion of the mental health field. Each resource is accompanied by a helpful, short description and two sets of ratings, one from Mental Health Net itself, and a "thumbs-up/thumbs-down" assessment from individuals (you can vote, too) who've actually used the site.

The joys of jurisprudence

The Social Law Library (www.socialaw.com) started off as a resource for Massachusetts attorneys, and developed into a one-stop clearinghouse for legal research of all kinds. Click one of the links under <u>Frequently Used Sites</u> for a direct connection to the U.S. Supreme Court; U.S. Circuit Courts; federal-level rules, regulations, and publications; and state tax forms. Or select any of the categories listed under <u>Internet Guide</u>, which include U.S. federal, state, and international law; legal publishers and publications; library catalogs; discussion groups; education; employment; and professional associations. Click <u>State Law</u>, for example, and you get an Alabama-to-Wyoming listing of codes, statutes, court opinions, legislative information, and other legal resources, with links for every one. It's enough to make a litigator's little heart go pitty-pat.

VC on your PC

Let's end this section on a cheerful note: Money. Venture capital is the late 20th century answer to bank loans and other forms of financing, for high-tech startups in particular. In exchange for funding your bright idea, venture capitalists often get a piece of the action and a seat on your board of directors. The Venture Capital Resource Library (`www.vfinance.com/`) provides a glimpse into the VC world, along with some good legal and general business advice.

Most of the dozen boxes at the top of the first screen lead to further lists o' links. Click Venture Capital (it is, after all, the theme of the site), and you get a list of VC firms in alphabetical order by company name, or by industry specialty. Click Software, for instance, to get a lovely list, complete with contacts and criteria, or descriptions of what each firm looks for when making an investment decision, and how much you can expect to get from them. One more click takes you to the VC's own Web site. Wear your best power suit, and good luck.

Web Rings: Ring Around the Web Sites

If you feel like you're going around in circles when you try to find something on the Web, you ain't seen nothin' yet. Thousands of people seem to think that the quickest way from Point A to Point B is not a straight line, but a circle — or, to be more precise, a ring. What's a web ring? A web ring is a linked collection of anywhere from three to several dozen individual sites, all focused on the same subject or theme. Each site is linked to the one before and the one after it in the chain. You navigate around the ring by clicking links to the next or previous sites. You can also skip links or ask to be taken to a random site in the chain.

The idea of a *ring* — like *band, crowd, circle, gang,* or *posse* — conjures up a picture of a bunch of like-minded enthusiasts — whether they be cat-lovers, classical music buffs, or Riven-driven game-players — hooked together with a few lines of HTML code. The guru pages we visited earlier in this chapter (see the sidebar, "A grab-bag of guru pages") are one way to identify experts and others with a deep interest in the subject you're researching. Web rings can connect you with dozens, even hundreds, of these people at once.

A ringing endorsement of RingWorld

The motto of RingWorld — emblazoned on the main page at www.webring.com — is "The shape of things to come." Clever; I like that in a site.

Browsing through RingWorld is the fastest and easiest way to grasp the web ring concept. From the main page, click on RingWorld, and then check out the broad categories and sub-categories. Looks sort of like a subject catalog, doesn't it? My cat, Flash, is sitting on the monitor as I type, demanding to be researched — actually, she's drooling onto the desk, but I'm fluent in feline and know what she's saying — so I pick Animals and Pets from the Miscellaneous category. (Alternatively, I could have typed **cats** into the search box at the top of the page.)

Whoa! Dozens of rings, some of them huge, with hundreds of individual links. Skipping past All Things Ferrety and the Horse Country Webring, detouring slightly to check out In the Company of Wolves, I take note of The CLAW Ring (my cats are *always* claw-ring the furniture), the Cat Lovers Ring, the Cool Kitties Web Ring (cyberpets permitted; I think I'll pass), Persian Breeders, the Ring of Cat Purrfection, and well over a hundred more.

Most of these listings include enough of a description to give you a sense of their style as well as their size. Some are geeky or amateurish (Hey, dudez! Check out my kool web ring! It's the BEST!), some are ultra-professional (RingWorld's directory reveals rings for Latin scholars, corporate managers, doctors, teachers, and ministers), and others just sound intriguing.

RingWorld gives you several entry points to the ring of your choice. After you've picked a site from the directory, you can click

- Index — for a complete listing of all the sites comprising that ring. Click any one and you're there.

- Home — to go to the master home page for the ring itself. Here, you often find an overview of the ring and its contents, plus instructions for adding your own ring. You can step out into the ring at large from this point, too.

- Random — which enables you to jump in and land at a site somewhere in the ring.

What's the advantage of web rings? Like guru pages, and the subject catalogs covered in Chapter 5, web rings provide a more focused and selective perspective on a topic. But they also have geometry going for them: You know how easy it is to click your way from one promising-looking link to another, while drifting farther and farther away from whatever it was you started out to find in the first place? Web rings, by their very nature, encourage you to stay within the circle. That means that unless you're seriously directionally impaired, you'll be able to find your way back to your starting point with a minimum of effort.

How do you find a web ring to match your interests?

✔ **The search engine approach:** Enter your keyword or phrase and the words *ring* or *webring* (sometimes web ring appears as one word, and sometimes the concept is referred to as simply a *ring*). Do a Boolean AND search, or specify that *all* your terms must appear. For instance:

> **ski and webring**
>
> **ski and ring** (this will pick up **ski** and **web ring**, too)

✔ **The Yahoo! approach:** Go to Yahoo! (`www.yahoo.com`) and drill down a few layers until you reach the subcategory <u>Computers and Internet: Internet: World Wide Web: Searching the Web: Indices to Web Documents: Rings</u>. There, you find a couple of ring directories plus a list of 300-some individual rings.

✔ **Beam yourself aboard the web ring mothership, RingWorld,** by connecting directly to `www.webring.com` (`www.webring.org` works, too). Why do I call it the mothership? See the sidebar, "A ringing endorsement of RingWorld."

Web ring member sites usually carry a couple of forms of ID. Most of them display a banner or symbol identifying them as a member of a ring. And virtually all of them present a standard set of navigation options that look more or less like Figure 6-1.

Other than that, web ring sites look just like normal Web pages. You may run across one in the course of your routine travels around the Web, or turn one up in a search engine or subject index search. Be on the lookout for those telltale navigation options; they'll lead you to other members of the family.

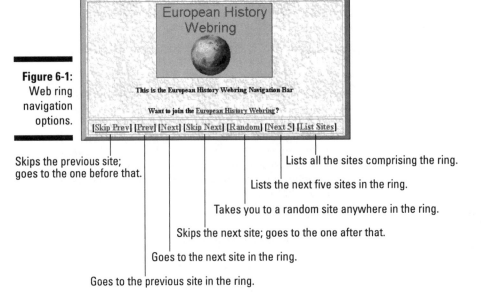

Figure 6-1:
Web ring navigation options.

European History Webring

This is the European History Webring Navigation Bar

Want to join the <u>European History Webring</u>?

[Skip Prev] [Prev] [Next] [Skip Next] [Random] [Next 5] [List Sites]

Skips the previous site; goes to the one before that.

Lists all the sites comprising the ring.

Lists the next five sites in the ring.

Takes you to a random site anywhere in the ring.

Skips the next site; goes to the one after that.

Goes to the next site in the ring.

Goes to the previous site in the ring.

Chapter 7

Ready Reference: Finding Facts Fast

● ●

In This Chapter

▶ Reference: Answering questions quickly

▶ Locating virtual reference books

▶ Finding the facts online

▶ Using primary sources

● ●

*T*he preceding chapters cover online resources that are a means to an end: Search engines, subject catalogs, guru pages, and web rings — all are tools to help find information that you can analyze and add to your understanding of your research topic. But sometimes you just need to get a quick fact or two to enhance your research and ensure its accuracy. That's what *reference* is all about.

Librarians know about the *ready reference* shelf — a section of books that they can reach without getting up from their desks; books that they keep handy because they use them a lot. You probably have something equivalent in your home or office — a *World Almanac,* a dictionary, an atlas, maybe a *Roget's Thesaurus, Bartlett's Familiar Quotations,* or an encyclopedia. In my house, we keep the *Compact Oxford English Dictionary* in the dining room, because we frequently get into debates about language at dinner. Okay, we're a strange family. But you've undoubtedly got your own quirky favorites: shop manuals, engineering handbooks, gardening books, *The Joy of Cooking,* your favorite *...For Dummies* guides — they're all ready reference, every single one, for somebody.

Reference: Research Light

When you hear the word *research,* you probably think of fairly complex, multi-stage research projects such as:

- ✔ What are the most effective treatments for Alzheimer's disease?

- ✔ Can I get a patent on my invention?

- ✔ Where should I go on vacation and what should I do when I get there?

- ✔ I'm having this persistent problem with Windows 95. . . .

For the answer to such questions, you almost certainly have to check more than one source, analyze and synthesize the information you find, and, most important of all, draw your own conclusions.

Not all questions require that much effort. You can find the answers to 84.7 percent of the questions that arise in the world every day — a statistic I just made up — in a handful of directories, almanacs, compendia, and guides. These are called *reference* questions. They involve very little analysis at all (except to ask yourself, "Can this statistic possibly be right?"). You have a question, you look it up in the appropriate source, and, assuming you've been good and the planets are all in alignment, you get the answer — almost without having to think about it.

Reference questions look like this:

- ✔ How tall is the Empire State Building?

- ✔ Where is Kenya, exactly, and what form of government does it have?

- ✔ What are Canada's chief exports?

- ✔ What's the population of Chicago?

- ✔ Who won the 1948 U.S. presidential election, and by how many votes?

- ✔ Who said "Neither a borrower nor a lender be"?

- ✔ Does *anal-retentive* have a hyphen?

- ✔ How many holes does it take to fill the Albert Hall?

If you find out the answer to the last two, will you let me know?

Virtual Reference Collections

A good way to familiarize yourself with reference books online is to browse the Net equivalent of that librarian's standby: the ready reference collection. These are collections of electronic resources similar to that handy shelf of well-thumbed volumes with which you and your local librarian are familiar. Dozens of such sites exist, and some of them are actually maintained by real live librarians. A few of my favorite starting points are:

The Internet Public Library

Figure 7-1 shows the comfy lobby or main reference area of the Internet Public Library (`www.ipl.org/ref/`). The picture is an *image map,* which means that you can click any of the labeled portions, such as <u>Education</u>, <u>Associations</u>, or <u>Arts & Humanities</u>, and go directly to a list of resources in that broad subject area.

Click <u>Reference</u> and you're transported to the general reference section and a list of subcategories: <u>Almanacs</u>, <u>Biographies</u>, <u>Census Data & Demographics</u>, <u>Dictionaries</u>, <u>Encyclopedias</u>, <u>Genealogy</u>, <u>Geography</u>, <u>News</u>, <u>Quotations</u>, and <u>Telephone</u>.

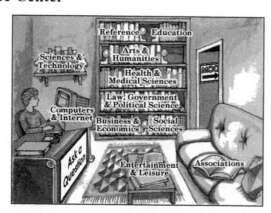

Figure 7-1:
The Internet
Public
Library.

WWWebster's

What better tome than that good ol' Merriam-WEBster to test how familiar reference books translate to the Net? You can click on the Internet Public Library's (www.ipl.org/ref/) <u>WWWebster Dictionary</u> link, or navigate directly to www.m-w.com/netdict.htm.

Key in your word, click Search, and enlightenment (in the form of a definition, pronunciation, word origins, alternate forms, and all those other lexicographical — look it up — goodies) awaits.

Don't overlook the hidden extras in some reference categories. <u>Dictionaries</u>, for instance, also includes non-English language dictionaries and dictionaries that translate from one language to another.

Now click <u>Dictionaries</u>. A list of 18 or so dictionaries of all kinds appears, ranging from well-known tomes such as the *Merriam-Webster,* to a rhyming dictionary, a dictionary of American Sign Language, a reverse dictionary (for when you know the meaning but can't think of the word), dictionaries of Net-related terms, early English, acronyms, and abbreviations.

One more click, on the dictionary of your choice, and you've got the virtual volume in your hands. Ready, set, go for it: *Thixotropic! Metonymy! Aphasia!* Or whatever words have got *you* scratching your head. For me, the possibilities are boundless.

Scroll a little farther down, past IPL's subcategory listing, and check out the uncategorizable reference tools below the listing: Calendars! Weights and Measures! Stylebooks! Loan rate calculators! How to write a research paper! This is info-junkie heaven, folks, and I'm about to OD.

The Virtual Reference Desk

The Virtual Reference Desk (thorplus.lib.purdue.edu/reference/index.html), a Purdue University Library production, is a no-nonsense listing of reference books in the categories shown in Figure 7-2. Some of these categories are quite different from the Internet Public Library categories described in the preceding section. You find this kind of inconsistency all over the Net — different minds, different ways of organizing information. What matters is that, ultimately, these differing categories lead you to many of the same resources.

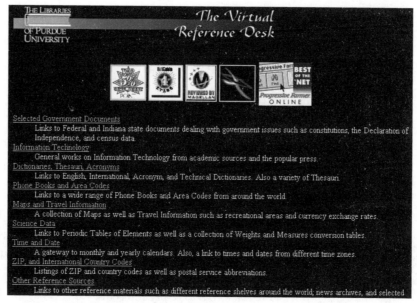

Figure 7-2:
The Virtual
Reference
Desk.

Consistent soul that I am, I click <u>Dictionaries</u> once more (actually, the category is <u>Dictionaries, Thesauri, Acronyms</u>, but who's keeping score?). The line-up here includes old standby, *Merriam-Webster,* a college slang dictionary (from 1989, though. That's so *over.* We can do better than that . . .), some specialized science and technology dictionaries, and several English-other language translation dictionaries. Again, one more click on the title of your choice, and a world of definitions awaits you.

Research-It!

Again with the exclamation points. Well, Yahoo! (`www.yahoo.com`) was there first. I'm not going to make any jokes about yelling in the library, either.

My only quibble with Research-It! (`www.iTools.com/research-it/research-it.html`) is that, given my earlier distinction between *research* and *reference,* they should have named it Reference-It! instead. But the site makes up for its lapse in nomenclature with the convenience of direct searching, right there, of dozens of individual reference sources. Enter your search term in the appropriate box, hit Enter, and there's your answer.

Figure 7-3 shows the top of the Research-It! reference collection. Besides dictionaries and thesauri, your options include

✔ Translations

✔ Acronyms

- ✔ Biographies
- ✔ Quotations
- ✔ Maps
- ✔ Phone books
- ✔ Currency converters
- ✔ Stock quotes
- ✔ Zip codes
- ✔ Package-tracking services (you won't find *those* on the shelves of your local public library)

. . . and more. Whew.

Okay, I know we're supposed to be about productivity here, but you know what they say about "all work and no play." Take a minute and scroll down Research-It! to one of my favorite time wasters, the Internet Anagram Server. I can rearrange my name to spell *Crab Shave, Brave Cash,* or *Brash Cave.* And you? Okay; time's up. Back to *real* ready reference.

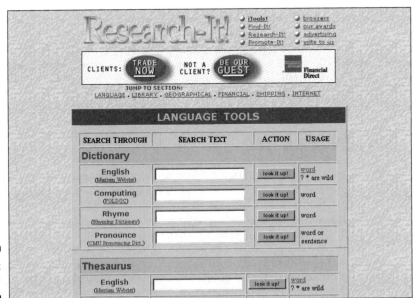

Figure 7-3:
Research-It!

The Yahoo! Reference Collection

Yahoo! is a great starting point for reference questions, and for many other kinds of info-quests as well. For a glimpse of the quick-lookup side of Yahoo!'s personality, go to www.yahoo.com and click Reference. You see the list of categories shown in Figure 7-4.

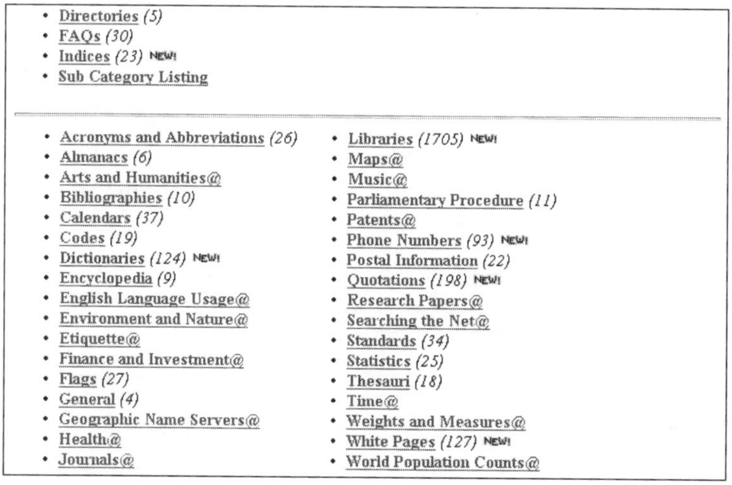

Figure 7-4: Yahoo! Reference categories.

- Directories *(5)*
- FAQs *(30)*
- Indices *(23)* NEW!
- Sub Category Listing

- Acronyms and Abbreviations *(26)*
- Almanacs *(6)*
- Arts and Humanities@
- Bibliographies *(10)*
- Calendars *(37)*
- Codes *(19)*
- Dictionaries *(124)* NEW!
- Encyclopedia *(9)*
- English Language Usage@
- Environment and Nature@
- Etiquette@
- Finance and Investment@
- Flags *(27)*
- General *(4)*
- Geographic Name Servers@
- Health@
- Journals@

- Libraries *(1705)* NEW!
- Maps@
- Music@
- Parliamentary Procedure *(11)*
- Patents@
- Phone Numbers *(93)* NEW!
- Postal Information *(22)*
- Quotations *(198)* NEW!
- Research Papers@
- Searching the Net@
- Standards *(34)*
- Statistics *(25)*
- Thesauri *(18)*
- Time@
- Weights and Measures@
- White Pages *(127)* NEW!
- World Population Counts@

Click Dictionaries (my current fixation) and Yahoo! presents a breakdown of dictionaries by type: English, foreign language, subject-specialized, slang. Each of those subcategories links to a list of titles. Pull one from the shelf, so to speak, and you're out on the Web, doin' the definition dance. (An added category points you to commercial dictionaries that you can buy in print and on CD-ROM.)

The Slang listing is a great read in itself. Check out the **College Slang Page** for the *real* 411.

Becoming a Reference Ace

Want to know how to keep track of the hundreds of reference works available to you online? Follow my tips for becoming a ready reference ace:

- ✔ **Spend some time poking around in virtual reference collections like the ones in the preceding section.** Get to where you can recognize the titles of some of the books that are shelved there. Develop a sense of the kinds of questions you can reasonably expect these books to answer, even if all you can say is, "oh yeah; I'm pretty sure I saw a reference site that may cover that."

✔ **Get to know both the content and the organization of the books you use the most.** Try them out with different kinds of questions.

✔ **Add your favorite online reference tools to your Bookmarks or Favorites list.** If your browser allows you to file your bookmarks in various folders, make one called **Reference**. Before you know it, you'll have your *own* online ready-reference shelf.

Hitting (A Few of) the Books

Obviously, I can't give you a personal introduction to every reference book you might ever need. But I'll introduce you to three that I find handy and return to again and again: an international country almanac, an encyclopedia, and a book of famous quotations.

World Factbook

Although they downplay the fact a lot more than they used to, the World Factbook (www.odci.gov/cia/publications/factbook/index.html) is produced by the CIA. Yes, *that* CIA — the U.S. Central Intelligence Agency. The CIA has been keeping tabs on countries all over the world, so why not share some of it with us-the-people? In fact, the World Factbook was one of the first published reference books to make its way onto the Net. For each country, it includes detailed data in the following broad categories:

✔ Geography

✔ Population

✔ Government

✔ Economy

✔ Communications

✔ Transportation

✔ Military

✔ Transnational Issues (including border disputes and so on)

Each country record includes a color map and flag as well.

To research a particular country, click <u>Countries</u> from the main Factbook page, and then choose one — say, <u>Kenya</u> — from the resulting alphabetical list. Remember the sample reference question earlier in this chapter about Kenya and the Kenyan form of government? The map at the top of the country description shows you where Kenya is located, and the Geography section that follows gives you the exact coordinates and more. Everything you wanted to know about the Kenyan government — at least the basic facts — is just a scroll away, in the section headed <u>Government</u>.

The World Factbook <u>Appendices</u> includes a detailed profile of the United Nations, various other international organizations and groups, information on selected worldwide environmental agreements, and weights and measures tables for the U.S. and metric systems.

Encyclopedia.com

Encyclopedia.com (`www.encyclopedia.com`) is based on the third edition of the *Concise Columbia Electronic Encyclopedia*. The articles are short but serviceable. You can browse through an alphabetical list of topics by clicking the A-to-Z-labeled volumes on the top page. Or you can search by keyword or phrase. You may have to browse a list of articles that mention your search term, and choose the ones that seem the most relevant.

Encyclopedias are wordy and expensive to put online, which is why many publishers have decided to go the CD-ROM route instead. Some leading encyclopedias, such as the *Britannica* (`www.eb.com/`), *Grolier Multimedia* (`gme.grolier.com/`), and Microsoft's *Encarta* (`encarta.msn.com/`), *are* available in online editions — for a fee. To get a taste of what these premier encyclopedias have to offer, check their sites for freebie introductory offers.

Bartlett's Familiar Quotations

The online edition of *Bartlett's* (`www.cc.columbia.edu/acis/bartleby/bartlett/`) is the old, familiar 1901 edition, which is great for looking up the classics. You can search by a distinctive keyword, or, if you're sure of it, the exact phrase (see Figure 7-5). You can browse famous quotes by author, as well. *Bartlett's* is great for getting the exact wording of a quotation when you only remember part of it, and for finding quotes that mention a specific word. If you can't find it here, check the quotations section of the virtual reference shelves (see the section, "Virtual Reference Collections" earlier in this chapter) for more up-to-date alternatives.

"Neither a borrower nor a lender be" turns out to be from Shakespeare. And all this time I thought it was Ben Franklin.

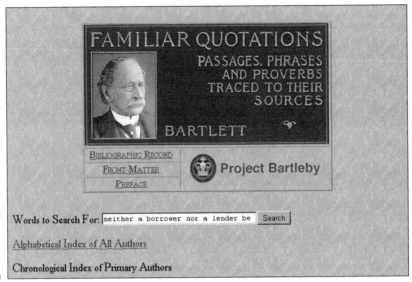

Figure 7-5:
Bartlett's
Quotations.

Random Reference Goodies

Net denizens are nothing if not helpful. Many individuals across the Web create and maintain sites that fall into the reference or quick lookup category. Sometimes these have printed book equivalents; often they do not. But they're all designed to give you an answer — fast.

How Things Work

The no-frills search form for How Things Work (www.phys.virginia.edu/ Education/Teaching/HowThingsWork/qsearch.html) enables you to search a database of questions and answers about — take a guess — how devices ranging from the very simple to the very complex actually work. I follow the simple directions, and key in **internal combustion engine** — my obsession since, oh, Chapter 2 or so — and get the exceedingly slick and useful summary shown in Figure 7-6.

Can't find what you're looking for? Back up a level to www.phys. virginia.edu/Education/Teaching/HowThingsWork/ and pose your query to the guy who wrote the book.

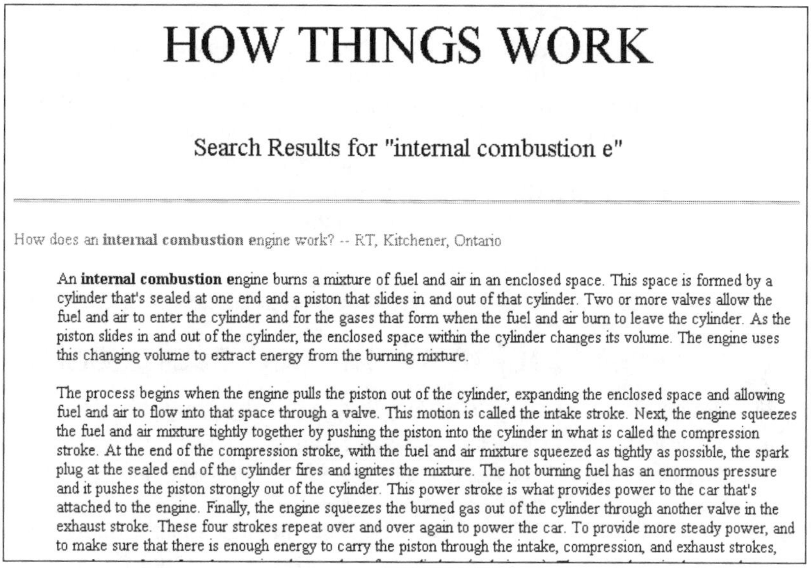

HOW THINGS WORK

Search Results for "internal combustion e"

How does an **internal combustion** engine work? -- RT, Kitchener, Ontario

An **internal combustion** engine burns a mixture of fuel and air in an enclosed space. This space is formed by a cylinder that's sealed at one end and a piston that slides in and out of that cylinder. Two or more valves allow the fuel and air to enter the cylinder and for the gases that form when the fuel and air burn to leave the cylinder. As the piston slides in and out of the cylinder, the enclosed space within the cylinder changes its volume. The engine uses this changing volume to extract energy from the burning mixture.

The process begins when the engine pulls the piston out of the cylinder, expanding the enclosed space and allowing fuel and air to flow into that space through a valve. This motion is called the intake stroke. Next, the engine squeezes the fuel and air mixture tightly together by pushing the piston into the cylinder in what is called the compression stroke. At the end of the compression stroke, with the fuel and air mixture squeezed as tightly as possible, the spark plug at the sealed end of the cylinder fires and ignites the mixture. The hot burning fuel has an enormous pressure and it pushes the piston strongly out of the cylinder. This power stroke is what provides power to the car that's attached to the engine. Finally, the engine squeezes the burned gas out of the cylinder through another valve in the exhaust stroke. These four strokes repeat over and over again to power the car. To provide more steady power, and to make sure that there is enough energy to carry the piston through the intake, compression, and exhaust strokes,

Figure 7-6:
An explanation from How Things Work.

New area code lookup

Trying to return a call to one of those new U.S. area codes, and you have no idea where you're calling? Or did you forget the new one that's been as-signed to *you* or to your nearest-and-dearest? Get thyself to www.nanpa.com, the home of the, ahem, North American Numbering Plan Administration. Click <u>Number Resource Information</u> on the left-side menu, then on <u>Area Codes</u>, and then, in the body of the text (they *don't* make it easy) on either <u>alphabetical order by location or service</u>, or <u>numerically by NPA</u> (NPA stands for Numbering Plan Area. All it means is Area Code. Bureaucratic jargon; yum). Finally, you reach a list of codes and their locations, or visa versa. Scroll down until you find your mystery code, or look for the city whose code you need to find, and *then* reach out and touch someone.

Any day in history

I love those "on this date in history" features. Any-Day-in-History (www.scopesys.com/anyday/) goes a step further, inviting you to pick any month and day, then displaying a loooong list of notable births and deaths, historic events, international holidays, and religious observances occurring on that date. They missed *my* birthday, but I forgive them.

Not all reference books are easy to use online. The information is there, but the lookup routine or query mechanism isn't always that precise. If a keyword search doesn't turn up the factoids you're looking for, you may have to browse, flipping virtual pages as you would in a real-life volume. You may have to fall back on other research methods, such as using search engines or subject catalogs. You may even have to wander over to one of those non-digital dictionaries, almanacs, atlases, or reference guides sitting on your shelf, or at your local library.

Literary lookups: Full-text books online

If you're a lit major or just happen to have a specific question that a quick look-up in a classic text might answer, check out some of these sites. Some of them offer full-text search capabilities, too.

The Internet Classics Archive (classics. mit.edu/) includes hundreds of English translations of classic Greek and Roman texts, featuring such all-time hits as Homer's *Iliad* and *Odyssey*, Virgil's *Aeneid*, Plato's *Apology*, and Ovid's *Metamorphoses*, plus links to other full-text book and manuscript sites around the Net.

The Online Medieval & Classical Library (sunsite.berkeley.edu/OMACL) features Chaucer, Icelandic sagas, song cycles, and other treasures of early literature. (Hey, if that's your thing, *this* is your site.)

Bulfinch's Mythology (www.showgate.com/medea/bulfinch/welcome.html) specializes in the classic tales of Greek and Roman legend.

Bibliomania (www.bibliomania.com/) encompasses a history of classic literature from 1607 to the 20th century, with complete HTML versions of novels such as *Little Women, Pride and Prejudice, A Tale of Two Cities*, and *Ulysses;* non-fiction works such as Adam Smith's *The Wealth of Nations* and Thomas Jefferson's autobiography; and poetry by William Blake, Walt Whitman, Oscar Wilde, and others.

Project Bartleby Archive (www.columbia. edu/acis/bartleby/) offers the complete texts of works by Agatha Christie, Emily Dickinson, Edna St. Vincent Millay, Thomas Paine, and more. For updates, keep an eye on The New Bartleby Library (www.bartleby. com).

Project Gutenberg (www.gutenberg.net/) showcases hundreds of classic novels, poems, plays, epics, and treatises, from all eras and cultures. Recent additions include works by Jack London, Joseph Conrad, Edgar Allan Poe, H.G. Wells, Charles Dickens, and the ever-popular Mr. Shakespeare.

Chapter 8
Visiting Libraries Online

· ·

· ·

*O*kay, you may be thinking — game's over, and the Net has won. Anything we may possibly want to know is just a few keystrokes away. It's all there, somewhere, online. Real-world libraries may as well close up shop, lock the doors, and stick a For Sale sign on the front of the building. Thanks for all your efforts; we appreciate your work; and will the last one out please turn out the lights?

Not . . . So . . . Fast.

You knew I was going to say that, didn't you? Libraries were on the Internet from the beginning, and despite the rise of do-it-yourself researching, they're not about to leave anytime soon. Libraries are *committed* to online information, and they're continuing to contribute in some very significant ways.

Libraries: Alive and Thriving Online

The "library" metaphor is a natural one for online research: The Internet is loaded with virtual reference shelves, subject catalogs, and libraries of this-and-that. But make no mistake: Right now, I'm talking about *real* libraries — actual institutions with buildings, and bookshelves, printed documents, and flesh-and-blood staff inside them.

Why are "old-fashioned" libraries still so important in this increasingly-digital world?

✔ **Libraries have more stuff.** You can find material in real-world libraries that you won't even find *pointers* to in a casual online search.

✔ **Libraries have deeper stuff.** No virtual library, no matter how rich, is as complete or deep as even the most modest neighborhood library.

✔ **Libraries have stuff the Net may never have.** No matter how fast the Web is growing, a lot of information — historical, esoteric, highly specialized, and often quite rare — will take a long time to migrate to the Net, if it makes it at all.

✔ **Libraries put good stuff on the Net.** Libraries are at the forefront of some pretty amazing projects to digitize at least a fraction of their collections — including rare manuscripts, old photographs, and other archival treasures — and make it available to everyone with a modem and a connection to the Net.

Although much of the material housed in real-world libraries isn't directly accessible online, you can browse through their catalogs and discover what's available, and then make arrangements through interlibrary loan, or a photocopy request, or document delivery order (I describe all of these procedures later in this chapter) to get hold of the actual document or a copy of the text. Library catalogs can also be useful for answering questions related to authorship, spelling, publication dates, and so on, and for compiling bibliographies or lists of publications by a particular writer or on a certain theme.

Finding Web-based Library Catalogs

Just about any kind of library you can name has a presence on the Web. Some library Web sites are purely informational: they give you the library's physical location, hours, policies, and a reminder to bring quarters for the photocopy machine. It takes serious money to implement a full-fledged interactive Web site and all the back-end software design and data entry that goes into one. And libraries, especially public libraries, are chronically strapped for funds. Support your local Friends of the Library. End of commercial.

But many library sites do provide a gateway into the collection itself. Not the actual *text* of all the books and periodicals housed there, but a record of what the library holds, searchable by author, title, or subject matter. The online catalog can be useful to your research in a number of ways:

✔ You can search for everything published by a particular author — and verify that she is, in fact, the expert she purports to be.

✔ You can search for documents by subject, and find publications that you didn't know existed.

✔ You can tap into special collections — works donated by a local patron, regional archives, or information about businesses, events, and people with ties to the area served by a particular library.

✔ You can verify author names, book titles, editions, publishers, and dates of publication for research papers and bibliographies.

✔ You can arrange to borrow books or order photocopies of articles.

Using WebCATS

To get a list of library catalogs on the Web, point your browser to WebCATS (`library.usask.ca/hywebcat/`), and then click either <u>Geographical Index</u> or <u>Library-Type Index</u>.

✔ The **geographical** tack brings up a list of continents and countries, in alphabetical order, under each one. Bet you can guess the next step: Click a country, get a list of libraries. Finally, click the name of a library. That should connect you to the library's Web site and its catalog.

✔ The **library-type** approach brings up this list:

> Armed Forces
> College and University
> Consortia
> Government
> Junior College
> K-12 Schools
> Law
> Medical
> Public
> Religious
> Special
> Unknown

Most of these choices are straightforward. If you're seeking something specific, such as a topic in the medical or legal area, you can head right for that category. A couple of categories, though, take a little more explanation:

✔ **Consortia** are groups of libraries, usually in the same state or geographic region, that band together for cataloging, book borrowing, and other cooperative efforts. If a consortium has put its joint, or *union* catalog online, you can cover dozens, even hundreds, of libraries at once. For instance, click <u>State of Iowa Libraries Online</u> (SILO — don'tcha love it?). Then, on the State Library of Iowa page, click <u>SILO</u>, and finally click <u>Silo Locator</u>. Key in your search, and the results list shows you what libraries in the consortium carry copies of the publication you're looking for. Click the record number for even more detailed information.

✔ **Special** libraries, in the U.S. at least, are usually corporate, government, or institutional collections — in other words, anything *other* than a public, university, or school library. In WebCATS, it's a catch-all category that may contain what you're looking for.

Online catalogs cover more than just books. You can also search for journal titles (though not specific articles) and discover how far back the library's collection extends, and which branch libraries subscribe to the journal or periodical. At some libraries you may have to select, and then search, a separate periodicals catalog. At others, you just select **journal titles** or **serials,** or a similar term, as a search option, or even easier, opt for a **title** search and key in the name of the publication.

Panning for gold at Penn

Penn, or the University of Pennsylvania — not to be confused with Penn State — is an excellent research institution that just happens to be my *alma mater.* It was founded by Ben Franklin himself, more than 250 years ago. Old Ben gets his payback in *Franklin/Web*, the name of Penn's online catalog. I'm sure he'd be thrilled.

To pay personal homage to Ben, get yourself to the Penn Library Web site (www.library.upenn.edu/) and click Franklin/Web. Your main search options are:

✔ Author/Title/Subject

✔ Keyword

✔ Guided Keyword

✔ Relevance Ranked

A **Help** button at the top of the Franklin/Web screen leads to detailed help and search hints for each of these options.

In addition, a **Set Search Limits** option lets you impose certain universal filters or restrictions, such as date or language, on a keyword- or relevance-ranked search.

That **Guided Keyword** search feature is a powerful one. It offers both Boolean AND, OR, and NOT operators, and *field searching,* which lets you restrict your search terms to certain *fields,* or parts, of a document record. Franklin/Web's fields include author, title, subject, series title, publisher name, conference name, and place of publication, among others. (See the Bonus Appendix on the CD for more about Boolean searching, field searching, and other powerful search aids.)

The Penn catalog is just one of thousands of online library catalogs worldwide. Each one has its own, sometimes unique, search features. To get the most out of a particular library collection, spend some time familiarizing yourself with how its online catalog works. Try looking up a particular author, or a subject you're researching or that currently interests you. Try out any special features offered by the catalog, such as Penn's Guided Keyword option. See whether relevance ranking or any other display options are useful for your purposes. As with any other research tool, the better you know a particular library catalog's capabilities, the more it can do for you.

Thinking locally

If your research plan involves finding resources that you might want to borrow or photocopy on your own, it makes sense to start locally, with the nearest university library. If you know — or can easily guess — the address of the university's home page, you can sometimes shortcut the search for its online library catalog. A <u>Library</u> link is usually visible from the main university page. From there, it's just a click or two to the catalog.

Sometimes local sources give you more than you bargained for. The Indiana University/Purdue University of Indianapolis Library (`www-lib.iupui.edu/`) offers IndyCat and IUCAT, which, between them, cover materials in all Indiana University Libraries. And that's not all. Click <u>Library Catalogs</u> for links to the Marion County (Indianapolis) public library, the Indiana State Library, and other university libraries both inside and outside the state.

Looking at the Library of Congress

The Library of Congress (`lcweb.loc.gov/`), the U.S. national library, is reputed to carry a copy of every book published in the country. It doesn't really. But it does contain more than 17 million books, including foreign publications, plus something like 111 million other items, such as maps, manuscripts, multimedia, and much, much more. If what you're looking for isn't listed at LC — as librarians fondly refer to it — well . . . are you sure you didn't *imagine* it?

Tapping into the catalog

In Figure 8-1, I've scrolled down to the bottom of the Library of Congress home page to show how easy it is to tap into our national library's catalog.

On that pull-down menu under <u>Research Tools</u>, I zero in on <u>Library of Congress Catalogs</u>. The next screen gives you several different ways to access the catalog; I pick Word Search, because it's the most straightforward-seeming option. After that, you get one more choice: <u>Simple Name/Title Word Search</u>, or <u>Advanced Word Search</u>.

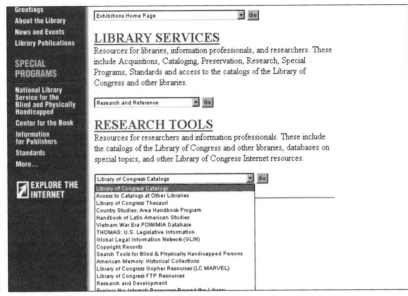

Figure 8-1:
Library of
Congress
Research
Tools.

✔ **Simple Search** lets you key in an author's name (last name only, or first and last), or words from the title of a book.

✔ **Advanced Search** allows you to extend your search beyond the book catalog into older, historical publications, original manuscripts, sound recordings, and other kinds of specialized research material. It also enables you to

- Search by subject as well as author or title.
- Specify an exact phrase, if you know it.
- Use Boolean ANDs, ORs, and NOTs to refine your search, as explained in the Bonus Appendix on the CD.

The Library of Congress catalog on the Web represents our tax dollars at work, fellow Americans. It's one use of those bucks that I can't argue with.

Steppin' out with Z39.50

The Library of Congress Web site is a good starting point for finding other library catalogs online, as are many other major library sites around the world. The Research Tools menu at the Library of Congress Web site includes an option called Access to Catalogs at Other Libraries. Click it, and you see a page headed **Z39.50 Gateway.** Z39.50 may sound like a sunscreen rating. But it's actually a standard that makes it possible to search other computer systems that subscribe to the same standard, without having to know the specific search syntax used by those other catalog systems.

Try it: Pick a library from the list, click, and you go — not directly to that institution, but to a uniform search form that transmits your query to the library you've selected.

Z39.50 is pretty cool, and definitely easy to use. But it does have a few drawbacks:

  ✔ **It's not universal:** Not all libraries subscribe to the standard, so it won't take you everywhere you might want to go.

  ✔ **It's not that sophisticated:** Its simplified interface eliminates some specialized catalog search features — you get the lowest common denominator only.

  ✔ **It doesn't show you everything:** You don't get to see what else the site has to offer — special collections and exhibits, information on borrowing privileges, reference books, shortcuts, and useful links.

Telnetting to OPACs

Lovely phrase, isn't it? Rolls trippingly off the tongue . . . telnetting to OPACs on a summer's day. Oh, you want to know what it *means?* Okay:

  ✔ *OPAC* **is librarian jargon for** *Online Public Access Catalog.* If you've checked out the Library of Congress, Indiana University, Penn, or any of the other library sites I mention in this chapter, you've already visited OPACs without even knowing it. That was easy, wasn't it?

  ✔ *Telnet* **is a means of connecting to another computer on the Internet.** Telnet is a text-based protocol that pre-dates the Web.

Libraries all over the world have put their catalogs — the electronic equivalent of the old three-by-five card catalog — online. Some are directly searchable on the Web. But not all of them. Some library catalogs can only be accessed via telnet. Some can be accessed through the Web as well as via telnet. Telnet can be faster, if you know how to use it and can stand the sometimes funky and awkward interface.

The telnet protocol uses a software application called a *telnet client.* You probably have a telnet client on your computer; it comes with both Macs and Windows machines, and is often included with the software package you get when you sign up with an Internet Service Provider, or ISP. If you can't find a telnet client on your computer, you can go to www.shareware.com and download one that works with your computer platform or operating system.

Most Web browsers are designed to work with a telnet client. If you click on a library catalog (or another Internet site) that requires the telnet protocol for access, telnet fires up and takes you to the spot. Internet Explorer seems to know how to find my telnet client automatically. I had to configure my copy of Netscape Navigator, though, by selecting Preferences from the Edit menu and, under Navigator, selecting Applications (then pointing Navigator to the path and filename for my telnet program).

Hytelnetting around

Many major library sites, especially university libraries, offer telnet access to other sites besides their own. Look for a link labeled **Other Library Catalogs** or **Internet Resources,** or something similar; or a link labeled **Hytelnet.** Hytelnet is a directory of telnet-accessible libraries and other information resources worldwide that some libraries have incorporated into their own sites. It allows you to search sites by geographic region (and sometimes by type of library) and to click and go directly to the library of your choice without having to type in its address.

You can also access Hytelnet directly at `www.lights.com/hytelnet/` and — ignoring the distressing message about the service closing down — click Library Catalogues, arranged geographically, or Search to locate them by name, type, or subject. Another route to Hytelnet is through `galaxy.einet.net/hytelnet/START.TXT.html`. Click Library Catalogs and, on the next screen, select either the geographic or the keyword-searchable approach.

Not all telnet sites expect outside visitors. They're set up for use primarily by the campus community, or whoever the library's main constituency is. It's by no means illegal to drop in; it's just that they don't always make it easy to enter, disconnect cleanly, or adjust the default display mode so that you can read the text on the screen. Telnetting to OPACs can be challenging, but who ever said travel to exotic lands was easy? At least you won't pick up intestinal parasites this way.

A short side trip to Malaysia

How far can telnet take me? I decide to find out. From the `www.lights.com/hytelnet/` site in the preceding section, I click Library Catalogues, arranged geographically. On the next screen I see:

The Americas
Europe/Middle
EastAsia/Pacific/South Africa

I pick Door Number Three, and am presented with an alphabetical list of exotic destinations, ranging from Australia to Thailand. I choose Malaysia, a place I've never been to, in virtual *or* in real life.

Next up: A list of half a dozen OPAC destinations. I select Universiti Sains Malaysia, because it sounds so very far away.

When I click, I get a brief set of basic directions:

✔ A link to the telnet address: Here, it's lib.usm.my

✔ The logon ID I need to key in: In this case, it's opac (remember this)

✔ The type of OPAC software used: This one says HOMEGROWN OR UN-KNOWN; doesn't that sound just fraught with intrigue? (you can probably ignore this information)

✔ The command used to exit the system (a good idea to remember this, too)

I click the link to lib.usm.my. My telnet software comes to life and spins into action. Whee.

Assuming I know the telnet address to begin with, I can get to the same point without Hytelnet, by just firing up my telnet client and typing in the address directly. How you do this depends on the telnet client you're using. On NCSA Telnet for the Mac, I hit ⌘-O and then type my destination in the **Host/Session Name** box. In Microsoft Telnet for Windows 95, I pull down the Connect menu, select Remote System, and then key in **lib.usm.my** or wherever I want to go today. From here on, everything's exactly the same as connecting via Hytelnet.

I can see telnet connecting to the faraway OPAC. It asks for my login. I type **opac,** and then I see Figure 8-2.

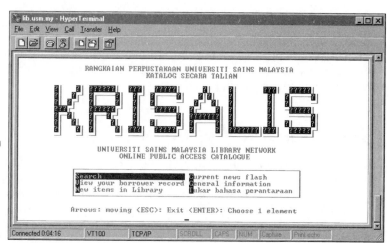

Figure 8-2: Welcome screen for Malaysian OPAC.

Having come all this way, I have to actually try *using* this thing. I do a title search and whaddaya know — 11 *...For Dummies* books! Hmmm, if I'm going to borrow from a library, I can probably find one a little closer to home.

So It's in the Online Catalog; How Do I Get It?

A library catalog is like a restaurant menu. It's educational, but it's no substitute for the real thing. When you're hungry you want a hamburger, or maybe a Caesar salad, not just a description of one.

So, how do you actually get hold of items that you've located in an online catalog? It depends, first, on whether you're looking for a book or an article from a magazine. Unless they're in a library where you have direct borrowing privileges, books (and some other materials, such as audio recordings) are subject to a policy called *interlibrary loan,* or *ILL.*

The ins and outs of ILL

Interlibrary loan is a process where your librarian acts as your agent, requesting a book on your behalf. In fact, librarians can sometimes shortcut your online catalog search by checking to see whether any library, anywhere in the region, state, or country, holds the book you want. You're responsible for returning what you've borrowed, in good shape, on or before the date it's due. Some materials, especially reference books and rare or expensive volumes, don't circulate at all. Beyond that, libraries have different policies regarding interlibrary loan; check with yours to see what other conditions apply.

ILL works most smoothly if you're affiliated with a university or college, or can deal with the main branch of your local public library. If you work for a company, your corporate library or information center can often handle ILL requests for you. Libraries may be part of a borrowing consortium, or have informal lending policies in place.

Buying instead of borrowing

You can use an online catalog to verify information about a book that's out of print or not widely available. You may want to buy a copy, not just borrow one. Supplying a complete and accurate description makes it easier for a bookseller to locate what you want.

The Web is home to hundreds of bookstores, many of which specialize in certain types of books, or provide added-value services such as searching for rare and out-of-print books. One of the best-known, Amazon.com (www.amazon.com), does a pretty good job of locating out-of-print titles. But my favorite starting-URL for hunting elusive volumes is www.powells.com/. That'll take you to the online home of Powell's, an amazing, multi-level bookstore in Portland, Oregon. Powell's catalog is a record of the bookstore's inventory, showing both new and used books that are actually on the shelves. And of course, you can order on the spot. Don't overlook your local independant bookstore, though, for special orders and other custom services.

Xerox is not a verb: Requesting article photocopies

Back issues of magazines, scholarly journals, and other periodical-type publications rarely leave the library — partly because if they're lost, they're very hard to replace. If you want to look through *Life* magazine from the 1940s, say, you may be able to make special arrangements to borrow those issues, but chances are you have to visit the library to see them.

But suppose you have a particular article in mind, and you at least know the author or title, and the issue in which it appeared. That's a different story.

- ✔ If it's fairly recent, you may be able to get a copy from the publisher, either in print or from their Web site.

- ✔ Commercial database services (see Chapter 9) include the complete text of articles, going back several years, from thousands of magazines, newspapers, and scholarly and professional journals. You can get a list of such publications from the online service itself or from individual database producers. The single best guide to what's available in these professional online venues is a comprehensive directory called *Fulltext Sources Online*. Your library may have a copy, or check www.bibliodata.com/ for details.

If neither of these alternatives works for you, it's time to turn to some not-exactly-cutting-edge technology — the good old photocopy machine. You can

- ✔ Make a photocopy at your library, assuming it has the periodical you want.

- ✔ Ask your librarian to submit a *photoduplication request* to another library.

- ✔ Pay a commercial document retrieval service to find and make a copy for you.

Document delivery services

That's right. There are businesses — lots of them — totally dedicated to finding, ferreting out, and photocopying articles on request. You pay for the service, of course — anywhere from a few dollars for something that's easily locatable, to $25, $50, or more, for an item that takes an extraordinary effort to locate. A significant chunk of this sum goes to cover copyright fees that the document supplier must pay on your behalf. (See Chapter 15 for more about copyright.)

Ordering a document can be as simple as picking up the phone: "One article to go, please; no anchovies." But the online approach works, too.

UnCover

UnCover (uncweb.carl.org/) enables you to search its database and place credit card orders; articles are delivered by fax. Setting up an account is hassle-free and nearly instantaneous. Rates are reasonable, too. Some items are available within the hour.

Click <u>Search the UnCover Database</u> to locate an article by writer, title, journal name, or subject; or to browse a particular journal by issue.

When you find the article you want, click it to see whether UnCover can supply it via fax. If so, you can order it on the spot. First, though, you have to fill in a Profile form and furnish that all-important credit card information. Oh, and your fax number, too, of course.

. . . and beyond UnCover

The downside to UnCover is that its article selection is limited. Because of copyright and licensing considerations, not everything in its database is actually available for ordering. You may have to pay a bit more and wait a while longer for service from an operation such as *EBSCOdoc* (www.ebscodoc.com), *Information Express* (www.express.com/), or *InFocus* (www.access.digex.net/~infocus/), which actually sends representatives out to libraries worldwide. For an extra fee, they even extend the quest to trade associations, conference organizers, and, if necessary, the authors themselves.

Hundreds of document delivery businesses exist worldwide. Some specialize in material from certain regions of the world, others in particular kinds of information. For leads to additional document delivery businesses, or to get an idea of what's available, go to the web site of the Association of Independent Information Professionals at www.aiip.org/. Click <u>AIIP Members Directory</u> and then use your browser's "Find on this page" function (in both Netscape Navigator and Internet Explorer, it's on the Edit menu; or simply hit Ctrl+F) to search for the phrase **document delivery** — or, for more comprehensive results, just the word **document**.

The Delights of Digital Libraries

Various projects are underway to digitize classic works and put them on the Net. (See the "Literary lookups: Full-text books online" sidebar in Chapter 7 for pointers to some of these projects.) Researchers use electronic editions — sometimes called *e-texts* — to locate information quickly, discover recurring themes, analyze patterns, and commit various other unspeakable scholarly acts. Some people just get a perverse thrill out of reading *Alice in Wonderland* on a monitor.

You won't find a single, universally-accepted definition of what constitutes a *digital library*. The term has been kicking around for years. Most people would agree that e-texts — like the ones at Projects Gutenberg and Bartleby that I mention in Chapter 7 — are part of the concept, however it's defined. But plain-text versions of familiar literary and historical works are ho-hum compared with some of the digital library initiatives that are emerging on the Net. Rare and even unique artifacts — including historical photographs, maps, hand-written letters, original manuscripts, and other image-based material — have begun to show up online.

It used to be that the only way you could examine such material firsthand was to travel to the library or archive that housed the collection and make special arrangements for access. You generally had to present acceptable academic credentials in advance; a mere undergraduate degree wouldn't do. You were strip-searched at the door, and your pens and other sharp objects confiscated until your departure. You were issued a gray smock to wear for the duration, and a blunt pencil for note-taking. Okay, I'm exaggerating, but only slightly.

Digital libraries take many forms, but they have one thing in common: They bring one-of-a-kind treasures and curiosities within everybody's virtual grasp. They're a boon for researchers who need primary source documents, such as photographs, sketches, maps, and manuscripts, to help fill in the gaps. The multimedia sound and video clips available at some of these sites are icing on the cake. Imagine being able to describe, in your own words, how Franklin D. Roosevelt or Winston Churchill spoke, and the gestures they used. Yes, you might have seen old film footage on TV, but a digital library enables you to view and analyze them to your heart's content.

In this section, I introduce you to just three of the many digital libraries on the Net. One is a comprehensive starting point (as well as a fascinating destination in itself); another is what librarians call a "special collection," concentrating on American history from colonial days to the present; the third illustrates the value of the Web in presenting photographs, drawings, and other graphical material.

SunSITE: The digital library motherlode

As a Berkeley partisan, I may be a wee bit prejudiced, but I'm convinced that the University of California's Digital LibrarySunSITE (`sunsite.berkeley.edu`) is the best place to start — and perhaps even end — your digital library explorations. It's an umbrella site (despite the Sun) covering not only several outstanding collections of its own, but also a set of research tools, pointers to other archival sites on the Net, and resources for exploring and building digital libraries.

Click <u>Collections</u> for an inkling of what SunSITE has in store. Two of my favorites are the Emma Goldman Papers, an archive of documents related to the early 20th century activist's life, and the Jack London Collection, which, among other things, includes some, er, stunning photographs of the author of *Call of the Wild.*

Speaking of which, remember what I said in the introduction to this section about having to submit to strip-searches (well, security checks, anyway) before being admitted to a research archive? I was thinking of my own experience, years ago, at the entrance to UC Berkeley's own Bancroft Library, a treasury of California and western history. Highlights from the Bancroft collection are now online at SunSITE; I click <u>Collections</u>, and then on <u>Pictorial Highlights from UC Berkeley Archival Collections</u>. Figure 8-3 gives a preview of what the Bancroft Library digital collection has in store. I'm on my way. And I get to keep my writing implements, too.

Figure 8-3: Highlights from the Bancroft Library Archives.

Pictorial Highlights From UC Berkeley Archival Collections

<u>The Bancroft Library</u> of the University of California, Berkeley is blessed with rich text and image collections. The images below are but a very small sampling of some of the Bancroft image collections. For more images and information, see <u>Archival Finding Aids</u> and <u>California Heritage</u> here on the Digital Library SunSITE. Or use the Digital Library SunSITE <u>Image Finder</u> to locate selected images both here and at other collections such as the Library of Congress and the Smithsonian Institution. Please note that clicking on an image below will bring up a larger version.

Salmon fishing on Deer Creek [Ishi], May, 1914. **Photographer/Artist:** Unknown **Original:**Photoprint **Collection:** C. Hart Merriam Collection.

Grandfather and grandson. **Photographer/Artist:** Lange, Dorothea **Original:** Photoprint **Collection:** War Relocation Authority records.

Migrant family of Mexicans on the road with car trouble, February, 1936. **Photographer/Artist:** Lange, Dorothea **Original:** Photoprint **Collection:** Farm Security Administration records.

The American Memory Project

Figure 8-4 shows the entrance to the Library of Congress American Memory Project (`lcweb2.loc.gov/ammem/`). You can go directly to any of the special exhibits highlighted under **Showcase,** or check out the featured **Sample Collection.** Once inside, you can walk through from the beginning, or go directly to a particular portion of what I intuitively picture as the exhibition "hall." (It's easier to find your way around if you think of a digital library as an actual place; the most successful ones are designed to encourage that.) Within the exhibit, you can read explanations, examine manuscripts, look at vintage photographs and illustrations, and even listen to sound clips and view movies of famous speeches and other historic events.

You can also do a keyword search to discover whether the American Memory archives hold anything on a specific topic. The search box is right there on the first page. To limit your query to a particular medium, like photographs, maps, motion pictures, sound recordings, or documents, click on the corresponding link.

If I click <u>Photos & Prints</u>, I can then enter keywords to find specific images, or browse a list of collections with descriptions for each one. American Memory starts with the ABC's — architecture, baseball, and California folk music — and goes on to list more than a dozen other graphical collections, including portraits of the Presidents and First Ladies from the 18th century on, pictures from the women's suffrage movement, and historical photos of Washington, DC. And that's just the beginning. Check out the early movies, audio clips, panoramic maps, and historical manuscripts, too.

Figure 8-4:
The American Memory Project.

To see the complete contents of the American Memory archive, click Browse, then scroll down to view the collection alphabetized by keyword. If you prefer to browse by exact title, click the alphabetized by TITLE link.

Images from the History of Medicine

A digital archive can be extremely specialized. For example, the National Library of Medicine (wwwihm.nlm.nih.gov/) has assembled an amazing collection featuring nearly 60,000 portraits, photographs, drawings, caricatures, cartoons and other forms of graphic art relating to the history of medical practice and its role in society. You can browse the collection by subject, or search by keyword.

My search on **Surgery** also turns up subject headings for surgery and art, military surgery, minor surgery, urogenital surgery (I'll pass), and surgical assistants. Each category contains at least one, often several, images. Clicking a category produces basic information about the size and medium of the original illustration(s), and a thumbnail (hmmmm . . . I think I'll leave that one alone) sketch for each one. I can click the thumbnail to see a larger version of the image.

Chapter 9

Knock, Knock: Gated Information Services

● ●

● ●

*M*uch as I hate that term *surfing the Net,* I've got to admit that it does feel like an ocean. It's deep, it's dangerous, and it's teeming with life — some very *strange* life forms, in fact. I do love riding those waves.

But there are times when I'd just as soon swim in a pool, in a more controlled environment, with some rules and boundaries. This pool may not be as colorful as the Net at large, but it's warm, and smooth, and clear all the way to the bottom. Someone takes care of it, too, adjusting the chemicals, skimming off debris, making sure the water's clean, and blowing the whistle when the kids by the diving board start getting rowdy.

Here's the analogy, and thanks for hanging in this far: If the Net is the sea, then the information sites and services I talk about in this chapter are pools — individual swimming spots, all neatly maintained

The metaphor I use (Oh no! Not another metaphor!) is *gated* sites, to distinguish these special sites from the open Web (see Chapter 1 for a quick summary of gated sites). Why *gated?*

✔ **Gates are usually locked:** You need a key, or a combination, to get in. (Picture one of those parking lot barriers that rise when you feed in your ticket. Am I the only one who hurries through thinking "Aaack! Automobile guillotine!")

✔ **Gates restrict access:** Most standard Web search tools are barred from entering and indexing the site; the information in gated sites is invisible from outside.

And it's good information, too — information you won't find duplicated anywhere on the open Web, *or* information organized so conveniently, or retrievable with such precise search tools, that you may actually be willing to spend the money to get it from a gated site rather than on the Web at large.

Getting Acquainted with Gated Sites

All gated sites have one thing in common: You have to register before you can access the information behind those gates.

Beyond that, they vary considerably:

- ✔ Some gated sites require a password; some don't.
- ✔ Some are free; others charge a subscription fee, or a fee for every item you view, download, or print.
- ✔ Some look and act just like ordinary Web sites. Others are actually proprietary online services with a highly specialized search language and a unique collection of documents and databases.

Proprietary services — and I'll say more in a minute about why I call them that — come in two flavors: consumer-oriented and professional. All of them require registration, password, *and* payment. The distinction between consumer and professional has to do with what the service is like once you get inside — the type and quality of information it contains, and the search tools you're given to work with.

Overall, my gated-site classification looks like this:

- ✔ **Web-based sites:**
  - • Registration required
  - • Registration plus a fee
- ✔ **Proprietary sites:**
  - • Consumer services
  - • Professional services

The word *proprietary* carries an air of exclusivity. That's the *gate* part. It also suggests a proprietor, or owner, who runs the place; and a set of standards and practices that are different from those that you find on the open Web. Many proprietary services still enable you to dial up directly to their own computers using a general terminal program, such as Procomm, or their own specialized software as an alternative to connecting through the Web. Some, such as America Online, *require* that you use their software.

Chances are you've already got access to the Web and have mastered the basics of getting around on it. For that reason, I take a Web-o-centric view of proprietary services in this chapter. You can often get enough information from a service's Web site (and if not, this book will help) to decide whether you want to invest time and disk space on a software front-end designed just for that service. In general, proprietary interfaces tend to be more flexible and powerful — and almost always faster — than using the same service through the Web.

Sampling Gated Web Sites

Gated Web sites run the gamut. Many are indistinguishable — once you're through the gate — from sites you find on the open Web. If it weren't for the extra step of registering and signing in, you wouldn't know the difference. Some gated sites, such as Consumer Reports (`www.consumerreports.com/`) provide even unregistered guests with useful information, reserving only the most detailed reports and value-added services for their paying customers. In effect, you can wander through the grounds of the estate and enjoy the gardens and landscaping, but you'll have to buy a ticket if you want admission to the mansion itself. Other gated sites, though, clang down those portals the moment you try to set foot inside. I can navigate to the front door of the Medical Economics Interactive site (`www.medecinteractive.com/pubpg/`), but I can't look up anything in the Physicians' Desk Reference without supplying a user name and password. And I can't get either of those without proving that I'm a practicing physician. Clang!

I've selected just three — of the thousands of gated Web sites that exist — to give you an idea of the different forms gated sites can take:

- ✔ **The New York Times on the Web** is easily recognizable as an online version of the printed publication of the same name.

- ✔ **The Wall Street Journal Interactive Edition** goes far beyond the publication on which it's based, encompassing other periodicals published by the same firm that produces the Journal, plus value-added services for investors, and access to a rich and varied collection of online databases.

- ✔ **Ei Village** goes even further, including not just published information, but access to human experts, colleagues, and other specialists who may be able to help.

The pros and cons of cookies

Web sites that require registration often do so to capture demographic data (you may be asked to complete a questionnaire) that the site owner uses to lure advertising support. But registration can work to your advantage, too. The site owner can keep track of your preferences and the parts of the site you use most heavily, and can direct you to new content in your areas of interest.

Customizing your interaction with a site is what the sometimes-controversial *cookies* technology is about. Cookies are software applications installed by the site-owner that can track your movement through the site and record the clicks and choices you make. Cookies are used to set placeholders and preferences so that, on subsequent visits, you can go directly to the portion of the site that interests you or to the point where you left off last time; Cookies are also used to record information, such as your password, so that you don't have to supply it every time you log on.

Some security risks are associated with cookies, as in any situation where you allow a program access to your disk. Privacy is also a concern. You may prefer to set your web browser so that you're notified whenever a cookie is about to be transmitted, and can reject it if you want to. Call me naive, but I've found cookies to be more helpful than not. Your mileage, as always, may vary.

For more information about cookies, check the mouth-filling and nutritious paper by Bill Helling entitled *Web-Site Sensitivity to Privacy Concerns: Collecting Personally Identifiable Information and Passing Persistent Cookies*. It appears in the online journal First Monday. Point your browser to `firstmonday.dk/`. Click <u>Archives</u>, and then <u>Vol. 3, Issue 2 (February 1998)</u>, and finally on the title of the paper. And also be sure to check out `www.cookiecentral.com/`, which attempts to be an objective and up-to-date voice in the cookie debate.

The New York Times on the Web

Prefer to read your daily newspaper online? *The New York Times* (`www.nytimes.com`) is only one — a high-profile one, for sure — example of the kind of thoughtful reporting and in-depth coverage of national and international issues that a general Web search won't turn up. You can read today's headlines, of course. You can also call up a year's worth of background articles — the news behind the news — and previous coverage to see just how an issue like the Northern Ireland peace initiative developed and played out — Who instigated it? Why was it done? Why were the warring factions willing, finally, to sit down and negotiate?

Suppose you want to pull up a series of stories by Jane Stevens, a science writer who went on board the Alvin, a deep-sea submersible craft. Start by clicking <u>Search</u> on the front page of the *Times* site (shown in Figure 9-1). Then enter the search query **Alvin and Stevens and (ocean or sea)** in the search form that appears next, and make sure the button labeled **Search all articles** — as opposed to **Search only today's articles** — is selected. (For help in formulating — or interpreting — that search request, click on Search Tips, or consult the Bonus Appendix on the CD of this very book.) You find 23 articles on your topic, and can click the titles to read any or all of them. Stevens' writing evokes not just the facts, but the first-hand feeling of being onboard this scientific research vessel.

If your research project can benefit from the detailed perspective you get from this kind of online journalism, remember to visit the *Times* and other newspapers on the Web. (Chapter 13 provides more information on research using online news sources.) Bookmark the sites you want to visit regularly. (See Bonus Chapter 3 on the CD for more about bookmarking as a technique for effective research.) Many newspaper sites, both national and small-town, require registration, which effectively cuts them off from the search engine spiders that crawl around the Web, looking for new content to index.

Figure 9-1:
The New York Times on the Web.

The *Times'* internal search engine lets you look for specific information in today's paper, or check back issues of selected sections, such as Books, Arts and Leisure, Autos, Real Estate and Travel. Or, you can read the way you do at the breakfast table, thumbing your way through from front page news to sports, business, and entertainment.

The *Times* on the Web includes an online-only section called *CyberTimes,* where you can find stories about life, business, and politics on the Net.

The Wall Street Journal Interactive Edition

Business researchers, corporate CEOs and managers, stock analysts and investors all regard *The Wall Street Journal* (www.wsj.com/) as the most complete and authoritative U.S. source of timely business and investment information. The daily edition of the *Journal* includes business news, in-depth profiles of companies and people, stock quotes and other investment data covering both domestic and international markets.

The Web edition of the *Journal* is equally comprehensive. Not surprisingly, all this information comes with a price tag attached. The Interactive Journal requires not only that you register, but that you pay a monthly, or annual, fee, which is actually pretty reasonable: $4.95 a month or $49 a year, or even less if you subscribe to the print edition, too.

The *Journal's Interactive Edition* (shown in Figure 9-2) includes not only the newspaper itself, but electronic editions of two other publications: *Barrons* and *SmartMoney*. Subscribers also get access to detailed company profiles, and to the Dow Jones Publication Library (see the section, "Beating the averages with Dow Jones Interactive" later in this chapter for more about the Publication Library). As Chapter 12 makes clear, *The Wall Street Journal* is an indispensable resource for business research. See that chapter for why that's so, and for some examples of how to use the *Interactive Edition* and the other resources provided at this site for your real-life business research needs.

Figure 9-2:
The Wall Street Journal Interactive Edition.

As a subscriber to *The Wall Street Journal Interactive Edition,* you have the option of setting up a *Personal Journal* to get customized information on the companies, industries, and stocks you want to follow. You can supply key words and phrases or the names of companies and industries to capture the news stories that interest you most. You can also select the *Wall Street Journal* columns and other regular features you want to see. You can create up to five portfolios to help you organize and track your investments. Once you've configured your Personal Journal edition, just click Personal Journal whenever you visit the site to enter your own private info-domain. Gates within gates, it sounds like to me.

Non-subscribers can take advantage of several free features on *The Wall Street Journal Interactive* site. These free features include career counseling, corporate annual reports, small business news, mutual fund information, and a year-end review of investments and the financial scene. Top business news is available in Spanish and Portuguese, as well.

Ei Village

A pride of pocket-protectors, a gaggle of geeks, an entire town full of badly-dressed people wearing glasses held together with tape. *Tweeeet!* Stereotype alert! But the founders of Engineering Information Village (www.ei.org/eihomepage/village/intro.html) are committed to bringing engineers and other techno-types together in a virtual environment that answers all their information needs. Figure 9-3 shows how seriously they take the small-town — or maybe campus — metaphor.

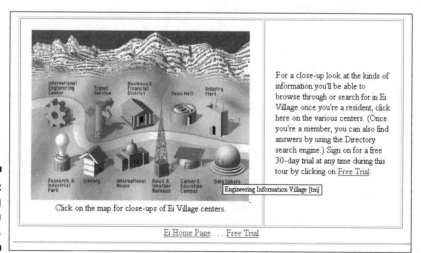

Figure 9-3: Engineering Information Village.

Subscribers enter the Village through a link marked <u>Residents' Entry</u>. You couldn't ask for a clearer indication that this is a gated site. Access is expensive; it's set up for multiple users within corporations and other institutions, and costs way more than my allowance covers. When I need engineering and technology information, I generally start with one of the databases described in Chapter 11, particularly the "Mere Technicalities" section and the sidebar called "Personal bests." Ei Village residents have access to some of this information from inside the gates of the site. Once enrolled, they can also sign up for technology news updates to stay current in their areas of interest; discussion groups for networking and information-sharing with colleagues; and document delivery services to provide copies of journal articles, conference proceedings and other material they may need to track down. Ei even provides formal research assistance with features labeled **Ask a Librarian** and **Ask a Senior Engineer.**

Ei Village is an interesting mix. It offers premium databases such as Compendex, a guide to engineering literature published since 1970. But it also features links to Web sites and other resources that you can navigate to, for free, on your own. Part of what Villagers pay for is the convenience of having all these related resources available in one spot. Another membership benefit is the chance to hang out and exchange information with colleagues who speak the same language. I talk more about that community aspect in Chapter 10.

Consumer Goods: Prodigy, CompuServe, and America Online

If I were writing this book two or three years ago, I would have given equal time — and quite a lot of it — to the so-called Big Three of consumer online services: CompuServe, Prodigy, and America Online (AOL). Each of these services still exists, but Prodigy seems to be turning into more of an Internet access provider than a destination in itself. And CompuServe, which AOL has acquired, faces an uncertain future. Even the formerly invincible AOL has lost ground — and subscribers — to the Web.

AOL, CompuServe, and Prodigy all have a presence on the Web. But each one charges a fee, and requires special software for full access to the service. That's part of the reason I call them *proprietary* services, as explained earlier in this chapter, in the section called "Getting Acquainted with Gated Sites."

These services are also proprietary in the sense that each one is a world unto itself. If you doubt that, talk to a long-time CompuServe forum member, or a denizen of AOL chat rooms. It takes a while to find your way around these services, let alone locate the precise information you're hoping to find. Given that there's so much information out on the open Web, why even consider signing up?

- ✔ **Ease into the Web.** If you're new to the online realm, these services are like training wheels when you're first learning to ride a bike. They give you a selected set of resources to begin with, and a kinder, gentler introduction to the wider world of the Net. It's way easier to contact a customer support person on these services (and maybe even get a response) than it is on the Web at large.

- ✔ **Get into the online community.** These services are *communities* as well as content providers. You can participate in forums and discussion groups, and tap into software libraries and other member-generated archives. If you enjoy the conversation enough to stick around, it makes sense to start your research there, too, in an environment that's friendly and familiar.

What do Prodigy, CompuServe, and AOL have to offer, research-wise, and what does it take to connect? I take a very quick look at each of these services in the next three sections. For more detailed information — and even more important, a sense of whether it's a comfortable fit for you — take advantage of each service's free trial membership offer.

Prodigy

For $19.95 a month (less if you sign up for a full year), Prodigy subscribers get access to fifteen or so broad content areas. Highlights include

- ✔ Technology news from hundreds of different sources
- ✔ Tips for keeping your computer running smoothly
- ✔ Investment information and portfolio tracking tools
- ✔ Associated Press wire stories and photos
- ✔ *Compton's Encyclopedia* Online

You can download the software you need from the Prodigy Web site (www.prodigy.com), or order a free CD-ROM. My personal opinion? Prodigy offers very little, research-wise, that you can't find elsewhere — often on the Web, for free.

CompuServe

CompuServe's traditional strength lies in its hundreds of Forums — discussion groups on subjects ranging from accounting to weather. Many of these groups have, over the years, developed into close-knit, supportive communities as well as founts of information on their respective topics. Clustered around those special-interest areas are pertinent publications, news stories, archives, and tools. In the personal finance area, for instance, you're likely to find investment newsletters, headlines relating to recent developments such as Roth IRAs, advice columns and feature articles, freeware or shareware accounting and portfolio-tracking software you can download, and, of course, those ongoing discussions about every aspect of personal finance you might imagine.

One of CompuServe's most useful hidden resources is Knowledge Index, a selection of databases covering business, news, medicine, science, and technology, drawn from the extensive Dialog collection described in the "Shopping at Dialog's supermarket" section, later in this chapter. KI uses a simplified form of the Dialog search language. At $21 an hour (with no additional charge for information retrieved) it may not sound cheap, but it's one of the best bargains around for serious researchers. ***Note:*** KI is intended for personal use and is subject to some contractual restrictions.

A full membership in CompuServe costs $24.95 a month for unlimited usage, or $9.95 for up to five hours, with additional hours at $2.95. To access the service you need CompuServe's proprietary software, which you can download from their Web site (`www.compuserve.com`) or order there, at no charge, on floppies or CD-ROM.

Beware of hourly charges when you're shopping for an online information service. It's easy to lose track of the ticking meter, and you can pile up a hefty bill before you know it.

America Online

If you've had any online experience at all, there's a good chance you had it with AOL. AOL claims to be the largest and fastest-growing online service in existence, and is particularly hospitable to novices. Not only that, AOL is almost impossible to avoid — if you subscribe to a computer-related publication, you've probably been inundated with generous introductory offers from AOL, complete with software disks or CD-ROMs good for up to 50 hours of free use. Thanks to AOL, I'll never have to buy blank diskettes again. They also make great coasters, or frisbees for very small dogs.

If you're one of the 27 people in North America who don't have at least one AOL freebie diskette lying around, you can find details about joining at www.aol.com/. AOL charges $21.95 per month for unlimited usage, less if you provide your own Internet access or sign up for one of the light- to moderate-usage plans.

Finding your way on AOL

America Online gained popularity right around the same time as the Web. Many people — several million, if you believe AOL's publicity — are still loyal to AOL despite the growing domination of the Web. That customer loyalty may have more to do with AOL's infamous chat room activity than with the quest for enlightenment. But if you poke around AOL, you can find some useful research tools — many of which lead you right back out to the Web!

"Poke around" is the key phrase there. AOL's information resources are widely scattered across the service's special-interest channels. You can use AOL's **Find** command to search for a particular publication by name or for a type of resource, such as an almanac. If you already know that what you want is on AOL, you can use the **Keyword** shortcut to go directly there.

Channel surfing on AOL

AOL offers a broad subject approach, too, letting you drill down through any of a dozen or so channels until you find what you want. Figure 9-4 shows the selection of channels you see when you sign on to AOL and click Channels.

Figure 9-4:
America
Online
channels.

Some channels that I've found useful as research starting points are:

The **Research & Learn** channel (I prefer its previous name, **Reference Desk**, but nobody asked me) includes atlases, country reports, links to Web-based encyclopedias, and resources in other areas such as history, science, health, and business. Click on **Business** to get:

- ✔ Recent company press releases from Reuters, Associated Press, PR Newswire and BusinessWire

- ✔ International country profiles and updates from the Economist Intelligence Unit

- ✔ A link to Hoover's Company Directory on the Web

- ✔ Searchable archives of *Inc.* magazine, *Home Office Computing,* and *Business Week*

- ✔ Links to patent and trademark information on the Web

- ✔ D&B@AOL — access to Dun & Bradstreet company profiles, financial information, and credit reports (many of these services cost extra)

The **Computing** channel includes information from and about a selection of high tech companies, arranged alphabetically by company name. You can also find links here to computer-related publications, most of them on the Web.

The **News** channel brings you current news headlines, as well as stories from today's *New York Times* and the most recent Sunday *Times Magazine,* plus back issues of selected sections. You can also find the most recent issue of *Newsweek,* with a searchable archive back to January 1995, and a pull-down list of other AOL channels, such as Sports, Family, and Personal Finance, with newsstands of their own. Click any of these channels to go directly to one of those subject-oriented periodical collections. The News channel's own Newsstand consists of links to a variety of publication sites on the Web.

The **Personal Finance** channel has a lot of information for stock-market groupies and would-be investors alike. It features recent market quotes and business headlines up front, but the real gold is in the **Investment Research** section. There, you find historical stock quotes, earnings estimates, financial statements, and company filings with the SEC (Securities and Exchange Commission, which regulates the affairs of publicly-traded U.S. companies). The Personal Finance channel offers some references for beginning investors, too — a dictionary of Wall Street terms, lessons in the basics of investing, and information on specific subjects, such as 401 (k) retirement plans, prepared by the American Association of Individual Investors.

The personal finance section was catapulted into stardom — no joke — by the arrival of the Motley Fool, an investment forum hosted by a couple of guys who could make a bear market seem like fun. If you're at all interested in investments, check out Fooldom and what it has to offer. Even if you keep your money under your mattress, The Motley Fool is a great example of an online resource that manages to be both informative and entertaining. The keyword **fool** takes you directly there. Chapter 12 tells you more about the Fool and other investment resources.

Calling in the Pros: Going Wide and Deep with Professional Online Services

I learned to search using proprietary services such as Dialog, LEXIS-NEXIS, and Dow Jones. This was way before the advent of the Web, and even before the graphical, point-and-click environment that's made millionaires of Messrs. Jobs and Gates. Monitors were monochrome, and mice were un-heard of (except in the rodent-based form). We had to trudge 20 miles to school, in the snow, uphill in both directions. Instead of clicking icons, we had to type — and know how to interpret — strange command strings such as **ss s1 and s4; t/3,k/1-5, 12,22.**

Dow Jones News/Retrieval, as it was then called, used the notorious *dot-dot* language, where you had to remember to type two periods before ..just ..about ..any ..command.

LEXIS-NEXIS gave smooshed-up and totally non-intuitive names to its databases. You were expected to remember these and type them in perfectly each time: BUSWK, FORTUN, ABAJNL (Um, I'd like to buy a vowel . . .).

After you connected to Dialog, you found yourself in a Zen-like environment: a totally blank screen with a question mark in the upper-left corner. *Now what?*

But y'know what? All these aggravating quirks were worth it. The early command-line database services were fast and powerful. Besides, they built character — they made us feel like gods for having mastered them.

Most of these services are easier to use now that you can search them on the Web or through their own point-and-click, pull-down menu software. But they're still complex; it takes time and practice to learn how to use them effectively.

The other downside to the professional online services, besides their built-in quirks, is *cost*. If you're used to browsing Web documents and downloading or printing them at will, beware — you're in a different environment now. You may not be paying by the hour or by the search, the way we did in the old days; but you're almost certain to be charged for each document you ask to see in anything other than its shortest or default format.

Some prose on the pros of the pros

These industrial-strength database services have several advantages over all the other online research tools I cover in this book:

✔ **Their search engines are extremely powerful and sophisticated.** They understand not only phrase searching and Boolean ANDs, ORs, and NOTs, but also relative adjacency — finding words near, or within so many words of, each other. They also support truncation; some even enable you to specify how many more letters to look for following the word-root you've supplied. *Result:* More precise searching, and more relevant answers. (See the Bonus Appendix on the CD for more complete descriptions of all of these search features.)

✔ **The information they contain is highly processed, down to the level of individual records or documents.** *Processed* may not be what you want in *cheese,* say, but in databases it's a good thing. Processing a database record enables you to search by author, or to look for words in specific parts of a document, such as publication name or article title. Some databases include keyword and concept indexes, so that you can search by subject, using a standard vocabulary, and find what you want even if your keyword doesn't occur in the text of the article itself. *Result:* More flexible searching, and a better chance of finding information you might otherwise miss.

✔ **The information tends to be more reliable than on the Web at large.** Much of the information originally appeared in a printed publication, so it's been subjected to fact-checking and editorial controls. *Result:* Though you can't believe everything you read in print, either, at least you know that somebody's taken responsibility for what you're pulling up. You've got a basic quality filter in place.

✔ **The information is often unique.** Sources include the complete text of legal cases, investment analyst reports and market research studies, as well as detailed summaries of conference papers, master's and doctoral dissertations, international scholarly journal articles, and more. Unlike the Web, the professional research services have a long memory, and maintain archives of documents that go back many years. *Result:* If you can't find it on the Web, or if there's a piece missing, you may well find it in a proprietary service.

> ✔ **They allow you to cover dozens, even hundreds, of individual publications and other information sources with a single search request.** You don't have to visit individual publication sites — many of which are closed to general Web search engines, remember — and run your search in each one, because proprietary services *aggregate* thousands of such resources under one roof. *Result:* It's the time-versus-money tradeoff: You may spend more money to get the answer, but you're saving yourself a lot of time.

Dealing with database depth

I've been talking about *professional online services* and *database services* more or less interchangeably. You've probably gathered by now that both terms refer to a much more complex research environment than single-publication sites such as *The New York Times on the Web,* and even the channels of information you navigate through once you're inside a service such as CompuServe or America Online.

Each of the services we're dealing with here can lay claim to housing at least as much information — *useable* information, anyway — as the entire Web. The head of Dialog claimed at the beginning of 1998 that their information content was 50 times greater than the Web's — six billion pages of text in more than 900 databases. Part of what makes all that information so useable is the database structure into which it's organized.

The information pyramid

The most basic unit of a database is an individual *record.* A journal article is a record. So is a patent, or a company directory listing, a legal case, or a profile of a chemical substance. A *database* — sometimes called a *file* — is a collection of individual *records.* A database may include records from a single publication only, or from a group of publications. Related databases may be grouped together into a larger database, or *group file.*

Before your eyes roll up into your head, just wait. I'm telling you this for a reason. The databases you select, and the level at which you select them, has a lot to do with how successful your search is. Too narrow, and you may get nothing because you've selected the wrong database. Too broad, and you may get more information than you can deal with.

Picture a pyramid, with the answer you're looking for — the ideal document — at the top, as shown in Figure 9-5.

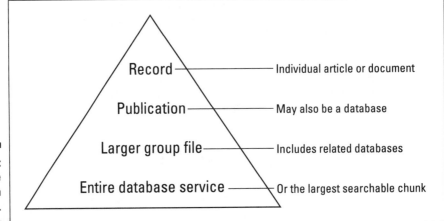

Figure 9-5:
The
information
pyramid.

Climbing up and down the pyramid

To find that ideal document, you can

- ✔ Try to guess what publication it may have appeared in. In some online services, each publication is a separate database. In others, you have to move down to the next layer to pluck the one you want from a larger selection.

- ✔ Select a category or type of publication that makes sense, such as major newspapers, computer magazines, medical literature, patents, or conference papers.

- ✔ Select an even broader category, such as News, Magazines, or Trade Journals.

- ✔ Opt to search the entire system, or as much of it as you can.

Different kinds of databases have different structures, even within the same online service. Searching patents and company directories together, for example, could produce weird and unexpected results. For that reason, some services block you from searching dissimilar databases at the same time. Trust me; it's for your own good.

The OTHER Online: Dow Jones, LEXIS-NEXIS, Dialog, and More

In this section I give you the briefest introduction, though it may not look that brief, to the *other* online — the research services that were around way before the Web, and that grew up independent of the Internet itself. My mission here is to convey why these services are important and what they can do for you. If you still opt not to use any of them, at least you know what you're missing.

Searching a proprietary database service is usually a three-step process. The order may vary, but the basic idea is the same:

1. **Pick your sources — the exact publication or group of publications that you want to search.**

2. **Key in your search query.**

3. **Determine the format — short, medium, or long — in which to review the answers.**

Before you opt to review your search results in *any* form, make sure that you know the costs, if any, for doing so.

Beating the averages with Dow Jones Interactive

Dow Jones Interactive (DJI) has a sisterly relationship — and an incestuous one, at that — with the *The Wall Street Journal Interactive Edition*. They have the same parent, the Dow Jones of Dow Jones Industrial Average fame, and considerable shared content, too. If you're a faithful reader of *The Wall Street Journal NONinteractive Edition* (also known as print), you may prefer to come in through the *Wall Street Journal* gateway that I described earlier in this chapter. If your information needs typically extend beyond what the *Journal* has to offer, you may prefer Dow Jones Interactive's more generic approach.

What'll it cost ya? $29.95 a year — comparable to the *WSJIE's* discounted rate for subscribers to the print edition. You can search and browse head-lines (including the lead sentence displayed with them) for free, but you pay $2.95 for every article you view, download, or print. In advanced search mode, where you have some additional format options, you pay $2.00 each for lead paragraphs and $1.00 for brief citations. Careful: it adds up. For an overview of the site, find the Dow Jones Interactive registration page (`nrstg1p.djnr.com/`), and then click <u>Take a Tour</u>.

DJI gives you not only the *Journal* itself, but a cluster of other information services, including today's top news stories, in-depth company and market research reports, historical stock quotes, links to other highly-rated Web sites, and CustomClips, an automatic update service for topics you want to follow.

DataBasics

Each of the proprietary services in this section contains anywhere from dozens to hundreds of individual databases. Some of them are highly specialized, with unique fields and features that drive even professional researchers back to Reading The Fine Manual. Yes, it *can* get that extreme. Searcher folklore is full of tips, tricks, and shortcuts that you won't really appreciate until you've been driven to distraction by the system's — or an individual database's — quirks. In the meantime, I highly recommend two coping strategies:

- Take any formal system training — online, or even in person — that's offered.

- Buy (unless it's free, of course) and *read* at least the basic system manual, plus detailed documentation for the databases or parts of the service that you plan to use the most.

The heart of DJI, though, is the **Publications Library,** a collection of nearly 4,000 newspapers, magazines, trade journals, and specialized business periodicals. You can find everything from *The Wall Street Journal* itself — remember that your subscription to the *Interactive Edition* gets you access to the Publications Library, too — to general newspapers such as the *Los Angeles Times,* *The Washington Post,* and some smaller city newspapers as well. You can also find a bulging magazine rack stocked with familiar periodicals such as *Esquire, Country Living, Field and Stream, Harper's, Redbook, The New Yorker, Sky and Telescope,* and *Smithsonian,* plus an array of more erudite titles, such as *American Behavioral Scientist* and the *Journal of International Affairs.*

Searching the DJI Publications Library

You can elect to run your search in a single publication, a generic category, such as **Top 50 U.S. Newspapers,** or a focused industry or regional grouping.

- Click any category name to get a list of the publications included.

- Click an individual publication title to see how far back it's carried, how frequently it's published and updated online, and the date of the most recent issue available through DJI.

- To see the titles of all publications in the library, click the All Publications link and then pick a letter, A to Z.

Figure 9-7 shows the default Dow Jones Interactive search form, which is labeled **Search by Words or Phrases.** To search — assuming you've already signed up for the service, surrendered your billing information, and logged in using your system ID and secret password — you need to do the following:

1. **Enter your keywords or phrases, using Boolean ANDs, ORs, and NOTs, if you want, between them.** (See the Bonus Appendix on the CD for more about Boolean searching.)

2. **Select the sources you want to search, by group or individual title(s).**

   Your default group file options are All Publications, Major News and Business Publications, Top 50 U.S. newspapers, or Wires: Press Release Wires. You can customize your selection by clicking on **change publications** and adding publications grouped by industry, type or region, or, drilling down still further, individual publications by title.

3. **Click the Run Search button.**

4. **Click any headline to read the full article.**

The pull-down menus on the search form allow you to

✔ Increase the precision of your search by limiting your terms to the **headline, headline and lead paragraph,** or **lead paragraph** only. This is based on the old journalistic adage (widely ignored in the New Journalism) that the *who, where, what, when, why,* and *how* of the story is supposed to be wrapped up in the first paragraph. On the other hand, you can go for broke — or maximum information retrieval, anyway — by looking for your terms in the **full article,** anywhere they might appear.

✔ Restrict your results to articles published this year or last, or between certain dates, or on a specific date. If you're looking for a particular article, or for very recent information, or for coverage published when a story was first breaking, this is the way to go.

✔ Sort the results by relevance or — if you want to see the most recent articles first — by date.

✔ Display the results in brief **(citation),** medium-length **(lead paragraph)** or **full article** format.

Click the <u>Examples</u> link above the search form to reveal some powerful and only semi-documented Dow Jones Interactive features. Besides the standard Boolean AND/OR/NOT operators, you find a bunch of handy *positional* or *adjacency* connectors, which allow you to specify how close to each other, and in what order, you want your search terms to appear. The Bonus Appendix on the CD tells you more about all these features and how to use them.

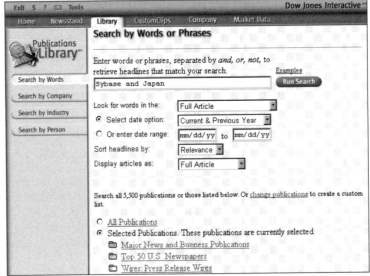

Figure 9-6:
Dow Jones
Interactive
search
form.

Dow Jones Interactive offers several other search options in addition to **Search by Words or Phrases.** These are listed to the left of the search form in Figure 9-7. Each option allows you to select specific publications to search, limit by date, and include any other terms that might be pertinent.

- ✔ **Search by company:** Enter the company name or ticker symbol.

- ✔ **Search by industry:** Select an industry from the pull-down menu.

- ✔ **Search by person:** Look for articles by or about a specific individual.

Want to stay up-to-date on a research topic? The major professional database services in this chapter all offer automatic alerting features that enable you to monitor topics on an ongoing basis. On Dow Jones Interactive, look for **Custom Clips.** The LEXIS-NEXIS equivalent is **Eclipse,** as in *e-lectronic clipping service.* Dialog's is called **Alert,** fittingly enough.

Learning the ways of LEXIS-NEXIS

As the name implies, the LEXIS-NEXIS service has two sides. The part that sounds like a luxury automobile (that's a sore point — a trademark infringement suit was actually filed over the similarity with *Lexus*) encompasses case law, U.S. and international governmental statutes, federal and state agency regulations, plus secondary material, such as bar journals, law reviews, and other lawyerly fare.

I'll be honest with you: Legal research is a science unto itself. If you're deeply involved in the law, you're probably already acquainted with Lexis or its chief competitor, Westlaw (www.westlaw.com). If you're *not* involved in the law, I'm not going to teach you here. I'm not looking for a lawsuit, myself. If you have need of legal research, it's best to contact an attorney or a qualified research professional, or buckle down and let LEXIS-NEXIS train you.

The other half of the service, Nexis, focuses on global news, politics and economics, company directories, financial filings, and other kinds of business, management and marketing information. The printed catalog of individual publication titles, divided into broad subject areas that LEXIS-NEXIS calls *libraries,* is almost 300 pages of very small and closely-spaced type.

LEXIS-NEXIS is particularly strong in full-text newspapers and general interest magazines, business and trade journals, international country and economic data, and market research reports. As with Dow Jones Interactive, you can cover dozens of publications at once with a single search query.

The LEXIS-NEXIS Web site (www.lexis-nexis.com) doesn't provide access to the system itself, but you can get a preview of what the service has to offer. Check out the **Sources** listings under **Products and Services.** Select any one of these categories: Business, Government, or Law. From the corresponding pull-down menu, highlight a subcategory of your choice. You're presented with a list — often a long one — of individual sources you can search on the LEXIS-NEXIS system.

LEXIS-NEXIS, alas, has not yet moved its entire grand edifice of legal and general news and information sources to the Web. The good news is that LEXIS-NEXIS offers some Web-based products for specialized kinds of research, as well as several different ways to search the full system using LEXIS-NEXIS's proprietary software. (In this context, *proprietary* means that its only function is to dial up and let you interact with the online service.)

Going online with LEXIS-NEXIS

For access to the full LEXIS-NEXIS service, you have to contract with the company, negotiate a payment plan (pay-as-you-go, or any of several subscription-type accounts), and get a copy of its imaginatively named **Research Software** package. The software gives you graphical help in selecting databases (Nexis calls them *files*), building and running your search, browsing through documents in various formats, starting new searches, saving your results, and signing off the system.

Low-volume users — that's me, and most likely you — often sign up for LEXIS-NEXIS's transaction-based fee schedule, which means that you're charged for every search you do. A group file such as ALLNEWS costs more to search than a single publication within that group file. The bigger the database, roughly speaking, the greater the cost per search. Bottom line: mistakes, even typos, can be expensivo.

LEXIS-NEXIS special searching features

LEXIS-NEXIS is a complex research service with dozens of specialized features. Like the other professional online services in this chapter, it utilizes the ol' Boolean AND/OR/NOT operators and many of the other power-searching capabilities covered in the Bonus Appendix on the CD. But LEXIS-NEXIS is unique in many ways. A full-fledged tutorial could take a whole book (and *does* — you can buy it from LEXIS-NEXIS). This section highlights some of its special features.

Automatic pluralization: LEXIS-NEXIS looks for both singular and plural forms of words, as long as the plural is formed by adding **s** or **es**.

Equivalents: LEXIS-NEXIS automatically looks for both U.S. and British spellings of common words such as **program(me)** and **colo(u)r**.

Truncation: LEXIS-NEXIS uses two different *wildcard* symbols. The **!** stands for any number of letters at the end of a word root. The asterisk (*****) stands for a single character anywhere in a word (except at the beginning).

> **wom*n** looks for both **woman** and **women**.

> You can use more than one wildcard symbol: **r**t** retrieves **root, rust, rent** and **rapt** — though I can't imagine why you'd want to.

You use asterisks at the *end* of a word to retrieve up to and including that many additional characters in the word: **bank***** retrieves **bank, banks, banker, bankers,** and **banking,** but not **bankrupt, bankruptcy,** or **bankruptcies.**

Case sensitivity: LEXIS-NEXIS enables you to search for uppercase letters anywhere in a word, for all-uppercase, or for lowercase-only forms.

> **caps (next)** retrieves references to NeXT computers — not all occurrences of the word *next* — though it will pick up the word *Next* if it happens to appear at the beginning of a sentence.

> **caps (Apple)** retrieves references to Apple computers, or the company, or people named Apple, or any occurrence of the word *apple* that happens to come at the beginning of a sentence.

> **allcaps (era)** retrieves references to the Equal Rights Amendment, and anything else with the same acronym, but not to uses of the word *era* as a measure of geological or historical time.

> **nocaps (era)** does the opposite.

atleast*n*: Your search term(s) must occur *at least* so many times in a document in order for it to be retrieved, which is a slick way of avoiding material in which your term is mentioned, but only in passing. If you specify a high value for *n,* you generally limit your retrieval to long documents. If you're looking for a good *short* article and not a whole treatise on the subject, try setting your **atleast** value in the 6–10 range: **atleast8 (kodak).**

Dow Jones Interactive offers an *atleast* feature, too.

Shortcut: You can stack commands — issue a whole sequence at once — by using a semicolon between them. Stacking saves time and tedium by bypassing the intervening LEXIS-NEXIS menus and prompts. Obviously, this works best when you've used the system for a while and can anticipate what the next two or three screens are going to tell you to do.

The sequence **news;curnews;gore w/seg global warming** selects the News Library and the Current News database within that library, and enters your search statement.

Dot commands: Save keystrokes by learning a few abbreviated alternatives to the commands you use most often.

.cl = change libraries

.cf = change files

.ns = new search

.ci (citation), **.fu** (full), or **.kw** (Key Words In Context) = change the format in which documents appear

.nd, .pd, or **.fd** = go to the next, previous, or first document in the current set of results

Focus (.fo): Enables you to look for occurrences of a new keyword within a set of documents you've already retrieved. Focus is a good way to zero in on the good bits buried in a steaming pile of not particularly glorious-looking articles. Focus helps you answer that ever-present question: Why on earth did I get *this?* Say you've done a search on **Caribbean** and realized, after pulling up hundreds of items, that you're really just interested in Caribbean cruises:

.fo cruise takes you to articles that contain both of those concepts

More: Allows you to tag a particularly juicy-looking document and tell LEXIS-NEXIS to "get me more like this one." Depending on your payment plan, you may be dinged for an additional search fee.

Takin' it free and easy

LEXIS-NEXIS offers two alternatives to the basic Boolean searching mode mentioned in the previous section and detailed in the Bonus Appendix on the CD.

Freestyle: Lets you enter your search query in plain English. You can specify any terms that *must* appear, add dates and other restrictions, and review the results in order of relevance. Freestyle is useful when your topic is abstract or you haven't yet come up with any industry jargon, distinctive phrases, or relevant names to pin it down. You can switch back and forth between Boolean (**.bool**) and Freestyle (**.fr**) modes during the course of a search.

Easy: Or guided searching, takes you by the hand and walks you through your search, prompting you at each stage of the way. Type **easy** after you've logged in to LEXIS-NEXIS to connect to the Easy menu system.

Other LEXIS-NEXIS access options

In the last few years, LEXIS-NEXIS has spawned a confusing variety of products, both Web-based and proprietary, aimed at various target markets — accountants, advertising, media, sales, marketing professionals, political consultants, pizza delivery persons, who knows. If you feel a bit daunted by the number and variety of sources and commands I describe in the preceding sections, don't worry. You may not *need* all that. If your main interest is business, government, international, or legal information, just click <u>Subscription Information</u> on the LEXIS-NEXIS home page and phone or e-mail the most appropriate-sounding contact point listed there. Tell them what you want to do, and let them recommend a service option suited to your needs.

LEXIS-NEXIS does offer a couple of remote-control ways to tap into the service. One of these simple alternatives may be all you need:

- ✔ **reQUESTer** lets you fill out a specially-designed search form and submit your search via e-mail or through your Web browser. You can tap into more than 7,000 Nexis sources, including newspapers, trade journals, market studies, and company financials. A companion product, **TRACKER,** keeps you current by automatically delivering updates on topics of interest.

- ✔ **InfoTailor** is a personalized daily briefing on as many as seven topics of your choice. You get up to 20 articles a day, delivered via e-mail.

Shopping at Dialog's supermarket

Searchers have likened Dialog to a supermarket of online wares. It's a fish market, a wine shop, a bakery, a hardware store, and a baby vegetable boutique — all under a single capacious roof. You want imported olives? No problem. Paper towels? They're on Aisle 4.

The sidebar "Dialog's well-stocked shelves" shows the variety of information you can get on Dialog. You can find most of the items stocked on Aisles 1 and 2 — in keeping with the supermarket metaphor, I'm just using the word *aisles* here to indicate broad categories of information — elsewhere as well, including the other gated sites and services we visit in this chapter. Although Dialog doesn't hold an exclusive on everything in the rest of the store, either, it's a convenient place to shop for them. You never know when you may get a craving for biotechnology patents or rubber chemistry. I know it hits *me* at the oddest times.

Aisles of files

Dialog identifies its individual databases in a straightforward way: It numbers them. The numbering is arbitrary, but easy to look up, and not that hard to remember. Well, not all 900 or so of them, but the ones you use most often.

The key to understanding Dialog databases lies in the *Bluesheets,* a brief but detailed guide to what each file contains, how far back it goes, and all the different ways you can search it. The Bluesheets (which really are blue) are also online at DialogWeb (`www.dialogweb.com/`), which we get to later in this section (see the section, "DialogWeb").

Dialog databases are highly structured. Each one has its own searchable fields. Some use special codes and index terms to make searching even more precise.

In **ABI/Inform** (File 15), a database of business, management, and marketing information, you can search for a specific slant or type of article:

> **ss cc=9110** for case studies
>
> **ss cc=9130** for theory
>
> **ss cc=9140** for statistical data

You can also use the made-up word **manycompanies** to limit your search to articles that survey, well, many companies in the same industry or involved in whatever topic the article is discussing.

In **Dun's Market Identifiers** (File 516), a company directory, you can look for firms with a certain number of employees, or annual sales above a certain amount:

> **ss EM=300** finds companies with 300 or more employees
>
> **ss SA=50M:100M** finds companies with sales in the $50- to $100-million range

In **Medline** (Files 154 and 155), which covers medical literature and related fields, you can use a **Limit** command to restrict your results to human subjects, or English language records, or both at once:

L12/human, eng

You can also link subject headings from the Medline index of terms to specific subheadings that closely define the topic:

ss arteriosclerosis (L) DT = drug therapy

ss arteriosclerosis (L) SU = surgical treatment

In **Claims/U.S. Patents** (File 340), you can search by inventor (the person who discovered it) or patent assignee (the person — or, more likely, the company — that gets the money from manufacturing or licensing it):

ss IV=Berlekamp

ss PA=Kodak

Actually, personal and company name searching on Dialog involves more than just entering what you assume is the correct name and specifying the appropriate field. Using the **Expand** command is a good idea because it shows you the various permutations of the name, with and without middle initials, and so on. You can pick the right one(s) from the Expand list and use them in your search.

What's that hissing sound?

Unlike Dow Jones or LEXIS-NEXIS, you have to tell Dialog every time you want to give it some terms to search on. Most search commands begin with **ss**. A single **s** works too, but doesn't give you a separate results listing for each of your search terms. One of Dialog's unique strengths is the ability to combine the *sets* it creates for all of the terms you enter. For example, if you're searching on **cats** (set 1) and forget to include the synonym **felines,** you can always search for it later and **OR** the two sets together:

ss cats and mice

>   set 1: cats

>   set 2: mice

ss felines

>   set 3: felines

ss s1 or s3

>   set 4: cats or felines

ss s4 and s2

>   set 5: cats or felines, and mice

Dialog's well-stocked shelves

Aisle 1: Business & Law

- International company directories, business and financial profiles, mergers and acquisitions, stock quotes, general business and economic news
- Market research data for industries and products
- Government contract opportunities, import and export statistics, census data
- Regulations and legislation
- Management theory and practice
- U.S. and international patents, trademarks; U.S. copyrights

Aisle 2: Current Events

- Wire service reports
- International, national, regional, and city newspapers
- Magazines and newsletters

Aisle 3: Science

- Mathematics
- Medical research and clinical trials
- Biotechnology, healthcare, pharmaceutical and chemical industry news and regulation
- Chemistry and chemical engineering
- Psychology and sociology

Aisle 4: Technology

- Aviation and aerospace
- Automotive engineering
- Civil, structural, and construction engineering

- Computers and electronics
- Materials science
- Government research & development

Aisle 5: Environment

- Geology, hydrology, oceanography, meteorology, zoology
- Oil and gas, nuclear energy
- Pollution

Aisle 6: Arts & Letters

- History, biography, public affairs
- Philosophy
- Art and architecture
- Language and linguistics
- Film
- Education
- Religion

Aisle 7: Reference & General

- Conference proceedings
- Dissertations
- Translations
- Quotations
- Books and periodicals in print
- Directories of associations, foundation grants, colleges, and more
- Public opinion polls
- Practice databases and Dialog search aids

If you were running an actual search, it would also show you how many hits Dialog found for each of your terms. If you're on the right track, an **OR** command increases the retrieval, because you're including more terms; an **AND** command reduces it, because you're imposing added restrictions. More about using ANDs and ORs is in the Bonus Appendix on the CD.

Stepping through a Dialog search

The standard drill for searching Dialog goes like this:

1. **Connect and log in.**

2. **Choose your database(s). You can string file numbers together, or select a broad category such as Papers to search many files at once.**

3. **Enter your search strategy. Remember that you can combine set numbers with ANDs, ORs, or NOTs to broaden or narrow the results.**

4. **Review interim results in one of Dialog's brief formats.**

5. **When you're satisfied that you're on target, print out or download your results.**

Special search features on Dialog

Dialog's search engine is based on essentially the same constellation of Boolean operators and proximity connectors used by Dow Jones and LEXIS-NEXIS. But each of those services offers its own refinements and specialized ways of handling certain features. Dialog is no different; here are just a few of its distinguishing characteristics.

The **Link** operator **(L),** which I used in the Medline example (see the section, "Aisles of files" earlier in this section), tells Dialog that your two terms must occur in the same *descriptor.* A descriptor is a standardized indexing term used throughout a particular database and assigned to documents dealing with a particular topic — such as **arteriosclerosis.** Usually, you link a subject heading with a sub-heading, such as drug therapy in the Medline example. You probably won't use the Link operator very often, but when you do you'll be glad it's there.

The **Field operator (F)** tells Dialog that both your terms must occur in the same part of the database record, for example in the title, in an *abstract,* or in the summary of the document. For more about field searching, see the Bonus Appendix on the CD.

The **question mark ?** is used for both internal *wildcards* and end-of-word *truncation:*

A **?** in the middle of a word is a wildcard: **wom?n** picks up **woman** and **women** (there you have it: my secret for picking up women) as well as the new-agey **womyn.**

A **?** at the end of a word can be tuned to pick up just one additional letter at most, or no more than a specific number of letters; or an unlimited number:

> **dog???** picks up anywhere from zero to three additional letters following the root word **dog.** You get **dog, dogs,** and **dogged,** plus anything else that starts with **dog** and contains up to three additional letters. Similarly, **dog??** or **dog????** would get you two- or four-letter endings, respectively; **dog?????** would get you up to five, and so on.

> **dog?** with a single **?** picks up everything in the world (and *don't* they?) from **dog** and **dogs** to **dogged, dogcatcher, dogfight, doghouse, dogleg, dogwood, dogmatic,** and **doggone.**

> **dog? ?** — that's a space between the first and the second **?** — gets just *one* more letter, max: **dog, dogs** — and **doge,** a Venetian nobleman. Won't *he* be surprised!

Target is Dialog's supplement to the Boolean search mode described earlier in this chapter and in the Bonus Appendix on the CD. Target searches and delivers results in order of their supposed relevance. You just key in your search words and indicate with an asterisk (*) which ones *must* appear. Type **target** while you're online to get a brief summary of commands.

Target works best when you want to get just a few key articles on the subject. You can use it in combination with a Boolean search. Say you've run a search, gotten more hits than you can use, and can't figure out how to narrow them down. **Target 4** (assuming set 4 is the last set of your Boolean search) re-ranks them in relevance (you hope) order and presents you with Dialog's top 50 picks.

Output options

Record Format: Dialog is big on numbers. It numbers its databases, and it also numbers the various formats for printing, displaying, and downloading database records.

- ✔ Some formats are very short and just intend to show you whether you're on the right track in the course of a search (typically, that's Format 6 or 8, and it's traditionally, although not always, free).

- ✔ Other formats give you basic information, such as author, title, publication name, and date (Format 3).

- ✔ Still others give you a brief summary or abstract (often Format 4 or 7, but it varies a lot).

- ✔ Other formats give you the whole schmear — complete text, all the numbers, coding and index terms, whatever's in the record (usually Format 5 or 9).

You can also roll your own — format your own format, in effect. Dialog's UDF (User-Defined Format) feature enables you to key in the fields or document sections that you want to see:

> **t/au, ti/1-5** tells Dialog to **type** just the **author names** and **article titles** for records **1 through 5** in the current set.

Dialog's pricing is based on which databases you search, the search commands you use how many documents you print or download, and the format in which you retrieve them.

In any given database, a brief citation costs less than an abstract; an abstract costs less than the full text (abstracts aren't available in all files).

If you display a document while searching, and order it later in the session, you pay for it twice. That's why it makes sense to keep your display format brief and order the complete item only if you're sure you want it. It's not like the Web, where you can browse and read to your heart's content!

UDF documents don't always save you money; if you specify a field that's otherwise only available in one of the higher-priced numbered formats, you're likely to pay that price — even if all you've ordered is one field.

Sorting: Dialog normally presents your search results in date order, with the most recent date first. You can override this order by specifying how you want the results to appear:

> **sort s3/all/au, py** tells Dialog to **sort all the documents in set 3** by **author,** and for each author, by publication **year**

Rank: The Rank command lets you determine the most common (highly-ranked) terms or concepts in a set of database results — without having to know what any of them are to begin with.

> ✔ You can use **Rank** after running a patent search to find out what companies hold the most patents in the area you're researching.
>
> ✔ You can use it in a search of the medical or engineering literature to identify prominent experts who've written a lot on the subject.
>
> ✔ You can search a company directory by geographic location to find out what kinds of businesses exist, or search by type of business and rank them by city.

The basic Rank syntax is easy: **rank pa** ranks the most recent set of search results by **patent assignee.** Substitute **au** for **author** or **cy** for **city,** and you're on your way — no longer a Rank amateur.

Rank is free in most databases, but in some, including patent files, you may be charged from 2 cents to 10 cents a record. That doesn't sound like much, but when you're ranking 5,000 records, it does add up.

Report: The Report feature lets you extract certain fields from database records and rearrange them into tables. Report is only available for databases where it makes sense to use it, such as in company directories.

> **report s5/co,cy,st,te/1-50** produces a tabular report with the headings **Company, City, State,** and **Telephone Number** across the top, and the information you've requested, for the first **50** records in **set 5,** arranged in columns.

Want the top 10 companies by sales? Or an alphabetical listing? Do a Sort on your final answer-set, and then run Report on the sorted set.

Offline delivery: You can download your search results as you go, or take delivery later via Dialmail (Dialog's proprietary e-mail system) or your own e-mail account on the Net. For details on these and other options, type **help email** when you get online.

DialogWeb

Dialog offers several connection options: You can dial up directly to the Dialog service using a standard terminal program, such as Procomm, or DialogLink, Dialog's proprietary software. You can telnet to `dialog.com` from somewhere else on the Net. You can use Dialog Select on the Web, or one of the Windows-based programs mentioned in the following section. Or you can search Dialog on the Web (`www.dialogweb.com/`).

DialogWeb is a great way to learn more about the Dialog system. You can poke around and read the copious help files, online Bluesheets, and other documentation, without having to pay a cent. It's like driving down a long and gently winding road until the **enter your password** gate clangs down.

DialogWeb makes it easy to browse through Dialog's database collection and see what it has to offer. I drill down through the **Food and Agriculture** category, to the **Food Sciences** subcategory (you're in a research supermarket, remember) and get a list of about a dozen databases that deal with that subject. I can select as many of them as I want to search at once.

I can click any of the individual database names to get the online Bluesheet (the digital version is blue, too) of detailed documentation on that particular file.

I can also use **DialIndex,** Dialog's mega-database index, either here in the **Food Sciences** subcategory or in the preceding, broader **Food and Agriculture** category, to identify databases that may be useful in my search (of course, you can try it in whatever category or subcategory interests you). If I enter a simple search statement such as **ss tomato?** and click on **Search DialIndex,** Dialog shows me a ranked list of databases that contain my search term. Of course, more isn't necessarily better — but DialIndex can help by pointing out files that I may have forgotten about, hadn't realized existed, or didn't know covered my subject.

After I've selected my databases, I click **Begin Databases.** At that point — but not until then — I have to enter my account number and password to log on and actually connect to the system.

If I know the database(s) I want, and have memorized their numbers, I can bypass the selection process and go right to **Command Search.** There, I use the **Begin (b)** command to specify the file or files I want to start with, and enter my first search statement at the same time. That's what's going on in Figure 9-7. (Note the **Dialog Command** help link to the left of the search box.) Now it's password time again.

After I've connected and logged on to the service, Dialog runs my search and displays how many results it got, in the databases I told it to search, for each of my terms. The bottom line *is* the bottom line — my *answer set,* or results. I can select a display format from the pull-down menu and click **Display** to look at any or all of the documents that Dialog has found for me. Or, if I'm familiar with Dialog commands and the formats described above in the Output Options section, I can specify one of those format numbers, and the number of documents to display, with a Type command such as **t/8/1-5.**

Easy answers

If you're impressed but a little daunted by the power and depth of the Dialog service, one of these alternatives may help:

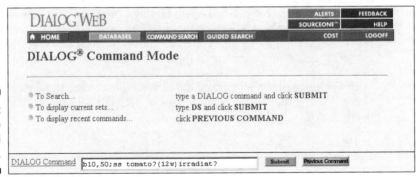

Figure 9-7:
DialogWeb
command
mode.

DialogWeb offers a **Guided Search** option that enables you to search the Dialog system without knowing any Dialog commands at all. I click on Guided Search, select my databases, and then fill in the appropriate forms to define and focus my search.

Dialog Select offers Web access — separate from DialogWeb — to selected Dialog databases. It uses pre-defined search forms and pull-down menus. For more details, get thee to the Dialog Select site (`products.dialog.com/products/dialogselect/`).

For information about Windows-based software packages that allow you to search selected Dialog databases without needing to know file numbers, formats, and system commands, check out the Dialog Corporation's Product Selection Guide at `products.dialog.com/products/guide/`. I can't vouch for any of these personally, since when I want Dialog, I want it *all*.

At the checkout counter

The moment of truth has arrived: How much is this load of groceries — or maybe just a bag of organic tomatoes — going to cost me?

Dialog pricing traditionally has two main components:

- ✔ **Connect charges:** how long you're connected to each database you search
- ✔ **Hit charges:** how many records you print, display, or download, and in what format

Most databases run $30 to $150/hour, pro-rated down to a fraction of a minute so that you pay only for the time you're connected.

Record charges vary. Some formats, such as title-only, are usually free. A full record typically goes for $1–$3 apiece, though government-subsidized databases are often less, and some business, financial, and specialized technical files can run considerably more. The gory details are all at `products.dialog.com/products/dialog/dial_pricing.html`.

I know that those hourly rates sound scary — they *are,* compared with the open Web, and with services such as Dow Jones Interactive that don't charge a connect fee at all. In reality, though, most Dialog searches don't take more than a few minutes to run. You're seldom connected to the databases for an entire hour, unless you're having a really bad day.

Just as this book was going to press, Dialog announced that it was dropping connect charges in favor of "Dial Units" (a measure based on the types of search commands issued during a search session). Dial Unit costs vary from database to database. The jury is still out on whether users will pay more or less overall for the service under the new Dial Unit plan.

Driving to databases

Many of the databases carried by Dialog and the other online services described in this chapter are also available through university libraries to affiliated students, faculty, and staff, and sometimes to members of the community on a walk-in basis. You may have to show up at the library and sign up to use a public terminal. If you're interested in exploring these resources but not ready to commit to a particular online service, check out the free-access angle through your nearest institution of higher learning.

Paging ProQuest Direct

If it's true that a picture is worth a thousand words, then ProQuest Direct is ahead of the game. It is a visual research experience, at least on the delivery end. The company behind ProQuest Direct is called UMI. Those letters used to stand for University Microfilms International. They started out microfilming doctoral dissertations, branched out into newspapers, developed some electronic databases of their own, and the rest, I guess, is history.

ProQuest Direct reflects — and respects — its roots. It covers more than 6,000 business, professional, technical, and general-interest periodicals, academic journals, newspapers, and more. And, as I hinted, some of those publications come complete with photographs and other illustrations, some in color, from the original articles. That's an exclusive; the other proprietary services surveyed in this chapter are almost entirely text-only.

You can connect to ProQuest Direct through a Windows-based software package, or on the Web (www.umi.com/proquest/).

Searching ProQuest Direct

ProQuest Direct enables you to search seven ways from Sunday, or at least four ways:

The default **Search by Word** option lets you key in a word or a phrase, then click Search, and off you go. Click the Help button to familiarize yourself with the ProQuest search language, which uses Boolean ANDs and ORs, field searching, wildcards, and the other power-search tools that are also explained in the Bonus Appendix on the CD.

Click the Search Options link if you want ProQuest to automatically search for word variants such as labor and labour, or to look for synonyms such as employment, job, and work.

Advanced Search is really a menu-assisted search mode. You can

- ✔ String together up to four words or phrases using Boolean AND/ORs
- ✔ Restrict your search terms to any of several different fields or portions of the document
- ✔ Limit the results by date

Search Assistant gives you a different kind of help. It's aimed at helping you narrow (and in some cases broaden) your search by importing operators, field qualifiers, and date restrictions into the box where you're working on your **Simple Search** or **Search by Word.**

Search for Publication is designed to help you locate copies of particular issues and articles within those issues. Click the button on the left side of the screen and then enter one or more words from the name of the publication. You get a list of matches; click your publication of choice and select an issue by date to look at its contents. Now you're at the article level, and you can click the item you want to read.

Scanning your search results

Figure 9-8 is what I call The Grid. You see this grid after you've done a **Search by Word** or an **Advanced Search.** Your articles are listed on the left. The five columns to the right indicate the five possible formats in which your document may be available. If the image in the box is filled in, it's available in that format; if it's grayed out, you're out of luck.

Figure 9-8:
ProQuest
Direct
results grid.

The first three formats, **Citation, Abstract,** and **Full Text,** are pretty standard. You run into them in other online research services, too. The other two are where it gets interesting.

Text+Graphics presents the text of the article, nicely formatted, with thumbnail (reduced-size) versions of photographs, diagrams, charts, or other illustrations that appear in the original article. If you're interested in the image, you can click it to enlarge it.

Page Image is a photographic reproduction of the article as it was originally published, complete with all the illustrations. You can download and print the pages, as you can in other ProQuest Direct formats.

The downside

ProQuest Direct pricing isn't geared toward small-time researchers. The service is marketed to libraries and other institutions that have a number of users to offset its high subscription cost. Ask around; maybe your library has access.

InSite straight

InSite is Information Access Company's Web-based database search service. Like ProQuest Direct, InSite is geared toward deep-pocket corporate and institutional users. Translation: It's not cheap.

InSite gives you easy, forms-based access to some of the best databases around for business and marketing information, computing, health and wellness, and general, consumer-type interests. Compared with the Big Three — Dialog, LEXIS-NEXIS, and Dow Jones Interactive, all of which carry the IAC files — InSite's coverage is fairly limited. But, as a working searcher, I always come back to these databases, over and over again. If you happen to work in a company that can afford what InSite has to offer, it may be a cost-effective solution for you.

For details, navigate to InSite (www.informationaccess.com/prods/insite/intro.htm).

Responsive to your needs

Responsive Database Services, producer of the Business & Industry, Business and Management Practices, and TableBase files available through Dialog (more about these databases in Chapter 12), has announced its own suite of Web-based products. Like InSite, the subscription price is steep for occasional users, but could be a bargain if you find that you're using these databases a lot. Check out www.rdsinc.com/ for more information.

How Do You Choose?

As you may have gathered by now, a lot of overlap exists, content-wise, among proprietary services. LEXIS-NEXIS, Dow Jones Interactive, and Dialog offer many of the same publication sources and database compilations. So how do you know which service is right for you?

It's mostly a matter of

- ✔ Preference
- ✔ Price
- ✔ Availability

Most professional researchers favor the system they learned first; typically, they have one home service and several supplementary ones that they use for unique sources and features they can't get elsewhere.

I recommend that you

- ✔ **Check out the pricing options for the service that appeals to you most.** If you're an individual, as opposed to a big corporation, and you anticipate using the service only occasionally and can't justify much out-of-pocket expense, it may be out of the running on economic grounds alone.

- ✔ **Check out the contents.** What does it have that you really want, and that you can't find (as far back, as complete, as fully searchable) on the Web or elsewhere?

- ✔ **Check out the look and feel.** Sign up for an introductory trial. Sit in on a class. Submit yourself to an online or disk-based tutorial. Take the system for a test drive any way you can. Are you comfortable with the steering? How's the air-conditioner? What kind of gas mileage do you think you're getting? Do you like the view? Hey! Watch out for that tree!

My own preferences? Oh dear. I grew up with Dialog, and can search it in my sleep — and on occasion, have. Although they've done a good job with DialogWeb, I much prefer the old user-hostile interface, the one that greets you with a **?** when you log in. It's fast, and flexible, and I can do just about anything with it that I want to. Dialog is the only alternative, as far as I'm concerned, for non-business searching (medicine, patents, science, and technology) and for databases that rely on codes and indexes for precision.

Dow Jones Interactive is a close second — maybe even number one when it comes to general business and financial research. I like its graphical interface, and I'd never go back to native-mode DJ searching — the *dot-dot* commands that I described earlier, in the section headed "Calling in the Pros" — again.

My friends at LEXIS-NEXIS know how I feel: Although their system may be the fastest, it's also the hardest for beginners to navigate and make sense of, because of the way the files are named and organized. If you do elect to sign up with LEXIS-NEXIS — after all, the system does contain a great deal of value — opt for the hourly pricing plan as opposed to the per-search plan. The latter charges you for every search you do, even when you've made a mistake and just want to start over. Sloppy typists pay the price! My opinion: For legal researchers, LEXIS-NEXIS is a must. For other types of inquiries, you can usually find the same information elsewhere.

Chapter 2 tells you how to think like a researcher: figuring out what you need, coming up with synonyms, broadening or narrowing your search results. You need that context to successfully tackle any of the industrial-strength gated services covered in this chapter. It helps to read and reread that chapter.

One Final Point

The key thing to realize about members-only Web sites and online services, whether or not they charge a fee, is that you have to know about them before you can take advantage of them. You won't just stumble across the information they contain, or even the fact that they exist, in a standard search engine search. The extra effort of bookmarking a great gated Web site — as I suggest in Bonus Chapter 3 on the CD — or signing up and becoming proficient with a full-featured proprietary service, is worth it — especially if you're serious about learning the research game. Bottom line: Remember that these services are around, and ask yourself whether your research project can use the boost.

Chapter 10
The Personal Touch

. . . .

. . . .

Maybe you've heard the joke: There are two kinds of people — those who divide the world into two kinds of people, and those who don't. As an analytical type, I've divided the world of online research into two kinds: *publication* and *people*. *Publication* includes most of the resources covered elsewhere in this book: Web sites, databases, virtual reference shelves, library catalogs, and indexes. But how do *people* figure into research? Think about how you find the answers to your questions in real life: Sometimes you do look at a book or visit your local library. But isn't it just as likely that you pick up the phone and call an expert — a doctor, accountant, travel agent, or somebody who knows a lot about the subject — or ask a friend for their opinion?

The Human Side of the Net

The online world does opinion really, really well — everyone has an opinion on everything. It's also an incredible source for fresh, fast, deep, and detailed information about subjects that haven't yet made it into print. People online are usually willing to help, if only because it gives them a chance to show off how much they know. That's not surprising when you realize that the first Net denizens were research scientists, university professors, and other brainy types who like nothing better than to argue, debate, and share their considerable knowledge with their colleagues worldwide. The human side of the Net is where you find first-hand reports, original data that never made it into print, controversy, alternative viewpoints, and hot-off-the-presses new developments.

People-resources are great when you're looking for hands-on perspectives and personal accounts:

- What's it like to sky-dive?
- Do I really want a career as a caterer?
- What should I pack for a holiday in New Zealand?
- How do I set up a salt-water aquarium?
- What laptop computer should I buy?
- How do I solve a particular problem with Excel?
- Are herbal remedies for weight control effective?
- Can someone recommend a good management consultant?
- Do U.K. residents think that peace in Northern Ireland is possible?

Where Do the Experts Hang Out Online?

You find knowledgeable and opinionated folks everywhere you go online. Depending on your perspective, you can carve up the territory in different ways, and the borders between neighborhoods aren't always clear. But the way I look at it, the Net has four main venues for conversation:

- Newsgroups
- Mailing lists or listservs
- Virtual villages and conferencing systems
- E-mail

Just like neighborhoods in your own town or city, each of these online hangouts has its own geography, flavor, and population, complete with local heroes, unsavory characters, and yep, village idiots. Each one has its own value for research, too, individually or in combination with other techniques.

For leads to *official* experts — people who are willing to lend their expertise, sometimes for a fee — check Kitty Bennett's Sources and Experts listing (`sunsite.unc.edu/slanews/internet/experts.html`).

Newsgroups

Don't let the name fool you. Newsgroups have very little to do with the updates you get from Dan Rather or your favorite nightly anchorperson. In fact, they're about as far as you can get from mainstream media while still staring at a screen. Newsgroups are closer to anarchy than they are to organized information. Think about a giant, messy bulletin board — the cork-and-thumbtack kind — where anyone is free to post notices, comments, and comments on *other* people's comments. Someone is trying to maintain order on a daily basis, but it's a constant battle against chaos and confusion. Sounds like a really promising place to do research, doesn't it? Actually, it can be, if you approach it correctly.

A newsgroup, singular, is an ongoing conversation devoted to a particular topic — quantum physics, body-piercing, snowboarding, tropical fish, you name it. Anybody who finds his way there can chime in, whether he's the world's leading expert on the subject, someone who just wants to register an opinion, or an online researcher, like you.

Browsing newsgroups with DejaNews

The DejaNews search engine is a window into the world of newsgroups (see Chapter 4 to read about what else DejaNews can do). For a quick flyover, pilot your Web browser (www.dejanews.com). Then,

1. **Click <u>Browse Groups</u>. This brings up a list of** Popular Top Level Groups, **which are the broad categories into which the vast majority of newsgroups are divided.**

2. **Click one of the** Top Level Groups, **say <u>rec</u> (short for "recreation").**

   The **Browse Group Results** screen, shown in Figure 10-1, presents a list of subdivisions. Each of these subdivisions corresponds to an individual newsgroup or collection of related groups.

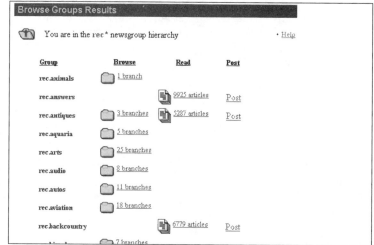

Figure 10-1:
DejaNews
view of
the rec
newsgroup
hierarchy.

The basic newsgroup hierarchy

rec — Hobby and recreational topics ranging from antique collecting to motorcycle riding. **rec.pets** is a fairly tame example of a newsgroup hierarchy; it's further subdivided into discussions on birds, cats, dogs, and reptiles. Check out **rec.music**, though, for a real taste of how deep and rich newsgroup discussions can be. I found 43 subdivisions when I looked, covering all the bases (and basses) from **rec.music.a-cappella** to **rec.music.hip-hop** to **rec.music.tori-amos**.

comp — Anything related to computers, from the mundane to the terminally geeky. You can get down as deep as **comp.graphics.rendering.raytracing**, if that's your fancy, or stay as straightforward and aboveboard as **comp.forsale**.

sci — Where the true scientists and science buffs hang out, in newsgroups ranging from **sci.aeronautics** to **sci.techniques.xtallography**.

soc — Social and cultural topics, such as politics, religion, and womens' issues, as well as international discussions grouped by country, region, religion, or ethnicity. The **soc.culture** sub-hierarchy covers Afghanistan to Zimbabwe.

talk — Think talk show; **talk** is the online equivalent, full of news reports, rumors, banter, and raging debate on current events and controversial subjects, such as abortion, gun control, and euthanasia.

misc — Just what it sounds like: a miscellaneous collection of discussions on topics such as transportation, writing, survivalism, kids, health, and so on, that don't fit anywhere else.

news — Updated information and bulletins about newsgroups and the Net itself. Check out **news.announce.newgroups**, **news.newusers.questions**, or the elegantly-named **news.answers**.

biz — Business-related topics and announcements. If you want to talk about accounting software packages or multilevel marketing opportunities, you've found one place to do it. Don't overlook **biz.jobs, biz.jobs.contract**, or **biz.jobs.offered** if you're in job-hunting mode.

alt — An alternative hierarchy, much looser than the ones listed above, and likely to include discussions on just about anything you can imagine. Anyone can start an **alt** group, on any subject. As soon as a certain purple dinosaur hit the scene a few years back, so did an **alt.barney.dinosaur** newsgroup. The Barney-hating contingent countered with **alt.barney.dinosaur.die**, and even more vociferous opponents spawned **alt.barney.dinosaur.die.die** and **alt.barney.dinosaur.die.die.die**. It won't surprise you to learn that the **alt** groups are almost singlehandedly responsible for the steep growth in the total number of newsgroups in the last several years.

A set of **k12** newsgroups exists for both teachers and kids from kindergarten through the 12th grade level. You also find a whole slew of international groups operating under their own country-based hierarchies (and native languages), and a collection of newsgroups in just about every U.S. state. A few places, such as Austin, Texas and the San Francisco Bay area, maintain their own newsgroups independent of state and national hierarchies.

You may also run into private newsgroups within corporations and organizations, or restricted to a group you belong to, such as customers of a particular Internet Service Provider. A company called ClariNet set up the **clari** hierarchy to supply actual news stories from sources such as UPI and the *New York Times*. It's a commercial service, though; for you to have access to the **clari** newsgroups, your ISP must subscribe.

Now look at the **Browse** column at the top of the screen. Do you notice that some newsgroups have a folder icon in this column, and an indication of the number of **branches,** and that some don't? The folders indicate that the newsgroup is divided into more specific sub-groups.

3. **Click one of the folders or branch links — rec.skiing, farther down the list, is a good example — to see the list of subgroups shown in Figure 10-2.**

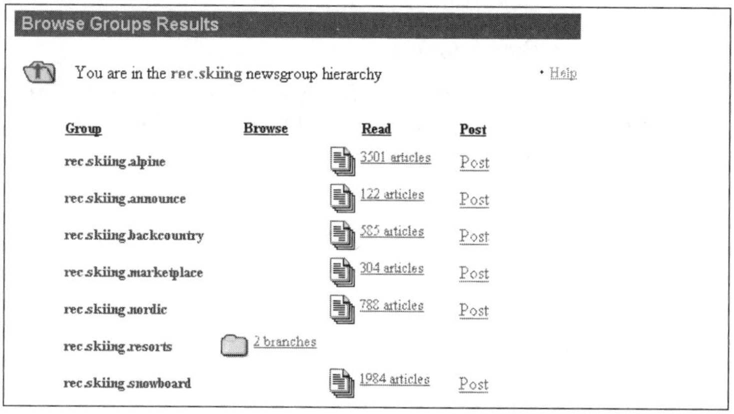

Browse Groups Results

You are in the rec.skiing newsgroup hierarchy   • Help

Group	Browse	Read	Post
rec.skiing.alpine		3301 articles	Post
rec.skiing.announce		122 articles	Post
rec.skiing.backcountry		585 articles	Post
rec.skiing.marketplace		304 articles	Post
rec.skiing.nordic		788 articles	Post
rec.skiing.resorts	2 branches		
rec.skiing.snowboard		1984 articles	Post

Figure 10-2:
rec.skiing
hierarchy.

Finding newsgroups with DejaNews

The Browse Groups approach is one way to locate newsgroups in your area of interest. But with thousands of newsgroups out there, some of them buried several levels down, it's not the most efficient way. Luckily, DejaNews offers a couple of more focused alternatives.

Say you're thinking about starting your own business. You want to find out where to pick up tips for budding entrepreneurs, and where people are talking, on a regular basis, about the joys and travails of running a small business. If the thought of running your own business leaves you cold, pick something that interests *you,* such as my skiing example.

1. **Point your Web browser to the DejaNews URL (**www.dejanews.com**).**

2. **Click Interest Finder.**

3. **Type** entrepreneur **in the Interest Finder search box, and click Find.**

Scan the resulting list of newsgroups (shown in Figure 10-3), ranked according to how frequently they mention the word *entrepreneur.* The higher the confidence rating in the left column, the more often your word occurs in that newsgroup. At this point, you have two choices:

- You can zero in on the newsgroups that sound as though they may be useful, regardless of their ranking (I'd go for *alt.business, misc.entrepreneurs,* and *alt.business.misc*).

- Or, you can just start at the top and go down the list, checking out each newsgroup in turn.

4. **When you decide on your strategy, click on the newsgroup name(s) and you see a list of individual messages in each group that mention the word *entrepreneur*.**

5. **Click on the message headers that seem promising to check out the information they contain.**

6. **If you find the content useful, click the corresponding Subscribe box on the Interest Finder results page to subscribe to the newsgroup and read it on a regular basis.**

Interest Finder Results   Help ❓ free homepages

You have found groups relating to entrepreneur

Confidence	Subscribe	Group
99%	☐	alt.business
71%	☐	alt.business.multi-level
61%	☐	alt.business.home.pc
60%	☐	alt.business.misc
49%	☐	comp.os.os2.games
46%	☐	misc.entrepreneurs
43%	☐	alt.business.home
29%	☐	comp.sys.ibm.pc.games.strategic
26%	☐	alt.make.money.fast
20%	☐	misc.immigration.canada
19%	☐	misc.jobs.offered
19%	☐	misc.jobs.resumes

Figure 10-3: DejaNews Interest Finder results.

Think about alternative ways to express what you want to find. If *entrepreneur* doesn't work for you, try *small business*. There's no telling what words, terms, and phrases people may be using to talk about your topic.

Reading newsgroup posts

Whether you **Browse, Interest-Finder,** or **Search** your way to the newsgroup of your dreams, you're still just standing at the doorway. Now it's time to enter and take a look at what's going on inside.

Searching for newsgroups

You can use DejaNews' **Quick Search** or **Power Search** features (see Chapter 4 for details) to get a complete list of newsgroup posts that mention your topic. This list isn't ranked by how often your term appears, but it does give you some leads you may not otherwise find. Scan down the **Newsgroup** column to see what catches your eye. You can click directly on individual message headers to see what they contain.

If you browse newsgroups as described a couple of pages back and get to either the **Browse Groups Results** screen shown in Figure 10-1, or a particular newsgroup hierarchy, like the one shown in Figure 10-2, here's what you do to start reading messages:

1. **Scan the** Read **column and click on either the pile-of-papers icon or the article count for the newsgroup you want. (An** *article,* **in newsgroup-speak, is an individual posting to the group.)**

   This brings up a list showing the headers or titles of recent posts made to the newsgroup, the date, and the person responsible for the posting.

2. **One more click on the title of an interesting-sounding post, and voilà! You're reading a newsgroup. Finally.**

If you use the DejaNews **Interest Finder** described in the last section to come up with relevant newsgroups:

1. **Click on the name of a newsgroup to get to the list of message headers.**

2. **Click on a title to start reading.**

If you do a **Quick Search** or **Power Search** (as described in Chapter 4), DejaNews automatically shows you a list of message headers (titles) relevant to your topic. Messages may come from a variety of different groups. Click on any title to start reading in the group in which that article was posted.

Click the **Author Profile** silhouette at the top of any individual post to see other newsgroups where that person has posted, which can give you a snapshot of that person's interests, enable you to follow their posts in other newsgroups, and establish whether they know what they're talking about.

Using a newsreader

The best way to keep up with newsgroups that you enjoy is to subscribe to them. In order to do so, you need a specialized software application called a *newsreader.* You don't necessarily have to install more software on your own computer, though. Both Netscape and Internet Explorer browsers have newsreaders built right in. DejaNews itself recently introduced its own Web-based newsreader, **My DejaNews.** You can register for it, free, at the DejaNews site (www.dejanews.com).

Taking the temperature of a newsgroup

A quick scan of newsgroup headers can reveal a lot, not only about the subjects being discussed there, but about the culture and customs of the group that you're about to join. Does it sound like a friendly place, helpful and welcoming to newcomers? Or is the atmosphere more smart-alecky and in-groupy? Some newsgroups even feel sort of dark and menacing — not the kind of neighborhood you want to visit unaccompanied, or at night. The less comfortable you feel with whatever seems to be the prevailing tone of the group, the more cautious you should be in your quest for information.

Headers can tell you other things about the group, too:

✔ **Do you see an abundance of current postings?** If so, the group is probably active and a good place to get current information on your topic.

✔ **Do you see a lot of off-the-subject banter and cross-talk?** The group may have outlived its usefulness as a research tool and deteriorated into a social hangout or a total waste of time.

✔ **Do the headers themselves give you a good idea of what people are actually talking about?** If so, it's probably going to be easier to find focused information there.

Before you post: The FAQs of life

If you've got a question, chances are someone else, somewhere in the world, has already wondered the same thing — or something very similar. That's a basic fact of online life; it has two implications you should be aware of:

✔ People get irritated when they're asked the same question over and over again.

✔ To minimize irritation, many newsgroups have compiled archives of Frequently Asked Questions, or FAQs.

Before you post your burning question, only to be met with a chorus of "Oh no, not *this* again" (or worse), check to see whether you can find a FAQ covering your subject. Trust me: It's worth the effort, and you may save yourself a lot of grief.

To locate FAQs online, you can

✔ Search DejaNews using your topic and the abbreviation FAQ.

✔ Try the Usenet FAQs listing (`www.cis.ohio-state.edu/hypertext/faq/usenet/top.html`). You can search using newsgroup names, subjects and keywords, or browse an alphabetical list.

✔ Check the even more elaborate Usenet Hypertext FAQ Archive (`www.faqs.org`).

When hunting for FAQs, keep your keywords general; for example, **skiing** produces better results than **bindings,** even if **ski bindings** is what you're ultimately interested in. Once you find a FAQ, scan through it, or use your Web browser's find-in-this-document function, to locate the specific term you're looking for.

Aunt Netty-Quette's priceless pointers for painless posting

Long-time Net denizens follow a code of conduct — sometimes referred to as *netiquette* — that's designed to preserve the core values of the Net: These values include non-commercialism (which sounds pretty funny in the context of the Web), consideration for one's fellow humans, and concern for the preservation and well-being of the Internet itself. Most experienced newsgroup posters subscribe to the same general values, and expect others to do the same. To help you avoid that awful feeling of blushing in front of your monitor — or sobbing, getting angry, or experiencing other strong negative emotions — my alter ego, Aunt Netty-Quette, has put together this handy list of tips:

✔ **Do your homework first.** Use DejaNews or look for a FAQ to see whether someone's already answered your question.

✔ **Lurk before you leap.** Each newsgroup has its own culture, customs, and taboos. Read the newsgroup for a while before you even *think* about posting, to get a sense of whether the group is friendly and tolerant, a little high-strung, or a bunch of barbarians to whom newbie blood is like mother's milk! Attune yourself to the dominant conversational style: Is the group scholarly and formal, or casually conversational? Do posters use smiley faces and acronyms, such as PMFJI (Pardon Me For Jumping In), or do they frown on such conventions?

✔ **Avoid commercial messages or shameless self-promotion.** Very few newsgroups tolerate blatant sales pitches, or even subtle ones.

✔ **If you're tempted to post your question in** *all* **the newsgroups that sound as though they might be useful,** *don't.* That's called *spamming,* and there's zero tolerance for it on the Net.

✔ **If in doubt, ask your question privately.** After you've hung out in a newsgroup for a while, it's easy to identify the people who know what they're talking about. Not only do their messages contain actual information, but others in the group tend to pay attention to what they're saying, direct questions at them, and treat them with respect. You may still be hesitant about speaking up in the group; if so, try an e-mail message directly to the designated expert.

✔ **Choose a descriptive subject header.** This holds for both public postings and private e-mail. A subject header such as **Help! Info Needed!!!** conveys nothing but urgency and desperation. That won't cut it in Newsgroupland. Chances are slim that a busy expert is going to stop to see what your message is about, let alone be favorably inclined to help you. You get better results with a header such as **Accounting Software for Start-Ups?** or **Best cross-country Ski Bindings?** Don't skimp on the specifics when you're packaging your information request. A clear subject header is as important as a good book title; it draws the reader in.

✔ **When it comes to the message itself, be succinct and considerate.** Use as few words as possible to introduce yourself, convey your question clearly, and indicate where you've already looked for information. Make sure that your request is reasonable — for busy people, time and attention are precious commodities. "Tell me everything you know" is going to be a lot less productive than "Can you recommend a good book or online starting point where I can find out more?"

✔ **Give something back.** Offer to share your findings with the group, or compile the answers and add them to the FAQ, or supply a pointer to wherever you plan to post your summary or research results. If you're dealing with an individual expert, offer to pay for postage and other costs, or even, if your request is non-trivial, to compensate them for their time. Informal promotion, such as referrals to their business or to books they've published, or a link from your site to theirs, is almost always appreciated.

Mailing Lists

Mailing lists are sometimes called *listservs,* a name taken from the software used to manage certain mailing lists. Sometimes they're simply called *lists.* I use all three of these terms interchangeably.

Newsgroups in action — a thrilling true-life scenario

A colleague of mine who specializes in international trade research needed to find out whether a market existed for electric food dehydrators in Eastern Europe. This example is typical of the exciting projects that independent professional researchers get to sink their teeth into every day of the week. She posted the question on a couple of newsgroups and, within 20 minutes, had three responses, all of which said that she and her client were thinking irresponsibly and should be investigating the market for *solar* food dehydrators instead. But within 24 hours, allowing time for the European work day to begin and for users in that part of the world to wake up and go online, she had two or three solid leads, one of which led to a business deal for her client.

Mailing lists are different from newsgroups in several ways:

- ✔ You have to subscribe to a mailing list in order to participate. You can't just wander in and start reading and posting.
- ✔ Messages come to you as e-mail. You don't need to go anywhere or use any special software in order to read and respond.
- ✔ Since subscribing generally means you have an interest in and commitment to a topic, mailing list discussions tend to be more focused.

Mailing lists come in assorted flavors. All are some combination of these types:

- ✔ **Private versus public:** Some lists are open only to members of a particular association, employees of a given corporation, or qualified practitioners in a certain field, such as computer security or nursing.
- ✔ **Moderated versus unmoderated:** Some lists have hosts or administrators who help direct the conversation and keep things running smoothly. Others are freewheeling, with nobody visibly in charge.
- ✔ **Open posting versus edited posting versus read-only:** Some mailing lists allow anyone to post directly to the list. With others, all messages go to the moderator, who screens them for usefulness before posting them to the list. Some lists don't allow posting at all; they're more like electronic newsletters where the publisher or editor talks, and your role is to read only (you can talk back, if you want, in private e-mail).

Many lists that allow open posting offer a digest version, too. Instead of seeing all messages as soon as they're posted to the list, you get a single long message, usually once a day, containing all postings in the order received. The digest version won't cut down significantly on your reading time, and it does interfere with your ability to respond to individual posts in a timely way. But some people prefer it because it cuts down on e-mail clutter.

Locating lists with Liszt

How do you find a mailing list to join? The easiest way, other than word of mouth, is Liszt (www.liszt.com), a comprehensive searchable directory of — at this point — almost 90,000 mailing lists worldwide. From this huge assortment, Liszt has culled a thousand or so lists that it believes to be public, active, and worthwhile. You can do a keyword search on the entire directory, or drill down through broad subject categories in the hand-picked **Liszt Select** collection.

The fast and easy search form shown in Figure 10-4 lets you enter your search terms and use the pull-down menu to select **any of these words, all these words,** or **this exact phrase.**

Liszt employs a junk filter to strip out as many private lists as it can identify, and to show you only the lists that you may be eligible to join. You can set the filter on **lots** if you want to retrieve only lists for which Liszt has detailed information. Or you can turn the junk filter off completely if you want to see what all is out there and are prepared to deal with whatever Liszt may dredge up.

Click **Go,** and Liszt displays the following information:

  ✔ Links to any Liszt Select subject categories that match your search terms

  ✔ Links to any Liszt Select lists (the actual mailing lists) that match

  ✔ Links to *all* lists in the Liszt directory that match your terms

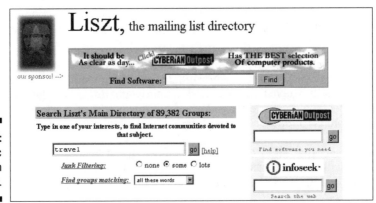

Figure 10-4:
Liszt basic
search
form.

Liszt's basic search feature works pretty well, but if you want more flexibility you can click **Advanced Search Options** at the bottom of the first page. Advanced mode allows for case-sensitivity, truncation, and several other features that, frankly, I don't think are all that important when you're looking for mailing lists.

Liszt's list listings — *that's* fun to say — are color-coded to help guide your selection:

- ✔ **Green** means that you get detailed information about the list when you click on its name.
- ✔ **Yellow** means that you get *some* information.
- ✔ **Red** means that Liszt has no information available.
- ✔ **White** means that Liszt hasn't asked for information, or has asked for but hasn't received any information.

From Liszt's search results page, you can click a Liszt Select subject category (assuming you got any matches) at the top of the page to see what lists Liszt has selected. Or you can click the name of a particular Liszt Select list or, below that, the name of a list from the larger Liszt directory, and get a description of its focus, purpose, and membership. Read that description to make sure it's the right group for you, and that you qualify for membership. If no description is available, Liszt supplies an e-mail address where you can request one.

The SELECTive approach

So far we've talked about locating mailing lists through keyword searches. If you prefer to browse by subject category through Liszt's own pre-selected collection, scroll down past the search form shown in Figure 10-4 to Liszt Select. Figure 10-5 shows the Liszt Select categories and subcategories, and how many lists each category contains.

I click <u>Recreation</u> and, on the next page, the subheading <u>Travel</u>. Liszt presents me with seven or so hand-picked mailing lists. Each record includes anywhere from a few words to a paragraph of additional information about the list. Some include a link to <u>more info</u>.

Netiquette revisited

Observing the local customs is just as important in mailing lists as it is in newsgroups; perhaps more so, because many mailing list subscribers are serious-minded, or deeply committed to the subject at hand. Some of them may be refugees from the noise and clamor of public newsgroups, and the last thing you want to do is re-introduce the kind of clueless behavior they thought they'd escaped from.

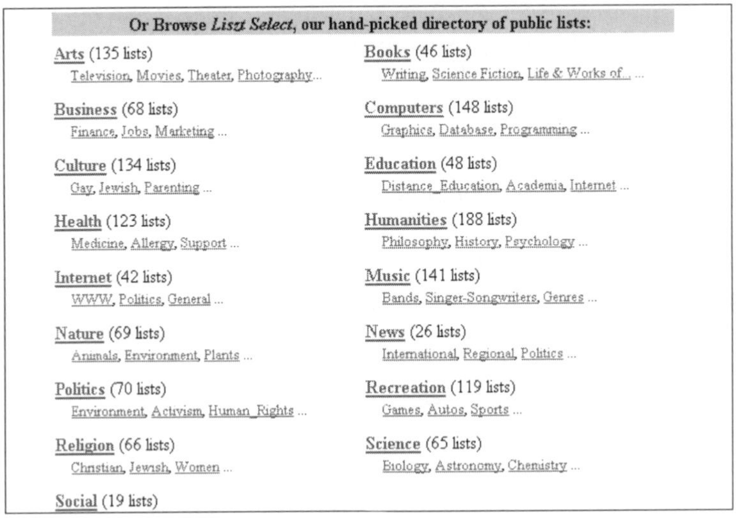

Or Browse *Liszt Select*, our hand-picked directory of public lists:

Arts (135 lists)
Television, Movies, Theater, Photography...

Books (46 lists)
Writing, Science Fiction, Life & Works of...

Business (68 lists)
Finance, Jobs, Marketing...

Computers (148 lists)
Graphics, Database, Programming...

Culture (134 lists)
Gay, Jewish, Parenting...

Education (48 lists)
Distance Education, Academia, Internet...

Health (123 lists)
Medicine, Allergy, Support...

Humanities (188 lists)
Philosophy, History, Psychology...

Internet (42 lists)
WWW, Politics, General...

Music (141 lists)
Bands, Singer-Songwriters, Genres...

Nature (69 lists)
Animals, Environment, Plants...

News (26 lists)
International, Regional, Politics...

Politics (70 lists)
Environment, Activism, Human Rights...

Recreation (119 lists)
Games, Autos, Sports...

Religion (66 lists)
Christian, Jewish, Women...

Science (65 lists)
Biology, Astronomy, Chemistry...

Social (19 lists)

Figure 10-5:
Liszt Select
subject
categories.

So, reread Aunt Netty-Quette's advice about how to behave in newsgroups. Ninety-nine percent of it applies to mailing lists as well.

Mailing lists do give you one additional way of screwing up in public: Be sure you know the difference between the e-mail address you use to *subscribe* and *unsubscribe* to the list, and the one you use to *post messages* to the group. They're different. You're unlikely to find a more embarrassing way to debut among your potential colleagues and experts, whose expertise you may want to tap, than to mistakenly send a **subscribe** request to all of them.

Dealing with info- and subscription-bots

You can get more information about a mailing list by sending e-mail to the address shown in the Liszt description. These messages are usually processed by *'bots* (short for robots; the apostrophe is optional), specialized software that sends out information in response to a precisely worded request. How you word your request depends on the type of software used to administer the list. Click the list commands link to verify the format used by the list in which you're interested. The info request typically looks something like **info Travel-L** (with the subject line of the message left blank). Sometimes you can get a help file by sending the single-word message **help** (I know; it sounds pathetic) to the same address. Remember that these messages are read by a dumb piece of software, not a smart human being. If you don't follow the rules, it won't understand what you're asking. Resist the temptation to say "please." If you don't, your mailbox will fill up, but with error messages, not listserv postings.

Mailing list subscriptions are handled the same way. The protocol often involves a command such as **subscribe Travel-L myname** in the body of the message, and nothing in the subject header. But do go through the robotic info-request routine first. The file you get back in e-mail will contain complete instructions for signing up — and signing off. Keep this file forever and ever, or for as long as you are subscribed to the list. The file tells you what address to use when you want to post a message to the other members of the list (or to the moderator, if it's that kind of list) and what address to use when you want to reach the list *server,* the 'bot responsible for the mechanics of subscribing and unsubscribing. As I said above, they're not the same, and the consequences of mixing them up may be embarrassing and frustrating to you, and annoying to others. 'Nuff said.

Most mailing lists only accept *unsubscribe* requests from the same e-mail account that you subscribed from.

Virtual Villages and Conferencing Systems

In Chapter 9, I mention online venues such as The Motley Fool, CompuServe forums, and Ei Engineering Village, where people get together to exchange information, assert their opinions, and generally hang out. I call such sites *virtual communities,* a phrase popularized by my friend Howard Rheingold in the early 1990s. Another term for them is *online conferencing systems.*

Thousands of such places exist online. Some are free; others charge a fee for access. Some are *mega*-systems, covering anything people may want to talk about. Others are more specialized, appealing to specific populations, such as doctors, lawyers, or parents.

Virtual communities are organized differently from newsgroups and mailing lists, although some newsgroups and lists have, over the years, developed somewhat of a community feeling. Virtual communities are organized in a three-tiered structure:

> ✔ **Virtual communities contain anywhere from half a dozen to a hundred or more individual *forums,* also referred to as *conferences* or *discussion areas*.** Each forum is devoted to a particular subject or interest. In a mega-conferencing system, you may find a Cooking forum, a forum devoted to Windows-based computers, and an Investment forum, right next door to each other and open to anyone on the system.

- ✔ **Each forum is divided into a number of *topics* or *threads* (America Online calls them *folders*).** Each topic is a separate conversation about some aspect of the forum's overall subject. In a Cooking forum, you may see topics on vegetarian cooking, barbecuing, cookware, Jell-O salads, and what to do with leftovers (put them in a Jell-O salad has always been my approach).

- ✔ **Each topic consists of a series of *postings*, or messages, from different users.** You can go back to see what others have written (in some communities, topics are preserved for years) or read a current discussion as it unfolds. You can lurk quietly, reading and never posting, or jump in and add your own comments.

The posting style in a virtual community is usually informal and conversational; it's basically just a bunch of people talking online. Communication isn't instantaneous as it is in a chat room — although when a hot discussion is going on, it can feel like a real-time environment. I was on a local conferencing system when a fire broke out in a nearby neighborhood; people were falling all over themselves, and each other, in their eagerness to ask questions and supply eye-witness reports.

Virtual communities can exist anywhere in cyberspace. Some are purely text-based, like the fantasy environments called MUDs (multi-user domains), and variations on that theme. They're distinguished by a sense of place, continuity over time, and a shared history — and maybe even *destiny,* too.

Virtual communities require a commitment. To get the most out of them information-wise, you have to build and cultivate relationships, and give back as much as you get. That's a lot harder than scanning listserv messages when they land in your mailbox, or hunting for a newsgroup FAQ. But these communities offer many other benefits — *besides* getting the answers to your questions — if you stick around long-term.

Exploring virtual communities on the Web

The most easily accessible communities, especially if you want to browse before you make a commitment, are on the Web. Most of these don't charge a fee, but do require you to register for full access.

Check out **Parent Soup** (www.parentsoup.com) for searchable message boards dealing with topics such as prenatal testing, attention-deficit disorder, parents of only children, and the catchall subject of parenting in the '90s (wonder what they'll call it when the millennium arrives?).

Third Age (www.thirdage.com) is aimed squarely at aging boomers. Not that *I* know anything *at all* about that demographic. Ahem. Third Age forums have names such as Money Matters, News & Politics, Tech Central, and Travel.

The Gate (www.sfgate.com) is jointly sponsored by two newspapers, the *San Francisco Chronicle* and *San Francisco Examiner.* Click <u>Conferences</u> on the main page. You see The Gate's operating philosophy stated right up front:

> This is a place to air your opinions and read what others have to say. Messages are posted, or written, "BBS style," with one written comment following another and are not "live" or real-time "chats" — they are more reflective and have the advantage of letting you respond when the time is right for you.

Participants at The Gate get to talk back to the newspaper columnists and reporters whose bylines they read every day. Newspaper journalists even host some of the Gate forums, which cover subjects such as business, books, current events (of course), movies, food, music, travel, health, technology, and the Net itself.

At **The WELL** (www.well.com/) (which stands for Whole Earth 'Lectronic Link, if you can believe that), discussion topics don't always stay in their neatly marked-off areas. Some conversations are linked between two or more conferences, and some topics seem designed to promote anything *but* linear thinking. A topic called Experts on the WELL is a prime example, with people carrying on interwoven conversations about building backyard ponds, how a capacitor works, whether recycling really helps the environment, and where to get the best espresso drinks in Berkeley (answer: the French Hotel). The WELL has both a Web-based interface and a text alternative called Picospan that I, being a dinosaur, prefer. You have to sign up and pay a monthly fee before you can fall into The WELL.

Agriculture Online (www.agriculture.com) is a real change of pace. Sponsored by a trade magazine, the discussion groups listed in Figure 10-6 are a window into what modern farming is all about. I click on Talk to get to this page. Next I click <u>Wildlife</u> (why not?) and fall into discussions about eagles, groundhog control, and Midwest fur prices. These were separate conversations, I hasten to add. Though I can imagine, sort of, how they might relate.

Farmers are online, bigtime, talking about crucial concerns such as weather, crop prices, and cattle deals. Other professions — including accountants, human resource specialists, librarians, and researchers — have their own online hangouts as well. Lawyers can subscribe to a private forum called CounselConnect (www.counselconnect.com/), while doctors can participate in Physicians Online (www.po.com/welcome.htm).

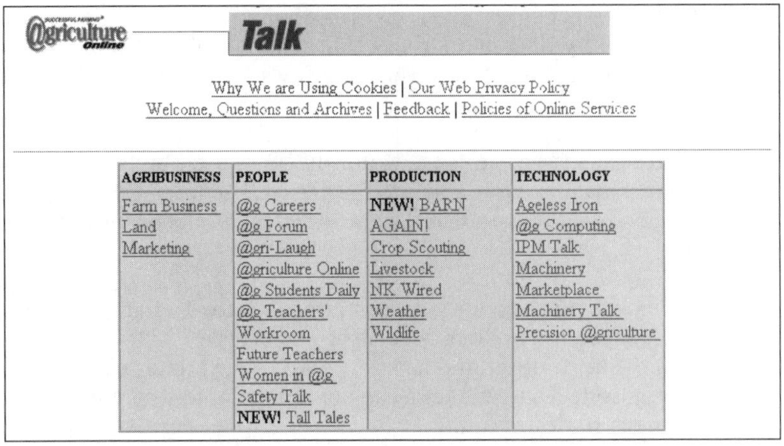

@griculture Online — **Talk**

Why We are Using Cookies | Our Web Privacy Policy
Welcome, Questions and Archives | Feedback | Policies of Online Services

AGRIBUSINESS	PEOPLE	PRODUCTION	TECHNOLOGY
Farm Business	@g Careers	**NEW!** BARN	Ageless Iron
Land	@g Forum	AGAIN!	@g Computing
Marketing	@gri-Laugh	Crop Scouting	IPM Talk
	@griculture Online	Livestock	Machinery
	@g Students Daily	NK Wired	Marketplace
	@g Teachers'	Weather	Machinery Talk
	Workroom	Wildlife	Precision @griculture
	Future Teachers		
	Women in @g		
	Safety Talk		
	NEW! Tall Tales		

Figure 10-6:
Agriculture
Online
discussion
forums.

Finding community online

How do you find a virtual community where you feel at home? Sometimes it just happens, as it did with me when I landed in The WELL in 1988. I got there via word-of-mouth from some people I already knew in real life. Friends and colleagues may tell you about the cool place they discovered, too.

You can survey the range of virtual community life through **Forum One** (www.ForumOne.com/). Forum One isn't all-inclusive, but it's a start. Once there, you can either

✔ Do a keyword search (simple or advanced) to identify online communities devoted to a subject, and relevant discussion topics *within* those communities.

✔ Drill down through the category listing shown in Figure 10-7 to get a list of communities only. The "Mega"-Forums category lists venues that talk about a variety of topics.

The HotBot search engine (www.hotbot.com) features a **Discussion Groups** search that links to the Forum One site.

Taking It to E-Mail

When people in a public venue, whether it be a newsgroup, mailing list, or virtual conferencing system, start going at each other too heavily, you hear the plea, "Hey, guys, take it to e-mail." Electronic mail is the best way, short of a phone call or face-to-face meeting, to resolve personal disputes.

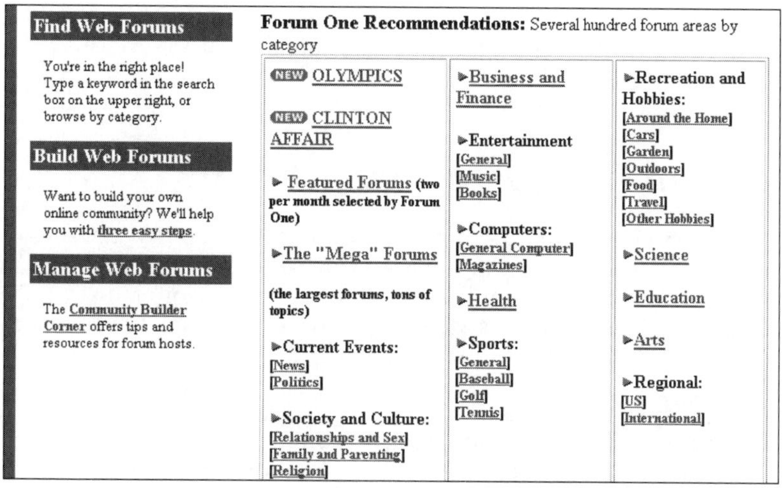

Find Web Forums

You're in the right place! Type a keyword in the search box on the upper right, or browse by category.

Build Web Forums

Want to build your own online community? We'll help you with three easy steps.

Manage Web Forums

The Community Builder Corner offers tips and resources for forum hosts.

Forum One Recommendations: Several hundred forum areas by category

(NEW) OLYMPICS

(NEW) CLINTON AFFAIR

► Featured Forums (two per month selected by Forum One)

►The "Mega" Forums

(the largest forums, tons of topics)

►Current Events:
[News]
[Politics]

►Society and Culture:
[Relationships and Sex]
[Family and Parenting]
[Religion]

►Business and Finance

►Entertainment
[General]
[Music]
[Books]

►Computers:
[General Computer]
[Magazines]

►Health

►Sports:
[General]
[Baseball]
[Golf]
[Tennis]

►Recreation and Hobbies:
[Around the Home]
[Cars]
[Garden]
[Outdoors]
[Food]
[Travel]
[Other Hobbies]

►Science

►Education

►Arts

►Regional:
[US]
[International]

Figure 10-7:
Forum One category listing.

E-mail is also the glue that keeps online relationships going. Allies in a debate or flamewar (more about flames in the next-to-last section of this chapter) encourage each other, plan their next move, and keep up a running commentary about other people's postings — privately, one-to-one, via e-mail.

As Aunt Netty-Quette pointed out earlier in this chapter, e-mail is a graceful way to ask for guidance when you're not sure whether your question is appropriate for the group at large, or when you hesitate to jump in because the pace of conversation is so frenetic or the group seems kind of intimidating. Pick someone who sounds supportive, and follow Aunt Netty-Quette's tips, especially the ones about being clear, concise, and considerate of people's time.

E-mail can take your research project to the next level, by putting you in touch with the experts. Start in a public space, such as a newsgroup or mailing list. Do your homework first, whether it's looking for a FAQ or reviewing the archives. Then follow up, selectively, with a politely-worded e-mail request. You can get maps, manuscripts, and countless helpful pointers simply by knowing how, when, and whom to ask.

Caveats and Cautions (Dealing with Human Nature)

I said at the beginning of this chapter that *people* research is different from hunting for documents or looking something up in a virtual reference book. You find information, and opinions, that you can't get anywhere else online.

But you also have to deal with some human factors that you won't encounter when you're dealing with books, subject catalogs, or other inanimate research aids.

From the horse's mouth?

There's nothing like getting your information directly from the source. But people are complex; they have all sorts of motives for helping, and all kinds of agendas to promote. They sometimes lie; they often distort. People aren't perfect; their memories are faulty, and they may, in all innocence, misrepresent the facts or leave out a crucial bit of data.

Unless you're dealing with the most straightforward, factual questions and answers, don't take what people tell you at face value. Examine their advice, and adjust for possible bias. Try to get a second, and even a third, opinion, ideally from someone who's not involved in your conversation and doesn't have an ax to grind. See Chapter 15 for more about judging the reliability of information.

The (low) signal to noise ratio

Ever try to pull in a ballgame broadcast on a funky old radio up in the mountains? Sometimes you have to filter out a lot of static in order to get the score. It's the same way online — lots of noise, relatively little signal, or hard information. A newsgroup, mailing list, or online conference can shortcut your information-hunt dramatically, if you know where to go and who to ask. Witness my research colleague's story, in the Newsgroups in Action sidebar earlier in this chapter, about the electric food dehydrators. If you're in luck and find a FAQ, you're golden. But hanging out online, hoping for enlightenment because the subject headers in a current thread sound promising, isn't the most efficient way to get research done. Depending on the group, you may have to wade through a lot of banter, byplay, and general silliness to get to the factual nuggets you need; search engines such as DejaNews can come in handy then.

Topic drift

You may scan a list of subject headers in a newsgroup or online conference and find one that sounds ideal. When you start to read the postings, though, you discover that the conversation has meandered far away from its original focus. Instead of discussing real estate, deep-space astronomy, or Middle Eastern politics, folks are talking about the cute thing their cat did yesterday, or the shoe sale in progress at Nordstrom.

This phenomenon is called *topic drift*. It happens in real life conversations — some say it's gender-related, but I deny that — and it happens online. Sometimes, especially in professional and technical forums, the moderator or host is expected to keep the discussion focused on its original goal. But drift comes with the territory, and in most places, it's inevitable. Some folks consider it an art form.

Topics that start out promising and disintegrate into drift can be frustrating for the researcher. As a participant, you can try, gently, to steer the conversation back on track. Or you can scroll back to the beginning of the discussion, before it went off on its tangent, to see what you can glean from the earlier posts.

Flame wars

Some people love to be provocative online. Others love to provoke them. Depending on where you hang out (newsgroups are particularly prone to this phenomenon), you'll eventually see a heated argument break out over *something*. When an online disagreement turns violent or abusive, it's called *flaming*. A full scale battle is called a *flame war*.

Flame wars can also break out as the result of simple misunderstandings. Online is a low-bandwidth medium. You don't have cues, such as facial expression and tone of voice, to tell you how someone is feeling, or to show the intent behind his words. All you have is text on a screen, and words can easily be misinterpreted, which is why some online denizens use smiley faces and other *emoticons* — smiles, frowns, and other facial expressions recreated, roughly, with keyboard characters: :-) — to give some context to what they post. I prefer clear writing to emoticons, but for some folks, emoticons are easier.

Abide by these two simple rules to avoid getting embroiled in a flame war:

- ✔ Do unto others as you would have them do unto you. (Where have I heard *that* before?)

- ✔ If you must disagree, attack the *argument*, not the *person*. For example, say, "I think your statement (or position, or reasoning) is idiotic," not "I think *you're* an idiot." It does help to think of a slightly less loaded word than *idiotic*. How about *fallacious, untenable,* or *flawed?* (This moment brought to you by *Roget's Thesaurus*.)

If all else fails, log out. That's right: Disconnect from your computer, catch your breath, and take a walk around the block until you calm down. Never post or send an e-mail message while you're angry or tired. Drop that bone, lighten up, give the other person the benefit of the doubt. Move on.

Overload

Flame wars or not, there are times when the online world gets overwhelming. There's just *too* much going on, too many people talking, too many annoyances, too much information to absorb.

When you reach that point — and you will — you can take comfort in knowing that you're not the only one who's ever felt this way. Software solutions abound: You can get spam filters to reduce the amount of junk mail, or bozo filters to silence those whose postings you can't bear to read. You can change your mailing list subscriptions to the digest version. You can set up filters in your e-mail program so that everything personal goes in one box, everything business-related in another, and all your mailing lists in a third, or however you want to set it up. For this, I use a program called Eudora Pro (`www.eudora.com/`). It's available for both PCs and Macs. Regard this as an unsolicited testimonial: Eudora changed my life.

Part III
Putting It All Together

The 5th Wave By Rich Tennant

"Quick, Igor, get online and find an authoritative science site without the flaming Bunsen burners!"

In this part . . .

If my name were Julia Child and you happened to be someone who'd never set foot in a kitchen, I could talk to you all day about chef's knives and wire whisks, reducing a sauce and clarifying a stock — and you still might starve before you'd figured out how to put a meal together. There's a reason why TV cooking shows are popular — you learn the tools and the techniques as you go, as part of creating a dish or an entire menu. And once you understand how and when to use them, you're on your way to becoming a competent, intuitive, and even inspired cook.

That's what I'm aiming for here. Parts I and II tell you all about search engines, subject catalogs, reference books, digital libraries, database services, newsgroups, mailing lists, and other tools and techniques for researching online. But without a sense of context — how and when to apply them to a particular research project — they're about as useful as a scalpel in the hands of a first-year medical student.

This part is all about context. Whether you've read the earlier chapters or not (don't worry — I'm not keeping track), here's where you discover how to apply those online search tools and tactics in a variety of real-life research situations, from tracking business competitors, to wending your way through government bureaucracies, to keeping up with the news.

Check the CD-ROM for even more examples. Bonus Chapter 1: Life Choices, shows you how to research important personal decisions such as choosing a college, buying a car, or picking a vacation spot. Bonus Chapter 2: Recreational Researching, shows how to research your own hobbies, interests, and leisure-time pursuits. If you *do* know how to cook, that chapter holds some tasty morsels for you, too.

Chapter 11

Strange New Worlds: Penetrating the Mysteries of Government, Medical, and Sci-Tech Research

*R*emember that old song, "Bewitched, Bothered and Bewildered"? I'm not sure what to do with the *bewitched* part, but bothered and bewildered am I. And you probably are, too — when it comes to dealing with the government, or trying to figure out what to do about your own or a family member's illness or newly-diagnosed medical condition, or solving a problem that requires getting hold of information in a highly specialized technical field such as engineering or computer science.

All of us are at a loss when we're operating in an unfamiliar environment, whether it's a strange country, a bureaucracy, or a scientific discipline where we don't know the rules and can't speak the language. We fall into sort of a trance — maybe *that's* where bewitched comes in — and often try ineffective, pointless, and sometimes counterproductive tactics before we give up and collapse into an exhausted, frustrated puddle.

Maybe you think the entire Internet is a foreign country. Trust me, unless you live there, these specialized research areas — I sometimes think of them as the Feds, the Meds, and the Ph.D.s — can be as rocky and inhospitable as the far side of the moon.

I'm not promising you any miracles. If I could cut through the morass of government bureaucracy, let alone all that other stuff, somebody would have noticed by now, and I'd be rich, retired, and wreathed in clouds of glory. What I *can* do, and show *you* how to do in this chapter, is gather information effectively from within the esoteric and often confusing realms of government, medicine, science, and technology.

How do you find information in a complex environment when you don't even speak the language? By looking at it through a researcher's eyes.

When you're investigating in an unfamiliar research environment, you need to know three things:

✔ Where to start

✔ What's available

✔ Where to get it

In this chapter, I give you a few starting points, an idea of what you can get from them, and the precise coordinates. Consider it a large-scale map of a foreign capital. When you walk around by yourself, you'll start discovering new neighborhoods, special attractions, and shortcuts of your own.

So pack your bags. Our flight's departing. Don't forget your passport.

We're from the Government, and We're Here to Help You

Getting information from the U.S. federal government may be both one of the most frustrating and one of the most rewarding experiences you can live through. And you *will* live through it.

You'd be amazed at the depth and variety of information collected by various agencies and analysts. When I worked for Information on Demand, a research company that tackled client projects using whatever combination of phone, online, and library visits it took to get the answer, I discovered government analysts whose sole job was to monitor water-pumping windmills, processed tomato products, or imports of wine and roses from Mexico (the last two occupied the same trade category, those romantics!). Some of these guys *lived* for a phone call from a private citizen who was actually interested in their work.

Budget cutbacks happen, and much of that data isn't collected in as much depth as it used to be — or at all. A piece of legislation called the Federal Paperwork Reduction Act resulted in the elimination of many kinds of reports. But savvy federal agencies (and some, you may discover, are a lot smarter and more responsive than others) realized that the then-emerging Internet was the answer to at least *some* of their budget- and policy-mandated restrictions: If it costs too much to publish and distribute reports in print, why not just put them online?

Mastering the info-maze with FedWorld

FedWorld (`www.fedworld.gov/`) is your gateway to the wide world of U.S. government publications, regulations, and sadistics . . . I mean, statistics. Figure 11-1 shows FedWorld's no-nonsense but option-packed front door. Without preamble — to the Constitution or anything else — it presents you with half a dozen search forms, each one an entryway to a particular star-cluster within the FedWorld galaxy. Click the category link, or pull down the menu, to discover what each one contains.

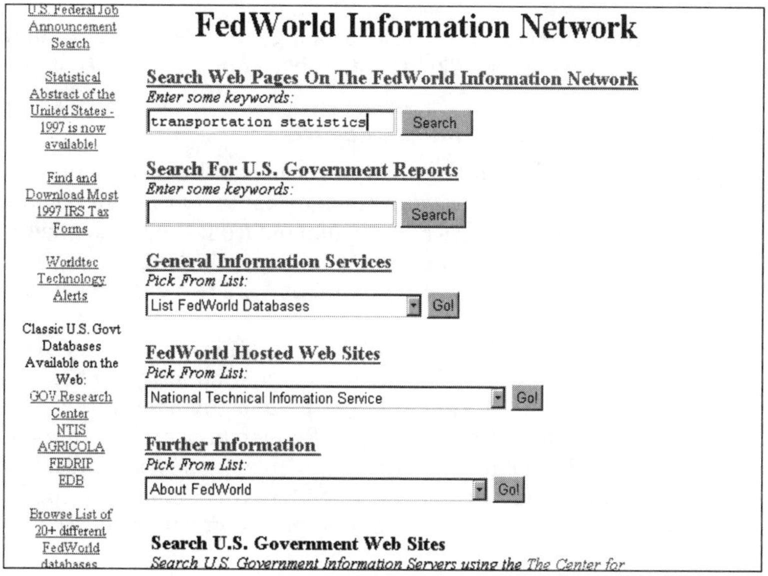

Figure 11-1: FedWorld search options.

Search Web Pages on the FedWorld Information Network

The first search box allows you to search the entire FedWorld network and zero in on the federal agency, and often the specific report or document, that can answer your question. (Click the title link for a list of individual sites you can search using the same form.)

A few quick searches demonstrate how, by entering a key phrase or concept that interests me, I can quickly identify the agency where I should start my research. FedWorld supports Boolean search logic, as described in the Bonus Appendix on the CD, as well as the phrase searching used in these examples.

- ✔ I key in **transportation statistics** and get a reference to the Bureau of Transportation Statistics, plus document titles such as *National Transportation Atlas.*

- ✔ I enter **child welfare** and get a publication about child support. When I click on the title, I find a reference to the Department of Health and Human Services, which oversees that area.

- ✔ What about **income tax evasion?** We know the answer to that, but you can prove it by clicking on the title of the first publication that comes up, and by discovering that it's — whaddaya know! — a section of the *Internal Revenue Manual.* And such fascinating reading it is.

A FedWorld-wide search is useful as a fogcutter. You may not find the answer online, but you can quickly identify the agency you need to contact.

Search For U.S. Government Reports

The National Technical Information Service is the distribution channel for thousands of reports funded in some measure by the federal government. It includes technical reports and documents from the Departments of Defense, Energy, Commerce, and Transportation, as well as agencies such as NASA, various government labs, and private universities and consulting firms.

The NTIS database, also up on Dialog and other proprietary systems (see Chapter 9), contains detailed abstracts, or summaries, of research studies in everything from management theory to civil engineering, space medicine, and library science. It even includes Published Searches (pre-packaged bibliographies or lists of documents, with summaries) drawn from the NTIS database itself. You can't get the complete text online, just the summaries, but you can order full reports and other documents from NTIS.

NTIS is one of the core databases for serious research in science and technology. You can also get to it directly from NTIS' own Web site (www.ntis.gov/).

FedWorld lets you do a limited but quite powerful search of the NTIS database using Boolean AND/ORs, phrases, and truncation (see the Bonus Appendix on the CD for more about these features). At the FedWorld site, click the U.S. Government Reports link to get a more detailed search form.

General Information Services

In bureaucrat-speak, *general* must mean *miscellaneous,* because this FedWorld search option, General Information Services, is a grab-bag of regulations, alternative access points, FTP archives (see Chapter 1 for more about FTP), and searchable databases. Interested in international trade prospects? Check the Export Administration Regulations Electronic Market-place. Are you a pilot? You can get to hundreds of Federal Aviation Admistration service, training, and regulatory documents. Supreme Court decisions? You can find them here. Looking for work? A searchable database of job announcements of government and some non-government positions is updated five days a week.

FedWorld Hosted Web Sites

What's the difference between **FedWorld Hosted Web Sites** and **Web Pages on the FedWorld Information Network,** which we looked at a couple of categories ago? Darned if I know. You find a lot of overlap, and I can venture all kinds of subtle semantic distinctions. But it doesn't really matter. You're here, and they're searchable, so go for it.

Check out the U.S. Commerce Department's online business bookstore, or the U.S. Business Advisor, for guidelines on doing business with the government. Planning a trip abroad? The U.S. Customs Service's popular *Know Before You Go* booklet is online at this site, telling you what and how much you can bring back. Need more information? The Customs Service has prepared a detailed FAQ (Frequently Asked Questions list): "What gives Customs the right to search me?" you may ask indignantly. The answer: Title 19 of the United States Code, Sections 482, 1467, 1496, 1581, and 1582. Will you please open that *other* suitcase now, ma'am? FedWorld gives you several access points for forms and other information from the Internal Revenue Service. But I prefer to hit the IRS site directly (`www.irs.ustreas.gov/prod/cover.html`). *Prefer* may seem an unlikely word to use in the same sentence as *IRS;* but I'm telling you, this is one fun Federal site.

I know you don't believe me. But when you bring up the Web site, look at it, and tell me if that looks like Fear and Loathing personified?

Behind the smiling facade you can find every tax form you'll ever need — and dozens that, if you're lucky, you've never heard of. The site offers explanatory publications ("How to Depreciate Property," "Tax-Exempt Status for Your Organization," "Your Rights As a Taxpayer"), a fax information service, a section endearingly entitled "Tax Regs in Plain English," and links to state forms and other information.

I never thought I'd say it, but I look forward to my visits to the IRS site. I'm learning to love Big Brother.

Search U.S. Government Web Sites

At the bottom of the main FedWorld page you'll find a searchable interface to an even wider range of government sites and servers. The Center for Intelligent Information Retrieval (the *best* kind of information retrieval, as far as I'm concerned) offers a sophisticated but easy way to use search engines covering hundreds of thousands of documents on all kinds of subjects. My search on **irradiated tomatoes** turned up everything from U.S. Department of Agriculture reports to food industry processing statistics, recipes for turkey-pita burgers, and inflight menus for space shuttle crew members. Fascinating, but maybe I need to focus my question a little better.

The first and last options presented on FedWorld's multisearch front page — **Search Web Pages . . .** and **Search U.S. Government Web Sites** — are your best prospects for getting to the information you need quickly when you don't know, or much care, where it's coming from.

Life beyond FedWorld

FedWorld is fine — more than fine — as far as it goes. But its charter is limited to research, regulation, and other activities that fall under the broad umbrella of the Executive branch of government. That includes independent and quasi-official agencies such as NASA, the Environmental Protection Agency, the Federal Reserve System, and the Small Business Administration.

Many of these agencies maintain their own Web sites where you can find additional information — a lot more information than you can get by probing at them through FedWorld. Once you know what bureau or department you're looking for, it always makes sense to visit it directly. FedWorld is just a starting point; many government Web sites are massive dataspheres in themselves. Some, such as the IRS, even have a distinct and engaging personality of their own.

How do you locate the government Web site you want?

- ✔ Sometimes you can find a link at FedWorld, or from FedWorld search results.

- ✔ You can take a quick guess at its URL. **WWW** and the agency acronym, followed by **.gov**, as in **www.nasa.gov**, gets you there a surprising percentage of the time.

- ✔ Or you can look it up in Thomas' comprehensive directory (`lcweb.loc.gov/global/executive/fed.html`). I introduce you to Thomas in the next section.

No doubting Thomas

Keeping an eye on Congress? Your best friend when it comes to insight into the legislative branch of government is named Thomas (see Figure 11-2). The Library of Congress's Thomas site (`thomas.loc.gov`), named in honor of Thomas Jefferson (you thought maybe Clarence Thomas?), enables you to track bills as they move through the House and Senate, read and download the text of pending legislation, and monitor roll call votes to help keep your local representatives honest, or at least accountable. Thomas has a sophisticated search engine that allows you to look for particular bills by name, number, subject, sponsor, and numerous other criteria.

Thomas features the text of the *Congressional Record* — actual transcripts of senators and representatives doing what we elected them to do, in their own inimitable individual styles. Read these for a while and you understand the saying about how nobody ought to have to watch how laws or sausage are made.

Thomas offers Congressional Committee reports, too. Committee reports are a handy way to identify experts on a particular topic. If you're looking for experts on global warming, say, you can search Committee Reports by word or phrase, click a resulting report title, then click Best Sections, and get the prepared statements of individuals who have testified before Congress on the subject.

Thomas also gives you background information, which is great for school reports, on how laws are made and enacted, and the text of great historical documents such as the Constitution and the Declaration of Independence.

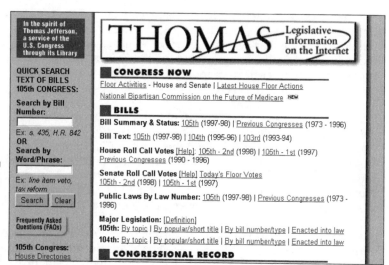

Figure 11-2:
Thomas:
U.S. Congress on the Internet.

Thomas offers an excellent collection of links to other sites for all three branches of government: legislative, executive, and judicial; plus state and local governments and related agencies on the Web. Sausage-making machinery aside, Thomas is worth a bookmark for this set of resources alone. It's as much a gateway to government goodies in its own right as FedWorld is.

Stalking statistical sources

People poke fun at the government for endlessly generating statistics. I happen to think that's one of its most useful functions. But of course, I'm an info-junkie. (*Doesn't say much;* I hear you.) The central clearinghouse for U.S. government statistics is the Economic Statistics Briefing Room (www.whitehouse.gov/fsbr/esbr.html). (Have you noticed that www.whitehouse.gov is getting to be almost as famous an address as 1600 Pennsylvania Avenue?) You can pick up stats there in any of these categories:

- ✔ Production, Sales, Orders, and Inventories
- ✔ Output
- ✔ Income, Expenditures, and Wealth
- ✔ Employment, Unemployment, and Earnings
- ✔ Prices
- ✔ Money, Credit, and Interest Rates
- ✔ Transportation
- ✔ International Statistics

Another good starting point for statistical information is the U.S. Census Bureau (www.census.gov).The Bureau not only collects, analyzes, and publishes the familiar age, gender, race, family size, and housing-type data that you see quoted in newspapers and magazines and on TV, but also a broad range of other demographic and economic facts and figures at both the federal and the local level.

The Census Bureau site features data from the current edition of the *Statistical Abstracts of the United States* (www.census.gov/statab/www/). You can download selected sections in Adobe Acrobat (PDF) format, which preserves tables and other special formatting, and print it out or read it using the free Acrobat reader software. The Census Bureau thoughtfully includes a link to the Adobe site, just in case you don't have a copy of the current version. (And I've made sure there's a copy on the CD.)

Stat Abs, as librarians fondly call it, is one of the few reference books I actually still own in print. If you need statistical information frequently, it's worth ordering a copy in print or on CD, since the Web site provides selected data only.

Just one more pointer before we leave the fascinating world of statistics. No, really. Like anything else, statistics *can* be fascinating once you unload your prejudices and spend some time with them. Statistics may lie, but they tell some pretty good stories, too.

Statistical Resources on the Web (`www.lib.umich.edu/libhome/Documents.center/stats.html`) is an awesomely rich, deep resource for statistical information from non-government and government sources alike, both domestic and international. The categories read like the sections of a good college bookstore: **Agriculture, Business & Industry, Consumers, Cost of Living, Demographics, Economics, Education, Energy, Environment, Finance and Currency, Foreign Economics/Government/Trade, Health, Housing, Labor, Military, Politics, Science, Sociology, Transportation,** and **Weather.** If you can't find the numbers you're looking for here, you may have to make up your own.

In Sickness and in Health

Maybe it's because I just got over the flu, but I've had medicine on my mind lately. If you're lucky, your encounters with the medical establishment will be casual ones, as most of mine have been (knock on wood, take two aspirin, and call me in the morning).

People flock to the Internet for medical information. Sometimes it's because they can't get the information from their own physicians, or are hesitant to ask. Often, though, it's a simple matter of self-empowerment: What better time to become an informed consumer than when your health, or the health of a family member, is at stake?

You can find some good medical advice online. You can also find some advice that's dubious, and worse. Before self-administering any treatment that involves ingesting, injecting, or for that matter, any practice more strange or controversial than a warm bath, check with your own health practitioner.

Tapping the medical literature with Medline

The U.S. National Library of Medicine is the mothership of the medical info-fleet. NLM is home to Medline, a venerable and highly-respected database of clinical and experimental medical literature, worldwide, that's been around since 1966. If you're looking for a research paper or an article from a medical journal, such as the *New England Journal of Medicine* or the *Journal of the American Medical Association,* Medline is a good first stop. Medline won't deliver the complete text, at least not on the first go-round, but you often get a detailed abstract or summary, and the NLM site tells you how to order a copy of the article.

Medline is available through Dialog and several other proprietary online services (see Chapter 9 to read about proprietary services). But it's searchable for free at the NLM Web site (www.nlm.nih.gov/). You have your choice of two versions: **PubMed** and **Internet Grateful Med.**

Power searching with PubMed

The PubMed approach to Medline assumes that you know what you're doing. It allows Boolean AND/OR/NOT search statements, including complex queries such as **multiple sclerosis AND (heat OR humidity).** You can search by author, publication date, and other parts of the document using field labels such as AU and DP, or selecting fields from the pull-down menu. (The Bonus Appendix on the CD tells you more about Boolean and field searching.) **List Terms** mode helps you improve and refine your search by displaying the portion of the database index surrounding your terms. But overall, PubMed doesn't give you much help, which is fine if you're an experienced medical searcher.

There's nothing like a Grateful Med search

Grateful Med is much, much milder, and won't upset your stomach. It uses pull-down menus and the step-by-step form shown in Figure 11-3. You can limit your search by date, language, and other restrictions, to make it more precise or to cut down on the number of items you retrieve. Grateful Med also offers separate searching of several supplementary NLM databases, including AIDS-related ones.

The search I did in Figure 11-3 resulted in 130 articles in the medical literature from 1995 to the present. I can click on any of the titles to read a more complete abstract or description. I can then print or download my results and/or order article copies from the NLM's document delivery service, Loansome Doc. The name *Grateful Med* is more than fine with me, but *Loansome Doc* is pushing it.

You can improve your search results by adding key words from MeSH, the official **Medical Subject Headings** used in the Medline database. Look at the indexing terms that turn up at the end of the best and most relevant items you've retrieved. Do another search that incorporates one or two of those terms in place of the corresponding words you came up with. If you get really serious about this stuff, you can download the MeSH headings list (www.nlm.nih.gov/mesh/filelist.html).

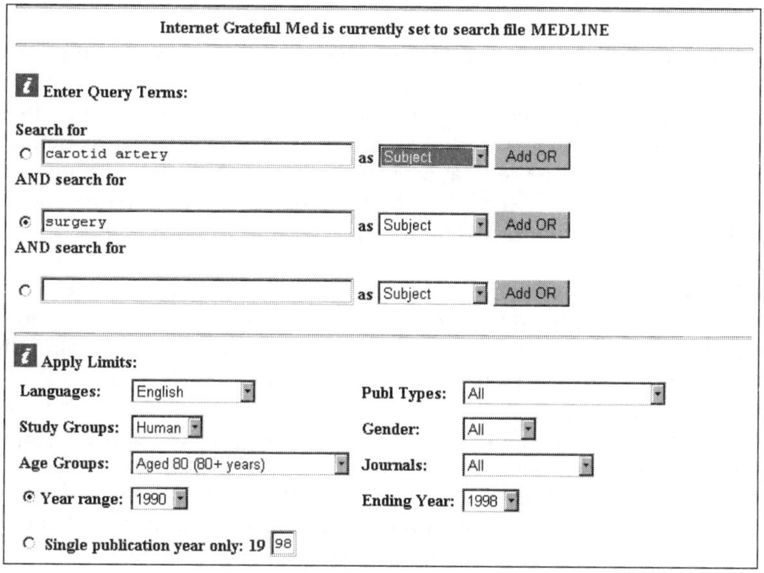

Internet Grateful Med is currently set to search file MEDLINE

i Enter Query Terms:

Search for

○ carotid artery   as [Subject ▾] [Add OR]

AND search for

◉ surgery   as [Subject ▾] [Add OR]

AND search for

○ [ ]   as [Subject ▾] [Add OR]

i Apply Limits:

Languages:	English ▾	Publ Types:	All ▾
Study Groups:	Human ▾	Gender:	All ▾
Age Groups:	Aged 80 (80+ years) ▾	Journals:	All ▾

◉ Year range: [1990 ▾]   Ending Year: [1998 ▾]

○ Single publication year only: 19 [98]

Figure 11-3:
Searching
the medical
literature
with Grate-
ful Med.

One of the slickest reasons to use a comprehensive database of medical
literature, such as Medline, is to identify individuals and institutions that
specialize in cutting-edge (no pun intended) treatments and procedures.
Each article includes not only the author(s), but also the name of the
institution with which they're affiliated. You can help your physician locate
specialists and treatment centers beyond their local referral network. You
can also search for papers published by a particular author, for example a
specialist to whom you or a family member has been referred, or for papers
published in a specific journal.

Exploring other medical information sources

Medline may be the mothership, but it's not the only ship in the medical sea.
It's not that hard to use, but it's difficult to master completely without
knowing medical terminology and all the subtle ins and outs that the
database offers.

More important, Medline doesn't give you any context for making informed
medical decisions. You can gather the facts — or the abstracts that lead to
the facts — but where do you go from there, other than directly to your
doctor?

Several other medical Web sites do give you more to go on.

Medscape

No, not *Netscape*. Medscape (www.medscape.com) is useful mainly for practicing physicians. In fact, it's set up very much like a magazine for doctors, with technical articles, news from the world of medicine, quizzes, conference and course information, and special reports. You can scan full-text articles in the medical literature by specialty, or search them using your own keywords or Medscape's own list of terms. No need to keep a medical dictionary at your elbow; Medscape has a searchable one built in.

Medscape doesn't cover nearly as many journals as Medline does, or the most authoritative ones; but it gives you useable information quickly. It does provide its own interface for searching Medline and other NLM databases — and some useful search tips — so I'd call it an even trade.

You can find consumer-oriented medical information at Medscape, too. The **Patient Information** section consists of the kind of simple explanations your physician may hand you in brochure form or leave in his waiting room for patients to read while they obsess about their symptoms. You can select from a broad menu of diseases, disorders, and medical conditions ranging from AIDS to Women's Health, and then zero in on the specific topic you want. The information is brief, clear, and basic.

Some portions of Medscape require registration. It's free, and it's worth doing.

Galaxy: Medicine

Galaxy is a subject catalog, similar to the ones I describe in Chapter 5, to information resources on the Web. Its **Medicine** section (galaxy. tradewave.com/galaxy/Medicine.html) allows you to drill down from very broad categories, such as **Diseases & Disorders, Health Occupations, Human Biology, Operative Surgery,** and **Therapeutics** (*treatments,* for us lay people), sometimes through several levels, to the exact topic you want.

The advantage of the drill-down approach is that you don't have to know much medical terminology to find the information you need. If you do have a term to start with, you can enter it in Galaxy's Simple or Advanced search form, and come up with a list of references.

The information available through Galaxy includes not only articles from the medical literature drawn from all over the Web, but pointers to other relevant sites and archives. You can also find cross-references to additional Galaxy categories and subcategories that may be relevant to your search.

Galaxy's **Advanced** option enables you to extend your search beyond the Web, to gopher and telnet sites (see Chapter 1 for more about these non-Web Internet resources). Click the Info & Help link for tips on effective searching.

Galaxy's Medicine section includes links to dozens of medical schools and centers, organizations, periodicals, newsgroups, and other medical sites on the Web. Click the **Merck Manual of Diagnosis and Therapy** to connect with searchable versions of both that authoritative reference and the new *Merck Manual of Medical Information — Home Edition*. You can get to both of these sites directly (www.merck.com/). The home manual on the Web includes extensive sections on medical terms, heart and blood vessel disorders, eye disorders, and women's health issues.

More medical pointers

The quest-for-health trend is probably part of the Aging Baby Boomer Syndrome. That huge chunk of the American population is growing older and becoming more concerned about their health, their symptoms, and getting and staying well. Whatever the reason, a massive amount of medical information exists online, for boomers and everyone else. I've got all my health-related sites in one folder in my browser's bookmark file, so I can find and remember them easily.

If you don't find what you're looking for at one of the sites I've already described, check out some of the sites I list below:

- Johns Hopkins University's **InteliHealth** (www.intelihealth.com/)
- **HealthGate** (www.healthgate.com/)
- The **Wellness Interactive Network** (www.stayhealthy.com/)
- **Health A to Z** (www.healthatoz.com/)
- **Pharmaceutical Information Network**, also known as **PharmInfoNet**, (www.pharminfo.com/pin_hp.html) (for drug and pharmaceutical news and information)

Seeking support for medical problems online

In Chapter 10, I explain how newsgroups and other electronic discussion forums can add a perspective and a depth of understanding that you won't find anywhere else online. That's true no matter what you're researching, and it's especially true when you're talking about illness and disability. What is more personal than your own or a family member's health and well-being?

Participants in newsgroups such as alt.support.mult-sclerosis and alt.support.cancer.prostate find support, commitment, and empathy, 'round the clock, seven days a week. Not only that, the level of information exchange — much of it more accurate, helpful, and current than what you find in print — is awesome.

If you or a family member could use this kind of support, look for pointers at the medical mega-sites mentioned in the last few pages, or visit DejaNews (www.dejanews.com/) and click the **Interest Finder**. Look for newsgroups with **support** in their name. Or click **Browse Groups** and look through the entire **alt.support** hierarchy. See Chapter 10 for more about reading and participating in newsgroups.

Mere Technicalities

If it weren't for scientists and engineers, you might not be online at all. That's obvious, but in a different way than you may think: The World Wide Web, without which online would be a whole lot harder and far less fun to master, was developed by a group of physicists as a way to distribute technical documents more easily.

Tech-types have been online since the beginning of the Net. Some of the earliest databases on proprietary online services, such as Dialog, were created by and for the scientific and technical community, 30 or more years ago.

That's all very admirable, you're thinking, but when does the average person — you, for instance — need sci-tech information?

Suppose you're

- A printer trying to figure out why a certain ink is causing problems
- A clothing manufacturer with a piece of equipment that keeps breaking down
- A golfer with an idea for an improved putter design
- A city public works administrator faced with rust on the concrete walls of the new civic auditorium
- An entrepreneur who wants to set up a fish-farming business
- A do-it-yourselfer who wants to build a second-story addition

What my examples are telling you is that even non-scientists occasionally need to wrap their minds around concepts such as thixotropic materials, metal fatigue, patentability, concrete reinforcement, aquaculture, load calculation, and, um, explosives.

Knowing where to start

The hardest part of sci-tech research for non-scientists is figuring out where to start. That's where consultants and freelance researchers earn the big bucks (consultants do anyway). They know where to find the information, and you pay them to deliver it.

It helps to develop your own network of colleagues. Scientists don't just *know;* they ask their colleagues on the Net or down the hall. Engineers (I've seen this in action) may spend hours mulling over a problem with the guy in the next cube. Then they pull out handbooks, open filing cabinets, look through textbooks that they've had since college — still in information-intake mode — before they actively start searching.

Your best resource is often someone who's faced the same or a similar problem, such as a member of your trade or professional organization, a fellow hobbyist, a person in a related field, a vendor, supplier, or customer. Failing that, you've got *me.*

Stop a minute and analyze the nature of the problem. It may turn out to be different from what you initially assume, but that's science for you. You've got to start somewhere. What category or branch of sci-tech knowledge do you think holds the answer?

Dividing and conquering

Engineers and scientists divide their realms into several broad disciplines. You'll encounter these when you start looking for scientific and technical information online, and it helps to have at least a general sense of where you're headed.

For engineering, you've got:

- **Civil/structural engineering:** Buildings, bridges, dams, and other structures, and the materials (most commonly concrete and steel) used to construct them
- **Mechanical engineering:** Anything that moves (because it's supposed to), such as gears, levers, engines, vehicles, and machinery
- **Electrical/electronics/computer engineering:** Wiring, electronic equipment, telephones, black boxes, and other mysterious stuff

Materials science is part of all three engineering disciplines. It refers to the use and properties (quality, strength, durability, and failure) of the concrete, steel, aluminum, rubber, silicon, duct tape, or bubble gum used in structures, machinery, or equipment.

In the sciences, you've got:

- ✔ **Life sciences:** Biology (including genetics and biotech), physiology, botany, zoology, and ecology
- ✔ **Hard (or physical) sciences:** Chemistry, physics, mathematics, and specialized fields such as hydrology, metallurgy, and optics

Actually, I classify chemistry with the *very* hard sciences. Once I get in above my knees, and that doesn't take long, I call in a colleague who specializes in the field. Learn to recognize, and respect, your limits, as well.

Patents are in a class by themselves. They play a role in almost every branch of science and engineering. Obtaining, or failing to obtain, a key patent can make or break a company's, or an individual's, fortune. I talk about patent research later in this chapter (see the section, "What about patents?").

The database approach

When I'm doing serious sci-tech research — and guess what? every one of those hypothetical examples at the beginning of this section (except for the kid with the bomb) was something a client actually asked me to help with — I *don't* go to the Web.

I head straight for a proprietary database service, usually Dialog, because of its wide range of science and technology databases. Unlike the Web, I can search hundreds of journals, conference papers, and reports at the same time. I can take advantage of the special keywords, concepts, and coding offered by each database to make my search more targeted and precise. If necessary, as it is for certain kinds of research, I can go back not just a couple of years, but decades in the scientific and technical literature.

Visit the Dialog Web site (www.dialogweb.com/) and click Databases. Then check these categories:

- ✔ **Technology**
- ✔ **Energy and Environment**
- ✔ **Medicine**
- ✔ **Chemicals**
- ✔ **Food and Agriculture**

Check out the subdivisions under these topics, too, for an idea of the number and variety of databases you have to choose from. If you really get into this, you can click the names of individual databases to read their complete profiles (which Dialog calls **Bluesheets**).

Which database(s) you select (often you need several to get the complete picture) depends on the exact nature of your question. Pay special attention to the **File Description, Subject Coverage, Sources, Dates Covered, Update Frequency, Document Types Indexed,** and **Geographic Coverage** as described in the Bluesheet, to make sure the database is appropriate for your search. And take a look at the **Sample Document** to see if it's the *kind* of information, generally speaking, that you're hoping to get. If you're expecting articles, a directory or standards database is not going to do the job, and vice versa.

Unlike the Web, many proprietary databases don't include the complete text of the document they reference. Instead, they provide summaries, or *abstracts.* Some give you less than that: just the author, title, publication name, volume and issue, and date of publication. These *bibliographic* or *abstract-and-index* databases are very useful for certain research projects: compiling a list of articles by a particular author, for instance, or doing a preliminary check to see what's been published on a specific topic. The database producers assume that if you want to see the complete article, you can get it in your local library, or order it from the publisher or database producer, or from a document delivery service. See Chapter 8 for more about document delivery.

Since bibliographic and abstract-and-index database records include far fewer words than the complete text, it's best to keep your search terms broad. Too specific a keyword or search query might eliminate useful documents. Better yet, check the standard indexing terms used in the database you're searching, either online or in a print thesaurus, and add the appropriate ones to your search statement.

What about patents?

A patent is a document that grants you, the inventor, or the party to whom the patent has been assigned (usually your employer), the rights to manufacture and market an invention. Patents are valuable because the holder of a patent controls the technology it describes, and the rights to that technology may be licensed or sold for massive amounts of money.

To be patentable, a process, design, device, or chemical composition has to be *useful,* which means that it's non-trivial, it's practical, and it works. It also has to be *novel,* meaning it hasn't been done before. That's why you do a patent search — to make sure nobody's beaten you to it.

But there's more to patent searching than searching patents. If you're checking for *patentability,* you also have to look for *prior art:* anything that may indicate that someone else had the same or a similar idea before you.

Engineering journals, conference papers, hobbyist, and popular magazines — they're all grist for a prior art search. That's one reason why those extensive backfiles — documents going back more than just a few years — in databases on Dialog are important.

Patent searching is hard; that's designed into the system. Think about it: A patent is supposed to disclose what's unique about an invention without revealing so much that a competitor can challenge its claims, file a competing patent, or improve significantly on the idea. Patents may hint at possible uses for the invention, but they seldom spell it out.

Personal bests

I started out as an engineering librarian, and over the years have gravitated toward a core group of sci-tech databases that provide what I need 99 percent of the time.

✔ **Ei Compendex** (Dialog File 8): We met Ei Engineering Village back in Chapter 9. Ei Compendex is the database around which Ei Engineering Village is built, and is the electronic edition of a long-time printed reference called *Engineering Index*. Compendex is a general engineering database covering all the main disciplines including automotive, nuclear, and aerospace engineering. It indexes about 4,500 journals, conference papers, reports, and other publications from 40 countries.

✔ **ISMEC: Mechanical Engineering Abstracts** (Dialog File 14): ISMEC is a more specialized database covering about 750 international journals; plus conference proceedings and reports in mechanical, production, and industrial engineering and engineering management.

✔ **INSPEC: The Database for Physics, Electronics and Computing** (Dialog Files 2-4):

Besides its advertised contents, INSPEC is good for information technology, computer science, and control engineering.

✔ **NTIS: National Technical Information Service** (Dialog File 6): If NTIS sounds familiar, it's because it's the same database you reach through FedWorld's **U.S. Government Reports** link. When I'm already using other Dialog databases, I search NTIS on Dialog as well.

✔ **Biosis Previews** (Dialog Files 5, 55): A leading database for the life sciences, but by no means the only one, Biosis is built around the print publication *Biological Abstracts*. It covers all branches of biology, microbiology, nutrition, toxicology, and the other life sciences, including biomedicine and bioengineering.

✔ **Chemical Abstracts** (Dialog Files 399 and 308-314): I may search this, but not happily, given my chemistry impairment. Serious chemistry researchers usually prefer the American Chemical Society's own version of the database, which is much more functional and complete.

Patent language is intentionally general and vague. The titles are almost useless. Would you guess that a patent having to do with a *flat planar surface* actually described a table? Patents have to fit into certain broad categories of subject and type, yet they impose no restrictions on the words that may be used to describe the invention. Those words are where most of the patent-searching action takes place, and where patent attorneys make their living. Patent litigation and defense (which is when someone claims that somebody else has infringed on his technology, or attempts to prove that his invention or use of a technology is entirely in the clear) is a big part of the professional patent-searching scene.

The U.S. Patent and Trademark Office

Got a bright idea? In the U.S., at least, the Patent and Trademark Office (PTO) Web site (www.uspto.gov/) is a good first stop. You can find basic information on patents, what they consist of, and how and when to file an application.

If you're located somewhere other than the U.S., click <u>Related Web Sites</u> and check the list of **Other Intellectual Property Offices,** worldwide. For international patent work, the Big Kahuna is the World Intellectual Property Office (WIPO) in Geneva, Switzerland (www.wipo.org/).

The PTO site offers free searching of U.S. patents from 1976 to the present, as well as a separate database of AIDS-related patents issued in the U.S., Europe, and Japan. You can do:

- A **Boolean Search** using pull-down menus, and look at the results in chronological or relevance-ranked order. But you're limited to two terms per search. (See the Bonus Appendix on the CD for details on Boolean searching.)

- An **Advanced Search** using whatever terms and qualifiers you want. Be sure to click <u>Help on formulating queries</u> to see how the advanced search syntax works.

The PTO site also includes patent classification listings that you can browse or search. A Patent Class is a broad grouping similar to a top-level subject category in a Web guide such as Yahoo!, or the channels in Excite.

Adding a Class number helps narrow your search to the right general field. For instance, if you want to search for patents on the kind of fork you use to twirl spaghetti, as opposed to forklift trucks, forks in roads, or robotic serpents with forked tongues, you can:

1. **Click Search US Manual of Classification.**

2. **Key in the search phrase** food and fork.

3. *Et voilà*: Class 30: Cutlery **is what you want to fold into your search. *Bon appetit* — or should I say *buon appetito*?**

Learning to speak Patentese

Synonyms are the key to successful patent searching. That's why the U.S. PTO's Advanced Search mode, or any option that allows you to enter multiple terms, is your best bet for patent subject searching. The more terms you can think of to describe your idea, the better. Keep them as specific as possible, and avoid using the word *device*.

Chemists joke about newbies who use the word *polymer* as a search term; that word appears in zillions of chemical database records, and has very little meaning on its own. *Device* is a similar deal — it's the patent-database equivalent of a *whatchamacallit*. You know, a thingy, a doodad. You get the idea.

To add a Class number to your patent using the PTO's **Boolean Search** form (`patents.uspto.gov/access/search-bool.htmlmenu`):

1. **Enter** fork **in the Term 1 box, leaving** Any Field **showing in the Field 1 window.**

2. **Enter** 30 **in the Term 2 box, selecting** Current U.S. Class **in the Field 2 window.**

3. **Click either** Chronologically **or** By Relevance **under** Rank Results **(I chose** By Relevance **in case I got a lot; many patent searches require a chronological listing instead).**

Figure 11-4 shows my search results. When I click on the title of that pasta-utensil item (Patent number 5,697,160), I find this Abstract or patent summary:

> An eating utensil used in cooperation with a fork to eat elongate type pasta in a manner which prevents splattering of pasta sauce onto the user. The utensil is comprised of a handle which carries a bowl which is formed with an upwardly concave center portion. A rim on the outer periphery of the center portion extends in an oval-shaped configuration, and a shield is mounted on one side of the rim. The shield is comprised of an upright wall having a curvature which conforms with the rim curvature. The height of the wall is effective to constrain the pasta and sauce above the bowl and within the shield as the tines of the fork, while being held and twisted by the user, turn and wrap the pasta into a bundle which can then be lifted away from the utensil for eating.

See what I mean by the language used in patents? And notice — the patent isn't even *for* a fork, but for a device intended to be used in conjunction with one.

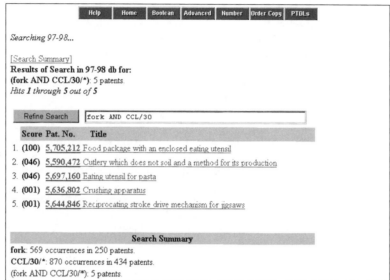

| Help | Home | Boolean | Advanced | Number | Order Copy | PTDLs |

Searching 97-98...

[Search Summary]
Results of Search in 97-98 db for:
(fork AND CCL/30/*): 5 patents.
Hits 1 through 5 out of 5

| Refine Search | fork AND CCL/30 |

Score	Pat. No.	Title
1. (100)	5,705,212	Food package with an enclosed eating utensil
2. (046)	5,590,472	Cutlery which does not soil and a method for its production
3. (046)	5,697,160	Eating utensil for pasta
4. (001)	5,636,802	Crushing apparatus
5. (001)	5,644,846	Reciprocating stroke drive mechanism for jigsaws

Search Summary

fork: 569 occurrences in 250 patents.
CCL/30/*: 870 occurrences in 434 patents.
(fork AND CCL/30/*): 5 patents.

Figure 11-4:
Patent
search
results from
the U.S.
PTO Web
site.

Other Web-based patent search sites

All U.S. patent filings come from the PTO, but the PTO isn't the only source for patent searching on the Web. The IBM Patent Server (www.patents. ibm.com/) goes five years farther back, to 1971, not 1976, and offers images of patent drawings, too, almost that far back. Images are a big plus; a picture *is* worth a thousand words, especially in Patentese.

The IBM Patent Server offers a simple Boolean search form, with a choice of fields for making your search more precise. The Advanced Text Search option allows you to enter more than two terms. (See the Bonus Appendix on the CD for more about Boolean and field searching.)

Micropatent's PatentWeb (www.micropatent.com/) is a commercial site that offers U.S. patents all the way back to 1964, and World patents from 1976 to the present. You must establish an account in advance and pay a fee for viewing or downloading patent documents. For occasional patent searching, especially of older filings that you can't find elsewhere on the Web, it's a useful alternative to coming up to speed on one of the propri-etary patent search services.

If in doubt, refer it out

Professional patent searchers use databases such as Claims/U.S. Patents and Derwent World Patents Index, which are available through Dialog and other industrial-strength online services. They can make these files jump through flaming hoops and do lots of other tricks that the Web-based patent databases aren't capable of doing. Patent searching is as much an art as a science, with a lot to discover. *I* still don't know it all.

You don't think it's worth the bother of making sure your patent search covers *all* the bases? Well, ask yourself what's at risk if you act without sufficient information? Income? Market share? Your professional or even personal reputation? Forgive me for getting all preachy on you, but if you don't want to take the time to come up to speed yourself, contract with a scientist, patent attorney, librarian, or independent information specialist who knows his way around the patent databases. You have to pay, but it's a sound investment.

The Association of Independent Information Professionals, an organization of research entrepreneurs, maintains a membership directory on the Web (www.aiip.org/). Click <u>AIIP Members Directory</u>, and then use your browser's **find text on this page** function (it's on the Edit menu in my versions of both Netscape and Internet Explorer), and look for the word **patent.** You may do better if you pick someone whose areas of expertise are in science and technology instead of all over the map.

Do-it-yourself is fine if you're just trying to satisfy your curiosity, wondering if anyone else has glommed onto your own best and brightest ideas. About that golf putter? You wouldn't believe how many duffers think they've come up with the ultimate solution. In fact, go ahead — that's a fun patent search to try on your own. Go back to the PTO and just key in **golf AND putter** as your two terms, then browse the titles. When I did it, I got 129 hits. Now try it on the IBM Patent Server, which gives you five more years of coverage. Make sure you click the button for 1971 to the present, and set **Maximum Results** to the top of the range. I got about ten times as many hits as I did at the PTO. Do you still think you've got a marketable new idea for a putter?

The discrepancy between IBM and PTO hits is interesting, and shows how careful you have to be not to accept search results at face value. When faced with a discrepancy such as this, I ask myself: Is there really such a big difference between the two search engines? Does IBM search more of each patent document than the PTO does? Can I find something in the documentation at the site that explains why I get so much from one, and relatively little from the other? Assuming this isn't just a glitch, I know which site I'd choose if I needed to do a comprehensive patent search. On the other hand, maybe there *was* an enormous upswing in golf-interest in the early '70s, and IBM's extra five years of coverage accounts for the difference. I doubt it, though.

Satisfying your scientific curiosity

Researching a scientific or technical topic is serious business. But just plain curiosity is something else. Early on, teachers discovered that the Web is a great tool for getting kids excited about science. If you don't know much biology but you've got a question-mark in your mind that you just can't dislodge, try baking powder and a vigorous scrubbing motion. No, sorry — try the Net.

Even professional scientists sometimes need a boost when they're investigating in a field other than their own. The Web abounds in general science mega-sites full of pointers to the best resources in various fields and disciplines. Some sites are for scientists, others for students, others for just plain folks. Nobody's checking I.D. or asking for your resume; use whatever sites work for you. If you find a great starting point, bookmark it, whether it's geared toward professionals or toward 12 year-old kids.

A couple of general science sites that I found worthwhile are Science World of Discovery and SciCentral.

Science World of Discovery

Meredith L. Huestis has created a one-stop resource (`members.aol.com/mlhuestis/sciworld/index.htm`) for anyone interested in science generally, or in search of more detailed information in a specific field. This site features individual sections for biology and the life sciences, including fossils, ancient artifacts, and early man; geology, weather phenomena, and other earth studies; chemistry, space science, and physics.

Exploring my new-found interest in astronomy (seeing a solar eclipse will make you an instant convert, too) I scroll down to the **Physical Science** center, and then click <u>Space Science: Astronomy Center</u>. I find resources ranging from **Ask an Astronomer** and **Hot Astronomy News** to a tutorial on basic astronomical subjects such as the solar system; to databases, dictionaries, observatories, and newsgroups, such as `sci.astro.amateur`, `sci.astro.planetarium`, and `sci.space.news`.

SciCentral

SciCentral (`www.scicentral.com/`) is a professionally-maintained gateway to more than 50,000 online resources in the biological and health sciences, earth and space science, engineering, chemistry, and physics. The site also features news stories, links to government agencies, universities and research institutes, and information on women and minorities in science.

When I follow my astronomy obsession through the frames of the SciCentral site, clicking first <u>Earth & Space Sciences</u>, and then <u>Astronomy</u>, I find many of the same items that I did at Science World but a lot of unique ones, too. Thumbs up to SciCentral; you're a bookmark now.

News from the world of science

Maybe you need your *Time, Newsweek,* or *People* magazine fix each week. I read *Science News.* To be perfectly honest, another name appears on the mailing label, but he lets me look at it when he's finished. *Science News* has a fine Web site (www.sciencenews.org/), though I prefer to browse it in print instead of on my screen.

A site I do like to look at online is *EurekAlert!* In fact, I just love to *say* it. EurekAlert! EurekAlert! EurekAlert! "Eureka!" is what scientists are supposed to say when they make a momentous discovery. It means "I have found it." Actually, the story I've heard is that all the great scientific discoveries were preceded not by a cry of "Eureka!" but by some guy in a lab muttering, "Hmmm, *that's* funny. . . . "

Anyway, *EurekAlert!* (www.eurekalert.org/) is produced by the American Academy for the Advancement of Science (AAAS). Its primary mission is to make sure that science writers and other journalists get the story right. To ensure this accuracy, it includes all kinds of auxiliary resources: links to dictionaries and scientific glossaries in various disciplines; pointers to image sources such as NASA and the Smithsonian Institution; and links to research sites, organizations, and science publications for professionals and lay people alike. But the heart of the site is its collection of news releases on a wide range of research fronts. Most of these news stories aren't of headline-making stature, like the discovery of ice on the moon. But scanning through them periodically gives you a good sense of what real scientists are working on, and how our knowledge of the world — and of worlds beyond our world — is increasing all the time.

Chapter 12

Strictly Business

• •

In This Chapter

▶ Gathering background information on a company

▶ Researching industries, markets, and products

▶ Identifying and tracking competitors

▶ Finding financial and investment information

• •

*F*or businesses, information is like oxygen. They inhale it constantly, without even noticing. It's in the air; it's a pervasive part of the environment. Unfortunately, the atmosphere in a few companies is on the stale side. Some organizations still haven't gotten the word that information is a vital part of their operation. They make decisions based on outdated facts and figures, and on assumptions about the marketplace and their competitors that they haven't tested in years. Check the business section of your local paper — you're sure to spot them. Look in the bankruptcy filings, for starters.

Once the Web got going, savvy corporations were among the first on board — if only to claim their domain addresses and plant their virtual brochures and business cards in cyberspace. But as the Web began to include real, substantial content along with sites and services geared toward the business community, *information* became a high-profile priority. Now that useful data for making business decisions is just a few keystrokes away, plugged-in business people know that staying informed is an imperative.

In this chapter, I show you how to find and use business directories, financial reports, public company filings with the Securities and Exchange Commission, stock quotes, investment analyst and market research reports, press releases, trade journal articles, and other forms of company, business, and marketing information. The open Web isn't always the most complete or efficient resource for business research, but it's a start. And once you're on the Web, it's much easier to tap into other useful online resources, especially the gated sites and proprietary services I wax rhapsodic about in Chapter 9.

Understanding Business Research

Business research takes many forms, depending on what you're hoping to accomplish. The main forms we look at in this chapter, along with an idea of what each one involves, are:

- ✔ **Company background:** Assemble a profile of a company, its history, and its lines of business. Obtain organizational information including location, top executives, major divisions, and subsidiaries. Get basic or detailed financial statements, and perhaps a credit history and rating as well. Collect news stories and press releases showing quarterly earnings, new products, management changes, and other timely information.

- ✔ **Competitive intelligence:** Identify companies competing in a particular industry. Scan analyst reports, market surveys, and trade journal articles to determine the market leaders and to get a sense of their strengths and weaknesses, current and long-term. Read closely to determine their market strategies, their research and development efforts, and their plans for the future.

- ✔ **Market studies:** Determine the market for a new product or service by checking to see what's already out there, who's selling it, and how much they're selling. Gather historical data to compare and determine trends. Is the demand for the product going up or down? Look at published market studies and articles in trade journals to identify the major players and their market share. Scan the consumer, regulatory, and broader business climate to identify opportunities and dangers.

- ✔ **Sales prospecting:** Build a list of potential customers by screening them according to location, size, type of business, or other meaningful criteria. Get names, addresses, and phone numbers so that you can contact them.

- ✔ **Stocks and investment research:** Gather current and historical quotes for stocks and other investments. Focus on a particular company's stock performance over time and its prospects for the future. Compare notes with other investors. Set up an alerting service to keep tabs on the companies and markets you follow. Manage your investment portfolio online.

- ✔ **Management theory and practice:** Learn new techniques for managing companies, people, and corporate operations. Discover other companies' methods and best practices. Read case studies, surveys, and executive interviews.

Getting a Company Backgrounder

Why gather background information on a company? Perhaps you're thinking about doing business with them, as a customer, partner, supplier, investor, or even a potential employee, and you want to be sure that they're stable and reputable — in other words, that they're going to *remain* in business and deliver on what they've promised you. A company backgrounder is like a resume, a quick-sketch portrait of the organization.

Company backgrounders are a fundamental part of business research. You may assemble one as part of a larger research project, zeroing in on a particular competitor, or potential client or joint-venture partner, after first surveying the field.

A basic company backgrounder includes this type of information:

- ✔ The name, address and telephone number of the company
- ✔ The names and titles of its top executives
- ✔ A general description of the company's products and services
- ✔ The number of employees
- ✔ Names and locations of subsidiaries and major divisions
- ✔ Annual sales and other financial figures
- ✔ Credit rating and history
- ✔ News about new product introductions, current earnings, executive appointments, and corporate strategies and goals

Strategizing a background search

Sounds like a lot of information, doesn't it? Luckily, you can usually find much of it in one place, in an online directory database or at the company's own Web site. It makes sense to start where you think you can get the biggest payoff.

Say you're gathering background information on Eastman Kodak Company. Your first stop is the Eastman Kodak site (www.kodak.com/). There you see, among all the product news and tips for taking great pictures, a header that says **About the Company.** Here you find the organizational lowdown you're looking for — or as much of it as the company wants to tell you. The site is theirs, after all, and they control the content.

Clicking the <u>About Kodak</u> link brings up information about the CEO, a history of the company dating from its founding in the late 19th century, an Investor's Center with complete financial information, a searchable collection of press releases, descriptions of individual business units, such as the Business Imaging Systems division, and a copy of the most recent company annual report — complete with photos, of course.

The fastest way to locate a company Web site, if you don't already have the URL, is to guess. For example, `www.kodak.com` is a no-brainer for Eastman Kodak. If you don't get it in a couple of tries, plug the company name into a search engine such as HotBot or Excite, or look it up in Yahoo!, or check a company directory site like CompaniesOnline, Hoover's, or CompanyLink (more about all three of these in the following section).

To gather background information on a company, you may have to go beyond its own Web site, looking for business directory profiles, credit reports, and opinions from investment analysts, competitors, suppliers, and writers for newsletters and other trade publications. It's a good idea to explore some of these alternatives, even if you did strike gold at the corporate site itself, because they add a different, more objective, perspective. A complete backgrounder often involves a three-stage effort:

1. I start with the most specific, structured sources — the kind where I can look up the business by name and *know that I'm getting everything there is to get*. Company directories and credit reports fall into this category, along with the company's own Web site.

2. After that, I broaden out to industry information sources that offer *a good chance — but not a guarantee —* of gaining more insight into the company and its doings.

3. Finally, depending on how much information I've gathered and how much more I think I need to get, I extend the search still further, to magazines, newspapers, and other publications that *may or may not* give me useful information. If I haven't found much at this point, I may even plug the company name into a Web-wide search engine.

Company directories and packaged reports

Company directories are not all alike. Some offer a detailed portrait of the firm, and sometimes links to additional sources of information. Other directories provide just a bare-bones sketch of what the operation is about.

Directories vary in their coverage, too. Some are strong on both public and private companies, while others focus on public companies only. Some are international in scope, while others restrict themselves to the U.S. or another specific country or region. Some have a minimum size cutoff, while others strive to be as comprehensive as possible, seeking out one-person operations as well as Gigundo Megacorp International Inc. and its corporate peers.

Bottom line: You may have to check more than one directory to get the complete picture, or to even *find* the company you're looking for.

Delving into Dun & Bradstreet

Dun & Bradstreet (D&B) is probably the single most comprehensive source of basic company information, worldwide. D&B maintains a huge database of business profiles, as well as a variety of more detailed reports, for both public and private firms.

Companies Online, a joint venture of D&B and the Lycos search engine folks, allows you to search for a specific company by name or ticker symbol, or to locate businesses that meet certain criteria. (I say a lot more about how to use criteria-screening in the "Prospecting for Sales" section of this chapter.)

Continuing my search for background information, I navigate to `www.companiesonline.com/`, type in **Eastman Kodak,** and click **Go Get It!** What's "it"? In this case, "it" is Kodak's mailing address and phone number, the name of its CEO, annual sales, number of employees, and other basic information about the company. If you haven't already visited Kodak's Web site, the URL is right there, ready for you to click and go.

Public versus private companies

I got lucky with Kodak. The Web site gave me all the background information I wanted, and more. But — confession time — I *knew* it would. Some companies are a lot more forthcoming than others. Publicly owned firms such as Kodak are required by law to divulge certain details about their operation, including financial information, to potential shareholders and government regulatory agencies like the U.S. Securities and Exchange Commission.

Privately owned companies present more of a challenge. Small, family-controlled firms may be the hardest to research because they're not required to divulge financial data or other details of their operations. Small companies — unless they're the latest hot high-tech startup, or involved in a scandal, or newsworthy for some other reason — tend to keep a much lower profile than large, well-known public firms.

Even some public companies, especially in highly competitive industries, are stingy with the details, although bona fide investors can usually get more information than window-shoppers like us.

Company name searching is a challenge. Sometimes the official corporate name is different from the name that most people use — **Eastman Kodak** versus just **Kodak.** If you know or can determine the *ticker symbol* (the abbreviation used to identify a public company's stock — Kodak's is **EK**) or its official name, you're in good shape. Otherwise, be prepared to pull up subsidiaries and branch offices along with the main headquarters location. You can usually identify the main office, which is almost certainly what you want for a background search, if you know where the company is based. And, simple but effective, look for phone number listings that end with a couple of zeros.

Companies Online offers you some extras, too. In this case, it's a link to free Kodak stock quotes and newswire headlines, and the option of purchasing an in-depth D&B Business Background Report and other, more detailed, information.

Click the Business Background link or aim directly for the main D&B Web site (www.dnb.com/) to see what else Dun & Bradstreet has to offer:

✔ The **Business Background Report** (BBR) includes contact information, sales figures, number of employees, lines of business, and top executive names and titles. But it goes considerably beyond that, including a history of the business, number of shares issued, background on senior management and their experience and education, and a brief description of any special circumstances, such as fires, floods, or major lawsuits, that may have affected the business in a significant way. A typical D&B BBR describes the corporate organization: parent company, subsidiaries, and branch offices; and provides an assessment of the company's financial condition in very general terms. A BBR costs $20 per report; D&B accepts credit cards from registered users.

✔ For the real dirt — I mean, for more detailed information on a company's stability and how well it's doing, you can order a **Supplier Evaluation Report** (SER). SERs cost $85 a shot, and the price reflects the value of the information offered. D&B offers various measures of a company's financial condition relative to other businesses in its industry and to businesses as a whole; and a ranking of how likely it is to default on payments to creditors, or go bankrupt or out of business completely. The ratings are based on factors such as payment history, liens and judgments, accounting statements, and corporate assets — most of which are also detailed in the report.

✔ For companies located outside the U.S., D&B offers a **GlobalSeek Report.** This $5 special includes basic locational information, business structure, names of key executives, year started, number of employees, net worth, annual sales, and profit/loss figures in both U.S. and the local currencies. This report is bare-bones, but is an easy way of getting relatively reliable international company information from a single reputable source.

Can't find it in GlobalSeek? Check out WorldPages (www.worldpages.com/) for links to individual business directories worldwide. You can find out more about WorldPages in Chapter 4.

America Online users have their own private channel to D&B reports through a service called D&B@AOL. To get there, enter the keyword: **business research** and click on Search Dun & Bradstreet.

Hoovering it up

D&B is formidable, but it's not the only game in town. Check Hoover's Online (www.hoovers.com/) for narrative company descriptions, information on key competitors, rankings (Kodak ranks 72nd in the Fortune 500), subsidiaries like Fox Photo and Kodak's German and U.K. operations, selected news stories, and more. Figure 12-1 shows the start of Hoover's **Company Capsule** on Kodak. Registered users can click Company Profile, Financials, or News to get more detailed information.

Hoover's is also available through America Online — keyword: **Hoovers.** You could've guessed.

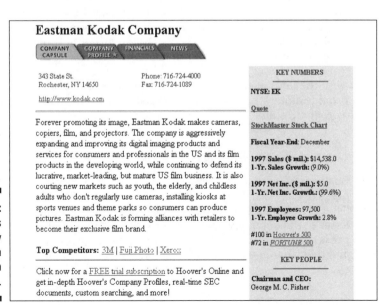

Figure 12-1:
Hoover's Company Capsule on Eastman Kodak.

Eastman Kodak Company

COMPANY CAPSULE | COMPANY PROFILE | FINANCIALS | NEWS

343 State St.
Rochester, NY 14650

Phone: 716-724-4000
Fax: 716-724-1089

http://www.kodak.com

Forever promoting its image, Eastman Kodak makes cameras, copiers, film, and projectors. The company is aggressively expanding and improving its digital imaging products and services for consumers and professionals in the US and its film products in the developing world, while continuing to defend its lucrative, market-leading, but mature US film business. It is also courting new markets such as youth, the elderly, and childless adults who don't regularly use cameras, installing kiosks at sports venues and theme parks so consumers can produce pictures. Eastman Kodak is forming alliances with retailers to become their exclusive film brand.

Top Competitors: 3M | Fuji Photo | Xerox

Click now for a FREE trial subscription to Hoover's Online and get in-depth Hoover's Company Profiles, real-time SEC documents, custom searching, and more!

KEY NUMBERS

NYSE: EK

Quote

StockMaster Stock Chart

Fiscal Year-End: December

1997 Sales ($ mil.): $14,538.0
1-Yr. Sales Growth: (9.0%)

1997 Net Inc. ($ mil.): $5.0
1-Yr. Net Inc. Growth.: (99.6%)

1997 Employees: 97,500
1-Yr. Employee Growth: 2.8%

#100 in Hoover's 500
#72 in FORTUNE 500

KEY PEOPLE

Chairman and CEO:
George M. C. Fisher

Linking up with CompanyLink

CompanyLink (`www.companylink.com/`), a service of NewsPage (Chapter 13 says more about NewsPage) provides news, research, and contact info for 65,000 U.S. companies. The site is searchable by company name, ticker symbol, state, or industry. Besides the basic company profile, CompanyLink offers links to press releases and news articles, financial filings, and stock quotes. Registered users can get additional goodies such as information on competitors and corporate operating units.

Tapping company and industry news sources

Business directories are just the foundation of a company background search. They're fine for the basic facts but, like their printed counterparts, most of them are updated annually at best — and a lot can happen in a year. Not only that, directory listings don't provide much, if any, insight into the company's activities, new product introductions, or changes in strategic direction.

If you're lucky, as I was with Kodak, you may find some of that supplemental information at the company's own Web site. But even then, all you're getting is their own perspective, and that's not enough. Organizations are notorious for tooting their own horns while gliding over not-so-wonderful news that may make their shareholders and customers unhappy.

For the complete picture, you've got to supplement your directory search with current corporate press releases, and see what the rest of the industry (or people and publications that follow the industry) and the larger business community are saying. The easiest way to tap into that broader perspective is through articles in trade, business, and general news publications.

Start with the links to news stories that Hoover's and CompanyLink thoughtfully provide along with their directory listings. From there, you can branch out to other sites and sources, such as

- ✔ The aforementioned NewsPage (`www.newspage.com/`), which lets you search for recent news by company or industry.

- ✔ BusinessWire (`www.businesswire.com/`), a corporate background and press release distribution service where client companies pay to be listed. For background, click Corporate Profile followed by the first letter of the company name, or browse the alphabetical listing. For press releases and related information, click Corporate News on the Net and then search by company name or browse the alphabetical listings.

✔ PR Newswire (www.prnewswire.com/), a press release distribution service similar to BusinessWire. Click <u>Company News</u>, and then key in the name of your company, or select it from an alphabetical listing.

✔ American City Business Journals (www.amcity.com/), a mega-site for the online editions of more than three dozen local business publications, such as the *Cincinnati Business Courier,* the *Philadelphia Business Journal,* or the *San Francisco Business Times*. City business papers are great sources for in-depth info on companies headquartered or doing business in a particular region. They're also excellent for gathering a variety of local opinions from the business community's perspective. The American City site allows you to search a particular publication, or all of them at once, and to restrict your search to the current issue or to cover an archive of back issues. Figure 12-2 shows the kind of information I got when I ran a search for Kodak in all 37 American City Business Journal publications. See what I mean about getting a variety of perspectives and something besides the company's official line?

America Online lets you search two weeks' worth of company news from Reuters and the Associated Press, along with 30 days' worth from PR Newswire and BusinessWire. This search method is a quick and efficient way to cover multiple newswires. The keyword **company news** takes you directly there.

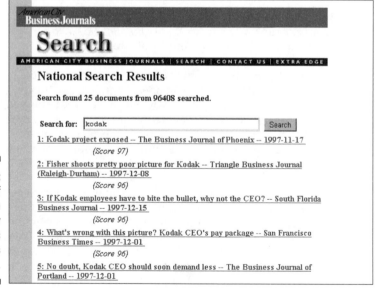

Figure 12-2:
Results of
American
City
Business
Journals
Search.

American City
Business Journals

Search

AMERICAN CITY BUSINESS JOURNALS | SEARCH | CONTACT US | EXTRA EDGE

National Search Results

Search found 25 documents from 96408 searched.

Search for: [kodak] [Search]

1: Kodak project exposed -- The Business Journal of Phoenix -- 1997-11-17
    (Score 97)

2: Fisher shoots pretty poor picture for Kodak -- Triangle Business Journal (Raleigh-Durham) -- 1997-12-08
    (Score 96)

3: If Kodak employees have to bite the bullet, why not the CEO? -- South Florida Business Journal -- 1997-12-15
    (Score 96)

4: What's wrong with this picture? Kodak CEO's pay package -- San Francisco Business Times -- 1997-12-01
    (Score 96)

5: No doubt, Kodak CEO should soon demand less -- The Business Journal of Portland -- 1997-12-01

Broadening your company background search

You've probably found enough background information to get you started by now, especially if the company you're researching is publicly traded, good-sized, or newsworthy in some way. But suppose you want more comprehensive information, or you still haven't filled in the blanks? Chapter 13 is all about tracking down information of all kinds in newspapers, magazines, and other periodicals. That chapter covers individual Web sites as well as online services and mega-sites, such as NewsTracker (`nt.excite.com/`) or the Electric Library (`www.elibrary.com/` or via keyword: **research zone** on AOL), that lead you to numerous publications at the same time. If you don't feel like turning pages yet, start with some of these key business and news sources:

- ✔ **U.S. business periodicals:** *Wall Street Journal Interactive Edition* (`www.wsj.com/`), *Forbes* (`www.forbes.com/`), *Fortune* (`www.pathfinder.com/fortune/`), *Business Week* ((`www.businessweek.com/`) or via keyword: **BW** on AOL)

- ✔ **International business periodicals:** *The Asian Wall Street Journal* (available through Dow Jones Interactive at `www.djnr.com/`), the U.K.-based *Economist* (`www.economist.com/`) or *Financial Times* (`www.ft.com/`)

- ✔ **National newspapers:** *The New York Times* (`www.nytimes.com/`), *USA Today* (`www.usatoday.com/`), *Christian Science Monitor* (`www.csmonitor.com`), or your local paper's Web site

Still coming up dry, or barely damp? It may be time for a needle-in-a-haystack search — the kind where you have no idea where information on your subject may appear, or how far back you may have to dig, but you'll take whatever you can get. If you haven't yet thrown the company name into a general-purpose search engine, or a meta-engine such as Inference Find, Dogpile, ProFusion, or the others I describe in Chapter 3, now may be the time.

But your best resource in a worst-case scenario is a comprehensive collection of business, trade, and general-interest magazines that indexes several years' worth of periodicals, not just several months. You can find such extensive databases on proprietary online services such as Dialog, Dow Jones Interactive, and LEXIS-NEXIS. I say more about these databases, which play a key role in other kinds of business information-hunting, in the "Planning a Competitive Intelligence Operation" section that follows, and the "Doing Market Research" section later in this chapter.

Planning a Competitive Intelligence Operation

What's *competitive intelligence,* anyway, and why is it staring at me like that? If a company backgrounder is a *portrait,* then a competitive intelligence, or CI, investigation is a *movie.* A backgrounder shows you what a business *looks* like; a CI report shows you what it's *doing* and where it's planning to go.

Like a movie, a CI investigation can reveal subplots and motivations. Like a movie, it's set against a backdrop — not an exotic locale, but a particular industry. And, like a movie, it features a supporting cast — other competitors, suppliers, customers, and regulatory and environmental issues — that play a role in determining the main character's fate.

Some corporations have entire departments set up to gather competitive intelligence. They monitor other companies in their industry, or companies that manufacture, distribute, or sell similar or complementary products and services. A good CI initiative helps companies anticipate what the competition is doing so that they can react quickly to changing conditions and profit from them — or at least minimize their losses. Suppose you discover, through a patent filing or a brief mention in a trade magazine, that your chief competitor in the upscale eyewear industry is thinking about introducing a model with windshield wipers so eyeglass-wearers can see better in the rain. You may want to crank up your own product development cycle and get *your* company's Wiper-Specs™ out on the market first.

A CI initiative is both broader and deeper than a company background investigation. It's *broader* because you have to look at the company in the context of the marketplace — other companies, consumers, and outside events and conditions, such as lawsuits or regulatory changes, that could affect its profitability and its strategic direction. A CI initiative is *deeper* because you go beyond the general background data that we gathered in the last section, and hunt for news — new plant construction, partnerships, management changes, patent applications, and so on — that may signal what the competition is up to.

CI reports are *analytical,* not just descriptive like a background report. You have to think like a detective, piecing together the facts, opinions, and analyses that you find, trying to discern meaningful patterns, and drawing conclusions based on the evidence you find.

How you approach a CI investigation depends to a great extent on the type of company you're researching and what you turn up as you go. For starters, though, we can retrace some of the same ground we covered in our company background search. This time we're going to pay closer attention to some areas that we brushed by last time around.

Using a company's Web site

Your first stop is the Web site of the company you're researching. I'm still interested in Kodak — maybe I'm a strategic analyst for Fuji Film, or an entrepreneur with my own hot ideas about digital cameras or imaging technology — because it's a global operation with a corner on at least the U.S. film market, but it has some significant weaknesses, too.

This time, we skip past the basic factoids and Kodak moments on the company Web site, and look for clues in areas such as

- **The company annual report:** This document is usually heavy on the horn-tooting, since it's designed to reassure shareholders that all is well with the company and that they should invest even more heavily than they already have. However, publicly traded companies are required to reveal the bad along with the good. You may have to read between the lines and deduct 50 percent for management-speak, but look for the truth in the shareholder report, financials, and management discussion sections. In Kodak's annual report, I zero in on the Year in Review, Letter to Shareholders, and Financial Review. I check key indicators, such as annual sales, comparative stock prices (ouch), and earnings per share, comparing the most recent year's figures with those of the year before. I read CEO explanations like this one with a critical eye:

  1997 was clearly a disappointing year for Kodak shareholders and employees. Sometimes, I am even asked why I can feel so optimistic about our future. The answer is simple: We are in a great business, with great people, great products and technology, and an unbeatable brand name.

  Uh-huh. I pay attention to the company's own spin on its new product introductions, acquisitions, joint ventures and partnerships with other firms, new facility construction, and directions for the future. I draw my own conclusions about whether they're expanding or consolidating, on shaky ground or firm footing, and whether the overall trend is up, down, or, as the Magic 8-Ball likes to say, *unclear at this time.*

- **Job listings:** Is the company hiring at all? If so, what kinds of positions is it advertising? What parts of the company are they in? Can I draw any conclusions about the extent of its listings in the marketing and technical areas? Is Kodak beefing up its marketing efforts, for instance, or hiring engineers in advanced digital design areas as well as its core chemical base? Obviously, the more you know about the company and its history and strategic directions, the more meaning you can read into its on-site employment advertising. And don't discount the possibility that it may be in a hiring freeze, and that all those ads may be outdated or strictly to keep up appearances.

✔ **New product announcements, press releases, and company news:** You can draw some conclusions, from the products and services highlighted at a company's site, about what it sees as its main business or its flagship product or line, and where its development and marketing efforts are centered. As long as you're at the site, you may as well tap into the firm's own press releases and flattering news clippings from other sources. You can find routine information, such as quarterly earnings, senior personnel changes, and other matters the company is required to report or doesn't mind your knowing about. You may also find rave reviews, from trade and consumer publications, of some of its products and services. For the real low-down, though, you have to use other news and business information sources. We talk about these sources in the following sections.

Finding alternatives to the annual report

Not all companies are as forthcoming as Kodak. Privately held companies — those that don't issue stock to the public at large — don't have to be, unless they're part of a heavily-regulated industry such as telecommunications or healthcare. Private companies are not accountable to shareholders in the same way that public firms are. Private companies may be required to file certain types of documents with the SEC or other regulatory agencies, but in general, they're not required to open their books or reveal the details of their operations across the board. Some private firms do publish annual reports or post financial statements on their Web sites, but you can't count on it, or on the strict accuracy of the information you do find there.

Hoover's Online (www.hoovers.com/) and Dun & Bradstreet are a couple of options for finding financial data and other leads on a privately-owned company's fiscal condition. For more detailed information, go to www.dnb.com/ and spring for one of those Business Background Reports or Supplier Evaluation Reports I describe in the section, "Delving into Dun & Bradstreet," earlier in this chapter. Besides the raw numbers, you can glean insights from the corporate history, management profiles, and even the description of the premises the company occupies.

The downside of a D&B report, and most other sources of financial information about private companies, is that the data tends to be self-reported. You get only what the company itself has volunteered, and the information isn't always accurate, complete, or timely.

Getting informed analysis

Investment banking and brokerage firms employ teams of analysts who follow individual companies and industries closely, tracking not just stock performance, but a constellation of other activities that may affect business operations, and issuing detailed reports. These reports focus on publicly traded companies, but also include private firms if they're significant players, have an interesting approach to the market, or own a promising technology.

Many of these investment reports are available online, both directly on the Web and through proprietary research services.

The Investext Group offers the complete text of company and industry reports from well-known investment firms such as Bear Stearns, Dean Witter Reynolds, Drexel Burnham Lambert, E.F. Hutton, Kidder Peabody, Paine Webber, and hundreds of others. Investext's **Research Bank** also includes reports from market research firms and trade associations.

You have several options for tapping into Investext:

- ✔ **Through the Web or direct dialup as an I/PLUS Direct customer** (see the Investext Web site at www.investext.com/ for details). You can also opt to subscribe and have Investext do the searching for you, but that seems like cheating, doesn't it? Either way, you can download complete reports, including tables, charts, and other illustrations, in Adobe Acrobat (PDF) format.

- ✔ **Through proprietary online services such as Dialog and Dow Jones Interactive,** which give you plain-text versions of complete reports or selected sections. On Dialog, select File 545 and confine your search to the company field. On Dow Jones, click <u>Company and Industry Center</u> to get to **Investext Company Reports,** and then enter the company ticker symbol and browse the tables of contents of individual reports until you find the complete report, or the sections you want. Figure 12-3 shows the kind of detailed competitive intelligence you can get from investment reports.

Be sure to study the database Bluesheet before searching Investext on Dialog. Unlike many databases where you go directly to the documents you've retrieved, Investext is designed so that you can browse tables of contents or zero in on the report sections you need by entering qualifying fields and phrases. Why the indirect approach? Complete reports can cost you $100 or more, and you don't always need the whole thing.

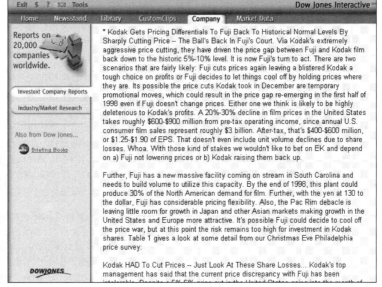

Exit $? ✉ Tools   Dow Jones Interactive℠

Home   Newsstand   Library   CustomClips   **Company**   Market Data

Reports on
20,000
companies
worldwide.

Investext Company Reports

Industry/Market Research

Also from Dow Jones...

🔵 Briefing Books

DOWJONES

* Kodak Gets Pricing Differentials To Fuji Back To Historical Normal Levels By Sharply Cutting Price -- The Ball's Back In Fuji's Court. Via Kodak's extremely aggressive price cutting, they have driven the price gap between Fuji and Kodak film back down to the historic 5%-10% level. It is now Fuji's turn to act. There are two scenarios that are fairly likely: Fuji cuts prices again leaving a blistered Kodak a tough choice on profits or Fuji decides to let things cool off by holding prices where they are. Its possible the price cuts Kodak took in December are temporary promotional moves, which could result in the price gap re-emerging in the first half of 1998 even if Fuji doesn't change prices. Either one we think is likely to be highly deleterious to Kodak's profits. A 20%-30% decline in film prices in the United States takes roughly $600-$900 million from pre-tax operating income, since annual U.S. consumer film sales represent roughly $3 billion. After-tax, that's $400-$600 million, or $1.25-$1.90 of EPS. That doesn't even include unit volume declines due to share losses. Whoa. With those kind of stakes we wouldn't like to bet on EK and depend on a) Fuji not lowering prices or b) Kodak raising them back up.

Further, Fuji has a new massive facility coming on stream in South Carolina and needs to build volume to utilize this capacity. By the end of 1998, this plant could produce 30% of the North American demand for film. Further, with the yen at 130 to the dollar, Fuji has considerable pricing flexibility. Also, the Pac Rim debacle is leaving little room for growth in Japan and other Asian markets making growth in the United States and Europe more attractive. It's possible Fuji could decide to cool off the price war, but at this point the risk remains too high for investment in Kodak shares. Table 1 gives a look at some detail from our Christmas Eve Philadelphia price survey:

Kodak HAD To Cut Prices -- Just Look At These Share Losses... Kodak's top management has said that the current price discrepancy with Fuji has been

Figure 12-3:
Company
report from
Investext
via Dow
Jones
Interactive.

Pre-packaged market research reports, such as those offered by Investext's MarkIntel division, are a terrific source of competitive intelligence information. In fact, CI and market research are similar in many respects, and often go hand-in-hand. See the "Doing Market Research" section for some specific leads on locating these reports.

Monitoring the news

Back in the Company Backgrounder section, I talk about using newspapers, magazines, and business publications to round out and lend some color to the bare-bones facts about a company and its operations. Competitive intelligence-gathering uses all of those sources — newswires, regional business journals, national and city papers, specialized trade periodicals — and more.

Now you're not just looking for background, but for specific information about a company's current and future directions. You may scan the same headlines, but you focus on news items that someone working on a broad-brush general picture of the company might dismiss as trivial and incidental:

✔ Plant openings that indicate expansion or new product lines

✔ Management changes that signal either a problem with turnover or a steady new hand on the wheel

✔ Contracts and agreements-to-purchase that clue you in on increases in production

✔ Licensing agreements, partnerships, and corporate acquisitions that tell you when a company is committing to new ventures and technologies

✔ Lawsuits, accusations, and regulatory actions that may spell trouble on the environmental, consumer, or new-product-approval fronts

Local color

For a deep and unvarnished look at how a company is faring, nothing beats the local paper in the town where that company is based. Think about it: among its subscribers are hundreds, even thousands, of employees and family members whose lives are influenced by that firm.

Once you have a headquarters address, check one of the newspaper mega-sites in Chapter 13 for newspapers in that city or area. You get more steady and detailed coverage of the company — especially if it's a major regional employer — than you do anywhere else. You also get information on issues, such as employee policies, internal politics, and concerns about environmental pollution, that the national press tends to overlook.

Don't just take my word for it. Aim your browser at the Rochester, N.Y. *Democrat & Chronicle Digital Edition* (www.rochesterdandc.com/), click Search, key in **Kodak**, and check the kinds of stories you pull up. The editors definitely did not run all of these stories by Kodak's public relations department.

Or go to the San Jose, California *Mercury-News* site (www.sjmercury.com/), and search the archives for articles on Netscape, say, or any other Silicon Valley or computer-industry firm.

Calling in the cavalry

Some of the best-informed and most valuable competitive intelligence insights come from articles in specialized industry newsletters and trade publications. Some of these periodicals do have Web sites with searchable archives, but it's tedious and time-consuming to visit them one by one. Besides, unless you're in the industry yourself, or have some bizarre personal interest in it, how are you going to know that publications such as *Chain Store Age, Chemical Marketing Reporter, Restaurants & Institutions,* and *Automotive Parts International* exist in the first place, let alone anticipate that any one of them might cover the company you're investigating?

If you're serious about competitive intelligence-gathering, it pays to invest whatever it takes to come up to speed on some of the heavy-duty trade and industry databases on Dialog and the other proprietary online services described in Chapter 9. These databases cover anywhere from dozens to

hundreds of periodicals in industries ranging from aerospace to zymurgy (look it up). They include articles ranging back 5, 10, 15 years or more, so that you can gather historical data, or compare a company's early stages with its present-day situation. And each database features a range of field options and specialized keywords and concepts, so that you can search not only by company name or ticker symbol, but by specific topics such as management philosophy, joint ventures, marketing, and new products.

Some of my favorite trade and industry databases are:

- **Dialog:** Business & Industry (File 9) and Trade and Industry Database (File 148) cover general business and specific industry publications worldwide, with a focus on companies, products, and markets.

  PROMT: Predicasts Overview of Markets and Technology (File 16) adds facts and figures from market surveys, investment analyst reports, government studies, and more general, business, and trade publications.

  IAC Newsletter Database (File 636) offers detailed coverage and insider analysis from industry-specific newsletters.

  Business Dateline (File 635) includes local and regional business journals, newspapers and magazines.

  Go to Dialog Web (www.dialogweb.com/) and check the Bluesheets (detailed database information) for the lowdown on how to use these resources. You may want to open a Dialog account and take their basic system training.

- **LEXIS-NEXIS:** In the Markets and Industry (MARKET) Library: Select the ALLNWS, CURNWS or ARCNWS group file, depending on whether you want coverage of all publications, just the most recent two years' worth, or archived (older) issues only. The MARKET Library contains hundreds of periodicals which you can slice and dice in a variety of ways. It gets pretty complex. If you sign up with LEXIS-NEXIS, you get documentation and training to help you figure out the most focused approach for a particular search.

- **Dow Jones Interactive:** In the Publications Library: Click Change Publications. Then, under **Publications by Industry**, select any or all of the broad industry categories shown.

The indirect approach

Competitive intelligence doesn't always come neatly packaged as *news*. You've heard of private investigators — some of them quite legitimate — who go through people's garbage or hire on as office workers or custodians to see what they can pick up. Don't worry; you won't be doing any dumpster-diving or undercover lurking here. But you can employ equally indirect methods to find out more about what the competition may be up to. For instance, you can

✔ **Monitor the patent databases** (see Chapter 11) to see what new technologies they may be exploring or planning to exploit. Search for the company as patent assignee, and include patent applications, for their early-warning value, as well as patents actually granted.

✔ **Check** *Commerce Business Daily* to discover any government contracts the competition has been awarded. CBD is on the Web at `cbdnet.gpo.gov/`, and is also available on a subscription basis at `cos.gdb.org/repos/cbd/`. Subscribers to that site can set up an automatic monitoring service and get daily updates. You can also search CBD on Dialog (Files 194 and 195), LEXIS-NEXIS (EXEC Library; CBD, CBDARC or CBDCUR files), and in Dow Jones Interactive's Publications Library.

✔ **Set up a current-awareness profile** on the Web or any of the proprietary online services to which you subscribe. New information on the company you're investigating is delivered to your e-mail box or waiting for you next time you log on to the site or service, without your having to re-run the search yourself.

  • In Chapter 13, I show you how to set up a Web-based alerting service on general news and business information sites such as NewsPage (`www.newspage.com/`).

  • On Dialog Web (`www.dialogweb.com/`), check the Help file topic Creating an Alert.

  • In LEXIS-NEXIS, type **sav** at the conclusion of a search and then follow the instructions to activate an **Eclipse,** or electronic clipping service.

  • In Dow Jones Interactive (`www.djnr.com/`) click Custom Clips to read all about it.

Competitive intelligence is serious business for many companies — both start-ups and long-established organizations. If you've taken on the responsibility, either on your own or on behalf of your employer, consider joining the Society of Competitive Intelligence Professionals (`www.scip.org/`). You can find out a lot more than I can possibly show you in this chapter.

Doing Market Research

What's market research? Is it that person with a clipboard in the mall, asking you whether you prefer the blue package or the red one? Is it a focus group where someone pays you $50 for your candid reaction to various scenarios and trial balloons? Is it the warranty card you fill out when you buy an electric toothbrush, or the questionnaire you're faced with when you register for a gated site on the Web?

Market research encompasses all of those activities, and more. Such efforts to measure and quantify consumer response are only a small part of the picture. Market research also includes:

✔ Industry overviews and background

✔ Surveys and descriptions of products and their manufacturers

✔ Product reviews

✔ Research and development

✔ New product introductions

✔ Competitive rankings and market share information

✔ Supply and demand indicators: production, shipments, imports and exports, and sales

✔ Overall market size in dollars or units sold

✔ Historical data, forecasts, and trends

✔ Market segments — how much to what kinds of customers

✔ Distribution channels

✔ Advertising and marketing strategies

What do the topics in the list above tell you? That you've changed your mind about tackling a market research project at all? Hang in there; I'm going to give you some shortcuts to make it a lot easier than it may look right now.

One thing that list indicates is that market research is concerned with *products and services* as much as, if not more than, with individual *companies*. In that way, market research is a change from the kinds of business research covered earlier in this chapter.

Another thing the preceding list suggests is that market research has a lot to do with numbers: quantitative information that takes time and money to compile. Your mission, if you choose to accept it, is to figure out how to get hold of the figures you need without re-inventing the wheel by going out and compiling it yourself. Hint: I can help.

Why do market research?

✔ Market research is a good first step in a competitive intelligence effort, helping identify the key and emerging players that you need to keep an eye on.

✔ Market research can overlap with CI, making sure you keep a broad picture of the industry in focus at the same time that you're monitoring your main competition.

✔ Market research can help you decide whether there's room in the marketplace for a new product or service.

✔ Market research can help you identify new opportunities — and warning signs, too —

as consumer tastes and market conditions change. Plow those tobacco farms into hemp fields, Mr. Marlboro Man.

✔ Market research provides quantitative information that you can plug into a business plan and use as the basis for revenue projections, mid-course corrections, and long-term strategic decisions.

✔ Market research is essential for convincing banks and other potential lenders that your business plan is sound and that they can expect to see a return on their investment.

Surveying sources for market research reports

Most of the market research information you find online is based on in-depth studies conducted by corporations, consultants, trade associations, investment analysts, and (duh!) companies that specialize in producing market research studies.

These in-depth studies, some of which were prepared originally as customized reports for a particular corporate client, are typically based on interviews with scores of industry sources or thousands of individual consumers, supplemented with the analyst's own proprietary research contacts and deep professional insights.

For all that service, you won't be surprised to hear, you're going to pay big bucks.

But you can find ways around shelling out dollars in the three-, four-, or even five-figure range (the going rate for many market research studies) for a report that may or may not tell you what you need to know. Here I introduce you, quickly, to some sources for packaged market studies online. Then I show how to save money by using precise database search techniques to extract from secondary sources (trade journals, published report excerpts, newspapers, and industry newsletters) exactly the facts and figures you need.

Next to news and technology info, market research is one of the most abundant forms of information online. But except for data on the growth of the Internet itself, you won't find more than a handful of good, detailed, current market research reports on the open Web. Remember, somebody paid a lot of money to collect, compile, and analyze all that data. They've got to recoup their investment. And they're not going to give it away.

For high-quality market studies, look to the gated sites and proprietary online services I introduce you to in Chapter 9. They allow you to search for reports that deal with a particular industry, product line, or individual company; you can browse a table of contents before buying to judge whether the entire report, or just the most relevant sections, is worth purchasing. Read about some of the major market research report suppliers in the next three subsections.

Investext

Investext (www.investext.com/) offers reports from more than 60 market research firms through its MarkIntel service. (See the section, "Planning a Competitive Intelligence Operation," earlier in this chapter to read more about Investext.) You can view reports online and download them in Adobe PDF format.

Investext reports are also available through Dialog (File 545) and Dow Jones Interactive. On Dow Jones, click <u>Company and Industry Center</u>, or the <u>Company</u> tab at the top of any page, to get to Investext company reports from investment analysts. Click once more, on <u>Industry/Market Research</u>, to access both investment reports and the MarkIntel collection.

DialogWeb

Dialog on the Web (www.dialogweb.com/) features a database category called **Market Research Reports Fulltext.** To get there, click <u>Databases</u>, and then <u>Business and Finance</u>. You can search the dozen or so files that comprise this category, either individually or as a group, or in any combination. Keep a hand on your wallet, though; remember that you can generally buy by the page instead of having to spring for the full report.

Profound

Profound (www.profound.com/), an online service that specializes in fulltext market research reports, is owned by M.A.I.D., a U.K. market research firm. M.A.I.D. acquired Dialog recently, and indications are that reports from Profound will be available on the Dialog service. Stay tuned, and in the meantime, check the Profound Web site for an indication of what that service has to offer.

LEXIS-NEXIS

The LEXIS-NEXIS (www.lexis-nexis.com/) MKTRES library includes reports from many of the same market research firms as you find in Investext, as well as other major U.S. and U.K. suppliers like Find/SVP, Freedonia, Frost & Sullivan, Business Communications Company, Nielsen, Packaged Facts, Datamonitor, and Euromonitor. For details on how to set up your account and get the required software, check the LEXIS-NEXIS Web site.

Before plunging into a market research spending spree, spend some time with the online Help files and database documentation on whatever service you've selected. Full-text market research is expensive, and you need to know the tricks that let you zero in on the sections that discuss market share — or whatever topics you're specifically interested in — and browse tables of contents before you buy.

Getting more for your money with secondary sources

I call myself a general researcher — I can handle just about anything *except* chemical structure searching. (A person's gotta draw the line somewhere.) But, to tell you the truth, 75 percent of the projects I've done over the years have been market research-related.

A typical client research request goes like this:

> I need to know the market for fountain pens. I've heard they're coming back, and people are even collecting them. How big is the market? How much has it grown in the last five years? What's the market like internationally? Who are the major manufacturers, and how much of the market does each of them control? What are the main retail outlets — stationery stores, department stores, gift shops, mail order? Why are people buying them; what in particular do they like? What's the outlook for the future?

Now that I've introduced you to Investext and those other grand and glorious sources for market research reports, I'll pull you up short by saying: I don't use them that much. Unless a client has specifically in-structed me to find *one* good, comprehensive study — and is willing to pay for it — I start from an entirely different angle. I use those massive database collections of business and industry periodicals that I mention in the section on competitive intelligence (see the section, "Planning a Competitive Intelligence Operation," earlier in this chapter).

Here's why: Market research firms release key findings — not necessarily all the details, but some good solid numbers — to writers and editors for those trade and general business publications. They do it to market *themselves,* to entice readers to buy the complete report, and maybe because they're good guys and want to contribute to the store of knowledge on the planet. Yeah, right.

In any event, I know that each of these trade and business databases uses standardized terminology or a set of codes and concepts that enable me to look for precisely the market data I need, for the product, service, or industry I'm interested in — and to retrieve whatever's available, regardless of what market research firm produced it or what publication reprinted the excerpts I'm hoping to find.

Digging into Dialog

I usually start with Dialog, because it allows me to use all those specialized database features in combination with its own powerful search language.

In **PROMT** (File 16) I can use Product and Event Codes to specify exactly what I'm looking for. These codes are cascaded, which means that when you enter a short code like **395 (Pens, Pencils and Related Equipment)**, it picks up all the more specific subcategories that begin with that number. I can enter **PC=395103** to search specifically for fountain pens. A broader category, **3951**, includes all kinds of pens and mechanical pencils. I may use both categories in this search, or even fold in the topmost **395** category. I can include the phrase **fountain pen(s)** to make sure that any general pen-market studies classified at the 395 or 3951 level do at least mention them.

Event Code 6 (which I search as **EC=6**) includes all kinds of market information — production, shipments, sales, orders received, and more. I can enter a more specific code like **EC=65** to focus on sales and consumption data only.

I can also use Dialog's **Limit** command (L/) to restrict my results to just the last couple of years. And, if I'm only interested in the U.S. market, say, or western Europe or Japan, I can limit using country and regional codes (like **4FRA** for France) to eliminate results from elsewhere in the world.

My search on the fountain pen market in PROMT looks like this (**ss** tells Dialog I'm entering a search term; read more about Dialog search language in Chapter 9):

```
1. ss pc=395103 or (pc=3951 and fountain()pen? ?)
2. ss [combined results of step 1] and EC=6
3. L/[combined results of step 2] 1996:1998
4. L/[combined results of step 3] 4FRA
```

Figure 12-4 shows some of the results, in brief form, for this search.

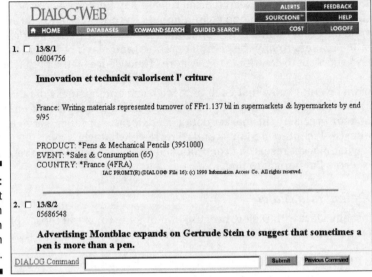

Figure 12-4:
Market
research
results in
PROMT on
DialogWeb.

PROMT's sister file, **Trade and Industry Database** (File 148), is also an excellent source of market research information. Recent records in T&I are indexed with PROMT's product codes so that you can easily search both databases at the same time. I like to include T&I's own indexing terms as well: Phrases like **Pen Industry — Marketing** do the job just fine.

Another set of siblings, **Business & Industry** (File 9) and **TableBase** (File 93) provide equally precise searching plus some unique sources and subject coverage. You search B&I much the same way you do PROMT, using product, concept or event, and geographic-type codes and terminology. The database includes a range of international business and industry publications, many of which PROMT doesn't cover.

TableBase is designed for hard-core number-junkies, people who want the cold, raw data without a lot of verbiage and explanation. You can search by industry, product, or service using the same codes as in the Business & Industry database, and specify exactly the kind of quantitative information you want to see — time series, market size forecasts, price trends, sales, and so on. Figure 12-5 shows just the facts, ma'am, for mass market sales of writing instruments and other stationery supplies.

Doing it with Dow Jones

I like Dow Jones Interactive for market research because the publications are pre-selected for their value and organized into industry categories that make it easy to select the ones that are most relevant for a particular search. Because of this up-front effort on Dow Jones' part, I don't have to spend as much time constructing a search with codes and keywords as I do

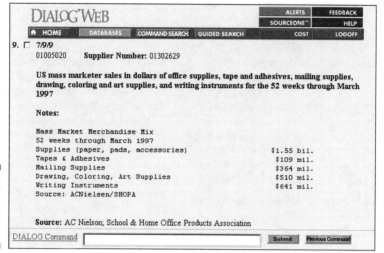

Figure 12-5:
Market data
from
TableBase.

on Dialog. I go to the **Publications Library,** click change publications and, under **Publications by Industry** — assuming I'm still on my quest for fountain pen market information — click to select the **Retail and Consumer Goods** category. I can go on to choose individual publications within that category, but this time I elect to search the entire group. I enter a simple search strategy (see Chapter 9 for more about the Dow Jones search language) and come up with a couple of promising-sounding items, shown in Figure 12-6. I click the titles to read the full text, and find just about everything my client wants to know.

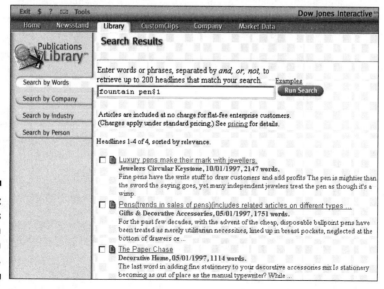

Figure 12-6:
Dow Jones
search on
the fountain
pen market.

Trademarking your new product

One important step in the market research process — after you've established that the idea is a "go" and before you've launched the big ad campaign — is to come up with a product name that's clever, memorable, and irresistible. Naming consultants charge big bucks to come up with winners like *Exxon, Telesis,* and *AirTouch.* Of course you can do better. No offense, but so could a roomful of monkeys typing at random.

But creative naming is only part of it. You're not going to launch a multi-million-dollar advertising effort — or even a multi-dozen-dollar one — without first making sure that the name you want is *available,* that is, that it's not owned or in use by somebody else.

I'm talking about *trademark searching.* You can do your own using the **Trademarkscan** databases on Dialog. The producer of Trademarkscan, Thomson & Thomson, offers trademark searching to subscribers — plus a lot of useful information about trademarks and intellectual property — on its Web site (www.thomson-thomson.com/).

Trademark searching, like anything else that involves money, identity, and pride, presents some quirks, wrinkles, and hoops-to-jump-through. A few important concepts to keep in mind are:

✔ **Degraded, phonetic, or cutesy spellings:** When it comes to trademark searching, **Quick = Qwik = Kwic.** The Trademarkscan database is smart enough to know this and builds at least the obvious equivalents in.

✔ **Embedded sounds or word-strings:** Trademarkscan allows you to search on a distinctive element that may appear anywhere in a word: **RECOR, PRECOR, TRECOR,** and so on.

✔ **Turning up an identical or oh-so-similar mark isn't necessarily the kiss of death.** Trademark law is based on the possibility of confusion in the consumer's mind. **Acme**

Scientific Instruments is no threat to **Acme Candy Company**, and vice-versa. (At least I hope not, but in this litigious society, who can be sure?) Use Trademarkscan's **Goods and Services** field to restrict the name you're researching to a category of relevant products and applications. Consult an intellectual property lawyer if you have any doubt. **Lexis**, the legal research firm, and **Lexus**, the car manufacturer, got into a trademark tangle a few years back. Some observers felt that, since the automobile might appeal to attorneys, there was indeed a potential for confusion. Ya never know.

✔ **No law says that names have to be trademarked.** It's stupid to gear up for production and actually get a product out there without registering its name. But many businesses, especially small regional ones, operate without protection of trademark for their *company* names, if not the products they manufacture. If you want to be sure of avoiding conflict with someone who might sue to protect a business name they thought of first, check business directories, professional magazines, and journals. A Web-wide search engine is great for picking up mentions of names that may not be trademarked but that could cause you problems because they were in use *first.*

✔ If you do find a conflict with the name you want, use Trademarkscan's **Status** field to discover whether the mark is active or abandoned. Each database record includes contact information for the trademark holder; so, if you really want to use a name that's registered to someone else, you can get in touch and negotiate. This works best when the trademark holder hasn't yet established a brand of his own. Don't try it with Marlboro, Ivory, or Black & Decker.

Prospecting for Sales

People often talk about sales and marketing in the same breath: *salesandmarketing, marketingandsales.* They may go together like a horse and carriage, but they're really two different things. Marketing is strategic; you do *market research* to identify where and how you want to advertise and promote your product or service. Sales is tactical, hands-on. Once you've identified a potential market — consumers at a particular income level, certain kinds of businesses — you focus more closely: get a list of people, families, or firms that meet your criteria, and start calling, writing, or dropping by.

Getting and screening that list of potential customers is called *sales prospecting,* and you can do it online.

At the consumer level, your best bet is to deal with a reputable mailing list broker who can generate a list of prospects — usually on labels, for a direct mail campaign — at a reasonable cost, often for no more than a few cents a listing. That's also true if you're contemplating a mass mailing to hundreds or thousands of businesses. You can find mailing list houses and direct mail firms in your local yellow pages, or online; check Yahoo!'s <u>Business and Economy:Companies:Marketing:Direct Marketing:Direct Mail:Mailing Lists</u> category, for starters. American Business Lists, Dunhill, and D&B — yes, *that* D&B — are a few that I know are reputable.

Yes, it *is* possible to harvest peoples' names and contact information directly from the Web, either from white page listings, site directories, or public discussion groups. I don't recommend it, unless of course you're looking for a particular individual or seeking to reach a highly-targeted group with an established interest in the type of product or service you're selling. Why do I discourage searching for sales prospects on the Web? Partly because gathering such listings is time-consuming, and the information is often out of date. But mostly because bulk e-mail — the way most online marketers logically decide to reach their prospects — can be incredibly annoying. It's known as *spam,* and it deserves the bad reputation it's developed. Companies are a different story, though, especially when you plan to contact a relatively small number of them individually, and your research has shown that they may actually be interested in what you have to offer.

Say you're a supplier of industrial shelving, and you want to find grocery and specialty food stores in your region to sell to. Or you manufacture a fine line of doggie chew-toys in your basement workshop, and you're looking for local pet stores that may want to carry them. Or you've developed a small business accounting software package that companies with one to five million dollars in annual sales would glom right onto, if only you could identify them. Or maybe you're a management consultant, seeking to promote your fine services to companies with a thousand or more employees, anywhere in the western U.S. You get the picture.

In Chapter 4, I show how you can use online business directories like BigBook (www.bigbook.com/) to locate certain kinds of businesses, such as banks, hardware stores, or pizza parlors, in a given geographic area. That approach works for sales prospecting, too, as long as you know the nature of the business you want to reach and can limit your prospects to certain cities, states, or regions. You get street addresses and phone numbers, and the maps and driving directions are a nice touch if you're planning to call on your potential customers personally.

But what if you've got broader or more subtle customer-screening criteria, like the management consultant or software developer I mentioned a couple of paragraphs back? You'd happily sell to anyone, regardless of their location or line of business, as long as they're a match — size-, revenue-, or otherwise — for your service or product.

Looking for prospects with CompaniesOnline

Way back in the Company Backgrounder section, I mention CompaniesOnline (www.companiesonline.com/) and its **Search by Criteria** feature. Instead of entering the name of a particular firm in the form shown in Figure 12-7, and retrieving a company profile as I did last time around, I can look for prospects using any or all of the following criteria:

- ✔ **Industry:** The pull-down menu gives me a choice of a dozen or so broad industry categories — **Manufacturing, Food & Clothing, Computers & Software, Travel & Transportation,** and more. I can select **ALL** if I don't want to restrict my search to a particular kind of business. For more precision, I can select the **Browse by Industry — Drill down into Sub-categories** option at the bottom of the page. That lets me refine my search from the too-general **Food & Clothing** category down to **Retail Food Stores.**

- ✔ **Annual Sales:** I can select from a series of ranges, starting with $0 to $99,999 and ending with a billion dollars or more.

- ✔ **Number of Employees:** I can target companies with a certain size workforce, starting with nine or fewer employees, and going up to 10,000 or more.

- ✔ **Location:** I can specify a city, or a state, or neither.

The main drawback to using CompaniesOnline for sales prospecting is on the output end: The list you get gives you just the company name, city, and state. You have to click each company name to get its complete mailing address and phone number. Of course, you pick up other useful information in the process, such as the number of employees and a contact person's name. But if you're dealing with several hundred prospects, this clicking-and-collecting can get tedious.

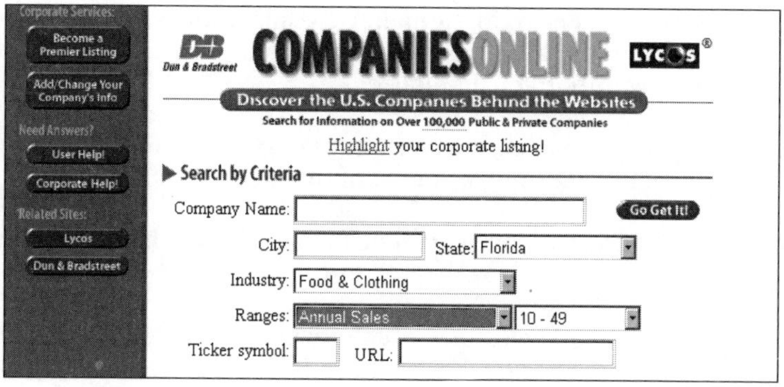

Figure 12-7:
Criteria
screening
with
Companies-
Online.

Have I got some alternatives for you.

The Dun's-on-Dialog alternative

The same Dun & Bradstreet database used by CompaniesOnline is also available, in a variety of packages, through the Dialog online service. Dialog's **Report** feature lets you

- Screen companies
- Sort them by criteria such as size, location, type of business, or alphabetically by name
- Select the elements of each record you want to display, such as name, street address, and phone number
- Generate a neat listing, in table form, of prospects

As a bonus, D&B on Dialog offers you much more precise screening criteria:

- Instead of just Retail Food Stores, you can use SIC (Standard Industrial Classification) codes or standardized line-of-business descriptions to specify supermarkets, convenience stores, butcher shops, fish stores, produce markets, candy stores, bakeries, health food stores, or what have you.
- You can target your search geographically, not just by city or state, but by county, metropolitan area, telephone exchange or area code, or zip code. You can even screen for cities of a certain population size.
- You can screen for — or screen *out* — branch locations and sole proprietorships.

Of the D&B databases on Dialog, Dun's Electronic Business Directory (EBD) (File 515) is the most complete and cost-effective for sales prospecting. It covers more companies than Dun's Market Identifiers (File 516) and Million

Dollar Directory (File 517), though it gives less information about each one. You can't screen by sales figures in EBD, but you *can* ask for — or eliminate — firms with fewer than ten employees.

For Canadian companies, check Dialog File 520, and for international coverage, File 518. D&B Europe, a subset of the international database, is File 521.

Dow Jones Interactive subscribers can use D&B WorldBase for international coverage.

For mailing lists and sales prospect screening, my friend — and business researcher *extraordinaire* — Mary Ellen Bates is keen on D&B Marketing Connection (www.dnb.imarketinc.com/), which provides more power and flexibilty than the freebie CompaniesOnline — at a fraction of Dialog's cost.

Investigating Investments

I'm timid when it comes to the stock market. I don't exactly keep my money under the mattress, but government-backed securities are about as risky as I want to get. I do have a lot of foolhardy . . . uh, investment-savvy friends, though, and they use online resources for everything from preliminary research on a potential investment to actual trades, portfolio-tracking, and Monday-evening-quarterbacking with fellow investors.

Taking stock

Investment information is easy to come by online. Dozens of Web sites purport to be your ideal pathway through the maze of stocks, securities, mutual funds, futures, IPOs, and dozens of other ways of losing your shirt — I mean, ensuring a comfortable retirement. Because I'm neither a committed investor nor a very knowledgeable one, I look for a site that (a) isn't too strongly associated with a particular brokerage firm or style of investing, and (b) gives me a lot of information in one place — not just recent and historical stock and money market quotes; but business, investment, and economic news, screening and analytical tools, expert opinions, investment tips, and links to other useful sites.

Daily Stocks

Stephen Tondreault, a CPA with McNulty, Garcia and Ortiz in St. Petersburg, Florida, first pointed me to Daily Stocks (www.dailystocks.com/), a downright folksy site, without a hint of a hidden agenda, that also happens to be awesomely comprehensive — way more so than its name implies.

In addition to the categories of information it bring up, Daily Stocks offers links to information on mutual funds, tech stocks, and futures, plus stock screening services. I can also get news headlines, today's corporate filings direct from the Securities and Exchange Commission, information on the U.S. economy, and columns by well-known investment analysts and advisors.

If I enter a company name or ticker symbol (the combination of letters that identifies the company on the stock exchange) in the Daily Stocks search form, I get an even more detailed range of choices, including dozens of sources for current, even real-time, quotes, plus moving averages, earnings estimates, stock split and dividend data, charts, analytical tools, figures that I can download into a spreadsheet, and a whole lot of other stuff I'll leave to my more sophisticated, and undoubtedly on-their-way-to-becoming-wealthy, friends.

Daily Stocks offers me some cool tools for general business research, too, including company profiles, income statements, and trade magazines and newspapers.

Dow Jones better-than-average

If you follow the stock market — or have read Chapter 9 — you know that Dow Jones is a major player in business information, especially when it comes to investments.

Other investment research starting points

Daily Stocks may be _too_ much information for the beginning investor — I know I feel a little woozy every time I visit. And you may not want to open an account with Dow Jones Interactive right away, especially if your interest in the stock market is as casual as mine. That's fine; you can check out a few even easier entry-points:

Yahoo! Finance (quote.yahoo.com/) offers neatly categorized financial news, headlines, stock reports, and other features, including investment reference tools.

TheStreet.com (www.thestreet.com/) gives you a magazine-style format, a running stock ticker, and links to online trading.

FinancialWeb (www.financialweb.com/ index.html) is a lively-looking place that features investment news headlines, columns, analytical tools, and links to major indexes and quotations.

Wall Street Research Net (www.wsrn.com/) claims half a million links to company research, stock screening, market and economic news, publications, brokerage firms, and other investor resources. Subscribers can download full-text brokerage reports from Multex.

InvestorGuide (www.investorguide. com/) includes some excellent background information on personal finance and investing, along with the standard links to stock quotes, investment research, and news.

The Dow Jones Interactive Web site (www.djnr.com/) is home to the <u>Historical Market Data Center</u>. Click on that link when you first enter the site — remember: you have to sign up with Dow Jones in order to get access — or on the <u>Market Data</u> tab from anywhere once you're inside. Use the pull-down menus and boxes to select the kind of report you want (Pricing History, Dividend, or Capital Change), the type of security (U.S., Canadian, or international stocks or market indices; government debt. bonds, mutual funds, options, or unit trusts), pricing intervals and duration, currency units, adjustment for stock splits and other events, and finally — pant, pant — the format of the report itself.

I like Dow Jones because I'm just a mouseclick or two away from information that helps me make smarter investment decisions, including Investext company and industry reports, hundreds of business journals and news sources, and of course *The Wall Street Journal.*

Digging deeper

Many of the sites I've just mentioned lead you to sources of detailed information on individual companies and industries. Don't overlook the ones we looked at earlier in this chapter — Dow Jones Interactive, Investext, and the other full-text research reports available through Dialog and LEXIS-NEXIS. In addition, PR Newswire (www.prnewswire.com/) features an **Investment Profiles** section — complete with tables, graphs, and downloadable reports in PDF format — for several dozen of its client companies.

America Online's **Company Research** section (you can use Company Research as the keyword to get there) includes current and historical stock reports, financial statements, earnings performance and estimates, company and market news, and Securities and Exchange Commission filings. You can also find personal portfolio management tools and a link to online trading, plus a handy dictionary of Wall Street terms.

Here's EDGAR

Speaking of the SEC (Securities and Exchange Commission), you've got to meet EDGAR. I haven't introduced you until now because so many of the other business research resources in this chapter link to him — I should say *it* — or utilize its data. EDGAR, or Electronic Data Gathering Analysis and Retrieval, is the electronic publishing arm of the Securities and Exchange Commission, which regulates the affairs of publicly traded U.S. companies in the U.S., the conduct of brokerage houses and other investment agents, and various other kinds of investment activity.

Public companies are required by law to disclose certain kinds of information to the SEC. This includes annual reports, proxy statements, and excruciatingly detailed financial reports of one sort or another, all of which are described on the SEC site (`www.sec.gov/`). These forms and filings, eye-glazing as they may seem, are packed with information of interest to potential investors. If you don't find what you need at the company's own Web site or at one of the business research or investment mega-sites I've described so far, EDGAR's your boy . . . er, site. He's a little fussy — it helps a lot to know what you're looking for, the exact name of the form, and of the fund or company you're researching. But he's thorough. EDGAR can help you retrieve any or all filings for a particular company, or run certain kinds of specialized searches, using pull-down menus.

EDGAR is a man . . . I mean, site, of many talents. For instance, a company filing an Initial Public Offering (IPO) with the Securities and Exchange Commission is required to disclose "risk factors," which can provide valuable industry insights for competitive analysis and other kinds of research. Get to know him — okay, *it.* EDGAR may be a business researcher's best friend.

Getting personal

I'll just bet you know somebody who's deeply into the stock market and can't wait to share (mild investment pun there) his or her hot tips. Your dentist, your brother-in-law, your neighbor down the block. Sure, you may get rich. You might also get burned.

The online world is full of amateur investors, and some of them even know what they're talking about. The way I look at it, there's safety in numbers. When you tap into an online investment discussion group, you get the benefit of many people's opinions, not just one. They can't *all* be wrong, or *all* be trying to sell you something — can they?

misc.invest

You want opinions? Newsgroups give you opinions — both informed and off-the-wall. The **misc.invest** hierarchy (see Chapter 10 for more about newsgroups, how they work, and what they can do for you) is where you go to eavesdrop on people who are talking about investments. Subgroups include **misc.invest.financial-plan, misc.invest.futures, misc.invest.mutual-funds, misc.invest.options, misc.invest.real-estate,** and **misc.invest.stocks** — among others. The latest edition of the **misc.invest** FAQ, a veritable encyclopedia covering all aspects of personal finance and investment — and a surprisingly slick document for a FAQ — is at `invest-faq.com/`. Before you plunge into a **misc.invest** discussion, invest some time in the FAQ.

The Motley Fool

The Motley Fool — despite its name — is probably the best-known online hangout for serious personal investors. It got its start on AOL, and is still accessible there (keyword: **fool**), but the Fool's now at home on the Web as well. The site (www.fool.com/) looks like a magazine, and offers some links to pre-packaged content such as stock quotes, news, and financials. But its main claim to fame is the value that human insight brings to the investment game, and the give-and-take among participants in its various forums. Don't miss the Fool FAQ, which will answer many of your investment questions without making you look foolish.

If it weren't for the personal touch — the touch of *many* persons, not just the two guys who started Fooling around in the first place — which sets it apart from the investment mega-sites I mention earlier in this section, I would have placed the Fool right up there as a starting point. Instead, I've saved the best for last. The Fool's motto is "to educate, amuse, and enrich," and that's almost enough to convince me to change my ultra-conservative investment ways. In fact, come to think of it, I *do* have a little extra this month. . . .

How Do You Manage?

I ask myself that every day. Seriously, effective company managers are constantly on the lookout for new techniques for improving their operations. Journals such as *Harvard Business Review* (www.hbsp.harvard.edu/frames/groups/hbr/index.html); the publications of the American Marketing Association (www.ama.org/pubs/index.html); traditional business magazines like *Forbes* (www.forbes.com/), *Fortune* (www.pathfinder.com/fortune/) and *The Wall Street Journal* (www.wsj.com/); and new-wave periodicals like *Fast Company* (www.fastcompany.com/), *Upside* (www.upside.com/), and *Red Herring* (www.redherring.com/) are full of ideas for innovation, change, and corporate fine-tuning.

If you're already in the habit of reading management periodicals that speak to your business and professional development needs — or feel like visiting publication Web sites like the ones I've mentioned, and browsing to see what bright ideas you can pick up — great. Well, not *great*, but okay.

But suppose you're grappling with a sticky accounting issue, or trying to implement a new benefits policy, or preparing for some major new initiative, like turning your company into a learning organization, or instituting a knowledge management program? You may pick up some insights in the course of your regular professional reading, but wouldn't it be useful to have just a few more data points — to know how other companies have faced similar challenges and dealt with them successfully? Sure it would.

My favorite one-stop source for strategic management information is a database called **ABI/Inform,** which is up on Dialog as File 15. ABI/Inform includes articles from hundreds of business and management periodicals, both general and industry-specific, worldwide. It covers subjects like employee recruitment and training, human resource policies, labor relations, production planning, quality control, facilities management, office automation, purchasing, data processing and MIS, finance and accounting, product development, marketing, and advertising. Whew.

You can research specific management topics in a certain industry (such as telecommunications or retail sales) or across all kinds of businesses, through a combination of standard keywords and codes. You can restrict your search to particular geographic regions, or to types of organizations: multinational corporations, small or minority-owned businesses, non-profits, or the public sector. You can specify the kind of information you're interested in, such as case studies of specific companies, broader surveys and reviews, statistical data, theoretical discussions, or interviews with management personnel.

If I want to see how companies in the financial services industry deal with management compensation, I can enter:

```
1. ss cc=8100 [financial services industry] and executive
        compensation
```

If I want to restrict my results to U.S. companies, I can add:

```
2. ss [combined results of step 1] and cc=9190
```

Depending on how much I'm getting (at this point, ABI/Inform has retrieved about 50 items for me to look at) I may want to limit my search by date to make sure that I'm getting the freshest data available:

```
3. L/[combined results of step 2]1997:1998
```

When I run this search, ABI/Inform gives me four good hits. I can browse them in a brief format (8) by typing:

```
t/8/all
```

To read the complete text of the third article, say, I tell Dialog that I want to see it in format 9:

```
t/9/3
```

This may seem like a lot to go through, but for managers in search of practical answers, it's not much effort at all. And in practice, running a search through a massive database collection such as ABI/Inform takes far less time than trying for equivalent results on the Web.

Chapter 13

Read All About It: News Media and Publications Online

*W*e're surrounded by news. It's on the doorstep when we go out for the morning paper, on the radio as we drive to work or school. During the day, our friends and colleagues talk about the latest out of Washington, Detroit, Silicon Valley, the City Hall crowd downtown, and in their own neighborhoods. We pick up weekly newsmagazines like *Time* and *Newsweek* at the corner newsstand, or from a co-worker's desk. At night, the evening news blares out of the TV. Maybe we go for one last recap before bedtime. Folks with satellite dishes or the right cable connection can watch the news 24 hours a day, from other cities and time zones around the country and the world. 57 channels, I hear you saying, and nothing on. Sometimes that's true, but you don't want to hear *my* rant about how the media's unflagging appetite can manufacture a big deal out of nothing; you've probably got a similar rant of your own. But when something important *is* happening, nothing compares with broadcast news, or the deeper coverage you get from a good daily newspaper. Nothing, that is — except online.

In this chapter, I start with the online equivalent of news the way you're accustomed to getting it — network news sites and the electronic editions of newspapers and news magazines. Then I lead you through some sources for finding a particular newspaper, tracking down stories from back issues, and digging into news archives to research people, stories, and events that may have made news months or years ago. I do the same for magazines. Finally, I wrap up with a glimpse at how the Net is changing the way we receive — and even think about — the news.

Chapter 12 shows you the value of online newspapers and magazines in business research, investigating companies, products, and industries. My own files are full of examples of research projects that I could not have completed successfully without searching magazines or newspapers or both:

- The recreational maze craze of a few years back, for an entrepreneur trying to decide whether to construct one of his own
- Local tastes in fresh-baked bread, and how it varies from city to city
- Accidents involving golf carts
- Coverage of a small, privately-held biotechnology company in Emeryville, California
- Background on a person who claimed to have no assets, but who showed up in the society pages as a lavish spender
- How banks market a new consumer investment product
- Various cities' experience with a certain shopping center developer
- Reviews of the same movie in different regions
- Identify reporters and writers assigned to the alternative energy beat, so my client could pitch a story idea of her own

Broadcast News

If you follow the news on TV, you probably prefer one network over the others. Your preference is probably based as much on style as on substance. Maybe you love Peter and hate Dan, or can't stand either of 'em, but can tolerate watching Tom (feel free to substitute your own names and combinations). Perhaps you watch CBS because the ghost of Walter Cronkite (who?) still hovers over the set. Or maybe you just think ABC's graphics are cooler than NBC's.

Each TV news program has its own look and feel. Content-wise, however, one may occasionally scoop the others on a breaking story, but by the time you've rolled through a news cycle or two, they're all covering pretty much the same events.

On the Web, network news sites look a lot like news magazines — but with the added value of real-time headlines crawling across the screen, new features added throughout the day, and the ability to search previous issues and dig up background on the crisis *du jour*.

Check out the following network news sites, for starters, and bookmark the one (or, for you hard-core news freaks, the *ones*) that you prefer.

Tuning in to the Big Three: ABC, CBS, and NBC

ABC News (www.abcnews.com/) offers breaking news headlines and in-depth stories in categories like Travel, World, Entertainment, and Sports. If the story you're looking for isn't right there at the top of the hour, you can search ABC News' multimedia archives by word, name, or phrase. Need to turn up a video clip of Monica Lewinsky? Want to judge for yourself whether Kathleen Willey was telling the truth? Want to see what Ken Starr looks like so you can avoid him at the next Washington party you're both invited to? (Can you tell what the hot story was when I was writing this chapter?) Just go to ABCNEWS.com and click <u>Search</u>. Then enter your terms, specify the sort order and how many items to display, and check the boxes for the media type — Video, Sound, Images, or Text — that you want to retrieve.

For a more linear look at ABCNEWS.com's offerings, click <u>Contents</u> and get a listing of recent stories, organized by general category, such as **World, U.S., Business, Science, Technology, Living, Entertainment, Sports,** and **Travel.** I can browse the **World** listings, click on a headline like **U.S. Eases Cuba Sanctions,** and read a detailed background story, complete with pictures.

CBS (www.cbs.com/) makes a bid to be your local news site by asking for your zip code the first time you visit — and spotlighting local affiliate content every time you log in thereafter. If you'd rather (no pun intended, Dan) view your news through the national lens, you can skip this step.

The content and organization of the site is closely tied to CBS programming. Click <u>CBS News</u> and then select your program from the pull-down menu. CBS gives you background reporting and some multimedia options. You want the video from last week's *60 Minutes?* No problem — assuming you've got the right web browser plug-in installed.

The **NBC News** site (www.nbc.com/), labeled MSNBC, is a joint venture between NBC and Microsoft. You get headlines, the option to scan **Quick News** — short blurbs on major stories — and your choice of stories in clickable categories such as **Commerce and Technology.**

NBC's Local News feature enables you to choose a region from a map and tune in to the NBC affiliate in that area, which is especially cool if you want broadcast news from your own city or somewhere else in the U.S. If you're a Windows 95 or NT user, you can get instant updates on topics of your choice using MSNBC's specialized News Alert software. (In the section, "Staying Current," later in this chapter, I show you some other automatic news update options.)

Viewing some other contendahs: CNN, Fox, C-SPAN

CNN (www.cnn.com/) gives you a choice of top news headlines and stories you can scan by category, all on the same page. Coverage of individual issues is deep, with lots of hyperlinks to background and related stories. You can search the CNN site using the Infoseek search engine.

Fox News (foxnews.com/) gives you headlines, too, plus background features arranged by category, a search function, and video for selected stories.

C-SPAN (www.c-span.org/) is for obsessive news-hounds and people who enjoy watching grass grow. The C-SPAN site mirrors its broadcast sibling, with coverage of congressional sessions and other stirring events. Watch Senate appropriation hearings in RealVideo, if that's your thing. C-SPAN's archives do include some interesting background documents and original source material on events currently in the news. When I last checked the site, they were featuring in-depth coverage of topics such as the **Situation in Iraq, Investigation of the President** — enough, already — and **Campaign Finance Hearings** ("Watch 41 of the tapes of Democratic National Committee Events, in their entirety." How can I resist?).

Getting the story worldwide

Much like CBS, the Canadian Broadcasting Corporation (CBC) site (www.cbc.ca/) is closely tied to its broadcast programming. You can click on Newsworld or go directly to its URL (www.newsworld.cbc.ca/) for scrolling headlines, summaries of top national and international stories, and in-depth background on topics of eternal interest, such as El Niño, the Middle East peace process, and Diana, Princess of Wales.

The British Broadcasting Corporation, or BBC (news.bbc.co.uk/), has always been a sterling source for news from an international perspective. I can listen to the famed BBC World News — a special audio edition produced for BBC Online — while I pretend to work.

News AND weather and sports

If you're a serious sports fan, you almost certainly know about ESPN. If you're a serious sports fan who's traveled *anywhere* online, there's a very good chance you've already visited ESPN's online home (ESPN.SportsZone.com/). If not, meet me back here in half an hour, okay?

The SportsZone is a one-stop gateway to real-time scores and other sports news as it happens, plus after-the-fact reports, analyses, breast-beatings, and lamentations. ESPN covers *all* sports — women's college basketball, fantasy leagues (they're not the same thing, guys), soccer, golf, tennis, auto racing, sailing, skiing, and so on. My sports consultant tells me they're weak on rugby and Australian rules football — but so's most of the world.

To tell you the truth, the only reason I sit through the sports segment on TV — unless the Giants are in the playoffs — is to get to my favorite part of the news: the weather report. As far as the Web is concerned, the Weather Channel owns not only the domain — www.weather.com/ — but the highs, the lows, and the entire range of meteorological forecasts and phenomena.

Weather is headline news, especially in an El Niño year, tornado season, or a winter marked by heavy snowstorms. You can program The Weather Channel site to show you your local weather whenever you log in. Or check the outlook for cities you're planning to visit, or to see what your friends up in Montana or out on the coast are having to put up with. You can also get special reports, such as ski conditions, allergy season, and aviation weather for pilots. The Weather Channel covers international weather as well — click <u>International City Forecasts</u>, and then choose your country from the pull-down menu and your city from the resulting list.

Newspapers Online

Newspapers online are even closer than your doorstep — assuming you've got a computer at home and it's not in some obscure corner of your attic or sub-basement. You don't have to freeze delicate body parts or get rained on while retrieving the daily web edition, and you won't have to scramble to get it out of the bushes or off the roof when the delivery person's having a bad arm day.

I don't think that reading the morning paper on the Net will ever replace the convenience of saving your favorite section, neatly folded, to peruse at your leisure on the bus or in some other, more private venue. Besides, what would you use to line the catbox? But it's handy to be able to scan the headlines and catch up with your favorite columnists online, especially when you've been out of town or missed a day.

Online newspapers (and magazines, too) offer some features you don't get in print — bonuses like *The New York Times* Cybertimes section, forums where you can talk back to journalists and debate with your fellow readers, searchable archives of back issues, and links to background information and other content that didn't make it into print for space or other considerations, but for which the Web edition has plenty of room.

Most of the online papers I've seen make an effort to emulate the graphics and section-by-section organization of the paper-and-ink original. The New York Times on the Web (www.nytimes.com/) uses the same familiar typeface and Gothic flag as the Great Gray Lady herself. Other major papers, such as *USA Today* (www.usatoday.com/), *The Washington Post* (www.washingtonpost.com/), and the *Los Angeles Times* (www.latimes.com/) look a lot like their print selves, too.

Appearances aren't supposed to matter, but the more the electronic version of a publication looks like what you're accustomed to, the easier it is to find your way around it. That's why I'm not making a big deal about how to interact with newspapers on the Web. You scan headlines, browse through sections, and read what catches your eye, just as you would in print. If you want to look for particular topics in current or past issues, you enter search terms just as you do in a general Web search engine, and scan the results the same way. See Chapter 3 for the basics of search engine searching.

City newspapers, large and small, are superb sources for in-depth information on events, and companies, in that region. You may not live there, but you can visit — and research — remotely. Consider the *LA Times* for movie industry coverage, for instance, and *The Washington Post* for inside-the-Beltway political news and gossip.

Finding your local paper online

If your daily newspaper is committed to a presence on the Web, you probably know about it already. If not, check the business section for promotional ads, or look for that telltale **www** on the masthead or in the tiny type that tells you how to get in touch with editors in various departments. Still nada? The newspaper mega-sites described in the next section can help you track down your daily newspaper.

Journalists' choice

AJR NewsLink (www.newslink.org/) has the professionalism of the respected *American Journalism Review* behind it. It offers links to both print and broadcast news sources, including college newspapers, alternative papers such as the *San Francisco Bay Guardian* and New York's *Village Voice;* magazines of all kinds, and other regional, national, and international categories. You can just drill down through the appropriate category to find the news source you want by type or region.

AJR NewsLink offers several different search options, too:

✔ You can do a keyword search of the site itself to locate links to particular publications or broadcast outlets.

✔ You can search the actual content of publications at several specialized news mega-sites, including NewsIndex and some of the others in the section, "Searching newspapers on the Web."

✔ You can search the entire Web using any of several leading search engines.

All the news, from everywhere

TotalNews got in some trouble a while back for linking to major news sites all over the Web, and framing their content so that it looked like it originated with TotalNews. Other news site owners were perturbed, to say the least. The issue has apparently been resolved, and it looks like TotalNews is going to stick around, which is good news as far as I'm concerned, because it provides a great service.

For a lead on your local news outlets — broadcast as well as print — go to `www.totalnews.com/` and click US Local, and then browse by state, or click on a state abbreviation. For international news, click World News, and then choose a region or click on the first initial of a country for sources in that area. Often the source is in the local language.

The TotalNews site is searchable, too. The archive of recent stories includes content from many gated sites that wouldn't turn up in a Web-wide search engine search.

Newspapers and more online

The name may seem straightforward, but Newspapers Online (`www.newspapers.com/index.html`) doesn't stop there. If you're a seeker-after-obscure-publications, you can appreciate this site's surprisingly broad scope. The streamlined, low-graphics pages offer links to classified ad papers (you may know them as shoppers' specials, pennysavers, or classified flea markets), ethnic and minority publications, religious periodicals, plus some titles that are both esoteric and weird. If you can't find it anywhere else, you may just find it here. Newspapers Online doesn't offer either site-wide or cross-publication searching, but that's not really its purpose. It's a thorough, well-organized guide to both essential and elusive publications on the Web.

Searching newspapers on the Web

The sites I survey in the preceding section are *pointer* sites. Their main mission is to point you to the web site of the individual newspaper you're hoping to find. Such sites are a good first stop when you're trying to track down your hometown paper or locate one in another region or in some specialized field. Many of these sites are comprehensive catalogs of newspapers and other news resources worldwide.

A different breed of newspaper mega-site focuses on finding the news, regardless of where it appeared originally. These *search* sites may not cover as many publications as the *pointer*-type sites in the preceding section, but if you care more about what's *in* the news than about a particular paper's perspective *on* the news, try one of the following sites first:

- ✔ **NewsLibrary** (http://newslibrary.infi.net/) enables you to search any or all of about three dozen newspapers, some going back as far as the 1970s. All are listed by geographic region, along with the extent of their archives. NewsLibrary gets a research gold star for better-than-average documentation. Pull-down menus make it easy to search NewsLibrary for any or all of your terms, do a phrase search, or use advanced features, such as Boolean searching, proximity operators, and wildcards (see the Bonus Appendix on the CD or click <u>Help</u> at the site for more about how to use these options). You can also limit by publication date, sort by date or relevance, and set a cap on the number of articles you want to see. Searching in NewsLibrary is free, but you need to get a *library card* and pay — usually $1, more for a couple of papers — to download the complete text of stories.

- ✔ **NewsHub** (www.newshub.com/) is light on actual newspapers, but it does cover news sites all over the Web. With updates every 15 minutes, it may be the freshest news mega-site around.

- ✔ **NewsBot** (www.wired.com/newbot/), *Wired* magazine's entry in the news-searching field, is a spin-off of the HotBot search engine. NewsBot is tailored to search general and international news, business, technology, and other specialized news sites. Coverage is pretty shallow — a week or so back — for most sources, but NewsBot includes more than two dozen major newspapers, as well as wire services, trade publications, and broadcast news sites.

- ✔ **NewsIndex** (www.newsindex.com/) features hundreds of U.S. and international newspapers, including *The New York Times, The Boston Globe, Vancouver Sun, Times of India*, and *South China Morning Post*. Coverage is limited, though, to today's edition only.

- ✔ Excite's **NewsTracker** (nt.excite.com) is a direct route into the Excite search engine site's **News** channel. NewsTracker features top news stories, headlines from Reuters and UPI, ongoing coverage of major stories, and links to newspapers and other news sites. Its master list of searchable sources (click <u>Sources</u> to see it) includes not only newspapers worldwide, but also an assortment of popular, business, and special-interest magazines on the Web.

After all this, the burning question I'm left with is: When are they going to run out of names beginning with **News___**?

The Electric Library, described in the section, "Search *for* and search *of*" later in this chapter, offers yet another channel into web-based newspaper searching.

Going deeper into the archives, part 1

Many, if not most, newspaper Web sites offer some sort of searchable archive. It may go back a few days, a week, a month, or as far as several years. You may have to register and/or pay a fee to search, or to search back beyond a certain point, or to retrieve the actual stories behind the headlines you've browsed.

Don't count on cover-to-cover completeness. Some archives include certain feature articles, bylines, or sections of the paper, and exclude others. Some index the Web version of the paper and ignore, or only occasionally pick up, stories that only appeared in print.

If you really need in-depth, comprehensive coverage, the only place you're guaranteed to get it is through a proprietary online service. LEXIS-NEXIS, Dow Jones Interactive, and Dialog all offer huge databases of full-text articles from hundreds of newspapers and other news sources, U.S. and worldwide. You can search any of them singly, or as a group or regional subgroup, or hand-pick your own assortment.

Individual titles go back years — in the case of *The Washington Post* on LEXIS-NEXIS, for instance, as far back as 1977. (The *Post* is no slouch on the Web, either; its archives there go back to 1986, which is highly unusual for a web publication.)

The content of these heavy-duty databases reflects what appeared in the actual printed newspaper, unlike the Web, where you often get a mix of print and electronic-only stories, or only stories that appeared in the Web edition and not necessarily in print. Using sources equivalent to the printed publication is important for research projects with legal implications, or whenever you're trying to be as official and comprehensive as possible.

Proprietary databases let you restrict your search by date, byline, dateline, or words that appeared in the title or another element of the article. You can also search a group of newspapers by region without having to specify their individual names. And you can do all this, and cover multiple papers at once, much faster and more efficiently than you can on the Web.

These are my starting points for searching newspapers on the leading proprietary services:

✔ On LEXIS-NEXIS, search the News Library and the MAJPAP (Major Papers) or PAPERS file. For international news in the language of the country, search the NONENG file, or specific country sources — NIEUWS (Dutch), PRESSE (French), ZEITNG (German), STAMPA (Italian), or MEXPUB (Spanish). At the LEXIS-NEXIS web site (www.lexis-nexis.com/), click Products & Services, and then select from the broad categories under **News/Business Sources** to get an idea of the publications that can be searched on their own or as part of a larger selection.

✔ On Dow Jones Interactive (`www.djnr.com/`) click <u>Publications Library</u>, and then select either **Major News and Business Publications** or **Top 50 U.S. Newspapers.** To customize your selection, click <u>change publications</u>. Then choose **Publications by Type,** followed by **All U.S. Newspapers.** Or choose **Publications by Region,** followed by the national, international, or regional grouping you want. Click on Add to include the entire category in your search, or click on any category or subcategory name and pick individual publications from the resulting list.

✔ On Dialog, search the **PAPERS** or **PAPERSNU** file (the latter covers U.S. newspapers added to the service since March 1997), or PAPERSMJ for major U.S. papers. Or select a regional grouping such as PAPERSNE for the Northeastern U.S. or PAPERSCA for all California newspapers. Search individual newspapers, whether U.S. or international, by their Dialog file number. For a list of newspapers on Dialog, go to `www.dialogweb.com/`, click <u>Databases</u>, and then <u>News and Media</u>, and finally a subcategory such as <u>Newspapers Fulltext</u> or <u>General News Sources</u>. Drill down another level or two for individual publication names and file numbers.

I Saw It in the Dentist's Office: Magazines Online

News comes in many guises — not always neatly packaged as a headline in today's or last week's newspaper or news magazine. What's news to *you* may have appeared anywhere — in a month-old magazine you meant to save but didn't, or a 2-year-old copy of a publication you don't even subscribe to.

In Chapter 8, I explain how professional *document delivery* services can track down an article from just about any publication, as long as you've got *some* idea of when and where it appeared. Professional document delivery firms typically scour the earth, or at least the earth's libraries, for articles in obscure scholarly journals or ancient issues of more popular magazines.

You can do your own document delivery — at least up to a point. Most mass-market magazines, like the kind you find at the supermarket or your corner newsstand, have, by now, set up a home on the Web. Typically, these Web magazines include feature articles from the current issue, perhaps some supplemental, cyber-edition-only copy, and a searchable archive of back issues going back a few months or, if you're lucky, years.

A Word about wires

Wire service bureaus around the world specialize in reporting breaking news stories and following up as they develop, around the clock. Wire stories often appear in printed newspapers and on news media Web sites. You can find coverage from U.S. and international wire services such as the Associated Press (wire.ap.org/), United Press International (www.upi.com/), Reuters (www.reuters.com/), Agence France Presse (www.afp.com/), the Russian news agency TASS (itar-tass.com/), the Japanese wire service, Kyodo (home.kyodo.co.jp/)

and mainland China's Xinhua (www.xinhua.org/).

Some wire services do provide stories and updates right at their site. Others don't provide direct feeds to non-clients, or require you to sign up for the service, or redirect you to a member newspaper or other subscriber site so that you can take your feed from there. Considering how easy wire service reports are to come by, I'd rather take them as I find them, at other news media sites — unless, of course, I have a reason to seek out coverage from a specific one.

You want newsmagazines? Check out these sites for starters:

- ✔ *Newsweek* (www.newsweek.com/) or keyword: **newsweek** on America Online
- ✔ *Time* (www.pathfinder.com/time/)
- ✔ *U.S. News & World Report* (www.usnews.com/usnews/home.htm)
- ✔ *The Economist* (www.economist.com/)

Locating magazines online

How do you find a particular publication online, or determine whether an electronic edition exists? I've got a few suggestions.

Take a guess

You can always try guessing a publication's URL the same way you can look for a company's Web site. If it's a multiword name such as *Business Week* or *Popular Science,* try running it together with a *.com* at the end: www.businessweek.com or www.popularscience.com (I'm not guaranteeing that either of those will work).

No go? Try hyphenating it — `www.business-week.com` or `www.popular-science.com`. Still no luck? Okay, think *abbreviations,* and give it one more shot: `www.busweek.com`, `www.popscience.com`, `www.popsci.com`. Don't get carried away; be sure to stop while you can still see straight.

And don't be surprised if you don't come up with anything. (*Now* she tells me!) If you do happen to hit it in the first couple of tries, using your intuition really is the fastest way. However, some magazines don't have their own separate address on the Web; instead, they're part of their publisher's domain. You'll find that especially true of some groups of trade publications, and journals published by professional associations.

Do a search

If the periodical's name is distinctive enough, or you can combine it with words from its *full* title such as **magazine** or **journal,** try running it through Infoseek, Excite, or another general search engine. **Database** alone isn't such a hot prospect, but **Database Magazine** may get it.

Or try Yahoo!'s subject guide approach: Starting with the <u>News and Media</u> category, drill down through <u>Magazines</u> to the subject you want to cover. When I click on the <u>News</u> subcategory, I find some of the usual suspects like *Time* and *U.S. News & World Report,* plus many international periodicals, and some web-only publications, such as the *Drudge Report* (more about *that* one in the "Zine Scene" section at the end of this chapter).

Check a media mega-site

Several of the newspaper mega-sites I describe earlier in this chapter do a pretty decent job of tracking magazines online, too. If you have a particular publication in mind, check the <u>Magazines</u> link at AJR NewsLink (`www.newslink.org`) first.

Looking for something more esoteric? Try the <u>E-Journal</u> site (`www.edoc.com/ejournal/`), which is actually a branch of the World Wide Web Virtual Library (a venerable institution that I describe in Chapter 5). E-Journal lists Web-based publications in all the categories shown in Figure 13-1. Start at the top and drill down, if necessary, to get to a list of titles, with a brief description for each. Click on a title, and click once more on its URL to transport yourself to the publication's own site. E-Journal offers a keyword search option, too, which I'm sure would be handy, but every time I tried searching, even for a publication I already knew was listed, I got the message No Matches Found. Despite that glitch — which may be fixed by now — the E-Journal site is a valuable resource.

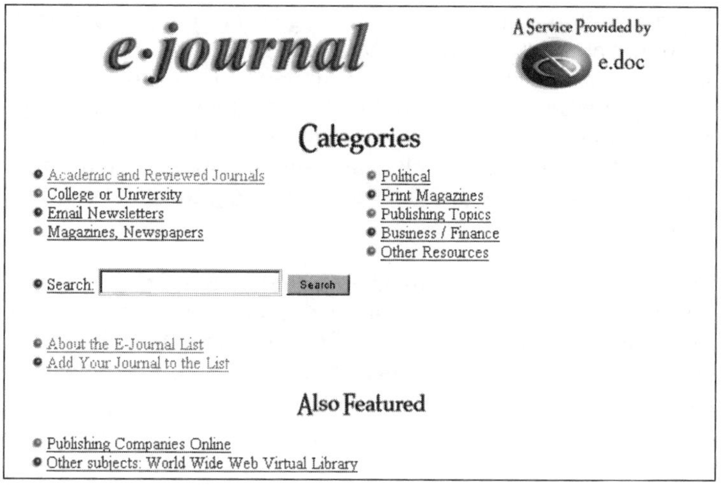

Figure 13-1:
E-Journal
category
list.

Peer into print

One of the best sources I know for determining whether a publication is online *anywhere* is a print directory called *Fulltext Sources Online* (FSO). FSO covers not only magazines, but newspapers, newsletters, wires, and broadcast transcripts. Published twice a year, FSO tells you whether the publication is available on the Web or on a proprietary online service, such as Dialog, Dow Jones, or LEXIS-NEXIS. For proprietary services, it tells you the month and year of the earliest issue available. For Web editions, it indicates whether a free archive exists or not. FSO isn't cheap, but as a subscriber, you also get access to a private section of the publisher's Web site at www.bibliodata.com/ where you can look up and link to those publications that have free archives on the Web.

Another print publication, *Net.Journal Directory,* covers much of the same territory, for Web-based periodicals only. Check the site (www.nasw.org/users/larryk/njdn.htm) for details.

Search for and search of

Say what? That's my succinct yet confusing way of introducing the Electric Library, a hybrid site that allows you to locate publications and search them at the same time. The Electric Library collection includes newspapers, wire services, and hundreds of magazines, ranging from professional publications like *American Demographics* (a great example of how to make statistical data fun — I'm not joking!), *China Business Review, Machine Design,* and *Training & Development,* to *Bicycling, Mother Jones,* and *Sports Illustrated.* For a complete listing, navigate to the Electric Library site (www.elibrary.com/) and click on a **Source Type** — magazines, newspapers or what-have-you — for a complete list.

You can do a Boolean or natural language search of the Electric Library collection, and sort the results by date or relevance. You can restrict your search by type of publication — magazines, books and reports, newspapers and newswires, and so on — and by broad subject category — business, health, politics, a couple of dozen in all — as well as specific keyword and date. You can search for specific elements or fields, such as author, title, or the name of a particular publication. Click <u>Help</u> to get more detailed hints for effective searching.

Suppose that I'm interested in whether baby boomers are still influential in the marketplace. I ask Electric Library to find articles about boomers, and I select **Business** on the **Specialized Content** menu. I get 30 promising references from such publications as *Business Week, Fortune, Money,* and *Nation's Business*.

Electric Library is a subscription-based site. You can try it out for free, or sign up for a 30-day trial. After that, the cost is $9.95 a month or $59.95 per year. This fee is a good deal for the casual researcher, especially when you consider that you can easily spend $60 for a single search of a general periodical database on a proprietary online service.

Speaking of proprietary services, the Electric Library is a bridge, as both a directory and a searchable collection of periodicals, between the locator sites we've visited so far and the heavy duty research databases I talk about in the very next section. Look out; here it comes.

Going deeper into the archives, part 2

So far, most of what I've described in this chapter is *information-gathering* — the kind you do every day when you leaf through the paper, catch the news on radio or TV, or burrow through the recycling pile looking for that article you meant to save last week. But what I've described is not really *research*. Random news-gathering and article-lookups is very different from tracking down elusive or historical information in a vast collection of periodicals when you're not even sure of the source.

Go back and reread — assuming you read it in the first place — the section, "Going deeper into the archives, part 1," about searching newspaper archives on proprietary online services, as opposed to searching them on the Web. If you haven't read it before, read it now. Everything I say there applies equally to magazines, journals, and other kinds of periodicals, too.

Proprietary services enable you to

✔ Go way back in the archives — many years, instead of a few months.

✔ Cover dozens, or even hundreds of publications, at the same time — including many that you can't search on the Web.

✔ Use special system and database search features that you won't find on the Web.

✔ Search faster and more efficiently.

✔ Search publications you not only don't subscribe to, but may not even have *heard* of. Though you can do this through the Electric Library and some of the news search megasites I've mentioned, services like Dialog, LEXIS-NEXIS, and Dow Jones Interactive provide a much broader and more complete selection.

In Chapters 11 and 12, I talk about tapping into databases of periodical literature in fields such as business, science, and engineering. If you're curious about the full range of publications available through any of these proprietary services, visit their Web sites and browse through the database and source listings.

For general news, current events, and popular magazines, though, you can find the greatest concentration of hits in these databases:

✔ On LEXIS-NEXIS, select the News Library, and then the MAGS and/or NWLTRS (newsletters) group file. Or select any of the individual publication files shown onscreen or listed in the printed *Directory of Online Services* (which you receive as a subscriber to LEXIS-NEXIS).

✔ On Dow Jones Interactive (www.djnr.com/) click Publications Library. Select Major News and Business Publications on the following screen. You can search the entire category or select individual titles. To search periodicals in a particular industry, click change publications. On the next screen, select **Publications by Industry** from the pull-down menu. Choose an industry grouping by clicking Add, or click the industry name to select individual titles within that group. If you want to search more popular, mass market, or special-interest magazines, click change publications, then select **Publications by Type** and finally **General Interest Publications.** You can click Add to search the entire category, or on the category name to select individual titles.

✔ On Dialog search **Magazine Database** (File 47), **Periodical Abstracts PlusText** (File 484), or **Readers' Guide Abstracts Full Text** (File 141), individually or in combination. For broad coverage of companies, products, markets, and management issues, check Trade and Industry Database (File 148) and the other business databases I describe in Chapter 12. Dialog also offers a huge variety of magazines and journals in technical, scientific, and other specialized fields. You can browse the entire collection on Dialog Web (www.dialogweb.com/) at no charge. Click Databases, and then select News and Media, and then Journals and Magazines or Journals and Magazines Fulltext. For coverage of business, trade and technical periodicals, select any of the industry-specific categories such as **Technology, Pharmaceuticals,** or **Food and Agriculture,** or the general **Business and Finance** division. Drill down to your desired level of specificity to browse databases pertinent to your field.

Staying Current

In library-land, we used to call them SDIs. In Ronald Reagan's '80s (*1980s*, I mean) those letters came to mean Strategic Defense Initiative. Imagine the confusion. But in a way, that's not so far off. The boring fact is that SDI originally stood for *Selective Dissemination of Information.* Ooo-eee; now *there's* a phrase you want to set to music and dance to. All it means is getting the right information to the right person at the right time — for defensive *or* preemptive use.

Today, we talk about *automatic updates, current awareness,* and the hyped-'til-it's-dead *push technology. Push* simply means that instead of you having to seek out databases or Web sites and check them periodically for updated information, the information is automatically delivered — *pushed* — to you. As I said, *push* is not a new idea. Dialog's Alert feature, LEXIS-NEXIS' Eclipse, and Dow Jones' Custom Clips have been providing push service for years.

E-mail is the easiest and most common form of push delivery. Hundreds of Web sites have jumped on the push bandwagon and now offer automatic delivery of new content — feature articles, columns, software, multimedia clips — filtered according to an interest-profile that you've set up in advance. You receive new pages, usually as HTML-coded documents, and you open and look at them — offline, if you prefer — in your browser's mail program or another HTML-compliant e-mail reader. For more information, you can connect and click through from the page you've been sent to additional content on the site.

Another delivery option involves logging into a special area of the publisher's Web site where new information that matches your personalized profile is stored. Other options are even more sophisticated, notifying you through a window or other signal on your desktop when you've got an update waiting — or even downloading new information automatically so that you don't have to go pick it up.

Sometimes the same site offers you a choice of delivery methods. Sites that provide push service — I still prefer SDI; it sounds so seriously geeky — usually advertise it prominently. They seldom use the word *push,* though; that sounds a little impolite, I guess. Instead, look for tip-off phrases such as *My Page, Personal Edition,* or *Custom News Alert.*

The real trick to staying current is selecting a service that meets your needs — for both content and delivery method. In this section, I outline just a few of the many options available to you.

The Daily Brief

The Daily Brief is nothing fancy. It's a plain ASCII text — no HTML — news-sheet that shows up in e-mail every business day. Supported by sponsors and voluntary contributions, the Brief presents a concise summary of world, national, business, entertainment, and sports news. When I don't have time to read the paper, I rely on the Daily Brief. To subscribe, send a message to **subscribe-db@incinc.net**

In-Box Direct

Netscape offers In-Box Direct, a one-stop subscription service for Web publications and other regularly-updated sites. Each new issue comes to you in e-mail, as an HTML-encoded Web page, direct from the publisher's own site. You can get

- Daily news summaries from ABC, CNN and *The New York Times*
- Customized news from My Yahoo! and other services
- Sports and entertainment updates from CBS Sportsline, Disney.com, *People,* and *TV Guide*
- Travel discount bulletins
- Notices of sales and specials at Internet shopping sites
- Business and personal finance newsletters
- Computer news, reviews, and advice — including tips from *Dummies Daily*
- Reports from diverse online venues, such as parenting support groups, and gay and ethnic communities
- A selection of global content from Africa, Australia, Europe, Latin America, and Asia

To sign up for the service, go to www.netscape.com and click In-Box Direct. Walk through the registration process and select the sources and services that interest you. Within a few days — depending on their publication cycle — you'll start receiving your e-mail updates.

NewsPage

NewsEdge, a company formed by the merger of two pioneering Net-news delivery services, offers NewsPage (www.newspage.com/), a subject-oriented approach to keeping current. You register at the site, then create your personalized edition by selecting from broad categories, such as

Business, Internet, or **General Interest.** Within each category, you can add or delete specific topics, fine-tuning your profile to pick up mentions of particular industries and even individual companies. The information you receive is drawn from hundreds of sources, including local, national and international newspapers and newswires, general business and specialized trade journals, and professional publications.

Basic NewsPage service is free; you build your personal interest profile, and then click My NewsPage whenever you visit the site for fresh content on the topics you've specified. For $6.95 a month, the Premium service delivers daily personalized updates via e-mail as well as holding them for you in your private area on the NewsPage site.

NewsHound

NewsHound (www.newshound.com/) focuses on information from newspapers in the Knight-Ridder chain, including the *San Jose Mercury News, The Miami Herald, The Philadelphia Inquirer,* and about a dozen others, plus wire service stories from AP, Reuters, and several business newswires. NewsHound is a sister of the NewsLibrary megasite described earlier in this chapter. Neither one is a dog.

You can train your NewsHound to sniff out predefined topics or keywords. Unlike most other news update services, NewsHound actually lets you construct a detailed search strategy using your own search terms, which produces more focused results than simply checking off categories and topics. You can increase precision even more by limiting your retrieval to stories ranked with a high degree of relevance, or to certain sources only. If you like the *Mercury News* coverage of Silicon Valley and other high tech topics, why waste your time plowing through stories from other publications?

Once you've created your profile, NewsHound scours the Net on a regular basis and brings back stories for you to look at. You can do so by logging in to your own private area of the NewsHound site. Or you can take delivery in e-mail — either HTML or plain text. A sum of $7.95 a month or $59.95 a year buys you up to five separate profiles, with no limit on the number of stories NewsHound can retrieve.

PointCast

PointCast (www.pointcast.com/) is for people who are serious about staying on top of things. The service delivers customizable news, weather, sports, and stock quotes from major news sources. The twist lies in *how* it delivers it. You download the free software, install it, and then watch PointCast take over where your flying toasters or psychedelic swirls used to be. That's right — PointCast's updates replace your screensaver, kicking in whenever you walk away from your machine. Uh, wait — what's wrong with this picture? No, really, that's the way it works; but you can read your PointCast updates any time you like, including scheduled off-peak hours, even when you're offline.

PointCast is cool, but it's a resource hog as well; it consumes a major share of computer system resources, to the extent that many companies have had to restrict or even ban its use. If the idea appeals, try it out and decide for yourself.

The Zine Scene: New Sources for News and Information

Not all online publications are replicas or special editions of something that first appeared in print. The Net has given rise to thousands of brand new periodicals that have no counterpart in the ink-and-paper world. These online-only productions are often referred to as electronic magazines, e-zines, or just *zines*.

Breaking news on the Net

The Internet is a global network — people are online 24 hours a day, seven days a week, exchanging news and information. Although some national governments have made efforts to control the flow of information into and out of their countries, the Internet is essentially a borderless network, too; when something big develops anywhere in the world — a war, a mass rebellion, a natural disaster — word travels around the Net almost instantaneously. During both the Persian Gulf War and the Chinese uprising in Tiananmen Square, the first news reports, and some of the best and most immediate continuing on-the-scene coverage, were carried over the Internet. Word spread, worldwide, in minutes. Newsgroups picked up early reports and promulgated them around the Internet. By the time conventional print and broadcast media got hold of the story, it was old news to many Net denizens.

Similar phenomena can happen locally, too. Northern California, where I live, has had a pretty rough time of it in the last few years,

with fires, earthquakes, and floods. I've found that I can log on to The WELL, my regional online community, and get the equivalent of a standup reporter on the scene — *many* reporters, in fact, each with a unique perspective on what's going on.

No way can I anticipate what may happen, or tell you where you should be standing — figuratively speaking — when disaster strikes. If a stock market crash is disastrous news for you, you can log on to the Motley Fool or one of the investment newsgroups in Chapter 12. If a natural disaster occurs, a local online pub — the WELL is that kind of hangout for me — is the logical place for folks to gather. Wars and civic disturbances play out in political newsgroups and forums all over the world.

The message is: When big news happens, don't just turn on your radio or TV. Try logging on to the Net and get the full, chaotic, unedited story, as it's unfolding. And come to your own conclusions about what's really going on.

Net publishing is cheap, especially compared with what it takes to reach a mass audience in print. Anyone with an opinion to express or a philosophy to further can rent server space and put a few Web pages out there for all the world to see. The Net is democratic that way, and much of its self-published content is refreshing, if not always reliable.

These three sites give you a taste of the alternative press, Net-style:

The Drudge Report (`www.drudgereport.com/`) is notorious for breaking hot political stories that may not always be firmly based in fact. Matt Drudge — that's his real name, apparently — does his own reporting, and also provides links to other popular columnists and commentators around the Web. He also links to an extensive list of wire services, major newspapers, and news-and-analysis magazines. Drudge is worth bookmarking for his outrageousness and occasionally valid scoops; his links to other top media sources are a bonus.

Salon (`www.salonmagazine.com/`) features solid background reporting by professional journalists on issues currently in the news, plus incisive analyses of the media itself and how it covers the issues. Regular columnists, feature articles, book, theater, and music reviews; and letters from readers — all contribute to a substantial package that feels very much like a *real* magazine. I subscribe to Salon's e-mail updates so that I always know what's new on the site.

The Onion (`www.theonion.com/`) is one of my guilty pleasures. Okay, you *can* subscribe in print, but The Onion really made its reputation online. These recent news headlines give you a hint of what The Onion is like:

> Free-Agent Clinton Signs Five-Year, $37 Million Deal With Argentina
>
> Albanian Village Bombed Forward into Stone Age
>
> U.S. Ambassador To Bulungi Suspected Of Making Country Up
>
> Microsoft Patents Ones and Zeros
>
> Area Twenty-something Disillusioned With Disillusionment
>
> Just-Opened Factory To Create 250 New Jobs, 170 New Cancer Cases
>
> Paula Poundstone Still Famous

Help — I can't stop! It's just too . . . delicious. Yes, The Onion is outrageous, irreverent, and occasionally offensive. I love it. The Onion is my favorite antidote when *real* world news gets to be too much.

Part IV
The Broader Picture

In this part . . .

Maybe you've gotten hooked on finding information online. Or maybe you're resisting even trying — not because it's hard, but because you figure you'll never be able to keep up with all the new Web sites, databases, and other research tools that keep popping up out there.

Not only that — you say to yourself — what about actually *using* all that information? Can I just go ahead and quote or make copies of what I find online, or incorporate it into a paper or presentation of my own? How can I be sure that I'm not breaking the law? And how do I know that the information I've located is worth using at all — that it's accurate, reliable, complete and up-to-date?

No kidding — when it comes to electronic information, plenty of hard and complex issues are still unresolved. This part sketches out some of the questions and challenges you'll run into, and gives you some pointers to help you cope.

Chapter 14

Keeping Up with the Online Jones(es)

. . . .

In This Chapter

▶ Subscribing to electronic updates

▶ Taking advantage of newsletters in print

▶ Getting by with a little help from your friends

. . . .

*J*ust in case you're not up on 1950s underground slang, a *jones* is an addiction. Not to make light of people struggling with real-world substance abuse problems, but the online habit can become addictive in its own way. This problem has been clinically documented and reported, sometimes over-sensationally, in the media. I know folks who are online far into the night and again first thing in the morning. It's not a pretty sight. Given the attractions of the Net, I understand and sympathize. But I can quit anytime. Right.

One of the first things you notice after you've been online for a while is that this thing is moving awfully fast. You can try saying "Slow down, honey" and threaten to fling yourself out the passenger door, but that probably wouldn't be too productive. I've often said that trying to keep up with the cyber-information scene is like changing a tire on a moving car. These days, it's like trying to change that tire while the car is moving *and* the road is still under construction beneath you.

Hardcore Net-addicts aren't the only ones who feel overwhelmed. Unless you're a member of a cloistered religious order, or you've resolved to live off the grid and away from civilization (in either case, I doubt you'd be reading this book right now) chances are that you suffer from information overload as much as I do. Fortunately, you don't have to turn your back on the outside world in order to get some relief. The solution lies in letting others do some of the filtering for you.

Help Is in the Mail: Electronic Resources

Electronic newsletters and other online subscription services are a convenient way to stay current on new developments online. You don't have to do anything. Just sit back, check your e-mail, and read the easily digestible summaries of changes that other intrepid cyber-scouts have discovered. Some of these publications appear weekly, some just monthly, and others several times a week. All the ones I'm about to describe are free.

Prefer to get your information on the Web? Many of these services offer a Web edition, too. All you have to do is bookmark the URL and remember to check in once a week or so.

Don't overlook the *push* option described in Chapter 13 for getting timely notices and, sometimes, actual fresh content from some of the Web sites you visit — or wish you *remembered* to visit — regularly. It's like the difference between subscribing to a magazine and having to remember to buy it at the newsstand.

I try to set aside one day every couple of weeks to follow up on the new sites and other developments that my e-subscriptions (shorthand for electronic subscriptions) have brought to my attention. I mark the date on my calendar just as I would a meeting, deadline, or any other obligation.

Netsurfer Digest

Netsurfer Digest tracks new and interesting Web sites regardless of their research value. Think of it this way: Even the hardest-working information hunter needs a break now and then. The issue that landed in my mailbox a couple of days ago featured sites for the newest dinosaur fossil discovery; updates on urban legends; video reviews; the inside story on what it's like to drive a cab or wait on tables for a living; Classical Greek history, art, and culture; and Scottish slang — plus several dozen others.

Netsurfer Digest's short blurbs are witty and informative. You need to use an HTML-compliant e-mail program, such as the ones that come with newer versions of Netscape and Internet Explorer, so you can click right through from Netsurfer's live links to the sites that they're describing. If you prefer, you can read the current issue or browse the archives on the Web (www.netsurf.com/nsd/). To subscribe to the e-mail edition, click on, you guessed it, <u>Subscribe</u>.

I use a freestanding e-mail program called Eudora Pro 3.0. This version isn't the latest one, but all the links are live, and that's the part that matters. In fact, because it *doesn't* display all the fancy, bandwidth-hogging Web graphics and special effects, it's faster than some fully HTML-compliant mail readers.

Net-Happenings

Net-Happenings makes a valiant effort to keep up with everything new on the Net. It does a particularly good job of tracking serious research sites as well as resources for kids and educators. Notices from Net-Happenings cover

- ✔ General reference sites
- ✔ State, federal, foreign government, and political resources
- ✔ K–12 (kindergarten through 12th grade) resources
- ✔ Sites that have moved or been updated
- ✔ New mailing lists and listservs
- ✔ Electronic magazines, newsletters, and journals
- ✔ Software
- ✔ Internet-related books
- ✔ Conferences in North America and elsewhere in the world
- ✔ Workshops, training, and seminars
- ✔ General information

Net-Happenings subscribers can contribute their own pointers to the list. As you can imagine, that makes for a very active list. To avoid terminal overload, I subscribe to the *digest* version of *Net-Happenings*. Instead of receiving dozens of individual messages a day, I only get three or four, each containing anywhere from a handful to a couple of dozen postings. See Chapter 10 for more about using digest mode for your mailing lists.

To subscribe to *Net-Happenings,* e-mail listserv@hypatia.cs.wisc.edu with the message **subscribe net-happenings** followed by your first and last name. When I signed up, I started receiving the digest version automatically. If you find dozens of messages cluttering up your inbox the first day, send a message back to that same listserv address saying **set net-happenings digest.** If you prefer the newsgroup environment (see Chapter 10 for more about newsgroups), you can follow *Net-Happenings* in comp.internet.net-happenings.

You can also sign up via the Web, or stick around and catch up with *Net-Happenings* there. Go to scout.cs.wisc.edu/scout/net-hap/ and click Today's Articles, This Month's Articles, or Article Archive. The archive is keyword-searchable, too.

New-List

You've got it — a mailing list about mailing lists. *New-List* is for announcements of new e-mail lists and significant changes in old ones. Much of the news in New-List does eventually make its way into other current awareness services like *Net-Happenings*. But if you want to sample the range of what people are talking about online, or you just want to be among the first to know, you can subscribe to New-List by sending e-mail to `listserv@ listserv.nodak.edu`. Leave the subject line blank, and in the body of the message type **sub new-list** followed by your first and last name. To get a weekly digest instead, send e-mail to the same address to which you subscribed, saying **set new-list digest.**

Getting really obsessed with listservs? Listing to port *and* to starboard? You can make sure you haven't missed anything by browsing the New-List archives on the Web (`listserv.nodak.edu/archives/new-list.html`). You can sign up for New-List via that Web address, as well.

Seidman's Online Insider

If you're interested in the companies, personalities, and wheeling-and-dealing behind the scenes of America Online and other consumer online services, Robert Seidman is your man. He's opinionated, well-connected, and a cat person. Recent issues of *Seidman's Online Insider* have covered topics such as Netscape's plans to market itself as an online service, a joint venture between Yahoo! and MCI; and excerpts from *Insider Talk,* Seidman's Web-based conferencing forum for online industry professionals.

I read Seidman for the same reason that I read the business section of my newspaper. The strategizing and maneuvering he describes have a direct effect on the online resources I use now, and the ones I'll be using in the not-so-distant future. For a text version of the newsletter, send e-mail to `insider-text-on@seidman.infobeat.com`. For an HTML version of the newsletter, send e-mail to `insider-html-on@seidman.infobeat.com`.

To unsubscribe from either version, send e-mail to `insider-off@ seidman.infobeat.com`. No subject line or body text is needed for any of the preceding instructions. If your e-mail program requires that something appear in the subject line or body of the message, it doesn't matter what text you enter. As a default, everyone is set to get the text version. If you wish to switch to HTML, use the command I just described to subscribe to the HTML version.

If you prefer, you can subscribe from the Web site, as well. While you're there, you can browse through back issues, or follow the <u>Insider Talk</u> discussions on topics such as The Browser Wars, Electronic Commerce, and Online Services. Don't miss the pictures of Seidman's cat, Brady.

Edupage

Edupage bills itself as "a summary of news about information technology." That may sound kind of ho-hum, but reading it is one of the best ways I know to keep up on some of the larger issues that affect the online realm. Three times a week, I get eight to ten well-written one-paragraph summaries on current topics — current at the time, anyway — such as Internet domain registration fees, proposals to tax the Net, and Microsoft's battle with the U.S. Justice Department.

Edupage's subscription instructions read like this:

```
To subscribe to Edupage: send mail to:
listproc@educom.unc.edu with the message: subscribe edupage
Andrew Carnegie (if your name is Andrew Carnegie; otherwise,
substitute your own name).
```

Edupage follows up with a capsule biography of that issue's honorary subscriber, whomever he or she happens to be. I've learned as much from those gratuitous celebrity bios as I have from the rest of the newsletter. Andrew Carnegie? A Scottish-born industrialist and social do-gooder who was largely responsible for the tradition of free public libraries in America.

For more information about Edupage or to read the publication on the Web or search back issues, check it out on the Web (www.educom.edu/web/pubs/pubHomeFrame.html).

Search Engine Report

The *Search Engine Report* is a monthly e-mail newsletter about new search engines, enhancements, and performance, as well as search techniques and underground trends, such as spamming keywords (loading a web site with hidden words to increase its chances of being retrieved) and pay-for-placement, that may affect your search results. I mention the Report and say more about Search Engine Watch, its Web-based home, back in Chapter 3.

You can subscribe to the Search Engine Report by sending a blank e-mail message — nothing at all on the subject line or in the body of the message — to **join-searchreport@lists.calafia.com.** Or use the sign-up form at the Web site (searchenginewatch.com/list.htm).

This advice may seem woefully obvious, but it's all too easy to overlook those "What's New" announcements, updates, and warnings that greet you when you log on to a Web site or an online service such as Dialog or AOL. Even if you're a frequent visitor and already know where you're headed once you connect, take a moment to check such notices — even if you have to stop and click a link to find out what's new.

Remember Paper? — Print Resources

Your best resource for keeping up with online may be *offline* — a print publication that specializes in pointing out what's new on a particular online service or on the Net at large. One advantage of print is that it's always around, even when you're logged off, reminding you by its very existence that the online world is moving on and that you've got some catching up to do.

Talk about pressure. But I refuse to give in until the pile of professional periodicals on my coffee table has toppled onto the floor at least four times. As long as the pile remains stable, I figure the situation hasn't yet reached the critical point.

System-specific newsletters

If you have an account with one of the major proprietary services, such as Dialog, LEXIS-NEXIS, or Dow Jones Interactive (Chapter 9 talks more about these services), you periodically receive mailings from them — *snailmailings*. Dialog, for instance, publishes the *Chronolog,* where you can read about new databases and take advantage of free-search-time get-acquainted offers. The *Chronolog* also spotlights database enhancements and new system features, offers tips for more effective searching, and announces upcoming changes in pricing, policy, and content. The *Chronolog* is must reading for Dialog users. Some of these publications, or the equivalent information, are available online as well. Check library.dialog.com/chron/ for an example.

The problem with Web-based newsletters is that you have to *remember* to go to the site and read them there. And in fact, some services, including most notably LEXIS-NEXIS, are not only mounting the latest edition of their newsletter on the Web, but moving in the direction of providing e-mail editions, with your choice of plain text or an HTML summary with links back to the full text on the Web.

Independent publications

For staying up-to-date on online developments, one of my colleagues swears by the publications he's always read — periodicals like *The Wall Street Journal* and *Business Week,* and even his local newspaper. His reasoning is that, by the time the news hits those general-interest outlets, it has to be of major importance, and therefore worthy of attention. He's got a heavy-duty information-filter in place, and it works for him. Personally, I'm glad I heard about, and had the opportunity to use, Netscape and Yahoo! before the companies went public.

Print magazines such as *Internet World* and *Wired* are closer to the center of what's happening online. So are the popular PC and Mac publications that occasionally run good feature stories and comparative surveys on online search tools and other resources. Even if you don't subscribe, scan them at the newsstand to see what they're covering, and buy an issue now and then to stay — or *get* — in the loop.

Information professionals rely on several publications to help them keep on top of changes in proprietary online services, research databases, and the Net. For a taste of what these periodicals have to offer, check the Information Today web site (`www.infotoday.com/`) for selected articles from *Searcher* and *Information Today,* and the Online, Inc. site (`www.onlineinc.com/`) for selections from *Online* and *Database* magazines.

My vote for MVP in the paper-based update world is an eight-page monthly newsletter called *The CyberSkeptic's Guide to Internet Research*. It's published by Bibliodata (`www.bibliodata.com/`), the same outfit that produces the guide to electronic editions of periodicals called *Fulltext Sources Online,* which I talk about in Chapter 13. *CyberSkeptic* is written and edited by information professionals who understand the relative strengths, weaknesses, and tradeoffs between professional research databases like those on LEXIS-NEXIS, Dow Jones Interactive, and Dialog, and equivalent (or maybe-equivalent) information on the open Web.

A typical *CyberSkeptic* issue might provide an in-depth profile of a valuable research Web site, such as The Library of Congress, DialogWeb, Hoover's, or Business Week Online; a comparison of Medline on the Web versus the same database on Dialog; brief sketches of useful Net resources in specific fields like Business/Finance, News, Legal/Government, Technical Industries, International, and the Information Industry itself; an article on a new or recently-enhanced search engine or some other research tool; plus editorial picks, tips, and techniques for effective searching. You can see why I like *CyberSkeptic* so much; it thinks the same way I do.

Human Resources

I'll never forget my first glimpse of the multimedia Web. I'd viewed it in text-only mode, using Lynx, the rudimentary browser I talk about in Chapter 1. But one day, my friend Howard Rheingold brought over a videotape from a friend of his in Japan. Joichi Ito had gotten hold of an early version of Mosaic, one of the first graphical Web browsers. We popped the tape into my VCR and I watched, rapt, as Joichi pointed and clicked and moved from page to image-bedecked page.

Kind of weird, huh, watching the Web on TV? Or maybe not — the people behind Web TV apparently think it's a natural. The point is, I found out about the Web from a friend, someone in the know, somebody who knew somebody who was a very early adopter of this new and enthralling technology.

Personal contacts are the best way I know to stay current on what's really happening online — and to distinguish the truly significant new developments from all the marketing hype, wishful thinking, and vaporware that's out there.

I belong to a private professional listserv run by and for members of the Association of Independent Information Professionals. When a colleague speaks up on the listserv about a new search engine, database, or resource on the Web, I listen. The technical forums on CompuServe have long had the reputation for informative, helpful discussions. WELL conferences, especially those devoted to Web technology, telecommunications, virtual communities, and libraries and information services, have been an incredible source of leads on cutting-edge developments in the online research field.

The trick is to hang out with people who are actually working with the new products and services they're discussing. Newsgroups are fertile ground for unfettered first-hand reports. If you're interested in search engines, hang out in `comp.infosystems.search`. Browsers? Try the `comp.infosystems.www.browsers` hierarchy. (For more about reading and participating in newsgroups, look at Chapter 10.) Remember — if you're reluctant to speak up in the public forum, you can always follow up in e-mail.

Whether you're a tax accountant or a graphic artist, a college student or a retiree, listen to your Net-knowledgeable friends. And if they don't volunteer the information, *ask* them. It's amazing what you can find out from a simple "What's new?"

The Researching Online
For Dummies Internet
Directory

The 5th Wave   By Rich Tennant

"It's amazing what a good search engine
can locate. There's your car keys behind
the sink and my ukulele in the basement."

In this directory . . .

This directory represents the best of the best — my own selection of more than 100 Web sites, online services, publications, and other resources that you'll find useful, and in some cases essential, for researching online. Most of these resources play a starring role elsewhere in this book. Here, I've arranged them conveniently by broad category according to what they do or the subject areas they cover.

Use this directory for quick reference, if you need to find a URL and don't feel like paging through the chapters or looking it up on the CD. Use it as a reminder, so you don't overlook any of the major research sites and services you want to factor in to your research project. Use it for inspiration when you want to try a new site or a different research approach. Use it to acquaint yourself with the amazing scope and depth of online research tools. I don't care what you use it for (actually, I can think of a couple of uses to which I'd rather not have you put it; let's just say that anything that involves tearing out the pages is off limits). But *use* it.

Researching Online For Dummies Internet Directory

- -

In This Directory

▶ Staying current in the online world

▶ Finding key resources in business, technology, government, and other research areas

▶ Locating search engines, subject catalogs, libraries, and Internet-navigation aids

▶ Tapping into news, magazines, and other media

▶ Getting up to speed on information quality

▶ Connecting with research pros and other online experts

- -

This directory is a quick and handy guide to some key resources for online research. It includes both general search tools, such as search engines, subject catalogs, and online services, and some more specialized resources in areas such as government, business, news, science, and technology. You also find suggestions for keeping up with the ever-expanding online world, and for assessing the quality of the information you find there.

I divide all these resources into broad categories, and arranged the categories alphabetically. Some of the larger categories are subdivided further, to make it easier for you to find a particular type of resource. Here are the main categories in this directory:

About the Net/Staying Current

Art, Literature, & History

Business, Finance, & Economics

Document Delivery Services

Government & Law

Libraries, Schools, & Universities

Magazines & Journals

Navigation Aids & Organizing Tools

News

Proprietary Online Services

Quality of Information

Reference Books

D-4   The Researching Online For Dummies Internet Directory _____

Research Groups

Science, Technology, & Medicine

Search Engines, Subject Catalogs, & Guides

Virtual Communities & Conferencing Systems

The sites and sources in this directory are just a small sampling of the three hundred or so online resources I talk about in this book and on the CD that's included with it. Reading the rest of the book will give you more ideas about how to use these resources in your real-life research efforts. Don't overlook the three bonus chapters and the Appendix on Boolean searching and other power-research techniques that you can find on the CD.

The CD includes a list of just about all the Web sites referenced in this directory and elsewhere in this book. Each listing consists of the name of the site and an HTML link to its URL or location on the Web. When you read about a site that intrigues you, use your browser's Find feature to look for its name (key in the most distinctive word from the site name for best results) and locate it quickly in the list on the CD. Then, click on the URL and — assuming you are online — connect directly to the site.

I've assigned mini-icons to many of these listings so you can tell at a glance what special features, restrictions, or claims to fame they possess:

This is a search engine site.

This is a subject catalog, guide, or mega-site.

This site (or the service it describes) features searchable databases.

The resource described here is a book, magazine, or other print publication.

Get in touch with experts here.

The site is (or directs you to) a list of frequently asked questions.

The site offers interactive conversations, chat, or other people-to-people contact.

The site offers files for downloading.

The site offers (or points you to) photos, illustrations, or other graphical materials.

The site features sound or video clips, or both.

You must register for access to some or all portions of the site.

$ You must pay for access to some or all of the information at the site.

About the Net/ Staying Current

One of the biggest challenges for researchers is keeping on top of all the changes in the online world. This section includes both print and electronic publications that report on the online industry itself and the companies involved in it; evaluate new research tools and enhancements to older ones; and that provide critical assessments of sites, search aids, and online services. See Chapter 14 for more about staying current on developments in the ever-changing online realm.

CyberSkeptic's Guide to Internet Research

www.bibliodata.com/

The *CyberSkeptic's Guide* is a printed newsletter, published 10 times a year, that evaluates Internet resources from a professional researcher's viewpoint. The publication compares Web sites with proprietary online databases and tells you in no uncertain terms when and why one is superior to the other for finding certain kinds of information. Check the Web site or e-mail ina@bibliodata.com for subscription details.

Database and Online

www.onlineinc.com/

Database and *Online* are like *Time* and *Newsweek* for information professionals. Well, bi-monthly versions of *Time* and *Newsweek,* anyway. Both are print journals published by Online, Inc.

Database focuses on content, whether on the Net, proprietary services, or CD-ROM. *Online* takes more of a systems approach, dealing with online services, new features, and broader information issues. To tell you the absolute truth, I've subscribed to these two publications for more than 20 years now, and I still have a hard time telling them apart. I guess that means I need both. Check the Web site for subscription details and selected articles from both magazines.

Information Today, Link-Up, and Searcher

www.infotoday.com/

Information Today covers the online industry, with opinion columns, product announcements, and in-depth reviews of new and enhanced resources. *Link-Up,* its sister publication, is geared toward do-it-yourself information-hunters rather than professional researchers. Format-wise, both are newsprint tabloids. *Searcher,* the third publication in this trilogy, is a glossy print magazine, and the editorial home of Barbara Quint, online researcher and gadfly *extraordinaire. Searcher* is must reading for most infopros I know. Look at the Web site for sample articles and subscription information.

Net-Happenings

scout.cs.wisc.edu/scout/net-hap/

Gleason Sackman, the man behind Net-Happenings, has been keeping track of Internet-related resources and events since before the rise of the Web. Net-Happenings' coverage of resources for schoolkids and teachers is particularly good, but Sackman's interests, and those of his contributors, range far beyond the K–12 set. You can subscribe and get Net-Happenings via e-mail (often several times a day — it *can* be a bit overwhelming), follow it in the comp.internet.net-happenings newsgroup, or check out the publication on the Web.

Netsurfer Digest

www.netsurf.com/nsd/

Netsurfer Digest reviews Web sites both serious and not-so. Its well-written (and often tongue-in-cheek) blurbs highlight significant developments in the online business, new and enhanced search tools, and destination sites for both research and recreation. Subscribe and get this extensive electronic newsletter (which includes HTML links to all the sites mentioned) weekly via e-mail, or browse to the above URL to read it on the Web.

Search Engine Report and Search Engine Watch

www.searchenginewatch.com

Search Engine Watch is the best way I know to stay up-to-date on the wonderful, and sometimes overwhelming, world of search engines. On the Web site, you can find current information about new search engines and changes to old favorites, as well as detailed, and often critical, performance comparisons. Search Engine Report is the e-mail supplement to the Search Engine Watch Web site. The Report provides periodic updates with HTML links to relevant sites, studies, and special reports. Check the Web site for the subscription how-to.

Seidman's Online Insider

www.onlineinsider.com/

When Seidman's newsletter lands in my e-mail box, it's as if a well-connected friend has pulled his chair alongside mine to share his weekly haul of online-industry gossip. Seidman schmoozes frankly about AOL, Compuserve, and other online services, their brilliant or ill-conceived marketing and pricing tactics, their alliances and enmities, their triumphs and defeats. Best of all, he analyzes what's going on, and tells you what it all means for you, the customer. Browse to the URL to read the Online Insider on the Web, or to subscribe to the e-mail edition.

Art, Literature, & History

The Web is so full of varied treasures — artistic, graphical, literary, and historical, not to mention just plain weird — that it's difficult to choose just a few representative sites. You can find out more about online collections of literary works and digital archives in Chapter 8.

The American Memory Project

lcweb2.loc.gov/ammem/

Put together by the U.S. Library of Congress, the American Memory Project is an electronic museum and exhibit hall featuring pictures, maps, and original manuscripts drawn from all stages of American history, from colonial times to the present. Add a multimedia dimension to your historical research by sampling the early twentieth century motion picture clips, and sound recordings of historic speeches, interviews, performances, and folk music.

Project Gutenberg

www.gutenberg.net/

Project Gutenberg started as a grass roots effort nearly 30 years ago, a labor of love by an army of dedicated volunteers. Its mission is to spread knowledge by digitizing classic works of literature, history, and science and getting them into the hands of online denizens everywhere. Check Project Gutenberg for electronic editions of writings by such well-known authors as William Shakespeare, Lewis Carroll, Jane Austen, and Joseph Conrad, as well as thousands of others, both ancient and modern.

Berkeley Digital Library SunSITE

sunsite.berkeley.edu

The University of California's SunSITE is a clearinghouse for digital library projects around the world. These rich collections of what scholars call *source material* — documents, maps, illustrations, and other artifacts actually created and used by historic figures and others who lived during the era being studied — enable researchers to examine and analyze rare, often one-of-a-kind resources that might otherwise be locked away in some remote and practically inaccessible archive.

World Art Treasures

sgwww.epfl.ch/BERGER/index.html

Spend enough time at the World Art Treasures site and you'll feel as though you're getting the equivalent of a Master's degree in art history. The bilingual (French-English), profusely illustrated (of course) site is packed with detailed lectures and essays on significant artists, periods, schools, and movements, from ancient times on. World Art Treasures encompasses Asia and the Middle East as well as the European tradition. The site is far from comprehensive (where are the moderns, for instance?), but as quirky, opinionated, and knowledgeable as a good university lecturer.

Business, Finance, & Economics

Online has become an indispensable resource for business research. In Chapter 12, I talk about how to use both proprietary databases and the Web for competitive intelligence, investing, market studies, sales prospecting, and other forms of business research.

American City Business Journals

www.amcity.com/

American City Business Journals pulls together more than three dozen weekly (usually) business newspapers from cities all over the U.S. You can search an individual publication or all of them at once. Local business periodicals such as the ones clustered at this site can give you deeper and more detailed information about companies and executives based in a particular location than you find in major national publications.

Commerce Business Daily

cbdnet.gpo.gov/

cos.gdb.org/repos/cbd/ (by subscription)

 $

Commerce Business Daily is your key to doing business with the federal government. You find not only requests for proposals, complete with instructions on how and where to submit your bid, but also announcements of contracts already awarded and other information to help you track your competitors and identify new and emerging market opportunities. CBD is available directly from the government, at no charge, at the first URL listed above; if you opt for the subscription version, you can get automatic updates tailored to your area of interest. CBD is also available through proprietary online services such as Dialog, LEXIS-NEXIS, and Dow Jones Interactive.

Daily Stocks

www.dailystocks.com/

I think of Daily Stocks as Everything You Wanted to Know About Investing But Were Afraid to Ask. This densely packed site is far more comprehensive than its name would lead you to believe. In addition to stock data, it includes hundreds of links to information on other investment markets, SEC filings, economic indicators, investment advice, and detailed company information, plus news headlines, magazine articles, and more.

Dun & Bradstreet

www.dnb.com/

$

D&B is one of the best-known names in business information and a source for financial and credit data on both publicly traded and privately held firms, worldwide. The main D&B Web site is your access point for purchasing several different kinds of detailed company reports. Don't overlook D&B's Companies Online (www.companiesonline.com/), which lets you search for companies that meet certain criteria, such as location, annual sales, or number of employees.

Hoover's Online

www.hoovers.com/

 $

Hoover's is a searchable online directory site that provides basic company profiles for more than 12,000 public and private firms worldwide. A typical profile includes a link to the company Web site, lists of competitors, and links to financial information, news stories, and stock

quotes. Subscribers to Hoover's get some additional features, such as detailed corporate backgrounds and financial data. America Online subscribers can get to Hoover's via keyword: hoovers.

Investext

www.investext.com/

$

Investext offers the complete text of in-depth reports on companies and industries, prepared by investment-house analysts and market research firms worldwide. Such reports can provide valuable insight into competitors' operations and business strategies, and can help you determine the potential demand for your company's products and services. You can tap into Investext through the Web, through its own proprietary I/PLUS Direct, or through other online services such as Dialog and Dow Jones Interactive.

misc.invest FAQ

invest-faq.com/

Investors are an opinionated and often quite knowledgeable bunch. One of the most thoughtful and comprehensive FAQs (Frequently Asked Questions lists) that I've seen represents the current collective wisdom of the misc.invest newsgroup hierarchy. Whether you're a novice investor or an old hand, you can search by keyword or browse by broad subject category and almost certainly come up with an answer.

Motley Fool

www.fool.com/

For an investment site with an abundance of personality, look into The Motley Fool. You find the Fool on the Web as well as at its original home, AOL (keyword: fool). The Fool's main draw is its lively online community, a collection of discussion forums devoted to every aspect of investing, including individual company stocks, industry outlooks, general advice, and personal financial management.

Statistical Resources on the Web

www.lib.umich.edu/libhome/ Documents.center/stats.html

Statistics make you queasy? This site eases your hunt for numerical data by providing a detailed index, subdivided by topic and issuing agency, to statistical sources all over the Web. In addition to well-known statistics-generating agencies such as the U.S. Census Bureau, you can find statistics from trade associations, research institutes, worldwide educational, environmental, and economic groups, and more.

Thomson & Thomson

www.thomson-thomson.com/

$ 📓 📊

T&T is about as synonymous with trademarks as Kleenex is with disposable facial tissue. Trademarks are a way of protecting your intellectual property rights — and the revenue associated with them — by registering the names of products or services you intend to market. Subscribe directly to T&T for trademark searching, or search their Trademarkscan databases on Dialog.

U.S. Securities & Exchange Commission EDGAR Database

www.sec.gov/edgarhp.htm

EDGAR is your entree into SEC corporate filings and other forms of disclosure required of U.S. public companies. SEC documents such as 10-Ks and 10-Qs can provide detailed insight into a company's

finances and operations. Such information is often valuable to competitors and potential partners as well as investors. EDGAR lets you search for corporate filings by company name or type of filing.

Wall Street Journal Interactive Edition

www.wsj.com/

$ 📓 📊

The online edition of *The Wall Street Journal* provides current business and economic news and feature articles, plus access to other Dow Jones publications and news stories and the thousands of periodicals in the Dow Jones Publications Library. (The Publications Library is described in Chapter 9 and in the "Proprietary Online Services" portion of this directory.) This subscription-only site also allows you to set up your own *Personal Journal* so that you can automatically receive your favorite WSJ columns and features, as well as custom-tailored information on the companies, products, and stocks you want to track.

Document Delivery Services

Document delivery companies specialize in locating articles, conference papers, and other items that you're unable to find online or at your local library. A document delivery firm can help when you're looking for something specific, know the name of the journal, book, proceedings volume, or other publication in which it appeared, and have a good idea of the author, title, and date. Chapter 8 mentions several such services; hundreds of others exist, all over the world.

UnCover

uncweb.carl.org/

$ ☑

UnCover lets you search for a particular article by author, title, publication name, or subject; order and pay for it with your credit card; and take delivery via fax. Uncover's REVEAL service keeps you current by automatically delivering the tables of contents of your favorite publications via e-mail and alerting you to new articles on topics you've specified as they're added to the UnCover database.

Government & Law

Federal, legislative, regulatory, and legal information is abundant online, and increasingly, on the Web. Chapter 11 (isn't that bankruptcy?) goes into detail about government information sources, and Chapter 6 talks about locating mega-sites for legal and related kinds of research.

Electronic Frontier Foundation

www.eff.org/

The Electronic Frontier Foundation is a cyber-citizens'-rights group charged with preserving freedom of expression in cyberspace for all of us. The EFF Web site includes news about free speech and censorship issues on the Net, information on ongoing campaigns, and background on the organization itself and its accomplishments to date. Members get a newsletter via e-mail and a warm, fuzzy, self-righteous glow.

FedWorld

www.fedworld.gov/

FedWorld is your gateway into a wide variety of U.S. government reports and other publications from executive-branch agencies such as NASA, the Department of Energy, the Environmental Protection Agency, and the Small Business Administration. FedWorld also leads you to individual agency Web sites where you can find even more information on your own.

Lexis

www.lexis.com/

 $

Lexis is the legal side of the two-headed online service known as LEXIS-NEXIS (see Chapter 9 and the "Proprietary Online Services" section of this directory for more about LEXIS-NEXIS). The Lexis service includes case law, statutory and administrative law, and special tools for citing, Shepardizing, and whatever else it is that legal researchers do. The Lexis Web site doesn't lead you directly into the full Lexis online service, but it gives you an idea of what Lexis offers and how you can get connected.

Social Law Library

www.socialaw.com

The Social Law Library is a legal mega-site offering links to Web resources for legal research of all kinds. From here, you can connect to the U.S. Supreme Court and a range of federal rules, regulations, and publications, or to state-by-state listings of codes, statutes, court opinions, and more. The site also encompasses international law, as well as other lawyerly resources such as legal publications, library catalogs, online discussion groups, educational and employment resources, and professional associations.

Thomas: Legislative Information on the Internet

thomas.loc.gov

Thomas Jefferson would be proud of his namesake site. It's as much a gateway into the legislative branch of the U.S. government as the aforementioned FedWorld is to the executive branch. Thomas lets you monitor the U.S. Congress in action (or is that *inaction?*), track pending legislation, and link to other government Web sites, whether federal, state, or local. The Executive Branch listing (lcweb.loc.gov/global/executive/fed.html) rates a bookmark of its own.

Libraries, Schools, & Universities

School and university Web sites can tell you as much about courses, faculty members, extracurricular activities, and student life as can an old-fashioned printed college catalog. This section includes sources for finding schools, and information about schools, online. University libraries — along with some public, government, and other specialized types of libraries — have their own distinct presence online as well, with searchable book catalogs and other research tools. This section gives you just a couple of examples. Chapter 8 tells you more about finding and using libraries online.

American Universities

www.clas.ufl.edu/CLAS/american-universities.html

College and University Home Pages

www.mit.edu:8001/people/cdemello/univ.html

These two sites provide copious links to college and university Web sites and sometimes to specific university departments, too. The College and University Home Pages site includes international schools as well. Between the two, you should be able to locate the Web site of just about any bachelor's or advanced degree-granting institution in the world — assuming, of course, that the school you're looking for *has* one.

Peterson's Directory of Colleges and Universities

www.petersons.com

Peterson's is the mainstay of high school guidance counselors everywhere. The online edition — which I put to use in the Life Choices chapter (CD-1) on the CD included with this book — lets you search for schools by curriculum or location. The rundown for each institution includes a description of specific programs, tuition and other fees, admission requirements, and contacts. Some of the schools let you request additional information, and even apply online, directly from the Peterson's site.

Spectrum Virtual University

www.vu.org/

$ 🗍

Spectrum Virtual U. is a school of a different color. You can enroll in online courses in subjects as diverse as computers, creative writing, genealogy, law, geography, history, and foreign languages. The school offers four to ten courses per quarter, and classes typically run for eight weeks. Fees are very low, and popular classes fill up fast. Subscribe to SVU's newsletter for notices of upcoming courses and campus — yes, I said campus — events.

U.S. Library of Congress

lcweb.loc.gov/loc/libserv/

Of all the possibilities covered in Chapter 8, I've selected the Library of Congress (LC) as the very model of a modern major library. The collection includes millions of books published in the U.S. and elsewhere, as well as maps, sound recordings, original manuscripts, and much more. LC's online catalog lets you search a great part of that collection by author, title, or subject, from the comfort of your own computer.

WebCATS

library.usask.ca/hywebcat/

WebCATS is a research tool for locating library catalogs on the Web. You can search geographically, by continent and country, or by library type. It's a great way to locate library catalogs close to home that you might actually want to visit or, if your research takes you there, library catalogs halfway around the world. You can also use WebCATS to identify special subject or regional collections to aid in a particular research project.

Magazines & Journals

Magazines — of all sorts — are one of the most common life forms on the Web. I talk about magazines generally in Chapter 13, about scientific, technical, and medical journals in Chapter 11, and about business periodicals in Chapter 12. Rather than fill up this section with my favorite online magazines (I'm tempted, but it would be wrong), I give you four different ways to find the periodicals you want online.

E-Journal

www.edoc.com/ejournal/

E-Journal leads you to popular magazines and scholarly journals on the Web. The site is divided into nine categories, and many subcategories, encompassing academic, political, and business publications, popular magazines, and even e-mail newsletters, as well as publishing topics and other periodical-related resources. Each subcategory contains an alphabetical list of titles. Click on a publication name to get a one-paragraph description, and on the URL to go to that publication or resource site.

Electric Library

www.elibrary.com/

$

The Electric Library allows you to locate publications and search them at the same time. Its collection includes newspapers and wire services as well as hundreds of magazines, both professional and popular. You can do a broad subject search or look for a particular article. Electric Library is a subscription-based site with a low monthly fee. You can try it out for free, or sign up for a 30-day trial.

Fulltext Sources Online

www.bibliodata.com/

$ 📖

My copy of *Fulltext Sources Online,* a print directory published twice a year and available by subscription, is one of the most heavily used books in my research collection. *FSO* covers both the Web and proprietary online services, such as Dialog and the others discussed in Chapter 9. For proprietary services, it tells you how far back the archives go; for publications on the Web, whether a free archive exists. Subscribers get access to a private section of the publisher's Web site where you can look up and link to those publications that have free archives on the Web.

Pathfinder

www.pathfinder.com/welcome/

Pathfinder, the Time-Warner media mega-site, illustrates how you can sometimes find several magazines clustered at their publisher's Web site. Pathfinder gives you access to *Time, Money, Fortune, People,* and *Entertainment Weekly*. Click a publication name, or use the pull-down menu, to browse the current issue or search back issues.

Navigation Aids & Organizing Tools

In the early days of the Internet, volunteers built and maintained their own resources for finding and organizing online information. Gophers were to the Net what search engines and subject catalogs, such as Infoseek and Yahoo!, are now — indispensible research aids. Many libraries put catalogs of their holdings online as well; even before the advent of the Web, researchers used a combination guide and navigation tool called Hytelnet to locate and connect to library catalogs. Both Hytelnet and much of Gopherspace (the portion of the Net defined and mapped by gophers) are now accessible through the Web. See Chapter 1 for more about gophers, and Chapter 8 for more about library catalogs and Hytelnet. The sites in this section provide web access to these resources. Type the address into your browser's Location or Address box just as you see it here.

University of Minnesota Gopher

gopher://gopher.tc.umn.edu

The original gopher was born at the University of Minnesota and named after the state animal and the school's mascot. Like most gophers, it contains a mix of information specific to that school or site, as well as links to information elsewhere on the Internet, and Internet search tools with names like Veronica and Jughead. For the flavor of another gopher, or an alternative jumping-off point into Gopherspace, try PEG, a Peripatetic, Eclectic Gopher (gopher://peg.cwis.uci.edu/).

Hytelnet

www.lights.com/hytelnet/

galaxy.einet.net/hytelnet/ START.TXT.html

Hytelnet is Peter Scott's contribution to cataloging and navigating through the rich resources of library catalogs online. Browse library listings by geographic area, or search the listings by name or subject. Click on a particular institution's telnet address to connect directly to its online catalog. Hytelnet is currently available through either of these URLs. Scott says, however, that he's no longer maintaining the service, but that he plans to replace it with something even better. We can hope.

News

News online comes in several different forms: broadcast media Web sites, individual newspapers, newsmagazines, and wire services. The news arena also features mega-sites that direct you to various news and current events resources, and services that will automatically keep you up to date. I've divided this section of the directory into broad categories and given you some leading examples of each kind. See Chapter 13 for more about finding and using news sources online.

Broadcast news

Many of the large broadcast networks, both North American and international, have a substantial presence on the Web. Typically, you can find real-time news headlines, feature stories, and tie-ins to the network's regular programs. If you're researching a topic that's currently in the news, broadcast media sites can provide the latest scoop, as well as background information and analysis of the *news behind the news*.

ABC News

www.abcnews.com/

Of the major U.S. networks, ABC's web presence is one of the most substantial. The site offers current news and background on ABC program content, a collection of recent stories arranged by topic, and a searchable multimedia archive with video and sound clips of people and events in the news. Check out the competition, too: CBS News (www.cbs.com/), NBC News (www.nbc.com/), Fox News (foxnews.com/), and CNN (www.cnn.com/).

C-SPAN

www.c-span.org/

C-SPAN rates a mention here because it's so darned thorough, especially where the workings of the U.S. government are concerned. You want continuing coverage of Congressional committee hearings? C-SPAN is your network. Click on top news stories for background and new developments throughout the day. C-SPAN offers sound and video clips, too.

CBC News

www.newsworld.cbc.ca/

The Canadian Broadcasting Corporation site covers breaking news in Canada and internationally. It provides an interesting perspective on events in the U.S., too. The site features links to detailed background information and commentary on issues in the news, plus audio newscasts, and interactive discussion forums and polls.

BBC News

news.bbc.co.uk/

For Americans, the British Broadcasting Corporation is a sometimes-necessary reminder that the world does not always revolve around the U.S. For the rest of the world, the BBC provides authoritative, thoughtful coverage of people, events, issues, and trends. The BBC Web site features not only news stories, features, and commentary, but also a special audio edition of its BBC World News program.

Weather Channel

www.weather.com/

Weather can be major news, not just a conversational opener. The Weather Channel Web site is a weather fan's delight, with major national and international weater-related stories, city-by-city forecasts, maps, skiing and air-travel reports, special weather briefings for pilots, and background on weather phenomena, such as El Niño.

Newspapers

Newspapers are a prime resource for many kinds of research. In addition to daily coverage of the news, newspaper sites frequently maintain searchable archives (in the old days, they were called *morgues*) of back issues. Local papers can provide deep insight into companies, industries, and individuals based in the region, and a different perspective on environmental, political, and social issues that particularly affect communities in their area. Besides the sites listed below, you can find hundreds of city newspapers on the Web. Even more extensive backfiles are available on proprietary services like Dialog, LEXIS-NEXIS, and Dow Jones Interactive, which allow you to search dozens of publications at once.

Los Angeles Times

www.latimes.com/

The *LA Times* is your window into the Southern California economy, Hollywood culture, and, of course, the film and entertainment industry. On the Web, you can read daily news headlines and hourly updates, browse particular sections of the paper such as business or regional news, do a keyword search for articles, or register to participate in online discussion forums.

The New York Times on the Web

www.nytimes.com

The *New York Times* is a national newspaper as well as a local one. The Web edition preserves much of the feeling of the printed *New York Times,* Gothic-script masthead and all. The CyberTimes section, a web-only exclusive, provides

in-depth, ongoing coverage of computers, online culture, business technology, and the high-tech industry.

Mercury Center

www.sjmercury.com/

 $

Backed by the San Jose, California *Mercury News,* Mercury Center is your doorway to Silicon Valley and the *Mercury News*'s coverage of high-tech happenings, issues, and personalities. Mercury Center also provides access to the NewsLibrary searchable archives, which covers the *Mercury News* as well as two dozen other newspapers, and the NewsHound personalized news-alerting service. Both of these resources are described in Chapter 13.

USA Today

www.usatoday.com/

The familiar graphics and editorial style of "the nation's newspaper" come through loud and clear on the *USA Today* site. I look forward to the U.S.-wide weather graphic whenever I travel to another city. Now I can get it on the Web.

Washington Post

www.washingtonpost.com/

$

The Washington Post gives you the inside scoop on doings in D.C. Read today's front-page stories online, or browse the paper by section. You can search the *Post*'s archives as far back as September 1986, and retrieve the full text of stories from the last two weeks, for free. For older stories, you must set up an account and pay $1.50 to $3 (depending on the time of day) to get the complete text.

News magazines

Weekly news magazines obviously aren't as timely as daily newspapers, but they often provide more detailed analysis and background.

U.S. News & World Report

www.usnews.com/usnews/home.htm

The *U.S. News & World Report* site provides stories from this week's print issue plus a searchable and browseable archive of back issues. The site also features additional content and analysis that you won't find in the print edition. Want to talk back to the journalists? You can register to participate in *U.S. News*'s online discussion forums. Prefer a different newsweekly? Never fear; your beloved *Time* (www.pathfinder.com/time/) is readily available on the Web. *Newsweek* has nailed down its URL (www.newsweek.com/) and promises to be there any day now. In the meantime, you can check it out on AOL — keyword: newsweek.

The Economist

www.economist.com/

 $

For an international perspective on the news, check out the U.K. publication, *The Economist. The Economist* Web site offers stories from the current issue and selected highlights, often cover stories, from some past issues. Register to search *The Economist* archive and get business and political updates via e-mail, too. Or subscribe to the web edition and get additional content such as surveys, reviews, and reference material.

Wired News

www.wired.com/

For news with a technology twist, put www.wired.com on your online reading list. The site, a *Wired* magazine venture, also covers world and national news, general business news, politics, and culture. I get my minimum daily adult requirement of *Wired News* by subscribing to the daily e-mail edition.

Wire services

Wire services are responsible for getting the story fast, distributing it to subscribing media outlets around the world, keeping on top of new developments, and filing continuous updates on rapidly changing events. TV and radio stations, news-oriented Web sites, and newspapers large and small all make use of wire service copy. You can benefit from their on-the-spot reporting even without visiting their sites. But you can also check out wire service sites directly when you want to monitor developments worldwide from the perspective of a local correspondent.

Associated Press (U.S.)

wire.ap.org

United Press International (U.S.)

www.upi.com/

Agence France Presse (France)

www.afp.com/

Kyodo (Japan)

home.kyodo.co.jp/

Reuters (UK and international)

www.reuters.com/

TASS (Russia)

itar-tass.com/

Xinhua (China)

www.xinhua.org/

News media mega-sites

How do you locate a particular newspaper or other news source on the Web? You start with a mega-site like one of those listed in this section or described in Chapter 13. These sites all provide more-or-less comprehensive listings of news media Web sites, with links to each one.

AJR NewsLink

www.newslink.org/

NewsLink is a production of the prestigious *American Journalism Review*. The site features links to both print and broadcast news sources, including not only the usual suspects, but also college newspapers and alternative papers such as the *San Francisco Bay Guardian* and New York's *Village Voice*. NewsLink covers magazines, too, and a variety of regional, national, and international periodicals that focus on news and current affairs.

Newspapers Online

www.newspapers.com/index.html

Newspapers Online isn't much to look at, but don't let that stop you. Instead of flashy graphics, you get lots of content at this site. The name Newspapers Online doesn't begin to describe its scope — classified ad "shoppers," religious periodicals, various ethnic and minority publications, and some downright strange stuff. If you're looking for an outside-the-mainstream periodical, you may well find it here.

News updates

Want to keep up with the news without having to drive all over the Web? You can get automatic updates in e-mail, or by logging in to your private, personalized portion of a news provider's site. Chapter 13 talks about a variety of update options. Here are three:

In-Box Direct

form.netscape.com/ibd/html/ibd.html

In-Box Direct is really a one-stop subscription service for web publications and other regularly updated sites. You register at the Netscape In-Box Direct site, pick the periodicals and services you want, and get each new issue via e-mail, direct from the publisher, as an HTML-coded page. Click on a link that interests you and go right to the site for the full story.

NewsPage

www.newspage.com/

 $

Register at the NewsPage site, then create your own personalized news edition by selecting specific topics, including companies and industries that you want to follow. Whenever you return to the site, you can click on My NewsPage to see updates that match your interest profile. The new information is drawn from newspapers, wire services, business and specialized trade journals, and other publications. For a small monthly fee, you can receive your daily customized news bulletins via e-mail, too.

Inquisit

www.inquisit.com/

$

Inquisit, which began life as a company called FarCast, lets you create *personal agents* to track companies, markets, technologies, stocks, and other topics that interest you. Inquisit draws from hundreds of sources, and delivers results via e-mail — or pager or cell phone, if you're so inclined. You can elect to take delivery of news as it happens, or at pre-defined days and times.

Proprietary Online Services

Proprietary services require you to register and to pay for the information you receive. In exchange, you often get access to unique research material, powerful search engines, and the ability to search hundreds, even thousands, of publications at once. Compuserve and America Online are classed as proprietary services, but the other four services listed here are really *industrial-strength* as far as serious research is concerned. Chapter 9 tells you a whole lot more about proprietary online services and how to use them.

Dialog

www.dialog.com/
www.dialogweb.com/

  $

Dialog offers hundreds of databases covering subjects as diverse as art, language, religion, psychology, sociology, business, news, chemistry, medicine, engineering, and technology. You can search the system several different ways; start with the first URL listed above to check out the various options. Or go directly to DialogWeb, the web interface to this awesome collection of information, read the detailed database descriptions posted there, and sample the range and depth of the resources that Dialog can provide.

Dow Jones Interactive

www.djnr.com/

  $

Through its Publications Library, the subscription-based Dow Jones Interactive service offers many of the same magazines, newspapers, and other periodicals as Dialog. But Dow Jones's main claim to fame is as a business research service. The Dow Jones Interactive Web site (the service is also available through a Windows-based software package) offers *The Wall Street Journal,* in-depth company and market research reports, historical stock quotes, and CustomClips, an automatic update service for topics you want to follow.

LEXIS-NEXIS

www.lexis-nexis.com

  $

LEXIS-NEXIS is the third of the top three professional research services covered in this section. It provides a broad range of business, news, trade, and international reports and publications, and the option of picking up case law and other specialized legal resources on the Lexis side. Though you can't yet access the full LEXIS-NEXIS service directly through the Web, you can get detailed listings of the sources available and contact points for more information.

ProQuest Direct

www.umi.com/proquest/

  $

ProQuest Direct provides searchable
access to the text of more than 6,000
publications, including academic journals, newspapers, and business, professional, technical, and general-interest
periodicals. Its real strength, though, isn't
text, but *pictures.* For a substantial
percentage of the articles in its collection,
ProQuest Direct offers photographs,
graphics, and other illustrations (some in
color), from the original articles, or actual
page images viewable with Adobe
Acrobat.

America Online

www.aol.com

 $

America Online, noted for its chatrooms
and almost unavoidable free trial offers,
offers several areas of interest to researchers. Use that freebie diskette and
the AOL proprietary software that comes
with it to log in and check out areas such
as the Business, Computing, and Research & Learn channels.

CompuServe

www.compuserve.com

   $

CompuServe is the home of Knowledge
Index, a slimmed-down version (in price
as well as content) of some of the same
highly useful databases offered on the
Dialog service. Don't overlook
CompuServe's traditionally excellent
discussion forums, with their accompanying libraries of software and information
in text form. Check the CompuServe Web
site for details on obtaining the necessary
connection software and opening an
account.

Quality of Information

Librarians, educators, and other interested parties have created several
excellent Web sites to help encourage
students, and information-users in
general, to think critically about the
information they find online. Some of
these sites contain bibliographies of
readings on the subject; some suggest
questions to ask and criteria to apply
when assessing documents and other
material you locate online; some take the
form of essays and presentations with
embedded links to examples and additional information on the topic; still
others are practical tutorials on how to
determine the quality of information in
electronic form. Read Chapter 15 for more
on information quality, and check the
sidebar in that chapter, "Evaluating
quality: some online resources" for some
additional sites on the subject.

Evaluating Quality on the Net

www.tiac.net/users/hope/findqual.html

Hope Tillman, library director at Babson
College, has posted her extensive presentation on assessing the quality of information on the Net. She covers the issues
involved in judging information quality,
suggests some criteria, points out
existing Net-based tools that can be used
in the evaluation process, identifies key
indicators of quality, and makes some
suggestions about how to proceed on
your own.

Evaluating World Wide Web Information

thorplus.lib.purdue.edu/research/
classes/gs175/3gs175/evaluation.html

This Purdue University site is a concise,
step-by-step guide to evaluating the

quality of information on the Web. It walks you through the various elements of a web page and suggests appropriate questions to ask at each stage: Who's the author? What's the institution? When was the document created or last changed? Who is the intended audience? What is the purpose of the information; is it intended to inform, explain, or persuade?

Evaluating Web Resources

www.science.widener.edu/~withers/webeval.htm

Evaluating Web Resources is a tutorial developed by reference librarians at Widener University. It includes lists of specific questions to ask and criteria to apply. The tutorial uses actual web pages as examples in showing how to assess the authority and accuracy, objectivity, currency, and completeness of a site. Other sample pages are used to illustrate some of the challenges that web information presents — for instance, pages that mix information with advertising or entertainment. Still other samples show the characteristics of certain kinds of sites: advocacy, business and marketing, information, news, and personal home pages. The site also includes a bibliography for further reading on information quality, and links to additional sites.

Reference Books

Some kinds of research involve just a quick lookup in what librarians call a *reference book* — a dictionary, encyclopedia, almanac, or directory of some kind. Chapter 7 tells you how to locate reference books online. Here's one site designed to help you find the reference book you need, and just four examples of the many reference volumes available to you online.

The Virtual Reference Desk

thorplus.lib.purdue.edu/reference/index.html

Purdue University's Virtual Reference Desk leads you to reference books all over the Web. You can find dictionaries, phone books, maps and travel information, resources in government, science and technology, and a fascinating collection of miscellaneous tools for looking up the answers you need. Click on a general category for a list of specific publications, with a brief and helpful description for each. Click once more on the title of the virtual volume and connect to it, wherever on the Web it resides.

Bartlett's Familiar Quotations

www.cc.columbia.edu/acis/bartleby/bartlett/

Bartlett's on the Web is an oldie but goodie — the 1901 edition, to be exact, of that standard reference work. You can search it by keyword or phrase, or browse by author through the collection of famous quotes. As a writer, I find Bartlett's indispensable for verifying the exact wording of a quote, or determining who said what. Of course, it doesn't help when I need to look up contemporary sayings, but that's where the Virtual Reference Desk (above) comes in.

Encyclopedia.com

www.encyclopedia.com

Encyclopedia.com is the virtual version of the *Concise Columbia Electronic Encyclopedia*. You can browse topics alphabetically or search by keyword or phrase. The articles are short, but serviceable. Like this description.

World Factbook

www.odci.gov/cia/publications/factbook/index.html

Despite the CIA's reputation for secrecy, its World Factbook was one of the first reference books made available on the

Net. The Factbook provides concise yet detailed profiles of just about every country in the world, complete with a color map and depiction of the country's flag. The information for each country includes geography, demographic and economic statistics, trade and commerce, form of government, communications and transportation networks, military strength, and any ongoing wars, border disputes, or other transnational issues.

Research Groups

Members of professional associations frequently trade tips with each other, participate in educational conferences, and create and distribute newsletters and other informative publications. Here are two such groups that cater to researchers who work on the kinds of projects described in this book.

Association of Independent Information Professionals

www.aiip.org/

The Association of Independent Information Professionals (AIIP) is an organization of professional researchers — not just online, but library, telephone, and document retrieval specialists as well. Members charge for their services, provide estimates of what a project might cost, and usually work on a not-to-exceed basis. The AIIP Web site includes a directory of members with descriptions of their research specialties and subject expertise. Interested in joining? You can sign up as an associate member, and upgrade to regular membership when you've gained some experience — and some clients — of your own.

Society of Competitive Intelligence Professionals

www.scip.org/

Members of the Society of Competitive Intelligence Professionals (SCIP) work either independently or as part of a company's strategic planning or competitive intelligence operation. If you're intrigued by the kind of business-information-gathering I describe in Chapter 12, you can learn a lot more by visiting SCIP's Web site, checking out its publications, and possibly even joining the organization.

Science, Technology, & Medicine

Originally, much of the online information needed by scientists, engineers, and medical researchers was only available in specialized databases on proprietary services such as Dialog. But many of these sources are now up on the Web as well. The Web has also proved to be a popular platform for science education, and for getting a basic understanding of particular scientific disciplines and issues. See Chapter 11 for the full range of scientific, medical, and technology-related research sources online.

SciCentral

www.scicentral.com/

SciCentral is a well-organized catalog of more than 50,000 online resources in the biological and health sciences, and in earth and space science, engineering, chemistry, and physics. You can also find science-related news stories, information on issues such as women and minorities in science, and links to government agencies, universities, and research institutes.

Galaxy: Medicine

galaxy.tradewave.com/galaxy/
Medicine.html

Galaxy: Medicine is a dense and detailed subject catalog of medical resources on the Net. You can search by keyword, or drill down from very broad categories, sometimes through several levels of increasingly-specific subcategories, to find the exact topic you want. For each topic, the site lists articles from medical journals that you can read directly. Galaxy: Medicine also links to medical schools and centers, organizations, periodicals, newsgroups, and other medical resources, both on and off the Web.

National Library of Medicine

www.nlm.nih.gov/

The National Library of Medicine is the home of Medline, a comprehensive database of article summaries from the international medical literature. Through the NLM Web site, you can search Medline in two ways: Grateful Med uses pull-down menus and a step-by-step search form. PubMed is for more advanced users. Grateful Med also provides access to several supplementary NLM databases, including AIDS-related ones. You can order copies of relevant articles through NLM's document delivery service, Loansome Doc.

U.S. Patent and Trademark Office

www.uspto.gov/

Think you've invented something? The U.S. Patent and Trademark Office is your starting point for background information on how the patent process works. The PTO can also be your gateway into *patent searching,* a necessary step in making sure that nobody else had the same bright idea first. The PTO Web site offers free searching of patents from 1976 to the present. That's a start, but to do a complete job, you may have to use a commercial patent database like those mentioned in Chapter 11.

World Intellectual Property Office

www.wipo.org/

For European and international patents, the recognized authority is the World Intellectual Property Office in Geneva, Switzerland. Its Web site can educate you in the intricacies of cross-border patent-granting, as well as copyright and other forms of intellectual property. The WIPO site also lets you do keyword searches or browse current and back issues of the *PCT* (Patent Cooperation Treaty) *Gazette,* a weekly publication highlighting new patent applications.

IBM Patent Server

www.patents.ibm.com/

IBM's experimental patent search site covers patents back to 1971. It offers images of patent drawings as well as text. That's worth knowing about, since the drawings can tell you more about an invention than a thousand words of obscurely-worded Patentese. The IBM Patent Server gives you a choice of simple or advanced search forms, with pull-down menus to make your results more precise.

Search Engines, Subject Catalogs, & Guides

Search engines, subject catalogs, and other guides to Net resources are as essential for online research as hammers, saws, and drills are for building a house. Chapters 3 through 6 cover these basic search tools in detail. This section highlights a few of the resources available to you in such categories as general and specialized search engines, meta-search engines, collections of pointers to search sites, subject catalogs, lists of FAQs (Frequently Asked Questions), guru pages, and mega-sites.

General search engines

General search engines enable you to do a keyword search over a broad range of sites, Web-wide. Each one works differently; each has its own special features and strengths. But no single search engine covers the entire Web. For best results, read Chapter 3 for details about each one. Then check out the search tips and other documentation at individual search engine sites, and do some sample searches to see how each one performs for you.

AltaVista

altavista.digital.com

AltaVista has a reputation for going deep, and pulling out references in web pages that are buried well below the top level of a site. Besides straightforward keyword searching, AltaVista lets you look for your search terms in specific portions of a document, such as the title or URL, or restrict your results to items in a certain language. You can also identify web pages that link to a particular site. AltaVista's translation feature is interesting, too, though sometimes the results are more amusing than enlightening.

Excite

www.excite.com

Excite is smart enough to look for terms and concepts closely related to the keywords you supply. That means you don't have to wrack your brain to come up with all possible synonyms for your search term. When you find a document that seems to be on target, click **more like this**. Excite uses the terminology in that document to further refine — you hope — your search, and to bring back even more relevant results.

HotBot

www.hotbot.com

HotBot allows you to search the Web at large, or to restrict your search terms to certain kinds of sites, such as current news, business directories, people-finders, stock quotes, or newsgroups and other discussion forums. You can also target your search by geographic region, or look specifically for images or other kinds of multimedia files.

Infoseek

www.infoseek.com

Infoseek lets you refine your first-round search results without running an entirely new search. Click **search only within these pages** and add one or more terms to make your search more specific. If you're looking for news stories or company profiles in particular, you can confine your Infoseek search to wire services, industry journals, national newspapers, and other web-based news sources.

Lycos

www.lycos.com

Lycos was one of the earliest web search engines and is still one of the easiest to use. Just enter a keyword in the search box. Click **Search Features** for fill-in-the-blank forms that allow you to limit your search terms to the title or URL, or to pages at a specific site. Lycos's Advanced Search lets you specify that your search terms appear in a certain relationship to each other.

Northern Light

www.nlsearch.com/

The Northern Light search engine covers not only the Web, but also a Special Collection of articles from thousands of sources not readily available outside proprietary database services like Dialog. Northern Light organizes your search results into Custom Search Folders, based on the Web sites and the types of information it turns up. You can look at your results arranged by folder, or browse a standard relevance-ranked list. Northern Light offers a subscription plan and a pay-as-you-go option, both very reasonably priced, for items from its Special Collection.

Specialized search engines

When you're looking for certain kinds of information — such as people, business listings, maps, software, mailing lists, newsgroup postings — it makes sense to start with a search engine designed for that purpose. See Chapter 4 for more information on putting these specialized search sites to work in your research projects.

BigBook

www.bigbook.com

BigBook is a company directory that lets you search by business name or by category. You can use BigBook to do market research, or investigate potential competition, by locating all businesses of a particular type in a certain city, zip code, or telephone area code.

Four11

www.four11.com

Switchboard

www.switchboard.com

Four11 and SwitchBoard are two of the leading people-finding aids online. Both sites let you look up e-mail addresses and phone numbers. Both sites offer business lookups as well. If you don't find the listing you want in one of these directories, try the other.

WorldPages

www.worldpages.com/

WorldPages offers an assortment of specialized searches, including attorneys, automobiles, restaurants, entertainment, and travel. Research-wise, one of its most valuable assets is its **International Search** link, which leads you to business directory listings in countries around the world.

DejaNews

www.dejanews.com

DejaNews is an essential tool for locating information that's been posted in the online discussion areas known as newsgroups. You can search for groups to join, or for specific information by subject, or for postings by a particular person. Chapter 10 (as well as Chapter 4) goes into more detail about how to use DejaNews.

Liszt

www.liszt.com

The Liszt search engine specializes in finding online mailing lists (sometimes called listservs) that deal with a specific subject such as accounting, physical therapy, travel, or library science. You can search by keyword or browse through broad subject categories to find the list you want. Once you've subscribed to a mailing list, you can stay up to date, and sometimes participate in discussions, via e-mail. See Chapter 10 for lots more about Liszt.

MapQuest

www.mapquest.com/

MapQuest is all about maps. The site features an interactive world atlas that lets you zoom in and out from a country-wide view down to street level. You can pinpoint a specific address, get driving directions from point A to point B, and locate places of interest such as restaurants, hotels, museums, theaters, and even ATMs. MapQuest also lets you create personalized maps, with your own landmarks and destinations, that you can print out or download.

Shareware.Com

www.shareware.com

Shareware.Com helps you locate publicly available software in archives and on corporate distribution sites around the world. You can look for a specific program name, or search by type of application, hardware platform, operating system, and other criteria. Once you've located what you want, another click or two downloads it to your computer. Unless you're absolutely sure of the source, it's a good idea to run a virus-checking program before installing shareware on your hard drive.

Meta-search engines

Meta-search engines run your search request through several search engines at once. You can cover a lot of ground quickly, though you don't get to take advantage of all the specialized search features that individual engines offer. Experiment with meta-search engines like the ones described here (and in Chapter 3), using simple keyword searches.

Ask Jeeves

www.askjeeves.com

Ask Jeeves is an unusual meta-search engine. To begin with, it encourages plain English search queries; just type in your question as if you were asking another person. Before going out and submitting your request to other search engines on the Web, Jeeves checks its own *knowledgebase,* or in-house Q&A collection, and attempts to match your question to the answers it already knows.

Sometimes the attempt succeeds, sometimes not. If not, Jeeves offers a set of results from other search engines which you can evaluate without traveling to the individual search engine site. When you find something good, click on the search engine name and go check it out in more detail.

Dogpile

www.dogpile.com

Dogpile runs your search through as many as 25 search engines at once, including newsgroup and newswire search sites and specialized tools for finding FTP files. You can select and prioritize the search engines you want to put to work. The more engines you select, though, the greater the odds of getting strange and unexpected results. For best results, keep your search query as simple as possible.

Inference Find

www.inference.com/ifind/

Inference Find is one of the easiest search interfaces I've found: Enter your key-words and hit the search button. Inference Find submits your search request to half a dozen of the top search engines, merges the results, removes duplicates, and groups the remaining items according to their main topic or the type of site they came from.

ProFusion

profusion.ittc.ukans.edu/

ProFusion presents a more complex picture than Inference Find. The pull-down menus offer you options galore. You can allow

ProFusion to select the best or fastest search engine for your current search, or choose your own favorites.

Search engine mega-sites

Unlike meta-search engines, the sites in this section don't actually run your search in several engines at once. Instead, they point you to a vast number of search engines, both general and specialized. You can explore, individually, the ones that interest you.

All-in-One Search Page

www.albany.net/allinone/

The All-in-One Search Page provides a simple search form for most of the hundreds of engines it lists, so you can submit your search from the All-in-One page. For the results, you're transported to the actual search engine site. All-in-One encompasses a dozen or so broad categories of search engine types, including Web and General Internet, Special Interest, Software, Publications, People, News/Weather, Technical Reports, Documentation, and Desk Reference.

Beaucoup Search Engines

beaucoup.com/

Beaucoup lists more than 1,000 search engines in two dozen or so different categories. These categories include Geographically Specific, Health/Foods, Social/Political/Environmental Concerns, Medicine, Science/Technology, and Politics/Government. Click on a category, then on a site listing to go directly to the search engine you want.

Search.Com

search.com/

Search.Com provides a directory of specialized search engines in categories ranging from Automotive to Travel. The site also includes an A-Z List of links to more than 100 individual search engine sites.

General subject catalogs

Web-wide subject catalogs lead you to selected resources by allowing you to drill down from a general category, sometimes through several levels of progressively more specific subcategories, until you find the site or sites you want. Chapter 5 tells you more about researching with subject catalogs.

Argus Clearinghouse

clearinghouse.net/

The Argus Clearinghouse is a catalog of *other* subject catalogs — and indexes, bibliographies, and guides — all over the Net. The categories often go two or three levels deep. Each resource is rated for content, design, organization, and overall usefulness. The Clearinghouse began as a joint project of students at the University of Michigan's library school.

Yahoo!

www.yahoo.com/

Yahoo! is the best-known online research tool. A fine starting point, especially when you don't know where else to begin,

Yahoo!'s broad subject categories and selective listings make it easy to find useful sites for most kinds of research.

Internet Public Library

www.ipl.org/

The Internet Public Library leads you to resources much as a real-world public library would. You can find a reference collection, special exhibits, resources for kids and young adults, and departments devoted to magazines and serials (arranged by subject category), newspapers (arranged by geographic region), and online texts. In the online texts department, you can do a keyword search, select author or title from an alphabetical list, or browse the collection by Dewey Decimal number.

World Wide Web Virtual Library

vlib.stanford.edu/Overview.html

The WWW Virtual Library was one of the first web organizing tools in existence. It covers topics from Agriculture and Education to Information Management, International Affairs, Regional Studies, Science, and Society. The catalog pages for individual topics reside on computers all over the world. Each one is different, but each is maintained by a certified expert in the field.

The Mining Company

www.theminingcompany.com/

The Mining Company hires real-life experts to identify and point you to worthwhile resources in their areas of expertise. Those areas run the gamut from Chinese culture to business management to geology, and beyond. Mining

Company guides also answer questions and keep you up to date through newsletters, e-mail, bulletin-board discussions, and scheduled online chats. Search the site by keyword or browse for your area of interest.

RingWorld

www.webring.com

www.webring.org

RingWorld is a catalog of a different color, or at least a different shape. Either of these URLs will lead you to this search-able catalog of *web rings*. A web ring is a group of related Web sites, linked to each other by a bit of HTML code, that form a circle or ring. See Chapter 6 for more about web rings and how to use them in your research.

FAQ finders

FAQs, or Frequently Asked Questions lists, are an Internet tradition. A FAQ is generally a collective effort by partici-pants in a newsgroup or other online discussion area, intended to provide the answers to . . . you guessed it. The right FAQ can sometimes tell you everything you need to know about a subject. Chapter 10 says more about FAQs and how to use them.

Usenet FAQs

www.cis.ohio-state.edu/hypertext/faq/ usenet/top.html

The Usenet FAQs site lets you search for a FAQ by newsgroup name, subject, or keywords. If you prefer, you can browse an alphabetical list, and link directly to the FAQ you want.

Usenet Hypertext FAQ Archive

www.faqs.org/faqs/

The Usenet Hypertext FAQ Archive lets you do an exhaustive, full-text search of actual FAQ contents. You can confine your search to newsgroup names, authors, subject headers, and keywords for greater precision. Or browse the FAQ listings by newsgroup name, hierarchy, or category.

Guru pages and mega-sites

Information on the Internet is organized in many different ways, including a great many volunteer efforts. Individuals, agencies, and professional organizations often post collections of links to useful sites that they've discovered. *Guru page* is my term for these personal labors of love; *mega-site* is the more formal, and all-encompassing, term. Chapter 6 talks about, and gives you more examples of, both kinds.

Awesome List

www.cais.com/makulow/awesome.html

John Makulowich's Awesome List began as an answer to questions like "What's so interesting about the Internet? Can you really find anything useful there?" It consists of links — now divided into two lists, the Truly Awesome and the (merely) Awesome — that show the incredible diversity of cool sites on the Web.

Sources and Experts

sunsite.unc.edu/slanews/internet/
   experts.html

Sources and Experts is a guide to online directories of experts in various fields, assembled by news researcher Kitty Bennett. The list is arranged by site, with a brief description of the areas of expertise covered by each one. Many of the sites let you search or browse by topic, and examine individual expert credentials in detail.

Internet Beatles List

www.primenet.com/~dhaber/
   blinks.html

Dave Haber's Internet Beatles List is fandom at its finest, and a classic guru page. The site generously includes links to other people's Beatles pages, as well as to more specialized information resources such as publications, song lyrics, fan clubs, collectibles, people and themes tangentially connected with the Beatles, and sites devoted to individual members of the Fab Four.

Virtual Communities & Conferencing Systems

Virtual communities and online conferencing systems are gathering places for Net denizens. Some of these cyber-hangouts you find have ongoing conversations on just about any subject you can imagine. Others are more specialized, dealing with particular issues

or catering to the needs of doctors, lawyers, and other professional and special-interest groups. Chapter 10 explains how participating in one of these online communities can deepen and enrich your research results.

Forum One

www.ForumOne.com/

Forum One is a guide to the variety of virtual communities and discussion groups or forums that exist online. You can browse the Mega-Forums category to find forums that talk about a variety of subjects. Or you can search by category or keyword to find discussion groups dedicated to a particular subject. Forum One's main categories include Current Events, Society and Culture, Business and Finance, Health, Computers, Science, and Education, plus a listing of regional forums, both U.S. and international. Forum One isn't totally comprehensive, but it's a very good start.

Parent Soup

www.parentsoup.com

As a member of Parent Soup, you can participate in real-time chats and ongoing discussions about all phases of parenthood and all aspects of being a parent. Non-members can still read discussion forums (or message boards) and search them by keyword for postings on a particular topic. Parent Soup's main discussion areas are arranged by age of child, from expectancy into the teens. Discussions deal with topics ranging from what to expect at various stages of pregnancy, to how to survive middle school. The Parent Soup site features such extras as a baby-name finder, a summer camp guide, a library of readings arranged by topics and subtopics, child-rearing-related news stories, and other resources.

D-30 Virtual Communities & Conferencing Systems

Third Age

www.thirdage.com

The Third Age site describes itself as *The Web . . . for grownups.* Translate that to mean mature adults and my generation of aging baby boomers. Third Age features ongoing conversations in broad subject areas like money, technology, news and politics, health, books, and relationships and other personal concerns. As a non-member, you can read forum messages and search archived postings by key-word, but you can't post your own responses until you register. Once you do join (it's free), you can participate in forums as well as both scheduled and impromptu real-time chat.

The Gate

www.sfgate.com

The Gate is a mix of publishing and community. The site offers news stories, feature articles, and columns from its two newspaper sponsors the *San Francisco Chronicle* and *The San Francisco Examiner.* Click **Conferences** to enter the discussion area of the site. Gate conferences cover business, books, current events, movies, food, music, travel, health, technology, and more. Newspaper writers and staffers participate in, and sometimes host, many of these discussions.

The WELL

www.well.com

    $

The WELL is my favorite online commu-nity, with conferences covering books, music, movies, politics, media, computers and technology, spirituality, and hun-dreds of other subjects. As one of the oldest communities in cyberspace (founded in 1985 or so), The WELL has had time to develop a distinctive culture of its own. You can sign up, choose from a variety of pricing plans, and explore the WELL for yourself, either through the Web or — my preference — a text-based interface called Picospan.

Chapter 15

The Big Issues: Copyright, Information Use, and Quality

"**I** found it on the Net." Well, put it *back*. No, that's not the extent of the advice you're going to get in this chapter. But too many people do think, just because they "found it on the Net" — apparently free for the taking — that they're entitled to use it in any way they want. It just ain't so. Copyright law and other legal and ethical considerations govern what you can and can't do with information — and, for that matter, graphics, video, sound, and other multimedia files — that you find online.

You wouldn't appropriate someone else's term paper, or a hot idea that someone came up with in a meeting, and claim it as your own. (If you *would,* go to your room; I don't want to hear about it.) The same standards apply to using information that comes from the Web or an online database. You must act responsibly with regard to information that someone else has created and respect their rights as owners of that intellectual property. Besides, it's just plain good manners — another aspect of the *netiquette* I talk about in Chapter 10.

I'll get off my soapbox now. In this chapter, I look at copyright and some of the other factors that affect how you can and should make use of information that you find online. I have something to say about information quality, too, and some pointers on how to judge whether what you've retrieved is even *worth* using at all.

Getting Right with Copyright

What is *copyright,* exactly? When you create an original work — an article, a poem, a book, or a painting, published or unpublished — you own it. With ownership comes the right to license others to use, copy, sell, or distribute it. That right is called copyright.

You may assign copyright to someone else, as writers do when they undertake a *work for hire.* That phrase indicates that the publisher, or whoever has commissioned the work, owns the rights to it. You may grant someone else the rights to your work in one medium, like print, while retaining the rights in a different medium, such as electronic.

Bottom line: Copyright belongs to the creator of a work, automatically, whether or not the work is marked with a © symbol, unless that person has explicitly assigned the right to someone else.

Fair use

Copyright seems pretty clear-cut, right? Wrong. Copyright law also includes the concept of *fair use,* which means that other people can make limited use of your work — as long as they're not profiting from it, plagiarizing it, or distributing it *en masse* to others — without asking your permission. Without fair use, it would be well-nigh impossible to hold a scholarly conference, bolster an argument with evidence, or even write that term paper.

I'm not a lawyer, nor do I play one in this book. But I can tell you this: You're usually on safe ground if you

- ✔ Quote brief portions of a work, as long as you credit the source.
- ✔ Quote longer sections of a work or incorporate them in your own work, as long as you both credit and *obtain permission from* the source.
- ✔ Point someone else to a URL or database citation so they can make use of the information directly.

You're stepping into dangerous territory if you

- ✔ Quote someone else's words without crediting the author.
- ✔ Incorporate someone else's words — or images, or multimedia creations — into your own work without obtaining permission (sometimes you have to pay a fee; sometimes a simple acknowledgment will do).
- ✔ Distribute someone else's work to others without obtaining permission.

Confusion, copyright, and the Net

Between the extremes of permissible and questionable conduct outlined in the preceding section lies a huge gray area filled with mass confusion. Copyright law came into being long before electronic publishing. Most experts hold that the law as it stands adequately covers this new medium. Even so, the issues and ambiguities that have arisen regarding copyright since the advent of the Net have created a Guaranteed Full Employment Act for attorneys that'll probably last for the next 20 years.

Even if the same legal principles apply online that apply to print — or to artworks created in paint or any other medium — the law, and our understanding of it, has to stretch to encompass realities such as these:

- On the Net, everyone's an author. But sometimes you can't even tell who created or holds the right to the information on a site.

- Computers and the Net have made it vastly easier to copy and distribute information. In the print world, you're limited by practical factors such as the number of copies your photocopier can crank out, and the time and effort involved in distributing them to your 500 closest friends.

- On the Net, a copy is indistinguishable from the original document, with no tell-tale second-generation fade. You can't detect whether you're looking at an original, a first-generation copy, or something that's been around the world and back. (Maybe if someone *would* invent an electronic document fading effect, we'd finally get rid of the Good Times Virus scare and all those other "oh no, not *that* again" mailbox-stuffers that never seem to die.)

- Electronic documents can be altered invisibly in ways that affect the author's meaning by omitting or changing critical information.

- Text from one document can be cut and pasted seamlessly into another document, as if it were part of the original.

- Electronic documents can be distributed around the world easily and instantaneously, or posted in online venues where thousands of people can read them.

Factor in other legal questions, such as what constitutes an original work, or whether a work is too short or otherwise uncopyrightable, and you've got enough loose ends to keep the intellectual property lawyers — not to mention their plaintiffs and defendants — preoccupied for decades.

In the public domain

What does it mean when a work is said to be *in the public domain?* Public domain has nothing to do with Internet domains — except that if the domain ends with *.gov*, it may be in the public domain. Huh? Okay, back up: You can use and disseminate freely a work that's in the public domain, such as most publications of the U.S. government, without having to worry about copyright. Our tax dollars at work.

Historic documents such as the Declaration of Independence, the Bible, and works of classical literature are usually — though not always — in the public domain as well. You don't have to ask Shakespeare's estate for permission to quote him. Most of the works in Project Gutenberg (www.gutenberg.net/), a full-text collection of literary and historic writings which I mention in Chapter 7, are there because they're in the public domain — no fees, no contracts, no legal wrangles involved in distributing them more widely on the Net.

Public domain is the exception, though, rather than the rule. Chances are that most of the information you want to use *is* covered by copyright. Sorry.

Copyright and the proprietary online services

Users of proprietary online services such as Dialog (see Chapter 9 for more about them) dealt with the copyright issue ages ago. The information climate in these online services is more controlled than on the Web. Dialog, for example, licenses the databases it carries from individual producers, who in turn negotiate contracts with the publishers whose content they use. The publishers, in turn, negotiate with authors — or should, in the best of all possible worlds — for the use of their material in electronic form.

When you pay — and pay you do — to download or print items from Dialog or another proprietary service, a portion of that fee goes back to the entity, usually the publisher, who holds the copyright on each item. In other words, you're covered for one-time, non-commercial, use of the information. But suppose you want to distribute it to your co-workers or publish it in an in-house newsletter? Dialog has a system in place for tracking and paying for multiple copies. These guys think of everything.

Copyright and the Web

Copyright works differently on the open Web. The rules aren't as clear, and the procedures aren't built in the way they are on a closed system such as Dialog. As a starting point, you can usually assume that downloading or printing a single copy of something you find on the Web (as long as it's for your own personal, noncommercial use) or quoting brief excerpts and giving credit where due, are okay.

Some sites, especially those run by publishers and other commercial organizations, spell out their copyright policies for you. If you click the copyright notice at the *New York Times on the Web* (www.nytimes.com/) you see:

> *All materials contained on this site are protected by United States copyright law and may not be reproduced, distributed, transmitted, displayed, published or broadcast without the prior written permission of The New York Times Company.*

> *You may not alter or remove any trademark, copyright or other notice from copies of the content.*

> *However, you may download material from The New York Times on the Web (one machine readable copy and one print copy per page) for your personal, noncommercial use only.*

> *For further information, see Section Two of the Subscriber Agreement.*

Section Two spells out the copyright terms in even more explicit, excruciatingly legalese terms.

The *Wired News* copyright policy (www.wired.com/) is a shade more liberal than that of the *New York Times on the Web*. See whether you can spot the differences:

> *This article is copyrighted by Wired Ventures, Inc. and may be redistributed provided that the article remains intact, with this copyright message clearly visible. Under any circumstances, this article may not be re-sold or re-distributed for compensation of any kind without prior written permission from Wired Ventures, Inc.*

Even when you don't see a copyright notice or the telltale © symbol, don't assume that what you find online is there for the grabbing. Remember, an original published work is automatically protected by copyright — it don't need no steenkin' symbol. If you don't find the terms and conditions of use spelled out somewhere on the site, and you'd like to use the material in a more extensive manner, such as distributing copies within your organization, you can e-mail the Webmaster, the site administrator, or the person responsible for the content. Ask permission. Sometimes that's all it takes.

You may occasionally encounter Web sites and other online distribution points that invite you to take what you want and distribute it freely. The site's owner wants to get the word out, promote her cause, or market her product, service, or professional expertise. What better way to spread the word than through an army of Net volunteers? I take explicit permission like this at face value.

For basic background on copyright law, check out the Electronic Frontier Foundation's lengthy FAQ (`www.eff.org/pub/CAF/law/copyright-FAQ`).

Using Information Responsibly

Your responsibility doesn't end when you clear the copyright hurdle. Even if you receive blanket permission to use material that you find online, or pay a fee, or determine that you're covered by fair use or that the material is in the public domain — you should still give credit where it's due.

When using or quoting online sources in a paper, talk, handout, or PowerPoint presentation, *attribute* the source. Attribution simply means that you supply the URL for a Web site, or the author, title, journal name, and date for a work that first appeared in print. Don't attempt to pass the work off as your own. Even if that's not your intention, not citing your sources is tacky and unprofessional.

If you got your information from a newsgroup, say so. If the author sent you a copy of a document, let you pick his brain (ugh; I hate that expression), or shared his random thoughts with you in e-mail, say that, too. Notes in printed books and articles sometimes reference a source by giving the person's name and adding the phrase *private correspondence with the author,* followed by the applicable date. You don't have to be that formal, unless you're writing for publication, too. But *do* share your sources. It's not just polite; it's the professional thing to do.

Hopping along the audit trail

Documenting your information sources isn't just good manners. When I worked at a research company called Information on Demand, some of our projects involved gathering information on the phone from dozens of industry experts and analysts, and then synthesizing what they told us into a narrative report. Along the way, we kept a complete list of everyone we talked to, their title, affiliation, and the date we spoke to them, as well as a record of what they said and whom they may have referred us to. We gave the client a copy of this contact list along with the finished report.

If a client questioned an assertion we'd made, we pointed them to the original source. If someone had doubts about the thoroughness of our work, we referred them to the complete list of everyone we'd spoken with — and also pointed out, where appropriate, that we could have done more with a bigger budget.

Keeping track of where you got your information not only increases your credibility with your audience, be it a client, a teacher, a trial judge, a graduate seminar, or a professional meeting, but covers your tail as well. That list of contacts and sources creates an *audit trail:* a route for you, and whoever else may be interested, to re-create your information-gathering process and validate what you found at each step of the way.

YOYOW: You own your own words

Folks on the WELL, the online community where I spend too much time, have a saying: *You own your own words.* The exact meaning of that statement is open to debate, and is debated so frequently, in fact, that we've come to abbreviate it YOYOW.

One interpretation of YOYOW is that you're responsible for what you say online. I can't argue with that. An alternative explanation — and they're not mutually exclusive — is that you, and only you, should determine how your online utterances may be used. They're not to be removed from the WELL and published or reposted in other venues without your permission. Some WELL-beings hold that what you say in one WELL conference shouldn't even be ported over to another without your explicit approval.

Putting aside the hair-splitting that always seems to accompany YOYOW discussions on the WELL, in practice it seems to boil down to good manners. Online conversation isn't fixed like a copyrightable work, and quoting someone probably won't run afoul of the law. Paraphrasing is safer than quoting directly. But it's still good form to ask. That goes even more strongly for private e-mail than for utterances in public conferences.

Thinking about Linking

One of the concerns behind the "you own your own words" philosophy described in the preceding section is that your words may be taken out of context. Web page owners have a similar concern. Anyone can link to somebody else's site just by including a simple bit of HTML code that points to the referenced site. Linking is what makes guru pages and mega-sites, like the ones I talk about in Chapter 6, such rich and robust resources.

In general, it's considered polite to ask permission before linking to someone else's site, especially if the potential linkee is an individual or small operation. Asking permission is less important if you're using a Web-wide resource such as Yahoo!, or a well-known site like the Library of Congress, which already gets thousands of hits a day.

Usually, the intention behind linking is helpful — to point you to other useful resources on a topic. But sometimes the motivation is not so benign. Consider the implications if a company's multimillion-dollar Web site were linked to an environmental group's list of corporate polluters, or a professional woman's management consulting page were linked to Babes on the Web, or the Boy Scouts of America home page were linked to a pedophile site. You get the idea — linking can subvert an author's original intentions, hold them up to ridicule, or completely change the way their message is perceived.

Inappropriate linking can work the other way around, as well. A site can gain credibility, or attempt to, by linking to other, more prestigious locations. We *do* judge people by the company they keep, and a marginal, shoddy, or unreliable operation can prop itself up with links to A-list, blue-ribbon companions.

What does this mean for you, the researcher? It means that you must think about *context* — maintaining an awareness of where you are as you move around the Web. Are you still under the IBM.com corporate umbrella? Or has your point-and-click meandering led you to a site that *parodies* IBM? Are you going to accept the content of the Drudge Report (see Chapter 13) as true on the strength of its prominent links to AP, UPI, Reuters, and other well-known news sources? Or are you going to examine Matt Drudge's allegations with the critical eye they require?

Linking has ties to the intellectual property issues raised by copyright and the you-own-your-own-words philosophy described in the preceding section, and to the *quality* issues I talk about in the next section.

Assessing Information Quality

At Information on Demand, the research firm where I worked for several years, we used the library, the telephone, computer databases, and various combinations of these three approaches to locate whatever our clients were paying us to find. Back then, business magazines were just beginning to run articles on companies like ours and the astounding feats we could accomplish with just a computer, a modem, and a connection to an online service.

As a result, we'd get a flurry of calls from prospective clients who wanted us to "pull something out of the computer" for them. But not every project was a candidate for what we formally referred to as an *online literature search,* and when we told callers that we might have to go to the library instead, or pick up the telephone and interview industry experts, they were sometimes horribly disappointed.

Even today, information that comes "from the computer" has a reputation for being cleaner and more reliable, somehow, than the equivalent material pulled together from dusty old books or an assortment of human experts. If you've ever had to deal with a screwed-up bank statement, you know that's not necessarily the case.

Garbage in, garbage out is an old saying from the early days of computers. It's true: The information you get from databases and other online resources is no more accurate than the information that went in. Professional searchers have struggled for years with typos, missing paragraphs, incorrect indexing, and countless other manifestations of *dirty data.* If I had to boil down 25 years of experience with online information quality into one rule of thumb, I'd say: *Never take anything at face value.*

We were luckier than we realized back when proprietary services like Dialog were our main online research tools. The information in those databases went through several stages of editorial review — first when an article appeared in print, and then again when it was converted to electronic form for inclusion in a database like Trade and Industry or ABI/Inform. Publishers took responsibility for fact-checking, verifying author credentials, and making sure that none of the statements or assertions made in the article raised a red flag, legally speaking. Still more editorial massaging and overall quality assurance happened later, when the document was added to the online database.

Judging quality and reliability on the Net

You can still find that level of reliability at some locations on the Internet. Well-known, reputable publications like *The New York Times, Forbes,* or *Consumer Reports* generally reflect the same high standards of editing and quality control online that they do in print. Professional associations, such as the American Bar Association, major universities, and government agencies, tend to put as much thought and care into their Web presence as they do into their real-world transactions. This level of attention to quality isn't always the case. I've seen some egregious lapses. But a recognizable brand name, whether it's a corporation, trade group, educational institution, or other official agency, is a good rough indication of quality and reliability.

A URL ending in *.gov, .edu,* or *.mil* is usually an indicator of quality, as long as it represents the official presence on the Net of an institution such as the Library of Congress, Harvard University, or the U.S. Army. But remember that the online accounts of students, enlistees, and government employees end with the same set of letters; and they, as a group, are no more reliable than us *.net*-heads and *.com*-mon folk.

What about the vast number of unbranded sites on the Net? How can you tell whether the information these sites offer is worth a second glance, let alone good enough to factor into an important personal decision, present at a business meeting, or offer as evidence in court?

Some things you may want to look out for are:

- ✔ **Accountability:** Who's responsible for the site? Is he who he purports to be? What are his credentials, his qualifications for presenting the information he presents? In the WWW Virtual Library (`http://vlib.stanford.edu/Overview.html`), for instance (I describe that institution in Chapter 5), an individual subject site typically identifies both the institution and the individual responsible for maintaining it. The Virtual Library banner is a brand name of sorts; it provides some credibility to begin with. But if you need more specifics, or have questions about the content of the site, the responsible party's e-mail box is just a click away.

- ✔ **Bias:** Even reputable publications have a slant. *The Wall Street Journal* is pro-business. *Mother Jones* leans to the left. It's a lot easier to judge the bias of a Web site, and to adjust for it accordingly, when you're familiar with, or can readily determine, its underlying philosophy. But it's easy to *conceal* agendas on the Web. Remember when laser printers first came out, and every document seemed so professional-looking and official? A document may not have been worth the paper it was printed on, but it looked so *good.*

Anyone can put up a substantial, handsome-looking Web site that purports to offer definitive, unprejudiced information. But unless you know the person or group, and the motivation, behind the site, you have to dig deeper, and read between the lines, to figure out whether to trust them.

- ✔ **Currency:** Information floats around the Net in a random and unpredictable way. Documents still in circulation may be outdated or superceded by more recent versions. The further you get from the source, the greater the possibility that what you're looking at is not the latest and greatest. Check to see when the Web site was last updated. Check back with the original author or issuing body to verify whether you've got the definitive edition.

Okay, that's easy enough. Now think about this one: Many Web sites are updated dynamically — throughout the day, even — on a continuous, rolling basis. The document you downloaded yesterday may already have been replaced by a later version, and by fresh, and maybe even contradictory, information. If you're going to rely on a Web site to bolster your position, be sure you know what's on the site *now*.

Gopher archives and FTP sites (I describe these pre-Web information resources back in Chapter 1) present even more of a problem, currency-wise, than the Web. Although many people still rely on such sites, some have been neglected or even abandoned entirely in favor of the more user-friendly Web. When you land at a gopher or FTP archive, poke around to see how current, in general, its files and documents appear to be. If they seem stale, be especially wary about getting outdated information.

✔ **Integrity:** The question of document integrity ties in to our earlier discussion about copyright and how easy it is to alter electronic information, whether intentionally or unintentionally. Do you remember "Whispering-Down-The-Lane" — the kids' game where the point was to see how distorted a saying could become after it had passed through a dozen sets of lips and ears? Documents on the Net may be incomplete, or altered from the original in some gross or imperceptible way. Text gets scrambled, sections get lost, new and sometimes incorrect information gets pasted in.

Widely-circulated items often lose all trace of their origin. Sometimes they even get credited to another source, with a totally bogus explanation. A perfect example of this was a speech that was supposedly made by the author Kurt Vonnegut at an MIT graduation ceremony. It was a great speech; I got 17 copies of it, myself, before the darned thing finally went away. But it turned out that Kurt Vonnegut had never addressed an MIT graduating class; the speech was a piece written by a columnist for the *Chicago Tribune*. Things are not always as they seem online.

Establishing expertise

The Net is full of self-appointed experts. Newsgroups are particularly fertile breeding grounds for people who claim to know what they're talking about, because the newsgroup population is often transient, and anyone can post. Before taking someone's assertions at face value, use the DejaNews search engine's **Author Profile** feature (see Chapter 10 for more about DejaNews) or click **Power Search** and enter the person's e-mail address in the **Author:** box. Doing this shows you where else the "expert" has posted, what she's said, and how deep and accurate her knowledge appears to be.

Evaluating quality: some online resources

Librarians and information specialists have put together a number of Web sites devoted to measuring and evaluating the quality of online information. To read more about this crucial issue, visit any or all of these sites:

Bibliography on Evaluating Internet Resources
`refserver.lib.vt.edu/libinst/critTHINK.HTM`

Evaluating Information Found on the Internet
`milton.mse.jhu.edu:8001/research/education/net.html`

Evaluating Quality on the Net
`www.tiac.net/users/hope/findqual.html`

Evaluating Web Resources (tutorial)
`www.science.widener.edu/~withers/webeval.htm`

Evaluating World Wide Web Information
`thorplus.lib.purdue.edu/research/classes/gs175/3gs175/evaluation.html`

Thinking Critically About Web Information
`www.ala.org/rusa/mars/ets98.html`

Thinking Critically About World Wide Web Resources
`www.library.ucla.edu/libraries/college/instruct/critical.htm`

Apply the same standards that you do when deciding whether to believe something you read in the newspaper or overhear on the street:

- Who's saying it?
- What are his credentials?
- Does he have proof for his assertion?
- How current and how valid are the facts or research on which the information is supposedly based?

You can use the search engines, people-finders, and other research tools described in earlier chapters of this book to check out experts and verify that they are who they purport to be. The guy's posting from a `columbia.edu` address? Can you find him in the faculty directory at `www.columbia.edu`? Is his home page linked off the Columbia server? Is he a graduate student or tenured professor? Or an undergrad or lower-echelon staff person just out to see what he can stir up?

Or maybe you've run into a purported medical researcher who's touting a radical new treatment. What's her track record? Run her name through Medline (on Dialog, or at `www.nlm.nih.gov/`) and see if anyone salutes.

Don't overlook e-mail as an investigative tool. If you're skeptical or need more documentation, get in touch with the person responsible for the statement or the site. Ask politely (of *course* you will), and chances are that the individual will be happy to help you. If he's defensive, or you don't hear back from him at all, well, that may tell you something, too.

Surveyors, geologists, and other field research types use the principle of *triangulation* to verify the location of an object in the landscape. As an online researcher, you should triangulate, too, by verifying the information you find in at least a couple of other sources. Check it in a book. Follow through on an article cited by the author. Find independent corroboration elsewhere on the Net. Ask a *different* expert.

Thinking critically

Want to know my single best tip for judging the quality of online information? Here it is in a nutshell: *trust but verify.* Leave yourself open to the possibility of knowledge coming from unexpected, and previously undiscovered, sources. But don't accept any of it at face value. Apply the critical filters that I give you in this chapter:

- ✔ Is it backed by a brand name or trustworthy reputation? If you're looking at a Web site, what can you find out from the URL?

- ✔ Can you verify an expert's credentials, or determine who's really responsible for a site, and what she's trying to accomplish?

- ✔ Can you determine whether the document in front of you is complete, unaltered, and current?

- ✔ Did a credible source point you to the site or information source in the first place? If not, can you verify the information in at least two other independent sources?

You may not want — or need — to go through the full interrogation every time you read and decide to use something you find online. But keep these questions in mind. Retain that skeptical edge. Don't believe it just because it "came out of the computer."

Part V
The Part of Tens

The 5th Wave   By Rich Tennant

"There's an idea in today's paper for your current issues research project: Teen anti-social behavior attributable to too much time online.'"

In this part . . .

So what's this Part of Tens business? It sounds vaguely medieval — *This kingdom shall henceforth be known as The Part of Tens* — or like what's next in line after the King of Hearts, the Jack of Diamonds, and the Queen of Spades. Maybe it's actually The Port of Tines — you know, the old forks' home. Or an unpleasant look on someone's face — the Pout of Tense. Or cookware — the Pots of Tin.

How much will you pay me to stop?

All right, already — this part is about lists. Lists that consist — astoundingly enough — of exactly ten items apiece. You'd almost think I planned it this way.

I enjoy making lists. I'm a world-class list-maker. I make lists of things I've already done for the sheer satisfaction of crossing them out. I make lists of lists. If it weren't for lists, I wouldn't remember where I put my car keys. In fact, where *are* my car keys? Oh, here they are, under the cat. I hope he wasn't out joy-riding again. I worry about him.

Speaking of joy-riding, this part is fast, fun, and easy to take. It's the thrill ride of the century. You must be *this* tall to read these chapters. Perhaps I exaggerate slightly. But I hope you hop in when the mood strikes you, and read a pointer here and there. You're sure to pick up some tips that, one way or another, will make your researching more interesting, effective, and rewarding.

Check the CD-ROM for Bonus Chapter 3: Ten Simple Tune-Ups for Streamlined Searching.

Chapter 16

Ten Timeless Truths about Search Engines

1 used to think that writing about search engines was like painting the Golden Gate Bridge — as soon as you've finished, it's time to start all over again. But I don't feel that way anymore. Now I think it's like painting the Golden Gate Bridge during an earthquake, with gale-force winds blowing, torrential rain, the usual traffic whizzing past in both directions, and a motley collection of software developers, graphic designers, marketers, and advertisers clambering over the railings and up the superstructure, pulling out rivets here, adding new cables there, replacing the roadway, and trying out new paint swatches right where I'm trying to lay down my own finest brushwork. Golden? Does it have to be golden?

Elsewhere in this book — mainly in Chapters 3 and 4 — I focus on some of the best, most useful, and most interesting search engines for various kinds of research. It's guaranteed: By the time this book reaches your hot little hands, some of what I say will have changed. Not substantially, I hope, but change is inevitable. It's ongoing. It's the way of the Net.

That's where this chapter comes in. It goes beyond the look, feel, and features of any particular search engine to capture some timeless — or, given the total unpredictability of the online world, semi-timeless — truths. Check out those earlier chapters and then come back here to put them in context. Or read this one first and then approach those chapters with your mind properly calibrated to deal with the only timeless truth: Change.

There's No One Best Search Engine

No single search engine covers the entire Web. For a variety of reasons, each search engine has weaknesses as well as strengths, which has as much to do with the Web as with the search engines themselves. But don't worry. We're not talking marriage, or any other kind of long-term commitment. If one search engine doesn't do it for you, move right along to the next one in line.

Search Engines Are Like Icebergs

Nine-tenths of a search engine's functionality is hidden under the surface. You may never see the algorithms or mathematical routines that actually analyze and process your search request. But you can explore the documentation on the other side of the Advanced Search, Power Search, Search Tips, or Help link for some powerful features that give you much more control over your search results.

Check the CD-ROM for a sample search engine tip-sheet from Northern Light.

Search Engines Are Like Snowflakes, Too

Every search engine is unique in that each one has its own special features, whether it's locating GIF files, searching newsgroup posts, finding people, or turning a fuzzy concept search into useable results. Save yourself time by researching the search engines before you start researching for real — and then choosing the right tool for the job.

Sometimes the Right Tool Isn't a Search Engine

When you think *research,* don't automatically think *search engine.* Depending on the project (I have a lot to say on this subject elsewhere in the book: see Parts II and III for more), starting with a subject catalog, a news-group, a specialized mega-site, or even a printed reference book, is often more effective than using a search engine. Don't underestimate the power of a well-placed phone call. Your telephone can sometimes be your most valuable research aid, and it doesn't even have to be connected to a modem.

Trust the Force

Obi Wan Kenobi's advice in *Star Wars* is a polite way of stating the K.I.S.S. principle: Keep It Simple, Stupid (I didn't make that up, and I'm not calling you stupid). Get to know a search engine and its capabilities before you start throwing it curve balls that you're not sure it can handle. Start with a keyword or two, or a simple phrase, and see whether the results, or at least some of the results, are on target. Don't overcomplicate your search query at the outset. You may be outsmarting yourself.

Use Meta-Engines Strategically

Meta-search engines — the kind that run your research query through several search engines at once — can be a time-saver when you're looking for a needle in a haystack. But a meta-search is just a rough first cut; you don't get the benefit of each individual engine's special features, and the results these meta-search engines deliver aren't always representative. A meta-search can play a useful part in your overall research strategy, but it's not a substitute for a focused, precision search using the right individual engine.

Know When to Specialize

You'll get a head start on many research projects if you look for search sites that focus on your broad subject area, and use the specially-tuned search engines you find there. Chapters 11 through 13 describe sites like FedWorld, Grateful Med, the IBM Patent Server, EDGAR, and the Electric Library. Starting with an appropriate subject collection like one of these is much more efficient than trying to pluck isolated references out of the Web at large.

Look Beyond the Web

The search engines used by proprietary online services such as Dialog offer more features, functionality, and control over your results than those in use on the open Web. See Chapter 9 for more about why you shouldn't overlook these heavy-duty research services.

The Only Constant Is Change

Search engine designers are constantly experimenting with their creations, adding new features, tweaking old ones, adjusting the interface for optimal results (and sometimes, I get the feeling, just for the heck of it). If you haven't visited a search engine site in a while, don't assume that its old limitations — or virtues — still apply. And if you tend to favor a particular engine, don't fall into a rut. What used to be *the best* may not, on closer examination, be worthy of that title anymore.

Say Hello to the New Kids on the Block

It seems like a new generation of search engines — general, specialized, meta-, and permutations yet unheard of — comes along every four days or so. Some of these newcomers are just variations on old familiar themes. But others do represent fresh and often improved approaches to the eternal problem of finding good information online. Read publications such as the *Search Engine Report* and others I suggest in Chapter 14 to keep up-to-date on the new kids on the block. Some of them may change the fundamental way that you, and I, do research.

Chapter 17

Ten Clarifying Questions for Better Research Results

In This Chapter

▶ Determining what you're really looking for

▶ Monitoring your research as you go

▶ Evaluating and fine-tuning your results

*R*esearch pros must deal with more questions than just the one they set out to answer. The pros ask questions at the beginning of a project, even before going online. They ask questions in the midst of the project, and still more at the end.

Why? Glad you asked that question. The first round of questions, which librarians call the *reference interview* (see Chapter 2 for more about reference interviews), is designed to sharpen your understanding of what you're hoping to accomplish, set your goals for the research session, and suggest some opening tactics. If you're working on behalf of a client, friend, or colleague, ask that person those reference interview questions, too.

You continue asking questions as you get underway with your search, in order to keep on track, and to adjust and regroup if necessary. That series of questions is more like a continuous feedback loop that plays throughout your search. If things are under control, they're like a low murmur in the background; if your research quest is getting out of hand, you may crank up the volume a little. Or a lot. If you find yourself getting in too deep, you may want to stop and ask yourself these questions out loud.

The final phase of self-questioning helps you evaluate the results you're getting, figure out whether you need to do more work, and decide when you've had — I mean *gathered* — enough.

Ask the right questions and you'll get the right answers. Uh-uh; I wish it were as simple as that. It's not. But by continuing to ask the right questions throughout your search, you can hone in on the right answers and come up with the high-quality research results that you need.

What Am I Trying to Accomplish?

A research query involves more than just searching for a simple list of keywords. Although keywords define the subject, they don't say anything about *why* you need the information. For example, if you're searching on *road rage,* are you interested in news stories about drivers going berserk, or do you need information about the psychological aspects of that behavior? For news stories about aggressive drivers, you might check some of the newspaper Web sites mentioned in Chapter 13. But for psychological studies on what triggers over-the-top aggression on the highway, you'd probably go to a proprietary online service like Dialog to search a scholarly database such as Psychological Abstracts. Or suppose you're searching on *tomatoes.* What is it about tomatoes that turns you on — growing them, throwing them, genetically engineering them, or cooking with them? Your purpose in asking the question determines where — and sometimes how — to look for the answer.

How Much Effort Is Appropriate?

Researchers have their own jargon for certain kinds of searches. Each kind requires a different level of effort:

- **Quick-and-dirty:** This type of search is fast, limited, and by no means definitive. A quick-and-dirty search gives you an idea of how much information is out there and how much time, money, and effort you can expect to spend on getting it.

- **No-stone-unturned:** Also known as a *scorched-earth search,* this type covers as many sources as you can manage, in as much depth as possible. The no-stone-unturned search is a common approach when preparing for lawsuits, resolving questions of liability, and researching business takeovers or other situations that involve large amounts of money.

- **Just-a-few-good-articles:** You conduct this type of search if you need a half dozen (or so) full-text stories from authoritative publications in the field. The ideal articles will provide background on a subject and an overview of current issues, trends, and problems. Busy people like to read someone else's analysis, rather than having to go through hundreds of articles and prepare their own.

✔ **A fishing expedition:** This type of search is an open-ended quest, undertaken when you're not sure what you're looking for and are hoping to stumble across some ideas, which you can then use to further refine your search. Fishing-expedition searches can be time-consuming and frustrating. Try to do some of that refining offline by reference-interviewing yourself (see Chapter 2 for more about reference interviewing).

✔ **Document delivery:** Conduct this type of search if you have a pretty good idea of when and where a particular article or document was published.

Answering a simple *curiosity question* requires a different level of effort than researching a high school term paper. That term paper, in turn, calls for a lower level of effort than preparing for a business deal, challenging a patent, or researching a doctoral dissertation (which is a good thing, especially if you're in high school). Know ahead of time what level of effort is appropriate for your project, and proceed accordingly.

What Else Should I Know About?

"What else should I consider?" is a catchall question intended to make you think about any special circumstances or unquestioned assumptions that you should factor into your search query. Examples include:

✔ **Whether the topic can be expressed in terms of trade jargon or other specialized terminology.** If so, adding such terms to your search query may help broaden, deepen, or focus your results.

✔ **Whether the definitive research on the subject may come from a non-English-speaking country.** If that's a possibility, you may have to search databases that cover international sources, or journals and Web sites based outside North America and the U.K. You may even have to engage a translator or someone fluent in that language to help you out.

✔ **Whether the event is recent or historical.** If your research depends on sources that are more than a couple of years old, you may have to search the archives in a proprietary online service rather than on the Web.

✔ **Whether the technology is cutting-edge or well-established.** You may find more on a new technology because it's hot, or less because few people know about it yet. You may find more on an older technology because so many people have paid attention to it, or less because it's so accepted now that nobody has anything left to say. The same applies to events and people in the news. Knowing whether your subject is "old" or "new" helps you determine where to look first, and whether it makes sense to search further back.

✔ **Whether the person or company is high-profile or publicity-shy.** A high-profile subject guarantees that you'll find a lot of information; one that shuns the limelight will take more effort to research.

If you're conducting research for somebody else, ask them where they've already looked, what they found, and how much information — if any — they expect you to find. For certain kinds of projects, like patent novelty searches, zero hits can be the best possible result.

You may be aware of some of these factors going in. Others you'll glean as you examine your preliminary search results, and adjust your approach accordingly. The important thing is not to assume you've thought of all the angles: Ask, analyze, and adjust.

Am I Likely to Find My Answers Online?

Some types of information generally aren't available on the Web. For example, you probably won't find this kind of information online:

✔ **Studies and surveys that cost a bundle for someone to produce and market:** Proprietary services like the ones I talk about in Chapter 9 do offer such reports, but you can expect to pay a share of that bundle.

✔ **Older material, such as magazine articles from the '80s or before:** Again, you may find some of this material in the proprietary services, but very little on the open Web.

✔ **Data that's highly labor-intensive to collect:** This type of information is especially hard to find online if it's ultra-specific in some respect. For example, you may be able to find sales statistics for flannel bedsheets sold in North America, but statistics for flannel bedsheets sold annually for the last ten years in Moose Jaw, Saskatchewan, broken down by king, queen, or twin-sized sheets? Dream on. Or commission your own study.

✔ **Confidential documents and privileged information:** Yes, top-secret, hush-hush material is sometimes leaked to the Internet, but not so routinely that you can count on finding it there. If you don't have a "need to know, " face it, you may never find out.

Is Online the Best Place to Look?

Don't discount the obvious. When planning your research, check your bookshelves for basic reference volumes like almanacs, phone books, dictionaries, and encyclopedias. Just because you *can* look up information online doesn't mean that you should. Picking up a book is often faster and more effective than going online and searching for the same information.

Remember that your local library is one of the best resources going, whether it's a neighborhood branch or a major university library. Although you *may* be able to find a 1950s magazine article on vintage aircraft somewhere on the Net (some aviation buff may have scanned it in), why not check with your library, too? As a bonus, libraries generally come equipped with *librarians,* who can point you to useful indexes and other reference tools — not to mention particular books and journals that you can't get access to online.

What's My Plan?

Where do you begin? We're talking about research strategy here. Some questions fall naturally into the search engine domain — and then you have to decide on the best engine for the job. Other research questions are candidates for the broader, more filtered *subject catalog* approach. Still other searches may benefit from the distillation of group expertise that you get in a newsgroup FAQ. Some answers reside only in proprietary databases. Some just require a quick lookup in a particular online reference book.

Knowing the form in which you expect your information to appear — a newspaper or news-wire story, or an article from a particular magazine — will often help determine your starting point.

Chapter 2 goes into much more detail about strategizing your search. The point is to stay aware of the dazzling array of research options available to you, and to deploy them in a way that makes sense for the project at hand.

Who's Likely to Know the Answer?

If you're wondering why your rose leaves are turning yellow, you don't search every book in your house for the answer — you go right to your gardening manual, or you ask Mrs. Green-Thumb next door. The same principle applies online: Draw on your own intuition and accumulated knowledge to go right to the source — or what you hope is the source — of the information you're looking for.

For example, if you need to find information on the housing industry, your thought process may go something like this:

> "Statistics on housing construction? The government publishes a lot of statistics. . . . I read about the FedWorld Web site in Chapter 11. . . . Before I slog through a search-engine search on the open Web, let's see what I can find at the FedWorld site."

Or perhaps your thoughts follow this course:

> "Who would know about housing construction? Builders! Maybe I can find a trade association. . . . Didn't I see a link to Associations on the Web last time I visited the Internet Public Library (`www.ipl.org/ref/`)? Yahoo! probably has an Associations category, too. . . ."

The point is to see if you can save time by taking a wild, intuitive leap (doesn't that sound like fun?) and landing right on, or near, the answer. Easy for me to say? When you get into the habit of thinking like a researcher, leaping to good conclusions should be easy for you, too.

What Have I Gathered So Far?

Answers come in many forms. Sometimes your goal is clear-cut — a phone number, a name, a statistic, a business directory listing. Often, however, you must piece together facts, comments, observations, and analyses from many different sources in order to come up with the complete picture.

If you think you're getting close to the finish line of your research session, stop searching and evaluate the information you've collected so far. Where are the gaps in your answer? What data do you still need? For example, if you realize that the only hole remaining is a single fact, a quote from the CEO, or a product description from one of the companies you're researching, you know that it's time to refine, refocus, and go after those missing pieces specifically.

Complex searches go through several iterations, from the general to the more specific, from one angle to another. Check your results periodically against your ultimate goal, and change your approach to pick up the parts you still require.

What Have I Overlooked?

Are you not finding what you need? Or do you just want to be sure you've covered all the bases? It's time to step back and double-check your search strategy, your starting assumptions, and the search tactics you've tried thus far:

- ✔ **Are you sure you've entered your search terms correctly?** Have you accounted for spelling variations, other forms of the word, synonyms, and related terms and concepts? Don't overlook British and American variations in spelling (labour/labor, aluminium/aluminum) and usage (lorry/truck, aubergine/eggplant). What about human error — are you certain you've spelled your search words correctly? Inconceivable as it may seem, could you have made a typo?

- ✔ **Have you imposed false assumptions or limitations on your search?** For example, a search engine may default to information published in just the last week or so, unless you tell it differently.

- ✔ **Are you checking the correct database?** Perhaps you're looking for an article that appeared in a magazine, but you've been searching in a newspaper article database. Or perhaps that once-reliable mega-site has gone stale since you last used it. You're not likely to pick up current pointers from a page that was last updated in 1996.

- ✔ **Have you utilized all the resources that you meant to?** What about that other search engine you intended to try? (See Chapters 3 and 4.) How about a Boolean search — you'll get different results than with relevance-ranking. (See the Bonus Appendix on the CD for more on Boolean searching.) Have you taken advantage of the special search engine features that let you focus your search more precisely? (See Chapters 3 and 4 again.) What about those links that you intended to follow before you went off in another direction? How about venturing into new territory, such as newsgroups or web rings (see Chapters 4 and 10 for newsgroups, and Chapter 6 for web rings) if those are sources you haven't explored before?

- ✔ **Can you locate broader data, or information from an allied field, that might shed some light on your search?** If you're not finding exactly what you need, try the indirect approach. What tangential indicators (such as sales of a related product, or statistics for a similar commodity) can help you develop a picture, however impressionistic, of the information landscape surrounding your topic?

How Do I Know the Information Is Good?

You can expect your research project (if it's typical) to pull up data, descriptions, and factoids from a wide variety of sources. Some of those sources will agree with each other. If the information matches from source to source, you have a built-in measure of reliability right there (either that, or you've put your finger on a widespread hoax).

However, some of the information you find is likely to be contradictory, or just not in sync. How do you weigh your catch and decide what's worth keeping and what you should throw back?

Chapter 15 has a lot more to say about judging the quality of the data you find online. Here are a few simple guidelines to get you up to speed:

- ✔ Scan for names you recognize. Look for acknowledged experts, reputable publications, institutions like government agencies and university departments, which have a vested interest in being right.

- ✔ Look for the most current version available. A title that matches the article of your dreams is worthless if it's out of date.

- ✔ Dig below the surface, if necessary, to find out what individual or organization is responsible for the site, what its agenda is, and whether it really is who and what it claims to be.

The Web can be a masquerade ball. Some folks delight in spoofing reputable sources and pretending to be what they're not. Develop your analytical skills, and learn to trust your intuition. An investigative reporter I knew always used to talk about the *JDLR factor* — if it Just Doesn't Look Right, it's probably not.

Chapter 18
Ten Trends to Keep an Eye On

● ●

In This Chapter

▶ Intelligent software at your service

▶ Breaking down barriers on the Web

▶ The next-generation Net

▶ Back to the future?

● ●

*P*redicting the future is a risky business. If you've ever read one of those old magazine articles with a title like, "Here's how we'll be living in . . . 1988!" then you know what I mean. Where's my self-cleaning house? Where's my personal jet-pack transportation machine? And if we're supposed to be getting all our nourishment from yummy food-like substances extruded from tubes, how come I still have to cook?

No matter how visionary we try to be, most of us haven't been issued a pair of magic goggles that enable us to peer far, far into the future. All we have to go on is the present and the past. Extrapolation is the name of the game: Futurists make predictions based on the current scene, and on new and possibly significant trends that have already begun to emerge.

Welcome to the edge. Read now about some emerging trends that may give us a preview of our future.

Smarter Search Engines

The next generation of search engines will be smarter and more specialized than what we have today. You won't have to exert as much effort to come up with synonyms or to ensure that your terms appear in the context that you intend. These search engines may employ a *cognitive net,* a matrix of alternative terminology and related concepts, plus an understanding of syntax, word usage, and other forms of linguistic analysis, to determine your meaning — much as a person who's listening to you knows what you mean without your having to spell it out in a literal, explicit way.

Personal Info-Bots

A *bot,* short for robot, is a clever piece of software that roams around the Net, bringing you the information you need even before you know you need it. Bots examine your selections and rejections, analyze your choices, and use that data to refine their own searching skills. Most of today's prototypes are still pretty rough, but the bot of the future may be your indispensable research assistant, with a personality you design to get along with your own.

Affinity Agents

Friends, colleagues, and fellow-enthusiasts can be your best source of information and informed recommendations. Specialized data collection and matching software, called affinity agents, can track your preferences, compare them with those of other people, and create a *community of taste,* a network of folks who share your opinions on books, music, software, or politics. The agent monitors the community's developing tastes, and continues to recommend resources that it thinks you will like, too.

Personal Programming

Whether it comes in over your Web TV, through a video window on your monitor, or directly onto your PC desktop, tomorrow's version of the customized news services and *push* channels described in Chapter 13 will be highly tailored to your needs. You want top headlines, international stock market reports, and local commute conditions every weekday at 6:30 a.m.? You got it. On weekends, you want weather forecasts, sports news as it happens, and movie schedules for your area, but not 'til 10:00 a.m.? No problem. The Net will live on your desktop, or wherever you've parked your PC. And so will the information you need, right now.

A Truly World Wide Web

The Web, already an international phenomenon, is rapidly becoming a multilingual environment. AltaVista and other search sites have begun to offer instantaneous — if not United Nations-style simultaneous — translations that should help break down the language barrier before it gets too high. They're not so hot right now, but expect to see smoother, faster, and more accurate translations as you move around the Web of the future.

Virtual Environments

Online has moved from text to pictures, and from static images to dynamic multimedia, in a very short time. The next step? Three-dimensional worlds that you can step into and move around in, or that create that illusion for you. Instead of typing on your keyboard, you'll manipulate data structures by picking them up and putting them over . . . there. You'll be able to visualize complex ideas by walking around them. And of course, you can meet all those people you've been talking to online in the flesh — or virtually so.

Fatter Pipes

The popularity of the Web has bogged down the flow of information through electronic pipelines that were never designed to carry that much traffic. Better connectivity, more bandwidth, and increased speed are essential for the future of the Net. Fortunately, much of the groundwork is already being laid to accomplish these improvements. Look for alphabet-soup solutions like ADSL (Asymmetric Digital Subscriber Line, or something like that —and thanks, but I'd rather not get into it right now), hardware alternatives like satellite and cable modems, and an entire fast-track network — much speedier than the current Internet but presently reserved for participating universities and other research institutions — called (are you ready for this?) Internet 2.

Online Everywhere

Early adopters — those clued-in folks whose noses are always in the air, sniffing the latest trends — are already bragging that they no longer own a desktop computer; they just use their laptop — or their palmtop — machines. Wireless telecommunication will free us from the tyranny — whoa! I'm getting a little carried away here — of modems, phone jacks, and power cords. Expect to see Net access blossoming everywhere, through devices that don't yet have a name, but that will be as commonplace and easy to use as a telephone or a TV.

Looking Forward to the Past

In the headlong rush to embrace the next big techno-thing, is anyone thinking about preserving the past? Every society needs a sense of its history in order to grow and thrive. That goes for cyberculture, too. Who are the custodians and historians of the Net? One venture, Alexa (`www.alexa.com/`), has made a small start on archiving the Web, and can supply you with copies of pages in its collection that are no longer available at their original site. The system's not perfect, and it raises lots of questions. But Alexa is a sign that someone's thinking about documenting the Web, present and past, so that we can learn from it in the future.

Internet Backlash?

Constant change can be tiring. You burn out on novelty after a while. The world is moving so much faster than it used to. Overnight delivery services take too long. You drum your fingertips on your desk while waiting for a fax in progress to finish. E-mail is convenient, but it speeds up communications even more — your correspondents know you're online, and they expect a response almost as immediately as if you were speaking with them face to face. What's next — Telepathy? Answering *before* you get their message?

I predict an online backlash, a reaction to all this rapid change and sudden acceleration in the pace of our work, school, and even social lives. Not a total withdrawal, but what stock market watchers call a *correction*. Watch for the terminally-wired to become the terminally tired. Taking time off, being out of touch, will be stylish. So pry those fingers off the keyboard, unplug yourself from the Net, and get away. At least for a few hours.

A Hiccup in the Continuum

Have you been counting? Okay, you get a bonus; this is trend Number 11. Real change comes from totally unexpected directions — a skipped beat, an extra measure, a hiccup in the continuum. Think back, if you can, to 1991 or so, before the Web burst on the scene. Would you have imagined that banks, movies, and manufacturers of sporting goods and fancy chocolates would all feature Web addresses prominently in their ads? Could you have conceived of the Internet — assuming you'd heard of it at all — being relevant in any way to your life?

The Web changed everything. Even those of us who were already living and working online didn't see it coming. We were blindsided. And it's going to happen again.

The seeds of change are all around us now. Let's see how many of them take root and grow.

Appendix

About the CD

· ·

*Y*ou can find a variety of software and other extras on the *Researching Online For Dummies* CD-ROM, including bonus chapters and an appendix that provide tips and examples for doing more powerful and effective online research. *This* appendix tells you what's on the CD and how to install and use its contents.

System Requirements

Make sure that your computer meets the minimum system requirements listed in this section. If your computer doesn't meet most of these requirements, you may have problems using the contents of the CD-ROM:

- ✔ A PC with a 486 or faster processor, or a Mac OS computer with a 68030 or faster processor

- ✔ Microsoft Windows 3.1 or Windows 95, or Mac OS system software 7.5 or higher

- ✔ At least 16MB of total RAM

- ✔ A CD-ROM drive — double-speed (2x) or faster

- ✔ A monitor capable of displaying at least 256 colors or grayscale

- ✔ A modem with a speed of at least 14,400 bps and an Internet connection

If you need more information on the basics, check out *PCs For Dummies,* 5th Edition, by Dan Gookin; *Macs For Dummies,* 5th Edition, by David Pogue; *Windows 95 For Dummies,* 2nd Edition, by Andy Rathbone; or *Windows 3.11 For Dummies,* 3rd Edition, by Andy Rathbone (all published by IDG Books Worldwide, Inc.).

Using the CD with Microsoft Windows

To install the items from the CD to your hard drive, follow these steps:

1. **Insert the CD into your computer's CD-ROM drive.**

2. **Windows 3.1 or 3.11 users: From Program Manager, choose File⇨Run.**

   Windows 95 users: Click Start⇨Run.

3. **In the dialog box that appears, type** D:\SETUP.EXE

   Replace *D* with the proper drive letter if your CD-ROM drive uses a different letter. (If you don't know the letter, see how your CD-ROM drive is listed under My Computer in Windows 95 or File Manager in Windows 3.1.)

4. **Click OK.**

   A license agreement window appears.

5. **Read through the license agreement, nod your head, and then click the Accept button if you want to use the CD (after you click Accept, you'll never be bothered by the License Agreement window again).**

   The CD interface Welcome screen appears. The interface is a friendly little program that shows you what's on the CD and coordinates installing the programs and running the demos. The interface basically enables you to click a button or two to make things happen.

6. **Click anywhere on the Welcome screen to enter the interface.**

   Now you're getting to the good stuff. The screen that appears lists categories for the software and the other added attractions on the CD.

7. **To view the items within a category, just click the category's name.**

   A list of items in the category appears.

8. **For more information about an item, click its name.**

   Sometimes a program has its own system requirements or requires you to perform a few tricks on your computer before you can install or run the program. This screen tells you what, if anything, you may need to do.

9. **If you decide not to install the program, click the Go Back button to return to the previous screen.**

   This feature allows you to browse the different categories and products and decide what you want to install.

10. **To install a program, click the appropriate Install button.**

    The CD interface drops to the background while the CD installs the program you choose.

11. **To install other items from the CD, repeat Steps 7 through 10.**

12. **When you've finished installing programs, click the Quit button to close the interface.**

    You can eject the CD now. Carefully place it back in the plastic jacket of the book for safekeeping.

Using the CD with a Mac OS

To install the items from the CD to your hard drive, follow these steps:

1. **Insert the CD into your computer's CD-ROM drive.**

   In a moment, an icon representing the CD you just inserted appears on your Mac desktop. Chances are the icon looks like a CD-ROM.

2. **Double-click the CD icon to show the CD's contents.**

3. **Double-click the Read Me First icon.**

   The Read Me First text file contains information about the programs and other contents of the CD, and gives you any last-minute instructions that you may need in order to correctly install the files from the CD.

4. **To install most items, just drag the folder from the CD window and drop it on your hard drive icon.**

5. **Some programs come with installer programs. With these programs, you simply open the program's folder on the CD, and then double-click the icon with the words "Install" or "Installer."**

   Sometimes the installers are actually *self-extracting archives,* which means that the program files have been compressed and bundled up into an archive with the software tool needed to un-compress and install them on your hard drive. This kind of program is often called an .sea. Double-click any file with .sea in the name, and it will run just like an installer.

   After you have installed the programs you want, you can eject the CD. Carefully place it back in the plastic jacket of the book for safekeeping.

What You Get on the CD

Here's a summary of the contents of this CD, arranged by category. If you use Windows, the CD interface helps you install software easily. (If you have no idea what I'm talking about when I say "CD interface," flip back a page or two to find the section, "Using the CD with Microsoft Windows.")

If you use a Mac OS computer, you can take advantage of the easy Mac interface to quickly install the programs.

Research help

Bonus Chapter 1: Life Choices

This chapter gives you insight into using online resources to research important personal decisions like choosing a college, finding a job, buying a car, or planning a vacation. To read the chapter, you need to have Adobe Acrobat Reader installed (see the "Multimedia Tools" section of this appendix for a description of Acrobat Reader). Put the CD-ROM back into the drive. Open Acrobat Reader, choose File⇨Open and then type **D:\CDCHAP1\CHAPTER1.PDF**

(*Note:* If your CD-ROM drive is not the D: drive, enter the correct CD-ROM drive letter instead.) Now you're ready to read!

Bonus Chapter 2: Recreational Researching: Hobbies, Interests, and Leisure-Time Pursuits

This chapter shows how you can find out more about your own hobbies and pursue new interests using the research tools and techniques presented in this book. Examples include movies, music, recipe collecting, bird watching, and a quick peek into genealogy. To read the chapter, you need to have Adobe Acrobat Reader installed (see the "Multimedia Tools" section of this appendix for a description of Acrobat Reader). Put the CD-ROM back in the drive. Open Acrobat Reader, choose File⇨Open and type **D:\CDCHAP2\CHAPTER2.PDF**

(*Note:* If your CD-ROM Drive is not the D: Drive, enter the correct CD-ROM drive letter instead.)

Bonus Chapter 3: Ten Simple Tune-Ups for Streamlined Searching

This chapter shows how you can get around network congestion, balky servers, missing links, and other roadblocks to effective searching by using both your Web browser and your time more effectively. To read the chapter, you need to have Adobe Acrobat Reader installed (see the "Multimedia Tools" section of this appendix for a description of Acrobat Reader). Put the CD-ROM back in the drive. Open Acrobat Reader, choose File⇨Open and type **D:\CDCHAP3\CHAPTER3.PDF**

(*Note:* If your CD-ROM Drive is not the D: Drive, enter the correct CD-ROM drive letter instead.)

Bonus Appendix: Boolean (and other) Basics

This important appendix explains in detail such power-research techniques as Boolean operators, proximity connectors, field searching, truncation, wildcards, and case-sensitivity. To read the chapter, you need to have Adobe Acrobat Reader installed (see the "Multimedia Tools" section of this appendix for a description of Acrobat Reader). Put the CD-ROM back in the drive. Open Acrobat Reader, choose File⇨Open and type **D:\CDAPP\APP.PDF**

(*Note:* If your CD-ROM Drive is not the D: Drive, enter the correct CD-ROM drive letter instead.)

Northern Light search engine tips

For a look at the often-hidden extra features that can make your research more precise and productive, open the North.HTML file as described in the following steps. Then click on <u>Click Here to Begin</u>. A collection of tips and handy information appears, telling you how to get the most from the Northern Light search engine. For search tips, click <u>Search</u>. And remember that useful, in-depth help for most search engines, not just Northern Light, is just a click away when you're online. Get into the habit of looking for help.

To read this HTML file, follow these steps:

1. **With the CD-ROM in your CD drive, launch your Web browser.**

   See the "Internet tools" section of this appendix to find more about the Web browsers included on this CD-ROM.

2. **Choose File⇨Open (Open File or Open Page, depending on your browser) and then type** D:\NORTHERN\NORTH.HTML

   If your CD-ROM drive is not the D: drive, enter the corresponding drive letter instead.

3. **Click OK.**

   Your browser opens the HTML file that contains the helpful search tips.

SurfSaver

SurfSaver, from askSam Systems, lets you store and search Web pages from your browser. You can quickly search and browse your saved pages, even when you're not connected to the Internet. SurfSaver gives you a permanent archive of your research results and a way of organizing them. The current beta version runs on Internet Explorer 4.0 only; versions for IE 3.0 and Netscape are in the works. For more information about SurfSaver, check www.surfsaver.com.

WebWhacker

WebWhacker enables you to save Web pages directly to your hard disk so you can open them with your browser and read them when you're offline. The software on this CD-ROM is a demo copy that expires after a certain period of time. If you like WebWhacker after trying it, you can download and purchase the software from the Web site, `www.bluesquirrel.com/whacker`.

Internet tools

Netscape Navigator 4.0 (for Windows 3.1/95/98 and Mac)

One of the two leading Web browsers, Navigator is a basic tool for, well, navigating the World Wide Web. To find out about the latest updates, please visit the Netscape Web site at `www.netscape.com`.

Internet Explorer 4.0 (for Windows 3.1/95/98 and Mac)

The other leading Web browser has essentially the same basic functionality as Netscape. Try them both and see which one you prefer. To find out about the latest updates, please visit the Microsoft Web site at `www.microsoft.com/ie`.

Eudora Light (Windows 3.1/95 and Mac)

Eudora Light is a freeware version of QualComm's popular Eudora Pro e-mail program. The Pro version includes additional features like automatic filtering of e-mail into different folders. Try out Eudora Light, and get more information about Eudora Pro at `www.eudora.com`.

Anarchie 2.0.1 (Mac)

Anarchie 2.0.1 (from Stairways Shareware) is a Macintosh shareware File Transfer Protocol (FTP) program. You can use Anarchie to find files on the Net and to copy files between your Mac and a computer on the Net. FTP programs were more useful before the World Wide Web took hold and made finding and downloading files a snap. However, FTP programs are still handy for activities not directly supported by the Web, such as uploading your own files and Web pages. To register the software, or just to find out more about the product, check out their Web site at `www.share.com`.

WS_FTP LE 4.5 (Windows 3.1/95)

WS_FTP is a File Transfer Protocol (FTP) program for Windows-based computers. This program lets you transfer files and Web pages between your computer and a computer on the Net. Portions of this software Copyright, 1991–97, Ipswitch, Inc.

Free Agent 1.11 (Windows 3.1/95)

If your Internet Service Provider has a news feed and you want to access some of the newsgroups spotlighted in this book using a program other than the Web-based Deja News reader, this program may interest you. Free Agent (from Forté, Inc.) is a Windows-based freeware program that lets you read and participate in ongoing newsgroup discussions. Tens of thousands of newsgroups exist, devoted to virtually every topic under the sun. Free Agent lets you read newsgroup articles offline, which can save you money and free up your phone line. For more information about how to use Free Agent, visit its Web site at www.forteinc.com.

Multimedia tools

Acrobat Reader 3.01 (Windows 3.1/95 and Mac)

Acrobat Reader 3.01, from Adobe Systems, is a free program that lets you view and print *Portable Document Format* (or PDF) files. Many Web sites on the Internet use the PDF format for storing and presenting certain kinds of information. PDF supports the use of assorted fonts, graphics, and elegant layouts that the HTML coding used in Web pages does not. You use Acrobat Reader to view the three bonus chapters and appendix on this CD, so you need to install this one for sure (see the "Research Help" section for more about reading the bonus chapters). You can get more information about the Acrobat Reader by visiting the Adobe Systems Web site at www.adobe.com.

Utilities

StuffIt Lite 3.6 (Mac)

StuffIt Lite is a shareware file-compression program from Aladdin Systems, Inc. This Mac program lets you squeeze large files (and small ones, too, for that matter) into a fraction of the space they normally take up, so you can store and transfer them more quickly and efficiently. For information about StuffIt Deluxe, the commercial version of the program, visit www.aladdinsys.com.

StuffIt Expander 4.0.1 (Mac)

StuffIt Expander 4.0.1 from Aladdin Systems, Inc., is a file-decompression shareware utility for the Macintosh. Many files that you find on the Internet or receive as e-mail attachments are compressed, both to save storage space and to cut down on the amount of time required to download them. StuffIt Expander can decompress many types of compressed files. Visit www.aladdinsys.com for more information about StuffIt Expander.

DropStuff with Expander Enhancer (Mac)

DropStuff with Expander Enhancer 4.0 from Aladdin Systems, Inc. is a shareware program that lets you compress files by simply dragging and dropping them on the DropStuff icon. Expander Enhancer allows you to expand a wide variety of Windows, Mac, and Internet file formats. You can use this program, if you prefer, in place of StuffIt Lite and StuffIt Expander. For more information about DropStuff with Expander Enhancer, visit `www.aladdinsys.com`.

WinZip 6.3 (Windows 3.1/95)

WinZip 6.3, from Nico Mak Computing, is a Windows-based file compression and decompression utility. Many files you find on the Internet or receive as e-mail attachments are compressed or "zipped" to save storage space and cut down on the amount of time it takes to download them. Once you have a compressed file on your hard disk, you can use WinZip to decompress it and make it useable again. To find out more about WinZip, visit `www.winzip.com`.

Knowing the Difference between Freeware and Shareware

Freeware is a program that the creator makes available for public use on a free-of-charge basis. You can download freeware from the Internet or get it on CD-ROMs like this one. You don't have to register your copy of the program, and you can use freeware for as long as you'd like with no obligations.

Shareware is another story. Shareware is not free — it's commercial software that you are allowed to use on a trial basis for no charge. After the trial period is over, you must decide whether to keep, and pay for, the shareware. If you decide *not* to pay for the shareware, you're expected to delete it from your computer. (Sometimes the copy you download becomes unusable upon expiration of your trial period.) If you decide to buy the shareware, follow the registration instructions that come with it.

Using the Internet Directory Links

The *Researching Online For Dummies* Internet Directory provides URLs and descriptions for more than a hundred of the sites that I mention in this book — plus a few extras that I thought may interest you. A picture (or a Web site) is worth a thousand words, so I recommend that you visit the sites that I describe to get a better idea of what they can do for you.

Rather than make you flip page by page through the Internet Directory to find these URLs and then type them into your Web browser navigation window, I figured I'd save you some time and typing. So I've created a list of links to all the sites in the Internet Directory, plus the others mentioned throughout this book, arranged by category. Here's what you do to use these links.

1. **With the CD-ROM in your CD drive, launch your Web browser.**

2. **Using the File menu in your browser, select the option that allows you to open a file.**

   The Open dialog box pops up.

3. **Select the LINKS.HTML file in the LINKS folder by clicking on it (if it appears in the dialog box, you're ready to click; if it doesn't appear in the dialog box, you can browse for it).**

   If you feel like doing a little typing, just type **D:\LINKS\LINKS.HTML** (if your computer uses another drive letter for the CD-ROM, enter the correct drive letter instead of D:).

4. **Click a link to view sites listed for different topics.**

   This action opens a second browser window, taking you to the topic you selected. The links page remains open in the original browser window so you can toggle back to select another topic. (Each time you select a new topic, the Web site selected pops up in that second browser window — so don't worry that you're going to end up with several browser windows open all at one time.) Now simply select the link you want to check out by clicking on it. Assuming your Internet connection is up and running, clicking takes you directly to the Web site you've selected.

Use your browser's Find in This Page feature to locate a particular site or resource whose name you know.

If You've Got Problems (Of the CD Kind)

I've tried my best to select programs that work on most computers with the minimum system requirements. But it's possible that (for whatever reason) some programs may not work properly on your computer.

The two most common problems are not enough memory (RAM) for the programs you want to use, or a conflict with other software on your system that affects the installation or running of a program. If you get error messages like Not enough memory or Setup cannot continue, try one or more of these tactics. Then try installing or running the software again:

- ✔ **Turn off any antivirus software that you have on your computer.** Installers sometimes mimic virus activity and may cause your computer to incorrectly believe that it is being infected by a virus.

- ✔ **Close all running programs.** The more programs you're running, the less memory is available to other programs. Installers may also update files and programs; if you keep other programs running, the installation may not work properly.

- ✔ **In Windows, close the CD interface and run demos or installations directly from Windows Explorer.** The interface itself may tie up system memory or conflict with certain kinds of interactive demos. Use Windows Explorer to browse the files on the CD and launch installers or demos.

- ✔ **Add more RAM to your computer.** Especially if you have an older computer, adding more memory can really help speed it up and enable more programs to run at the same time. Check with your local computer store or with a friend who knows how to add memory to your computer.

If you still have trouble installing items from the CD, please call an IDG Books Worldwide Customer Service Representative at 800-762-2974. Outside the U.S., call 317-596-5430.

Index

(continued)

Notes

Notes

IDG Books Worldwide, Inc., End-User License Agreement

READ THIS. You should carefully read these terms and conditions before opening the software packet(s) included with this book ("Book"). This is a license agreement ("Agreement") between you and IDG Books Worldwide, Inrÿ ("IDGB"). By opening the accompanying software packet(s), you acknowledge that you have read and accept the following terms and conditions. If you do not agree and do not want to be bound by such terms and conditions, promptly return the Book and the unopened software packet(s) to the place you obtained them for a full refund.

1. **License Grant.** IDGB grants to you (either an individual or entity) a nonexclusive license to use one copy of the enclosed software program(s) (collectively, the "Software") solely for your own personal or business purposes on a single computer (whether a standard computer or a workstation component of a multiuser network). The Software is in use on a computer when it is loaded into temporary memory (RAM) or installed into permanent memory (hard disk, CD-ROM, or other storage device). IDGB reserves all rights not expressly granted herein.

2. **Ownership.** IDGB is the owner of all right, title, and interest, including copyright, in and to the compilation of the Software recorded on the disk(s) or CD-ROM ("Software Media"). Copyright to the individual programs recorded on the Software Media is owned by the author or other authorized copyright owner of each program. Ownership of the Software and all proprietary rights relating thereto remain with IDGB and its licensers.

3. **Restrictions on Use and Transfer.**

   (a) You may only (i) make one copy of the Software for backup or archival purposes, or (ii) transfer the Software to a single hard disk, provided that you keep the original for backup or archival purposes. You may not (i) rent or lease the Software, (ii) copy or reproduce the Software through a LAN or other network system or through any computer subscriber system or bulletin-board system, or (iii) modify, adapt, or create derivative works based on the Software.

   (b) You may not reverse engineer, decompile, or disassemble the Software. You may transfer the Software and user documentation on a permanent basis, provided that the transferee agrees to accept the terms and conditions of this Agreement and you retain no copies. If the Software is an update or has been updated, any transfer must include the most recent update and all prior versions.

4. **Restrictions on Use of Individual Programs.** You must follow the individual requirements and restrictions detailed for each individual program in the "About the CD" Appendix of this Book. These limitations are also contained in the individual license agreements recorded on the Software Media. These limitations may include a requirement that after using the program for a specified period of time, the user must pay a registration fee or discontinue use. By opening the Software packet(s), you will be agreeing to abide by the licenses and restrictions for these individual programs that are detailed in the "About the CD" Appendix and on the Software Media. None of the material on this Software Media or listed in this Book may ever be redistributed, in original or modified form, for commercial purposes.

5. Limited Warranty.

(a) IDGB warrants that the Software and Software Media are free from defects in materials and workmanship under normal use for a period of sixty (60) days from the date of purchase of this Book. If IDGB receives notification within the warranty period of defects in materials or workmanship, IDGB will replace the defective Software Media.

(b) **IDGB AND THE AUTHOR OF THE BOOK DISCLAIM ALL OTHER WARRANTIES, EXPRESS OR IMPLIED, INCLUDING WITHOUT LIMITATION IMPLIED WARRANTIES OF MERCHANTABILITY AND FITNESS FOR A PARTICULAR PURPOSE, WITH RESPECT TO THE SOFTWARE, THE PROGRAMS, THE SOURCE CODE CONTAINED THEREIN, AND/OR THE TECHNIQUES DESCRIBED IN THIS BOOK. IDGB DOES NOT WARRANT THAT THE FUNCTIONS CONTAINED IN THE SOFTWARE WILL MEET YOUR REQUIREMENTS OR THAT THE OPERATION OF THE SOFTWARE WILL BE ERROR FREE.**

(c) This limited warranty gives you specific legal rights, and you may have other rights that vary from jurisdiction to jurisdiction.

6. Remedies.

(a) IDGB's entire liability and your exclusive remedy for defects in materials and workmanship shall be limited to replacement of the Software Media, which may be returned to IDGB with a copy of your receipt at the following address: Software Media Fulfillment Department, Attn.: *Researching Online For Dummies,* IDG Books Worldwide, Inc., 7260 Shadeland Station, Ste. 100, Indianapolis, IN 46256, or call 800-762-2974. Please allow three to four weeks for delivery. This Limited Warranty is void if failure of the Software Media has resulted from accident, abuse, or misapplication. Any replacement Software Media will be warranted for the remainder of the original warranty period or thirty (30) days, whichever is longer.

(b) In no event shall IDGB or the author be liable for any damages whatsoever (including without limitation damages for loss of business profits, business interruption, loss of business information, or any other pecuniary loss) arising from the use of or inability to use the Book or the Software, even if IDGB has been advised of the possibility of such damages.

(c) Because some jurisdictions do not allow the exclusion or limitation of liability for consequential or incidental damages, the above limitation or exclusion may not apply to you.

7. U.S. Government Restricted Rights. Use, duplication, or disclosure of the Software by the U.S. Government is subject to restrictions stated in paragraph (c)(1)(ii) of the Rights in Technical Data and Computer Software clause of DFARS 252.227-7013, and in subparagraphs (a) through (d) of the Commercial Computer–Restricted Rights clause at FAR 52.227-19, and in similar clauses in the NASA FAR supplement, when applicable.

8. General. This Agreement constitutes the entire understanding of the parties and revokes and supersedes all prior agreements, oral or written, between them and may not be modified or amended except in a writing signed by both parties hereto that specifically refers to this Agreement. This Agreement shall take precedence over any other documents that may be in conflict herewith. If any one or more provisions contained in this Agreement are held by any court or tribunal to be invalid, illegal, or otherwise unenforceable, each and every other provision shall remain in full force and effect.

Installation Instructions

• •

Please see the Appendix for full details on the CD and its contents.

Using the CD with Microsoft Windows

1. Insert the CD into your computer's CD-ROM drive.

2. Windows 3.1 or 3.11 users: From Program Manager, choose File⇨Run. Windows 95 users: Click Start⇨Run.

3. In the dialog box that appears, type D:\SETUP.EXE

   Replace *D* with the proper drive letter if your CD-ROM drive uses a different letter.

4. Click OK, read through the license agreement, and then click the Accept button if you want to use the CD.

5. Click anywhere on the CD Welcome screen to enter the interface.

6. To view the items within a category, just click the category's name.

7. For more information about an item, click its name.

8. If you decide not to install the program, click the Go Back button to return to the previous screen.

9. To install a program, click the appropriate Install button.

10. When you've finished installing programs, click the Quit button to close the interface.

Using the CD with a Mac OS

1. Insert the CD into your computer's CD-ROM drive.

2. Double-click the CD icon to show the CD's contents.

3. Double-click the Read Me First icon. (The Read Me First text file contains information about the CD's programs and other contents.)

4. To install most items, just drag the folder from the CD window and drop it on your hard drive icon.

5. Some programs come with installer programs. With these programs, you simply open the program's folder on the CD, and then double-click the icon with the words "Install" or "Installer."

   Just double-click any file with .sea in the name, and it will run just like an installer.

Discover Dummies Online!

The Dummies Web Site is your fun and friendly online resource for the latest information about ...*For Dummies*® books and your favorite topics. The Web site is the place to communicate with us, exchange ideas with other ...*For Dummies* readers, chat with authors, and have fun!

Ten Fun and Useful Things You Can Do at www.dummies.com

1. Win free ...*For Dummies* books and more!
2. Register your book and be entered in a prize drawing.
3. Meet your favorite authors through the IDG Books Author Chat Series.
4. Exchange helpful information with other ...*For Dummies* readers.
5. Discover other great ...*For Dummies* books you must have!
6. Purchase Dummieswear™ exclusively from our Web site.
7. Buy ...*For Dummies* books online.
8. Talk to us. Make comments, ask questions, get answers!
9. Download free software.
10. Find additional useful resources from authors.

Link directly to these ten fun and useful things at
http://www.dummies.com/10useful

For other technology titles from IDG Books Worldwide, go to
www.idgbooks.com

Not on the Web yet? It's easy to get started with *Dummies 101*®: *The Internet For Windows*® *95* or *The Internet For Dummies*®, 5th Edition, at local retailers everywhere.

Find other ...*For Dummies* books on these topics:

Business • Career • Databases • Food & Beverage • Games • Gardening • Graphics • Hardware
Health & Fitness • Internet and the World Wide Web • Networking • Office Suites
Operating Systems • Personal Finance • Pets • Programming • Recreation • Sports
Spreadsheets • Teacher Resources • Test Prep • Word Processing

IDG BOOKS WORLDWIDE
BOOK REGISTRATION

Register This Book and Win!

We want to hear from you!

Visit **http://my2cents.dummies.com** to register this book and tell us how you liked it!

- ✔ Get entered in our monthly prize giveaway.

- ✔ Give us feedback about this book — tell us what you like best, what you like least, or maybe what you'd like to ask the author and us to change!

- ✔ Let us know any other *...For Dummies*® topics that interest you.

Your feedback helps us determine what books to publish, tells us what coverage to add as we revise our books, and lets us know whether we're meeting your needs as a *...For Dummies* reader. You're our most valuable resource, and what you have to say is important to us!

Not on the Web yet? It's easy to get started with *Dummies 101*®: *The Internet For Windows*® *95* or *The Internet For Dummies*®, 5th Edition, at local retailers everywhere.

Or let us know what you think by sending us a letter at the following address:

...For Dummies Book Registration
Dummies Press
7260 Shadeland Station, Suite 100
Indianapolis, IN 46256-3945
Fax 317-596-5498

BUSINESS AND
GENERAL
REFERENCE
BOOK SERIES
FROM IDG

COMPUTER
BOOK SERIES
FROM IDG